ARE MIRACULOUS GIFTS FOR TODAY?

Four Views

With much appreciation and affection
we dedicate this book
to our wives
Jean Gaffin
Margaret Grudem
Debra Oss
Nancy Saucy
Ann Storms

CONTENTS

PREFACE

How is the Holy Spirit working in churches today? Is he really giving miraculous healings and prophecies and messages in tongues? Is he giving Christians new power for ministry when they experience a "baptism in the Holy Spirit" after conversion? Is he driving out demons when Christians command them to flee?

Or are these events confined to the distant past, to the time when the New Testament was being written and living apostles taught and governed—and worked miracles—in the churches?

There is little consensus on these questions among evangelical Christians today. There are many Pentecostals who say that Christians should seek to be baptized in the Holy Spirit after conversion, and that this experience will result in new spiritual power for ministry. But other evangelicals respond that they already have been baptized in the Holy Spirit, because it happened the moment they became Christians. Who is right? What are the arguments on each side?

In addition to these questions, there are many differences over specific spiritual gifts. Can people have a gift of prophecy today, so that God actually reveals things to them and they can tell these revelations to others? Or was that gift confined to the time when the New Testament was still unfinished, in the first century A.D.? And what about healing? Should Christians expect that God will often heal in miraculous ways when they pray today? Can some people still have a gift of healing? Or should our prayer emphasis be that God will work to heal through ordinary means, such as doctors and medicine? Or again, should we mostly encourage people to see the sanctifying value of sickness and pray that they will have grace to endure it?

9

There is even less consensus on the gift of speaking in tongues. Some Christians say that it is a valuable help to their prayer life, others say it is a sign of being baptized in the Holy Spirit, and still others say it does not exist today because it is a form of verbal revelation from God that ended when the New Testament writings were completed.

We could go on with more questions—questions about whether the Holy Spirit guides us today through feelings and impressions of his will, about casting out demons, and about seeking spiritual gifts, or questions about claims that evangelism today should be accompanied by demonstrations of God's miraculous power. But the point should already be clear: This is a large and interesting area of discussion, one of immense importance to the life of the church today.

THE FOUR POSITIONS

Is there any way forward from this array of questions and different views? The first step should be to define clearly what the main positions are that are currently held in the evangelical world. If this book succeeds only in that task, something valuable will have been achieved.

But what are the main positions? Can the entire evangelical world be classified into four positions on these questions? As I discussed this matter with editors Stan Gundry and Jack Kuhatschek at Zondervan Publishing House, some positions became immediately clear.

The *cessationist* position argues that there are no miraculous gifts of the Holy Spirit today. Gifts such as prophecy, tongues, and healing were confined to the first century, and were used at the time the apostles were establishing the churches and the New Testament was not yet complete. This is a well-defined and often-defended position within evangelical scholarship.

There are cessationists within both the Reformed and the dispensational segments of evangelicalism. Reformed cessationism is represented by many of the faculty at Westminster Seminary, especially Richard Gaffin. Dispensational cessationists hold similar positions on this question but are in different institutions; they are represented by institutions such as Dallas Seminary and The Master's Seminary. Within the Lutheran tradition, conservative groups such as the Missouri Synod also hold mostly to a cessationist position.

Standing in clear opposition to the cessationist position are three groups that encourage the use of all spiritual gifts today: *Pentecostals*, *charismatics*, and *the Third Wave*. Although sometimes people have used the terms "Pentecostal" and "charismatic" indiscriminately to refer to all of these groups, the terms are more accurately understood in the following way:

Pentecostal refers to any denomination or group that traces its historical origin back to the Pentecostal revival that began in the United States in 1901, and that holds the following doctrines: (1) All the gifts of the Holy Spirit mentioned in the New Testament are intended for today; (2) baptism in the Holy Spirit is an empowering experience subsequent to conversion and should be sought by Christians today; and (3) when baptism in the Holy Spirit occurs, people will speak in tongues as a "sign" that they have received this experience. Pentecostal groups usually have their own distinct denominational structures, among which are the Assemblies of God, the Church of God in Christ, and many others.

Charismatic, on the other hand, refers to any groups (or people) that trace their historical origin to the charismatic renewal movement of the 1960s and 1970s and that seek to practice all the spiritual gifts mentioned in the New Testament (including prophecy, healing, miracles, tongues, interpretation, and distinguishing between spirits). Among charismatics there are differing viewpoints on whether baptism in the Holy Spirit is subsequent to conversion and whether speaking in tongues is a sign of baptism in the Spirit. Charismatics by and large have refrained from forming their own denominations, but view themselves as a force for renewal within existing Protestant and Roman Catholic churches. There is no representative charismatic denomination in the United States today, but the most prominent charismatic spokesman is probably Pat Robertson with his Christian Broadcasting Network, the television program "The 700 Club," and Regent University (formerly CBN University).

In the 1980s a third renewal movement arose, a movement called *The Third Wave* by missions professor C. Peter Wagner at Fuller Seminary (he referred to the Pentecostal renewal as the first wave of the Holy Spirit's renewing work in the modern church, and the charismatic movement as the second wave). Third Wave people encourage the equipping of all believers to use New Testament spiritual gifts today and say that the proclamation of the gospel should ordinarily be accompanied by "signs, wonders, and miracles," according to the New Testament pattern. They teach, however, that baptism in the Holy Spirit happens to all Christians at conversion[1] and that subsequent experiences are better called "fillings" or "empowerings" with the Holy Spirit. Though they believe the gift of tongues exists today, they do not emphasize it to the extent that Pentecostals and charismatics do. The most prominent representative of the "Third Wave" is John Wimber, a pastor of the Vineyard Christian Fellowship in Anaheim, California, and leader of the Association of Vineyard Churches.[2]

Those are the well-defined positions: cessationist, Pentecostal, charismatic, Third Wave. But these hardly represent the entire evangelical world. There is yet another position, held by a vast number of evangelicals who think of themselves as belonging to none of these groups. These people have not been convinced by the cessationist arguments that relegate certain gifts to the first century, but they are not really convinced by the doctrine or practice of those who emphasize such gifts today either. They are open to the possibility of miraculous gifts today, but they are concerned about the possibility of abuses that they have

---

[1]John Wimber, in his book on Christian doctrine, writes: "How can we experience Spirit baptism? It comes at conversion. . . . Conversion and Holy Spirit baptism are simultaneous experiences" (*Power Points* [San Francisco: HarperCollins, 1991], 136).

[2]As an editor, I was not satisfied with the name "Third Wave" for this movement, because it does not have a surface meaning that refers to any distinctive emphasis of the movement. I considered the term "expectant evangelicals" because one distinctive emphasis is a high level of expectancy for God to work in miraculous ways today, but the authors rejected it as completely unfamiliar. One recent spokesman for this group has chosen the term "empowered evangelicals"—not implying that others are not empowered, any more than the term "Baptist" implies that others do not baptize or "Presbyterian" implies that others do not have elders— but implying that empowering by the Holy Spirit is a prominent emphasis in the teaching and practice of this group: see Rich Nathan and Ken Wilson, *Empowered Evangelicals* (Ann Arbor, Mich.: Servant, 1995). Perhaps this is the best alternative. But the consensus of the four authors, including Dr. Storms, was that at this time "the Third Wave" is the most familiar term and would work best for this book.

seen in groups that practice these gifts. They do not think speaking in tongues is ruled out by Scripture, but they see many modern examples as not conforming to scriptural guidelines; some also are concerned that it often leads to divisiveness and negative results in churches today. They think churches should emphasize evangelism, Bible study, and faithful obedience as keys to personal and church growth, rather than miraculous gifts. Yet they appreciate some of the benefits that Pentecostal, charismatic, and Third Wave churches have brought to the evangelical world, especially a refreshing contemporary tone in worship and a challenge to renewal in faith and prayer.

As the Zondervan editors and I talked, we realized that this last group was gigantic in the evangelical world, but it did not have a name. For purposes of this book, we have called it the *open but cautious* position. It represents the broad middle ground of evangelicals who do not fall in one of these other camps. I suspect it is the position held by the majority of evangelicals today, at least in the United States.

We were left, then, with five positions: (1) cessationist, (2) open but cautious, (3) Third Wave, (4) charismatic, and (5) Pentecostal. To have five essays, however, seemed unsatisfactory, because three of them would have affirmed the validity of miraculous gifts today, making the book imbalanced on the central question it addresses. So we combined positions (4) and (5) and asked the Pentecostal author to represent both the Pentecostal viewpoint and, where it differed, the charismatic viewpoint. This left us with the four views that are now represented in this book: (1) cessationist, (2) open but cautious, (3) Third Wave, (4) Pentecostal/charismatic.

THE AUTHORS

In order to get the best possible statements of the four positions, my goal as the general editor was to find the most responsible representatives of these four positions among evangelical Protestant scholars today. I wanted the essays to interact seriously with scholarly questions, so the search was confined to individuals who had academic doctorates and who had, in previous research and writing, demonstrated considerable competence in biblical exegesis. I also looked for people who had reputations for representing fairly the positions of those with whom they disagreed, but who would nonetheless state and defend their own convictions firmly. Both the Zondervan editors and I hoped that when the book was published, every reader would think that the author representing his or her own opinion had done so skillfully and fairly. The authors of the four essays are as follows:

(1) *Cessationist:* For the cessationist position we approached Dr. Richard B. Gaffin, professor of systematic theology at Westminster Theological Seminary in Philadelphia. He has already published a book-length defense of cessationism, *Perspectives on Pentecost: Studies in New Testament Teaching on the Gifts of the Holy Spirit* (Phillipsburg, N.J.: Presbyterian and Reformed, 1979), which has had considerable influence since its publication. He is a graduate of Calvin College (A.B.) and Westminster Seminary (B.D., Th.M., Th.D.), where he taught New Testament for twenty-three years and has now taught systematic theology since 1986. Dr. Gaffin is a minister in the Orthodox Presbyterian Church.

(2) *Open but cautious*: For the challenging task of representing the broad center of evangelicals we invited Dr. Robert L. Saucy, Distinguished Professor of Systematic Theology at Talbot School of Theology in California, where, in a teaching career that now spans thirty-four years, he has instructed many of today's evangelical leaders. He is a graduate of Westmont College (A.B.) and Dallas Seminary (Th.M., Th.D.) and has published three books and numerous journal articles. Dr. Saucy is a member of a Conservative Baptist church.

(3) *Third Wave*: To represent this most recent viewpoint within evangelicalism we invited Dr. C. Samuel Storms, the president of Grace Training Center, a Bible school connected with the Metro Vineyard Fellowship of Kansas City and also an associate pastor of the Metro Vineyard Fellowship. Dr. Storms is a graduate of the University of Oklahoma (A.B.), Dallas Seminary (Th.M.), and the University of Texas at Dallas (Ph.D.), has over twenty years of pastoral experience, and is the author of six books. He has recently written and spoken about his decision to affiliate with the Vineyard movement.

(4) *Pentecostal/charismatic*: To represent these views we invited Dr. Douglas A. Oss, professor of hermeneutics and New Testament and chairman of the division of Bible and theology at Central Bible College (Assemblies of God) in Springfield, Missouri, where he has taught since 1988. Dr. Oss is a graduate of

Western Washington University (A.B.), Assemblies of God Theological Seminary (M.Div.), and Westminster Seminary at Philadelphia (Ph.D.). He has two books forthcoming, *The Hermeneutical Framework of Pentecostalism* and a commentary on 2 Corinthians, and has published several journal articles. Dr. Oss is a member of an Assemblies of God church.

(5) *The general editor*: To complete the information given above about the other contributors, I should add that I am currently professor of Biblical and Systematic Theology at Trinity Evangelical Divinity School, Deerfield, Illinois, where I have taught since 1981. My educational background includes degrees from Harvard (B.A.), Westminster Seminary (M.Div.), and the University of Cambridge, England (Ph.D.). For most of my life I have attended "open but cautious" churches, with three exceptions:

During my college years I had the privilege of working one summer in Mt. Vernon, New York, as an assistant to the Rev. Harald Bredesen, who was by that time a prominent spokesman for the charismatic renewal. Then, during my seminary years, I served as a summer intern at a "cessationist" Orthodox Presbyterian Church in Westfield, New Jersey—pastor Robert Atwell, himself a cessationist, simply asked that I not make my convictions about spiritual gifts a matter of controversy in the church. Finally, during the years 1989–1994 my wife and I were part of one Vineyard church and also helped to start another one, but the 45-minute drive finally proved too far for effective church involvement. For that reason we began attending a wonderful Southern Baptist church near our home, where we are now members.

From this varied background, I have gained a deep appreciation for the sincerity and the Christian lives of people who hold each of these "four views." This does not mean that I think these matters are unimportant or that the positions are all equally persuasive—but the question as to which view is most faithful to Scripture, I now leave to readers to decide!

THE PROCESS

The Essays

Each author first wrote a fifty-page position paper, which could not be changed after the final copy was turned in. (This was to be fair to the other authors, who could then be sure that their responses would refer to the actual essays as they would appear in the book.) The authors had to cover the following topics in order, though the space devoted to each one could vary:

(1) baptism in the Holy Spirit and the question of post-conversion experiences;
(2) the question of whether some gifts have ceased;
(3) a discussion of specific gifts, especially prophecy, healing, and tongues;
(4) practical implications for church life;
(5) dangers of one's own position and that of the others.[3]

These position papers were then circulated to the other authors, and each author wrote an eight-page response to the other position papers. By this point, the positions had been defined, defended, and criticized. Many other "Four Views" books have ended at this point.

The Authors' Conference

However, after the position papers and critiques had been written and circulated, the four authors and I (as editor) met in a two-day, closed-door conference in Philadelphia, on November 14–15, 1995. The purpose was for the authors to talk together at length after they had written and read so many pages about these things. Perhaps a more accurate understanding of one another's positions would result (it did). Perhaps authors would find that they were being understood in ways they did not intend (they were, in one or two places). Perhaps the discussion could be carried on in more detail than was possible in the essays (it could be and was). Perhaps the authors would even change their positions (they did not).

---

[3]The authors and I together decided that we would not attempt to discuss the question of the "Toronto Blessing" in this book, because (1) it is a topic distinct from the subject of the book, which focuses on certain gifts of the Holy Spirit today; (2) it is a specific historical event, but we are writing about continuing, everyday church life; and (3) even within the four positions represented by this book, there are differing assessments of what has been happening in Toronto. However, some comments and bibliography may be found in Dr. Storms's essay (p. 182) and in Dr. Saucy's essay (p. 142).

People have asked me why these four men who all believe the same Bible and all have deep personal love for our Lord could not reach agreement on these things. I tell them that it took the early church until A.D. 381 (at Constantinople) to finally settle the doctrine of the Trinity, and until A.D. 451 (at Chalcedon) to settle the disputes over the deity and humanity of Christ in one person. We should not be surprised if these complex questions about the work of the Holy Spirit could not be resolved in two days!

On the other hand, I think everyone was stretched in trying to understand and interact with the other positions. Face-to-face dialogue is immensely valuable, especially when not interrupted by telephones, appointments, and classes to teach.

During this conference the five of us engaged in seventeen hours of intense discussion, with Greek New Testaments often in hand and with alignments shifting as the topics of discussion went from baptism in the Holy Spirit to guidance, prophecy, tongues, healing, spiritual warfare, and several related matters. Again and again we returned to the question of whether the New Testament church, as described in Acts and the New Testament letters, should provide the pattern for our expectations of church life today.

Of course, the four authors and the Zondervan editors knew that I had previously written in defense of one of these positions, but they accepted my pledge to remain as impartial as possible in my editing and in moderating our two-day conference. I hope I have succeeded in that attempt. I should explain that when we actually got into the two-day conference, from time to time I stepped out of my "moderator" role and participated actively in the discussion (especially on the gift of prophecy, on which I had written quite a bit), but Dr. Gaffin and Dr. Saucy, who differed with me on this matter, were well able to defend their own positions, and I don't think my participation skewed the discussion in any significant way. In any case, my primary role as moderator was to keep the discussion focused on one issue at a time—and to tell when it was time to stop for supper!

How did the authors respond to this conference? I think one spoke for all when he said at the end, "I wouldn't have missed this for anything." More detailed evaluations can be found in each author's "Concluding Statement," which was written after this conference.

VIEWS NOT REPRESENTED IN THIS BOOK

Circulating within the evangelical world, especially at the popular level, are several views that find no representation in this book. For example, no one in the book argues for any of the following positions:

(1) If a person has not spoken in tongues, he or she is not truly a Christian.

(2) If a person has not spoken in tongues, he or she does not have the Holy Spirit within.

(3) People who speak in tongues are more spiritual than those who do not.

(4) If someone who is prayed for is not healed, it is probably the fault of the sick person for not having enough faith.

(5) God wants all Christians to be wealthy today.

(6) It is always God's will to heal a Christian who is sick.

(7) If we simply speak a "word of faith," God will grant what we claim with this faith.

(8) There are apostles today in the same sense that Peter and Paul were apostles.

(9) If we are truly guided by the Holy Spirit, we do not need to follow the directions of Scripture.

(10) We should follow anointed leaders with fruitful ministries even if they deny the inerrancy of Scripture.

(11) Speaking in tongues is usually demonic in origin.

(12) In guiding us, the Holy Spirit never uses our intuitions, promptings, and feelings.

(13) God should not be expected to heal today in answer to prayer.

(14) God never works miracles today, because those ceased when the apostles died.

(15) Charismatics and Pentecostals are not evangelical Christians.

(16) The charismatic movement is part of the New Age religion.

(17) The Third Wave movement (or the Vineyard Movement) is nonevangelical (or is a cult).

(18) Charismatics are generally anti-intellectual.

(19) Cessationists in general are rationalistic and their faith is mostly dry intellectualism.
(20) It is legitimate to criticize another position by telling anecdotes of mistakes made by untrained laypersons.

I believe it is fair to say that all four authors would unite in their rejection of these teachings. These positions, as far as we know, are defended by no academic leaders in any branch of the evangelical world. In some cases they are misrepresentations of the teaching of Scripture, and in others they are caricatures of other positions, but in every case they are teachings that we think hinder and disturb the body of Christ, not building it up or strengthening it in truth and in faithfulness to God's Word.

COMMON GROUND SHARED BY THE AUTHORS

Finally, though significant differences remained on some important questions, I think it will be clear in the pages that follow that these four positions share much common ground. We agree in affirming the total truthfulness of Scripture and agree that it is our absolute rule in all matters of doctrine and practice. We agree that God answers prayer today. In our discussions together, we also came to recognize much more fully the fundamental unity we share as brothers in Christ, and we realized that our unity in Christ is not destroyed by our differences on these questions, as important as they are to the life of the church today.

We realize that this book might become the basis for many subsequent discussions among Christians who read it and who differ over these matters. It is our hope that the evident blessing that God gave to our discussions, whereby we could differ clearly and directly for seventeen hours over these matters without anyone even once losing his temper or resorting to personal attacks, and with everyone continuing earnestly to seek to understand Scripture more accurately, may also be evident in all the discussions that follow from these essays.

Now it is the hope of all five of us, as we release this book, that the Lord will be pleased to use it to clarify the continuing discussion over these matters, to provide responsible statements of the main positions, and to show clearly where there is common ground and where the remaining differences lie. Perhaps out of that foundation there will eventually be further progress in the church's understanding of these matters, "until we all reach unity in the faith and in the knowledge of the Son of God" (Eph. 4:13).

Finally, I want to give special thanks to my teaching assistant, Jeff Purswell, for compiling the author and Scripture indexes and for painstakingly correlating the numerous internal cross-references within the book, to my secretary, Kim Pennington, for faithfully coordinating correspondence and manuscript transmission to and from all four authors, and to Stan Gundry, Jack Kuhatschek, and Verlyn Verbrugge at Zondervan for prompt and accurate editorial help at each stage of this project.

WAYNE A. GRUDEM
TRINITY EVANGELICAL DIVINITY SCHOOL
DEERFIELD, ILLINOIS
FEBRUARY, 1996

ABBREVIATIONS

EvQ	*The Evangelical Quarterly*
GTJ	*Grace Theological Journal*
ICC	International Critical Commentary
IDB	*Interpreter's Dictionary of the Bible*
IDBS	*Interpreter's Dictionary of the Bible Supplement*
JETS	*Journal of the Evangelical Theological Society*
JPT	*Journal of Pentecostal Theology*
JSNTSup	Journal for the Study of the New Testament Supplement Series
KJV	King James Version
LW	*Luther's Works*
LXX	Septuagint
NASB	New American Standard Bible
NEB	New English Bible
NICNT	New International Commentary on the New Testament
NICOT	New International Commentary on the Old Testament
NIDNTT	New International Dictionary of New Testament Theology
NIGTC	New International Greek Testament Commentary
NRSV	New Revised Standard Version
NIV	New International Verson
SBLSemPap	*Seminar Papers of the Society of Biblical Literature*
SJT	*Scottish Journal of Theology*
TDNT	*Theological Dictionary of the New Testament*
TDOT	*Theological Dictionary of the Old Testament*
TynBul	*Tyndale Bulletin*
VoxEv	*Vox Evangelica*
VT	*Vetus Testamentum*
WBC	World Biblical Commentary
WTJ	*Westminster Theological Journal*

Chapter One

A CESSATIONIST VIEW

Richard B. Gaffin, Jr.

A CESSATIONIST VIEW

Richard B. Gaffin, Jr.

SOME PRELIMINARY REMARKS

1. The designation of the view I have been asked to represent in this symposium suggests only that I am against something. So, before anything else, let me try to be clear about what I am for in the ongoing debate about the work of the Holy Spirit in the church today. As much as anything, I am for the truth expressed in John 3:8, the truth that in his activity the Spirit is like the blowing wind, sovereign and ultimately incalculable. Any sound theology of the Holy Spirit, I take it, will be left with a certain remainder, a surplus unaccounted for, an area of mystery. The cessationist view I hold is least of all driven by a rationalistic desire to have everything about the work of the Spirit tied up in a tidy, comfortable little package.

At the same time, we ought not to embrace a kind of "whimsy of the Spirit." The Spirit-wind of John 3:8 does not move in a vacuum. Scripture as a whole teaches that in his own sovereignty the Spirit has seen fit to circumscribe his activity and to structure it according to the patterns revealed there. Those patterns, not what the Spirit may choose to do beyond them, ought to be the focus and shape the expectations of the church today.

Typically, the cessationist view is reproached with something like trying to "put the Spirit in a box." But according to Scripture, as I will try to show below, the Spirit has sovereignly chosen to "box" himself in; the ardor of the Spirit, we may say, is an "ordered ardor" (cf. 1 Cor. 14:33, 40).

2. The context of John 3:8—Jesus' interchange with Nicodemus about the new birth—prompts another observation. At issue in this symposium is not whether the Spirit of God is at work today in a powerful, dynamic, supernatural, and direct way. No work of the Spirit, I hold, is more radical, more impressive, more miraculous, and more thoroughly supernatural than what he does—now, today—with people who are nothing less than "dead in ... transgressions and sins" (Eph. 2:1, 5). Beyond any human capacity—rational-reflective, intuitive-mystical, or otherwise—the Spirit makes them "alive to God in Christ Jesus" (Rom. 6:11).

This activity, as Jesus later in John's Gospel (e.g., John 5:24–25; 11:25–26) and Paul (e.g., Eph. 2:5–6; Col. 2:12–13) make plain, is nothing less than a work of *resurrection*—no less real, no less miraculous, no less eschatological than the future, bodily resurrection of the believer at Christ's return. The cessationist view I and many others hold will yield to no one in stressing that the present activity of the Holy Spirit in believers is of "incomparably great power ... like [on the order of] the working of [God's] mighty strength, which he exerted in Christ when he raised him from the dead and seated him at his right hand" (Eph. 1:19–20).

To put it mildly, then, one ought not simply suggest that all cessationist positions result from captivity to "common sense" realism,[1] or are "an intellectualized quasi-deism" (with the hardly subtle suggestion that it falls under the annihilating indictments of Jesus in Matt. 22:29 and Paul in 2 Tim. 3:5),[2] or betray an "anti-supernatural hermeneutic" in interpreting Acts,[3] or are so bound up with an unbiblical, outdated Enlightenment worldview that, though "incensed at Bultmann's 'rationalism,'" they have nonetheless "adopted their own brand of rationalism."[4]

[1]H. I. Lederle, "Life in the Spirit and Worldview," in Mark W. Wilson, ed., *Spirit and Renewal: Essays in Honor of J. Rodman Williams* (Sheffield: Academic Press, 1994), 29.

[2]J. Ruthven, *On the Cessation of the Charismata: The Protestant Polemic on Post-biblical Miracles* (Sheffield: Academic Press, 1993), 204, 206.

[3]J. Deere, *Surprised by the Power of the Spirit* (Grand Rapids: Zondervan, 1993), 111–12.

[4]G. D. Fee, *God's Empowering Presence: The Holy Spirit in the Letters of Paul* (Peabody, Mass.: Hendrickson, 1994), 887–88; Deere, *Power of the Spirit*, 112, also draws the link with Bultmann.

In what follows I will do what I can to allay such misconceptions. But we must be clear here. Western philosophy since the Enlightenment has by and large denied the power of the resurrection confessed above. Along with other cessationists, of course, I am well aware that in our attitudes and lifestyles, we often compromise that power and grieve the Holy Spirit (see Eph. 4:30); we need to be warned about that and to remain open to such admonition. But to write our position off as quasi-deism closed off from the supernatural or as part of the debris left by the Enlightenment's commitment to the autonomy of human reason will not help us.

In fact, there is good reason to ask whether the tables do not need to be turned here, at least for some who speak from a charismatic perspective. In a recent Festschrift for J. Rodman Williams, for instance, Henry Lederle is encouraged that charismatic spirituality, as he understands it, involves a worldview that has affinities with postmodernism, insofar as this philosophical movement seeks to recover "a sense of the whole and the interrelatedness of knowledge and experience."[5] In other words, he believes, what has been suppressed so long in much of modern Western rationalistic philosophy since the Enlightenment—the nonrational and intuitive aspect of human spirituality—is now being taken into account more adequately in contemporary philosophy.

But is this postmodern emphasis really an advancement? Is not Lederle's a spirituality that has become rather comfortable with the spirit of the times? Have we really gained anything for the gospel by rejecting one form of philosophy, only to identify with a different form that, though it seeks to limit, still affirms rational autonomy?[6] Such an approach hardly does justice, for instance, to Paul's unsparing opposition of his Spirit-taught wisdom to the wisdom of the world (1 Cor. 1:18–3:23), or his endeavor to "demolish arguments and every pretension that sets itself up against the knowledge of God" and to "take captive every thought to make it obedient to Christ" (2 Cor. 10:4–5). What is called for is confrontation, not limitation or containment by expansion.

---

[5]Lederle, "Spirit and Worldview," 26.
[6]Cf. ibid., 24.

Postmodern philosophers have rightly rejected the emphasis, especially since Descartes, on human reason being neutral and unbiased. But so far as I can see, they are still committed—in some instances, even more resolutely than the Enlightenment—to human autonomy. Any assertion of autonomy, rational or otherwise, whether it be from the seventeenth century or the late twentieth century, effaces the creature–Creator distinction. And human wholeness cannot be recaptured unless every vestige of autonomy is abandoned in submission to the Triune God of the Bible. Pentecostal power and postmodern pretensions have nothing to do with each other.

3. The cessationist position is most often associated with the name of B. B. Warfield, both because of his commanding stature as a theologian and because of his book, *Counterfeit Miracles*.[7] Understandably, then, opponents have concentrated on this book and suppose that by refuting it, they have refuted the cessationist position as a whole.[8] In other words, they think that the cessationist position for the most part stands or falls with Warfield's argument for it.

The case that I will be making stands squarely in the tradition of Warfield; at the heart of his position, I believe, is a fundamentally sound insight into Scripture. Still, a couple of initial observations, frequently overlooked on both sides of the debate, need to be made.

(a) Warfield did not intend to make an exegetical case; *Counterfeit Miracles* is primarily a study in church history and historical theology, as even a perusal of his table of contents shows. To be sure, he does give brief indications of how he would argue exegetically,[9] but he does not develop that argument, nor, as far as I know, does he elaborate on this issue anywhere else in his writings. It is wrong to suppose, therefore, that it is impossible to make a more extensive and cohesive exegetical defense of the cessationist position.[10]

---

[7]B. B. Warfield, *Counterfeit Miracles* (Edinburgh: Banner of Truth Trust, 1983 [1918]). Deere is typical in calling him "the greatest of the cessationist scholars" (*Power of the Spirit*, 268, n.9).

[8]E.g., most recently, Ruthven, *On the Cessation*.

[9]Primarily in chapter 1 (e.g., 3–5, 21–23, 25–28).

[10]This point is missed even by Ruthven in his major work on Warfield's views. He finds it "astonishing that he [Warfield] fails to address almost all of the impor-

(b) Warfield not only did not argue exegetically but also, in my judgment, probably could not have made the best exegetical case for his position. That is primarily because he did not have an adequate conception of the *eschatological* nature of the work of the Holy Spirit. (By *eschatological* I mean "characteristic of the 'age to come'"; see Matt. 12:32; Eph. 1:21; Heb. 6:5.) Briefly, one of the most important developments in biblical studies in this century has been the rediscovery of the already/not yet structure of New Testament eschatology. This broadened understanding of eschatology, which has now virtually reached the status of consensus, has brought a growing recognition that for the New Testament writers (most clearly Paul), the present work of the Spirit in the church and within believers is inherently eschatological. The Holy Spirit and eschatology, rarely related together in traditional Christian doctrine and piety, are now seen as inseparable.[11]

The eschatological reality of the Spirit's activity today is usually seen by noncessationists to be decisive for their view.[12] But as I will try to show below, this perception has to be challenged; in fact, that reality is fully compatible with, perhaps even essential, to the cessationist view. At any rate, to ask what constitutes the eschatological essence of the Spirit's present work in the church serves to focus a pivotal difference between cessationists and noncessationists.

---

tant Scriptures bearing on his cessationist polemic" (*On the Cessation*, 111); "it is ironic," in view of Warfield's stand for the authority and inerrancy of Scripture, "that in only a few scattered pages of *Counterfeit Miracles* does he seek scriptural support for his cessationist polemic" (194; cf. 197). But that was not Warfield's main intent in this book.

[11]Noteworthy historically is the fact that among the first to perceive the significance of this point, especially in Paul, was Geerhardus Vos, Warfield's (cessationist) Princeton Seminary colleague (and regular walking companion for over two decades); see his "The Eschatological Aspect of the Pauline Conception of Spirit," in R. B. Gaffin, Jr., ed., *Redemptive History and Biblical Interpretation: The Shorter Writings of Geerhardus Vos* (Phillipsburg, N.J.: Presbyterian and Reformed, 1980), 91–125, and *The Pauline Eschatology* (Grand Rapids: Baker, 1979 [1930]), 44, 58–60, 159–71. If, as Fee says, the latter is "a book that was some years ahead of its time" (*Empowering Presence*, 803, n. 1), how much more so the former essay, which appeared nearly two decades earlier in 1912.

[12]So, e.g., Fee, *Empowering Presence*, 803ff., esp. 822–26.

A. SECOND EXPERIENCES?

Virtually everything the New Testament teaches about the work of the Holy Spirit either looks forward or traces back to Pentecost. In other words, what really happened on that day is the all-important question. For instance, do the remarkable events of Pentecost provide a model challenging each New Testament believer, regardless of time and place, to seek to receive the Spirit in power as a distinct experience accompanied by speaking in tongues, either at the same time as or subsequent to conversion? Pentecostal denominations and those in the charismatic movement answer this question affirmatively. Many Pentecostals encourage *Christians*, who have already been born again, to be "baptized in the Holy Spirit," and they claim support from events in Acts 2 (Pentecost), 8 (Samaria), 10 (Caesarea), and 19 (Ephesus). Just as Jesus' disciples were first born again and then *later* baptized in the Holy Spirit at Pentecost (so their argument goes), we also should seek a Pentecostal "second experience" in our lives today.[13]

But is Pentecost intended to be a model for us to use in this way? In attempting to answer that question here, I will broaden the discussion somewhat by also keeping in view the question to what extent, if at all, Pentecost is about power experiences in the church today, postconversion second blessing or otherwise.

1. **Why Pentecost is unique.** D. A. Carson has observed, "The essentially salvation-historical structure of the Book of Acts is too often overlooked."[14] This is particularly true of those who find in chapter 2 (and elsewhere in Acts) enduring paradigms for Christian experience. The problem with second blessing and other empowerment theologies is not that they appeal to the narrative material in Acts to make a doctrinal point (as some cessationists have argued); Luke–Acts is equally as theological as, say, Paul's letters. The problem, rather, is that such theologies misunderstand Luke's theology.[15]

---

[13]See, representatively among more recent proponents, J. R. Williams, *Renewal Theology*, vol. 2 (Grand Rapids: Zondervan, 1990), 181–236, and the secondary literature cited there.

[14]D. A. Carson, *Showing the Spirit: A Theological Exposition of 1 Corinthians 12–14* (Grand Rapids: Baker, 1987), 150.

[15]In this respect, note Carson's pointed critique (ibid., 151) of R. Stronstad's *The Charismatic Theology of Luke* (Peabody, Mass.: Hendrickson, 1984).

This is a major premise

What, then, is the significance of Pentecost within the redemptive-historical framework set out by Luke? In order to answer that question, we must remember the basic distinction between the history of salvation (*historia salutis*) and the order of salvation (*ordo salutis*). In theological terms, the phrase "history of salvation" refers to events that are part of Christ's once-for-all accomplishment of his work of earning our salvation. The events in the history of salvation (such as Christ's death and resurrection) are finished, nonrepeatable events that have importance for all of God's people for all time. But the phrase "order of salvation" refers to events in the continuing application of Christ's work to individual lives throughout history, events such as saving faith, justification, and sanctification. When individual believers appropriate Christ's work in their own lives, those experiences are part of the "order of salvation," not (to use theological terms) part of the "history of salvation." (Another term for "history of salvation" is "redemptive history.")

Now in terms of that distinction, Pentecost belongs to the history of salvation, not to the order of salvation. That can be substantiated from a couple of angles. Jesus' words in Acts 1:5 ("For John baptized with water, but in a few days you will be baptized with the Holy Spirit") link John's ministry/baptism (Luke 3) and Pentecost (Acts 2) as sign to reality, prophecy to fulfillment. "I baptize you with water. But one more powerful than I will come. . . . He will baptize you with the Holy Spirit and with fire" (Luke 3:16). It is not difficult to see from the immediate context that the promised baptism with the Holy Spirit and fire[16] highlights not just one aspect, however important, but the Messiah's impending activity *in its entirety*. John's prophecy is his response to the basic messianic question in the crowd's mind as to whether he is the Christ (v. 15). His reply meets that question on the level on which it was asked and so surely intends to

---

[16]Interpreters have long debated whether "Holy Spirit" and "fire" have in view two baptisms, one positive and one negative, or one baptism with a dual outcome. The latter is almost certainly the case, esp. in view of v. 17: The metaphoric parallel to the messianic baptism is the *one* threshing floor with its dual result (wheat and chaff); see esp. the discussion of J. D. G. Dunn, *Baptism in the Holy Spirit* (Napierville, Ill.: Allenson, 1970), 10–14, who speaks of "the fiery *pneuma* in which all must be immersed" (13). The entire range of Dunn's insights on this passage (8–22) remains especially stimulating.

provide an equally basic perspective: Spirit and fire baptism is to be nothing less than the culmination of the Messiah's ministry; it will serve to stamp that ministry as a whole, just as, in comparison, water baptism was an index for John's entire ministry (Luke 20:4; Acts 10:37).

From this prophetic vantage point, Luke suggests, Pentecost is at the heart of Christ's finished work, at the core of the salvation brought by the coming of the kingdom of God (cf. Luke 7:18–28); in other words, it is an eschatological event.[17] All that Christ came to suffer and die for, short of his return, reaches its climax in his baptizing with the Holy Spirit and fire. Without that baptism Christ's once-for-all work of salvation is unfinished.

Looking in the other direction from Acts 1:5, Peter's Christ-centered sermon on the day of Pentecost confirms what we find in John's prophecy. In 2:32–33, following out of his focus on the earthly activity, death, and especially the resurrection of Jesus (vv. 22–31), Peter closely conjoins, in sequence: resurrection–ascension–reception of the Spirit[18]–outpouring of the Spirit. The last element, Pentecost, is climactic and final. It is not some addendum; there is nothing "second" about it. Resurrection–ascension–Pentecost, though distinct in time, constitute a unified complex of events, a once-for-all, salvation-historical unity; they are inseparable.

---

[17]Luke 3:17 ("His winnowing fork is in his hand to clear his threshing floor and to gather the wheat into his barn, but he will burn up the chaff with unquenchable fire"), too often neglected or misunderstood in discussing Pentecost, reinforces its eschatological (as well as forensic) significance. Here the messianic baptism is pictured under the metaphor of the threshing floor/harvest, a favorite biblical image for eschatological judgment (e.g., Isa. 21:10; 41:15–16; Jer. 51:33; Matt. 13:30, 39; Rev. 14:14–20). Grammatically, the subject of the subordinate clause in Luke 3:17 is the subject of the main clause of v. 16b; the Spirit-and-fire baptizer is, *as such*, the eschatological harvester-judge. Pentecost, then, is essentially a matter of judgment. Whatever may be its full significance and outworkings, the point of departure for a proper overall understanding of Pentecost is to see it as a part and within the context of eschatological judgment. See R. B. Gaffin, Jr., "Justification in Luke–Acts," in *Right With God: Justification in the Bible and the World*, ed. D. A. Carson (Grand Rapids: Baker, 1992), 108–12.

[18]At the Jordan Jesus receives (i.e., is himself baptized with) the Spirit as endowment for the messianic task that lies before him (Luke 3:21–22); in the ascension he receives the Spirit as reward for the completed task behind him and for baptizing others with the Spirit.

Second experiences as analogies to Pentecost? Pentecost, then, is no more capable of being a repeatable paradigm event than are the other events. Given this structure, it is anomalous, to say the least, to view one of these events (Pentecost) as a repeatable model for individual Christian experience and the other three (Jesus' resurrection, ascension, and reception of the Spirit) as nonrepeatable, once-for-all events.

According to H. L. Lederle (to cite one charismatic reaction at this point):

> No one would want to argue for a literal repetition of Pentecost, but one wonders if the symbolic value of the events of salvation history needs to be totally abandoned? In the Reformed tradition the ethical concepts of mortification and vivification have always been developed as analogies of Christ's death and resurrection. Perhaps a "coming" of the Spirit could be seen in the same way.[19]

Such a response misses the point and highlights what is at stake here. Reformed theology, more importantly, the theology of Paul that it seeks to reflect, does not view either Christ's death or his resurrection as being "symbolic" or providing "analogies" for particular experiences, whether subsequent to conversion or distinct from the initial experience of salvation.

The apostle makes that point clear within the overall flow of his argument in Romans 6:1ff. Without doubt, union with Christ in his death and resurrection has experiential implications and outworkings in the ongoing life of the believer (vv. 15ff.; cf. Phil. 3:10). But that union takes place at the inception of the Christian life, inseparable from justification (and through the same initial act of faith). Union with Christ in his death and resurrection is not a matter of replicating these events, by analogy, in our ongoing experience; believers do not have a death experience as distinct from a resurrection experience—whether

---

[19]Lederle, *Treasures Old and New: Interpretations of "Spirit-Baptism" in the Charismatic Renewal Movement* (Peabody, Mass.: Hendrickson, 1988), 2–3. Much more typical among Pentecostal/charismatic writers is Williams' flat, unqualified assertion: "Unlike the coming of Christ in the Incarnation, which was a once-for-all event, the coming of the Holy Spirit would occur an unlimited number of times" (*Renewal Theology,* 2:184); the Spirit's coming at Pentecost is "the first in an unlimited number that came later" (n. 10).

temporally or causally. Rather, at conversion we are definitively united to the exalted Christ and so continue to share in who he is as the crucified and resurrected Lord.

Similarly, a share in the Spirit takes place at conversion. Paul says as much in 1 Corinthians 12:13, the only New Testament reference, apart from those in Luke–Acts, that speaks of being "baptized with the Spirit." There Paul shows how the epochal, once-for-all event of Pentecost subsequently becomes effective in the life of the individual believer. Two points are plain: (a) "All" (in Christ's body, the church, cf. v. 12), not just some, have been Spirit-baptized; (b) that experience takes place at the point of coming "into" the fellowship of Christ's body (that is, at conversion), not subsequently.[20]

In other words, the primary significance of Pentecost is redemptive-historical and Christological, not experiential.

Other New Testament perspectives on Pentecost. That significance is not unique to Luke–Acts but also emerges elsewhere in the New Testament. In John 14:16–17, for example, Jesus' promise to send the Spirit,[21] premised on his imminent departure or ascension (14:12; cf. 7:39; 16:7; 20:17), carries another promise that in fact is not a different one: "I will not leave you as orphans; I will come to you" (14:18). For the Spirit to come will be for Christ to come.[22] The Spirit is the "vicar" of Christ. He has no agenda of his own; his role is basically self-effacing and Christ-enhancing (see esp. 16:13–14). His presence in the church is, vicariously, the presence of the ascended Jesus.

Again, in Matthew's Gospel, the resurrected Jesus (to whom universal authority has just been "given"[23]) declares: "I

---

[20]It appears that increasingly even Pentecostal commentators recognize that Holy Spirit baptism as a distinct postconversion experience is not taught here; see, e.g., the clear-headed exegesis of Fee, *Empowering Presence,* 178–82.

[21]I will leave aside here the relationship of the "Johannine Pentecost" (John 20:22) to Acts 2; see R. B. Gaffin, Jr., *Perspectives on Pentecost* (Phillipsburg, N.J.: Presbyterian and Reformed, 1979), 39–41.

[22]The Second Coming or, alternatively, Jesus' brief, temporary resurrection appearances hardly qualify as the coming of Christ in view here, which from the immediate context (vv. 17–23) is so closely conjoined as to be virtually identical with the imminent ("a little while," v. 19; cf. 16:16–19) dwelling/showing/being of the Spirit (and the Father, v. 23) in/to/with believers, in distinction from the world.

[23]That is, power he did not have previously but now does, as a result of the resurrection (cf. Acts 2:33, 36).

will be with you always, to the very end of the age" (Matt. 28:20). These well-known words from the Great Commission are not, at least primarily, an affirmation of divine omnipresence but a promise of Pentecost and its enduring consequences. The presence of the Spirit will be the presence of Christ; Jesus will be with his church in the power of the Spirit. If it means anything, Pentecost means the exalted Jesus is here with his church to stay.

In a similar vein, Paul asserts that by virtue of his resurrection and ascension, "the last Adam [became] life-giving Spirit" (1 Cor. 15:45c, author's translation) and "the Lord is the Spirit" (2 Cor. 3:17a).[24] These, in effect, are one-sentence commentaries on Pentecost and its significance.[25] Without in any way diminishing the personal distinction between them, the exalted Lord Jesus and the Spirit are one in the activity of giving resurrection life (1 Cor. 15:42ff.) and eschatological liberty (2 Cor. 3:17b).

In 1 Corinthians 15:45 "life-giving" contemplates Christ's future action, when he will resurrect the mortal bodies of believers (cf. v. 22). At the same time, it seems difficult to deny, in light of the overall context of Paul's teaching, that his present activity is also implicitly in view. The resurrection life of the believer, in union with Christ, is not only future but also present (e.g., Gal. 2:20; Col. 2:12–13; 3:1–4). The resurrected Christ is already active in the church in the resurrection power of the Spirit.[26]

---

[24]The meaning of these statements, in context, is much disputed and cannot be discussed in detail here. In particular, I will have to forego interacting with Fee's diverging exegesis (most recently in his *Empowering Presence*, 264–67, 311–14 and "Christology and Pneumatology in Romans 8:9–11—and Elsewhere: Some Reflections on Paul as a Trinitarian," in *Jesus of Nazareth: Lord and Christ*, ed. J. B. Green and M. Turner [Grand Rapids: Eerdmans, 1994], 319–22). Though I share fully his opposition to the sort of functional Spirit-Christology argued by James Dunn and others, his insistence that the "whole point" of 1 Cor. 15:45 is "soteriological-eschatological" ("Christology," 320) underplays in my judgment the profound Christological and pneumatological dimensions also present. See further H. Ridderbos, *Paul: An Outline of his Theology*, trans. J. R. de Witt (Grand Rapids: Eerdmans, 1975 [1966]), 88, 225, 539, and R. B. Gaffin, Jr., *Resurrection and Redemption: A Study in Paul's Theology* (Phillipsburg, N.J.: Presbyterian and Reformed, 1987), 85–97.

[25]The "is" of 2 Cor. 3:17, far from expressing an unqualified or timeless predication, rests on the "became" of 1 Cor. 15:45.

[26]It is gratuitous to find in these passages a "functional" Christology that denies the personal difference between Christ and the Spirit, one that is irreconcilable with later church formulation of Trinitarian doctrine. The personal and parallel distinction between God (the Father), Christ as Lord, and the (Holy) Spirit—underlying subse-

For Paul, there is no work of the Spirit within the believer that is not also the work of Christ. That appears, for instance, in Romans 8:9–10, where "you ... by the Spirit" (v. 9a), "the Spirit ... in you" (v. 9b), "belong to Christ" (v. 9d, virtually equivalent to the frequent "in Christ"), and "Christ ... in you" (v. 10a)—that is, all the possible combinations—are used *interchangeably*; they do not describe different experiences but the same reality. There is no relationship with Christ that is not also fellowship with the Spirit; the presence of the Spirit is the presence of Christ; to belong to Christ is to be possessed by the Spirit. For a person to be strengthened "through his Spirit in your inner being" is for Christ to "dwell in your hearts through faith" (Eph. 3:16–17).[27] And that is true in the ongoing experience of believers (*ordo salutis*) only because of what is true, antecedently, in the once-for-all experience of Christ, because of who he is/has become in his exaltation, "the life-giving Spirit" (*historia salutis*).

Conclusion: Pentecost completes Christ's finished work for our salvation. Without Pentecost, the accomplishment of redemption is incomplete and meaningless. To maintain the significance of Pentecost as a power experience enjoyed by some believers in distinction from others, one that is "beyond" salvation (seen only as the forgiveness of sins),[28] is seriously inadequate. Such an appraisal makes too little, not too much, of Pentecost. Without Pentecost there is no salvation. Period. Why? Because without Pentecost there is no (resurrection) life in the Spirit, and without that eschatological life,[29] sinners remain "dead in [their] transgressions and sins" (Eph. 2:1, 5).

---

quent doctrinal formulation—is clear enough in Paul (e.g., 1 Cor. 12:4–6; 2 Cor. 13:14; Eph. 4:4–6; cf. esp. Fee's excellent discussion, *Empowering Presence*, 827–45). We should emphasize that the salvation-historical focus of Paul's argument must always be kept in view. He is concerned not with the ontological question of who Christ is (timelessly, eternally) as God's Son (e.g., Rom. 1:3; 8:3, 32), but with what he *became*, what has happened to him in history, and what his identity means as "the last *Adam*," "the second *man*" (1 Cor. 15:47), that is, in terms of his true humanity.

[27]That Paul does not intend an absolute identity between Christ and the Spirit is clear later on in Romans 8: the Spirit's interceding here, within believers (vv. 26–27), is distinguished from the complementary intercession of the ascended Christ there, at God's right hand (v. 34).

[28]So, e.g., Williams, *Renewal Theology*, 2:177, 189, and esp. 205–7.

[29]Paul's metaphors for the Spirit as "deposit" (2 Cor. 1:22; 5:5; Eph. 1:14) and "firstfruits" (Rom. 8:23) highlight the inherently eschatological nature of his presence and work within believers.

Pentecost publicly attests that the saving work of Christ is complete, that he has become "the life-giving Spirit." Pentecost is the redemptive-historical Spirit-seal (cf. Eph. 1:13) of Christ to the church on the forgiveness and eschatological life secured in his death, resurrection, and ascension. To put it in formal, doctrinal categories, the "newness" of Pentecost is not, at least not primarily, anthropological-experiential but Christological and ecclesiological-missiological. Above all Pentecost means two things: (a) The Spirit is now present, at last and permanently, on the basis of the finished work of Christ; he is the *eschatological* Spirit; (b) the Spirit is now poured out "on all people" (Acts 2:17), Gentiles as well as Jews; he is the *universal* Spirit.[30]

2. **But what about second experiences in Acts?** But still, after all this (and some charismatics will agree with much of what has just been said about the significance of Pentecost), the question persists: What about the undeniably remarkable experience of the 120 at Pentecost and of others subsequently involved in the rest of the Pentecost event-complex as recorded in Acts (e.g., 8:14ff.; 10:44–48/11:15–18; 19:1–7)?

In answering this question, it becomes especially crucial not to ignore the redemptive-historical framework of Acts. Too often Acts is read as a more or less random collection of episodes from the primeval glory days of the church, as a rather loose anthology of vignettes from "the good old days when Christians were *really* Christians." This reading not only fosters an anachronistic "Back to Pentecost" nostalgia, but almost inevitably an exegetical inductivism, without adequate attention to context, also takes hold. As a result, Acts is mined for experiential nuggets that are fused (I would have to say, forced) together to provide an ongoing, standard model for individual empowerment.

The whole of Acts is unique. As a document, Acts, like Luke–Acts as a whole, is carefully crafted. Whatever the multifaceted purpose of this book, a primary concern is surely to show that history unfolded just as Jesus said it would: "You will be my witnesses in Jerusalem, and in all Judea and Samaria, and to the ends of the earth" (Acts 1:8). Acts intends to document a *completed* history, a unique epoch in the history of redemption—the

---

[30]See my *Perspectives on Pentecost*, 13–41.

once-for-all, *apostolic*[31] spread of the gospel "to the ends of the earth." There is no need for a Part Three to Theophilus. The outcome for the apostle (Paul) is left unresolved, but not for the apostolic gospel; it has covered the earth (cf. Col. 1:6, 23). Although there will be a postapostolic future,[32] the history that interests Luke is *finished*.

It is in terms of this controlling perspective that the miraculous experiences of those at Pentecost and elsewhere in Acts have their meaning. These miracles attest the realization of the expanding *apostolic* program announced in Acts 1:8: Jerusalem and Judea, Samaria, the ends of the earth—or, in ethnic terms, Jews, half-Jews, non-Jews/Gentiles (note the parallelism of "Gentiles" and "ends of the earth" in Isa. 49:6, cited in Acts 13:47).

This perspective seems clear enough in those passages most often discussed in chapters 2, 8, 10/11, and 19. The redemptive-historically restrictive textual markers that control these passages are unmistakable: "God-fearing Jews" (2:5), "Samaria" (with reference to "the apostles in Jerusalem," 8:14), "the Gentiles" (10:45; cf. 11:1, again with reference to the apostles, 11:18; 15:8). The ethnic identity and (redemptive-)historical locale of the individuals involved may not be brushed aside as essentially indifferent to their power experiences described in these (and related) texts.[33] Acts 2 and the subsequent miraculous events that Luke narrates are not intended to establish a pattern of "repetitions" of Pentecost to continue on indefinitely in church history. Rather, together they constitute, as already intimated, an event-complex, complete with the finished apostolic program they accompany.

It would certainly be wrong to argue, on the one hand, that Luke intended to show that miraculous gifts and power experi-

---

[31]Note that Acts 1:8 is not a promise to all believers or to every generation of the church indiscriminately, but only to the apostles; grammatically, the antecedent of "you" in verse 8 is "the apostles" in verse 2. In Colossians 1:6, 23 Paul hints at the completion of this worldwide apostolic expansion of the church through his own ministry.

[32] "Without hindrance," the final word in the Greek text, is the note Acts ends on (cf. 2 Tim. 2:9: Paul is in chains, "but God's word is not chained").

[33]This applies as well to the incident in 19:1–7, which addresses a salvation-historical anomaly: disciples of John the Baptist who knew (or should have known) of the prophecy that stamped his ministry/baptism (Luke 3:16–17) but were still unaware of its fulfillment.

ences ceased with the history he documented. But it is no less gratuitous to suppose that he was implying that they would continue beyond. That issue is simply not in his purview and will have to be settled on other grounds.

In this respect, to observe that in Acts others than apostles exercise miraculous gifts (e.g., 6:8) is beside the point. To offer that as evidence that such gifts continue beyond the time of the apostles[34] pulls apart what for Luke belongs together. Others exercise such gifts *by virtue of the presence and activity of the apostles*; they do so under an "apostolic umbrella," so to speak.[35] Their activity, too, belongs to Luke's global concern, intimated at the outset (cf. 1:1–2): what the exalted *Christ* is doing by the *Holy Spirit* through the *apostles*.

More troublesome is the argument for continuation based on the assertion that in Acts signs and wonders do not so much attest the bearers of the gospel as the gospel itself—that is, that the primary referent of miracles is the message, not the messenger.[36] This notion again injects a disjunction foreign to Luke. But it also carries the potential for subverting the very apostolicity of the church he is concerned to demonstrate.

Do the apostles (and others) proclaim the gospel because it is true? Of course. But equally important, the gospel is true *because* the apostles proclaim it, and others do so *only derivatively*, in *dependence* on that apostolic witness. As Luke makes clear from the outset (Acts 1:15–26), material authority (the gospel message) and formal authority (the apostles) belong together.[37]

---

[34]As do, e.g., Deere, *Power of the Spirit*, 68, 244; W. Grudem, *Systematic Theology: An Introduction to Biblical Doctrine* (Grand Rapids: Zondervan, 1994), 358–59, 362.

[35]Note (pace Warfield) that I am *not* arguing that only those the apostles actually laid hands on exercised these gifts; the text will not sustain such a "mechanical" conclusion.

[36]E.g., Deere, *Power of the Spirit*, 103–4, 249, and, more cautiously, Grudem, *Systematic Theology*, 359. In their handling of Acts, I believe, both authors illustrate the questionable inductivism spoken of above.

[37]A wide-ranging debate continues over the background and nature of apostleship in the New Testament. For one, the exact relationship between the apostles appointed by Christ and the Jewish šᵉlîah of that time is disputed. Suffice it here to say that the latter institution at least provides a backdrop for understanding the apostles and their authority; akin to persons today with power of attorney, they are legally authorized representatives of the exalted Christ. In an original, nonderiva-

In fact, they stand or fall together; the only gospel Luke knows is the *apostolic* gospel, attested as such by signs and wonders.[38]

The non-uniform nature of Acts experiences. In my view, those who order the material in Acts to provide a model for a distinct postconversion power experience too easily gloss over problems in the text that make such a position all but impossible. For instance, is the experience in view in fact postconversion? (Acts 2: yes; ch. 8: likely, but debatable; chs. 10/11: no; ch. 19:?—Do John's disciples lack saving faith?) Do people experience the Spirit at the time of or subsequent to water baptism? Is it with or without prayer and the laying on of hands? Such questions do not have a consistent answer, so that any quest for an experiential paradigm in Acts is seeking what it does not intend to provide.

The experience of the disciples on Pentecost (Acts 2) was undoubtedly postconversion. But how does that fact make individual conversion a prerequisite or even a presupposition for the coming of the Spirit on each of them there? Shall we say, then, that their conversions were likewise a precondition for the death, resurrection, and ascension of Jesus (the other events with which Pentecost forms a once-for-all event complex, 2:32–33) to take place?! Involved is the unique, sign-laden experience of that generation, of which by the nature of the case there could only be one. Theirs was the experience of those who happened to live at that time, "when the time had fully come" (Gal. 4:4), when God's Son actually became incarnate, suffered, died, was raised, ascended, and, inseparably and in consequence, sent the Holy Spirit to the church.

Finally here, it strikes me that Pentecostal/charismatic authors have remarkably little to say about the closing words of Luke's Gospel (Luke 24:52–53). This, after all, is the note Luke

---

tive way, he speaks through them (2 Cor. 13:3); their word is God's word (1 Thess. 2:13). See, e.g., H. Ridderbos, *Redemptive History and the New Testament Scriptures* (Phillipsburg, N.J.: Presbyterian and Reformed, 1988 [1955]), 12–15.

[38]The ongoing debate about biblical authority shows what is at stake here. (1) Does God/the Bible say so because it is true? Or, (2) is it true because God/the Bible says so? A false dilemma surely; both must be affirmed. But in biblical theism, where the image-bearing creature remains permanently dependent for knowledge as well as existence on God the Creator, the proposition contained in (2) is more ultimate: God is the source of all truth.

chooses to end on, the impression he wishes to leave with Theophilus until Part Two arrives. This closing includes the following: The apostles and other disciples, having just had contact with the resurrected and ascended Jesus, with hearts inflamed (v. 32) and minds opened (v. 45), worship "with great joy," "praising God [continually]" and publicly ("at the temple"). All this sounds impressive to me and is in full continuity with their (Spirit-filled) experience *after* Pentecost (cf. Acts 2:46–47). This is just one more indication how little the primary point of Pentecost is individual Christian experience, postconversion or otherwise.

3. **Because of Pentecost, we experience the Holy Spirit's work.** Emphasizing the once-for-all, redemptive-historical, Christological significance of Pentecost may leave the impression of being "eager to move away from giving any experiential significance to Spirit-baptism."[39] That impression, however, I am eager to dispel. Undeniably (and I will have more to say on this below), the Spirit that came at Pentecost is the author of rich and profound experiential realities in believers; he is the source of all Christian experience. There can be no question from the viewpoint of the New Testament: Not to experience the Spirit—in a vital, transforming, and thus powerful way—is not to have the Spirit at all. That is not at issue in this symposium.

B. CESSATIONISM

1. The issue of cessation needs to be focused. I certainly do not hold that all gifts of the Spirit have ceased or that the church is devoid of such gifts today—a point I will return to below. Suffice it here to say that the question is not *whether* but *which* spiritual gifts continue today.

Nor do I argue that miracles have ceased. Defining "miracle" adequately is difficult and would require extensive discussion. For our purposes I will accept that a miracle occurs when God does something "less common" or "extraordinary" and "highly unusual."[40] I do not question that such activity contin-

[39]So Lederle, *Treasures Old and New*, 2.

[40]So Grudem, *Systematic Theology*, 355; D. A. Carson, "The Purpose of Signs and Wonders in the New Testament," in *Power Religion: The Selling Out of the Evangelical Church?* ed. M. S. Horton (Chicago: Moody, 1992), 114, 118 (n. 6).

ues today. More specifically, I do not deny that God heals (miraculously) today. He may choose to do so, no matter how hopeless and terminal a prognosis is medically, in response to the individual and corporate prayers of his people. James 5:14–16, for instance, points us to that, no matter how we settle the details of their interpretation.

I do question, however, whether the gifts of healing and of working miracles, as listed in 1 Corinthians 12:9–10, are given today. I note here at least two factors sustaining that doubt. (a) Within the New Testament the only specific instances of the actual exercise of these gifts, given by the ascended Christ, are documented in Acts (cf. Heb. 2:3b–4). But these (whether by the apostles themselves, by those they laid hands on, or by others), as noted above, accompany the unique and finished apostolic spread of the gospel that concerns Luke. In this sense they are "the [signs] that mark an apostle" (regardless of the correct interpretation of 2 Cor. 12:12), and their continuation into the postapostolic era may not simply be presupposed. That must be established on other grounds, which, so far as I can see, the New Testament does not provide. (b) James 5 contemplates a different sort of scenario. There healing is not dependent on or effected by an individual empowered to do so but takes place through prayer, not only that of the elders (and then without distinction among them) but of all believers as well.

2. My main concern is the cessation of all revelatory or word gifts. By *word gifts* I have in mind (with a view to the lists in Rom. 12:6–8; 1 Cor. 12:8–10, 28–31; and Eph. 4:11) prophecy and its assessment, tongues and their interpretation, the word of wisdom, and the word of knowledge. Since it is generally recognized that a certain amount of overlap exists among these gifts (according to 1 Cor. 14, for instance, prophecy and interpreted tongues are functionally equivalent), we may view them together, generally, as prophetic gifts.

A full case for the cessation of these revelatory gifts cannot be made here.[41] It turns, to note just one key passage, on the salvation-historical understanding of the church and its apostolicity expressed in Ephesians 2:11–21. There the church is pictured as the construction project of God, the master architect-

---

[41]See my *Perspectives on Pentecost*, 89–116.

builder, underway in the period between the ascension and return of Christ (cf. 1:20–22; 4:8–10, 13). In this church-house the apostles and prophets are the foundation, along with Christ as the "cornerstone"[42] (v. 20).

In any construction project (ancient or modern), the foundation comes at the beginning and does not have to be relaid repeatedly (at least if the builder knows what he's doing!). In terms of this dynamic model for the church, the apostles and prophets belong to the period of the foundation. In other words, by the divine architect's design, the presence of apostles and prophets in the history of the church is temporary.

How are the apostles and prophets the foundation of the church? The redemptive-historical specs for the church-house provide the answer. According to 1 Corinthians 3:11 (the metaphor varies slightly but with no significant theological difference), Christ is the foundation of the church. How? Not in a general sense or in his person considered in the abstract, and not even primarily because of his present activity in the church. Rather, Christ is the foundation "already laid" (v. 11); that is, he is the foundation because of his death and resurrection (e.g., 1 Cor. 1:18, 23; 2:2; 15:3–4; 2 Tim. 2:8). All that he now is for and in the church depends on and derives from his being the crucified and glorified Christ. He is the foundation of the church because of his *finished* work.

The apostles and prophets, then, are not the foundation because they make up for some lack in Christ's work. What is essential and otherwise lacking is an adequate witness to that work—in a word, a gospel witness. The apostles are Christ's authorized witnesses, appointed by the resurrected Christ himself to bear authoritative testimony to his resurrection and its implications (e.g., Acts 1:2, 8, 21–26; 1 Cor. 9:1; 15:1–4, 8–11; Gal. 1:1, 15–16).

The apostles (and the prophets[43] along with them), in other words, are the foundation of the church because of their

---

[42]Especially given its close proximity to the foundation, "keystone" hardly fits the context; cf. Fee, *Empowering Presence*, 688, n. 100.

[43]That New (not Old) Testament prophets are in view is seen from the word order (not: "the prophets and apostles," i.e., the Old and New Testaments) and especially from Ephesians 3:5, where the same expression occurs with the word "now" (in contrast to "other generations" in the past).

witness—their inspired, revelatory witness (note Eph. 3:5: "now
... revealed by the Spirit to God's holy apostles and prophets").
In terms of the deed-word correlation that marks the giving of
revelation throughout redemptive history, their witness is the
foundational witness to the work of Christ; to the once-for-all
work of Christ is joined a once-for-all witness to that work. Here
is the matrix for the New Testament canon, for the emergence of
a new body of revelation to stand alongside what eventually
becomes the Old Testament.[44] With this foundational revelation
completed, and so too their foundational role as witnesses, the
apostles and, along with them, the prophets and other associated revelatory word gifts, pass from the life of the church.

Various objections to this construct, along with evasions of
its implications, will be taken up during the course of the discussion that follows.[45] Here we may note briefly that "apostolic
succession" in a personal sense, however conceived (whether
institutionally or charismatically), is a contradiction in terms. At
issue for the New Testament is the redemptive-historical "once-
for-allness" of the apostolate, the unique noncontinuing presence of apostles in the life of the church. The apostolicity of the
"one, holy, catholic ... church" (Nicene Creed) is revealed wherever the church holds faithfully to and builds firmly on the finished apostolic-prophetic witness to Christ's finished work and
to the implications of that witness for faith and life. This complete, foundational witness is preserved, in its full scope if not
its entire extent, as the New Testament.

3. To maintain the continuation of the prophetic gifts today
stands in tension with the canonicity of the New Testament,
particularly the canon as closed. Inevitably such continuation
relativizes the sufficiency and authority of Scripture. Many con-

---

[44]That several New Testament documents were not written by apostles is
beside the point. Parallel to what we saw above about signs and wonders in the New
Testament era, apostolicity, though not strictly a criterion of canonicity, is undeniably the medium or matrix for canonicity; see R. B. Gaffin, Jr., "The New Testament
As Canon," in *Inerrancy and Hermeneutic*, ed. H. M. Conn (Grand Rapids: Baker,
1988), esp. 172–79.

[45]Ruthven's rebuttal effort (*On the Cessation*, 216–20), for example, is marred
generally by an inadequate conception of apostolic authority as well as a less than
accurate representation at points of the position he is opposing (e.g., "the preaching
of Calvinistic soteriology" renders the exalted Christ "presently inactive," p. 113!).

tinuationists, I am well aware, vigorously deny this assertion. But I ask for their patience as I try to point out why it may not be simply dismissed as a "red herring."[46]

Many continuationists are in fact cessationists, in that they recognize there are no apostles[47] today.[48] That reflects an appreciation of the unique authority of the apostles and the tie between that authority and the authority and (closed) canonicity of the New Testament.[49] That awareness, in turn, implies the legitimacy of distinguishing between an apostolic and postapostolic era of church history, or what parallels it, between an open and closed canon period.

Everyone who accepts this distinction has to think through its ramifications. A flat "all the gifts are for today" will not do (and in fact is not the position of many continuationists). But what is the connection between gifts like prophecy and the presence of the apostles? Is it coherent exegetically and theologically to maintain, on the one hand, the cessation of the revelatory word gift of apostleship (for surely it was primarily that, cf. Gal. 1:11–12; 1 Thess. 2:13) and, on the other, the continuation of the prophetic gifts? Would not such continuation take us back to the open canon situation of the early church,[50] and do so without the control of a living apostolate?

---

[46]As does, e.g., M. Turner, "Spiritual Gifts Then and Now," *VoxEv*, 15 (1985): 55.

[47]The New Testament uses the Greek word *apostolos* in more than one sense. In view here are those appointed by Christ and invested with his authority (see above, n. 37), those who are "first" in the church (1 Cor. 12:28; cf. Eph. 2:20; 4:11; 2 Cor. 11:13): the twelve, Paul, and perhaps others.

[48]E.g., Carson, *Showing the Spirit*, 91, 156; Grudem, *Systematic Theology*, 906, 911. Note in this regard the qualified, less than emphatic conclusion of even so resolute an anticessationist as Ruthven (*On the Cessation*, 220). Grudem's proviso that apostleship is "an office, not a gift" (1019, n. 6; cf. Deere, *Power of the Spirit*, 242) is hardly sustainable (if nothing else, in the light of the activity of the ascended Christ in view in Eph. 4:8, 11: "he . . . gave gifts to men"; "he . . . gave some to be apostles") and makes a disjunction Paul would not recognize. All gifts are not offices (a point, by the way, too often missed or glossed over in current debates about women's ordination), but all offices are gifts.

[49]E.g., Grudem, *Systematic Theology*, 60–63.

[50]I should emphasize that, during the foundational, apostolic period of the church, its "canon" (i.e., where I find God's word and revealed will for my life) was a fluid, evolving entity, made up of three factors: (1) a completed Old Testament;

4. Those who maintain the continuation of the prophetic gifts today are substantially at odds about these gifts, especially their authority. On the one hand, there are those who hold that these gifts are fallible in their exercise and have an authority lower than that of the Old Testament canonical prophets and the New Testament apostles. On the other side, Gordon Fee, for instance, dismisses this position as "controlled by factors that do not interest Paul at all" and "speaking to a lot of concerns that are quite different from Paul's."[51]

According to Fee, "[Paul] undoubtedly saw 'the New Testament prophets' as in the succession of the 'legitimate' prophets of the Old Testament ... and the only 'prophets' Paul ever refers to who are not part of the present Spirit-inspiration are the prophets whose oracles become part of his Bible (Rom 1:2; 3:21)."[52] While Fee does call this "slender evidence to go on," in context it seems difficult not to read him to be saying that, as far as we can tell, we are unable to distinguish, in inspiration and authority, between New Testament prophets and inscripturated prophets.

The view of Williams is similar to Fee's (a view that, I take it, is widely held among Pentecostals and charismatics). Though he maintains that any expression of the gift of prophecy is "subordinate revelation" and not "on the same level with Scripture," at the same time he asserts that it "is directly from God and is spoken with divine authority," that "the words are divinely inspired," and that "true prophecy is the very utterance of God."[53] If such is the case and if such prophecy continues today, then it is difficult to see how the sufficiency of Scripture or its canonicity (other than relatively, as a complete collection of authoritative documents) can be viably maintained. Clearly, the

---

(2) an eventual New Testament and other inspired documents no longer extant (e.g., the letter mentioned in 1 Cor. 5:9), as each was written and then circulated (cf. Col. 4:16); and (3) an oral apostolic and prophetic voice ("whether by word of mouth or by letter" [2 Thess. 2:15] points to this authoritative mix of oral and written). The church at that time lived by a "Scripture plus" principle of authority and guidance; by the nature of the case, it could not yet be committed, as a formal principle, to *sola Scriptura*.

[51]Fee, *Empowering Presence*, 892 (with specific reference to the view of Wayne Grudem).

[52]Ibid.

[53]Williams, *Renewal Theology*, 2:382, 386; cf. 1:43–44.

issue here is more than whether contemporary prophecy *contradicts* Scripture.

It may well be that "no one ... wants to open up the possibility of someone adding to Scripture."[54] But if prophecy today, as claimed above, is of divine inspiration and authority, then, whatever the intention, in effect Scripture has been added to.[55] Now the "canon" (i.e., where God's word is found today) becomes not only what God has said in Scripture but also what he is saying beyond Scripture, and we are bound to attend and submit to both of these. In fact, the latter will likely prove more compelling because of its perceived contemporaneity and immediacy to our situation. To see here a relativizing threat to the canon and its authority is anything but a red herring.[56]

Fee, in the context just cited, believes that "questions such as those raised by people with 'canonical consciousness' lie totally outside his [Paul's] frame of reference," and that "he has no interest at all in the questions raised by our existence in the church some 1900 years later."[57] But are such sweeping statements sustainable? Paul's redemptive-historical, eschatological frame of reference,[58] with his keen sense of living "between the times," comprehends the period between Christ's resurrection and return in its entirety, no matter how long it may prove to be (or how short Paul himself, in response to the revelation he

---

[54]Deere, *Power of the Spirit*, 241 (after reading him I am still not sure whether his view of prophecy and its authority is closer to that of Fee or of Grudem); cf. Williams, *Renewal Theology*, 1:44.

[55]Williams emphasizes (with italics) that there is nothing more, prophecy included, to be added to the special revelation attested in Scripture. But just two sentences later he describes prophecy as "a disclosure of some message for the contemporary situation that adds nothing essentially to what He has before made known" (*Renewal Theology*, 1:44). Surely it is not carping to observe that, however nonessential, an addition is still an addition. Further, it has to be asked: what really is the disqualifying, limiting force of "nothing essentially," when it is God's own utterance, possessing divine inspiration and authority? I don't see how Williams' position has a satisfactory answer to this question.

[56]Ruthven, for instance, speaks of "the eternally-sealed limits of the biblical canon" (*On the Cessation*, 194). I accept and value this affirmation but have difficulty seeing, not only in terms of his overall position but also the immediate context, how he can maintain those limits in a theologically (and practically) significant way.

[57]Fee, *Empowering Presence*, 892.

[58]Few have commented on this more ably in our day than Fee himself.

received and communicated, may have anticipated it would be). Paul is an apostle for all seasons, regardless of the number of ensuing generations. He writes for all who are in the position of having "turned to God from idols to serve the living and true God, and to wait for his Son from heaven, whom he raised from the dead" (1 Thess. 1:9–10). Paul can hardly be said to be indifferent to the (legitimate) theological concerns of the church at the end of the twentieth century.

Moreover, the Pastoral Letters with their nonapostolic addressees (Timothy, as much as anyone, is fairly seen as Paul's direct, personal successor, cf. Phil. 2:20–22, but Paul never calls him an apostle), show a concern for a postapostolic future. Specifically, the injunction to guard the (apostolic) "deposit" (2 Tim 1:14; cf. v. 12; 1 Tim. 6:20) evinces at least an incipient "canonical consciousness."

5. But what about the lower, fallible authority view of prophetic gifts?[59]

(a) This view does not have an adequate explanation for Ephesians 2:20; 3:5 (the prophets as part of the church-foundation, discussed above). Wayne Grudem, for instance, has argued at length that there the "prophets" are not the prophets mentioned elsewhere in Paul but the apostles ("apostle-prophets," "apostles who are also prophets").[60] But, grammatically, that is unlikely.[61] Nor is it likely contextually, for in 4:11, Paul's next reference to prophets, in a related context (concern with the makeup of the church), he clearly distinguishes them from the apostles (4:11; cf. 1 Cor. 12:28).

Grudem goes on to maintain that even if the prophets are distinct from the apostles there, Ephesians 2:20 still does not have "much relevance" for deciding whether prophecy continues today.[62] That is because, despite his effort to minimize the

---

[59]E.g., Carson, *Showing the Spirit*, 91–100; R. Clements, *Word and Spirit: The Bible and the Gift of Prophecy Today* (Leicester: UCCF, 1986); W. A. Grudem, *The Gift of Prophecy in the New Testament and Today* (Westchester, Ill.: Crossway, 1988); *Systematic Theology*, 1049–61; cf. 1031–43; G. Houston, *Prophecy: A Gift for Today?* (Downers Grove, Ill.: InterVarsity, 1989); cf. Turner, "Spiritual Gifts Then and Now," 15–16.

[60]See his *Gift of Prophecy*, 45–63.

[61]See esp. D. B. Wallace, "The Semantic Range of the Article-Noun-KAI-Noun Plural Construction in the New Testament," *GTJ*, 4 (1983): 59–84.

[62]Grudem, *Systematic Theology*, 1051, n. 4.

point,[63] he abandons the unity of New Testament prophecy by positing, in effect, two gifts: noncontinuing ("foundational"), infallible prophecy and continuing, fallible prophecy. That amounts to a basic, categorical difference, for which there is no evidence in the New Testament, particularly in the lists of gifts.

(b) The two explicit instances of nonapostolic prophecy in the New Testament do not support the view that it was fallible. These are the prophecies of Agabus in Acts 11:28 and 21:10–11. Grudem, for one, has gone to considerable effort to indict him with well-intentioned, minor errors in the latter instance.[64] In general, this attempt suffers from the demand for pedantic precision imposed on Agabus.[65] Here[66] I can only observe further that Acts 21:11–14 must be read with an eye to Luke's overall narrative flow, noted above (the worldwide, foundational, apostolic spread of the gospel to include non-Jew as well as Jew). Read in that framework, what transpired at Caesarea, including Agabus's prophecy, is most naturally read as a fuller account that parallels the tightly compressed description of what was said to Paul earlier at Tyre (v. 4—urged "through the Spirit" not to go on to Jerusalem).

Both these instances, in turn, illustrate the sweeping truth expressed earlier by Paul himself in giving the Ephesian elders an overall account of his unique ministry: "I only know that in *every* city *the Holy Spirit* warns me that prison and hardships are facing me" (Acts 20:23). The fact that on both occasions disciples (perhaps even Agabus himself and others who prophesied) sought to dissuade Paul in no way compromises the Spirit-breathed, infallible truthfulness of what was prophesied. Also, if Agabus made errors, that apparently was lost on Luke. There is no indication that he records this incident other than as it serves his overarching purpose to show the advance of the

---

[63]Grudem, *Gift of Prophecy*, 63–64.

[64]Ibid., 96–102; see also his *Systematic Theology*, 1052–53; so also Carson, *Showing the Spirit*, 97–98; Houston, *Prophecy*, 114–16.

[65]J. W. Hilber observes pertinently, "If one's judgment is rigid enough, similar 'errors' in OT predictions can also be cited" ("Diversity of OT Prophetic Phenomena and NT Prophecy," *WTJ*, 56 [1994]: 256).

[66]For a more extensive response to this view, see my *Perspectives on Pentecost*, 65–67 (whether that response "does not pay close enough attention to the text" [so Carson, *Showing the Spirit*, 98] the reader will have to judge).

gospel from Jerusalem to Rome. What Agabus says is "what the Spirit says to the churches" (cf., e.g., Rev. 2:7). In sum, the fallible prophecy view is unable to offer a single supporting New Testament example.

(c) Some brief comments may be made about several texts frequently offered as evidence that (nonapostolic) prophecy has a lower, fallible authority. In 1 Corinthians 14:29 the verb applied to prophecy (*diakrino*) has a broad semantic range; it may be construed in a variety of ways, depending on the particular context, and is variously translated "evaluate," "test," "judge," and "weigh." Here there is nothing in Paul's usage to demand that, because what is prophesied is subject to "testing," it is therefore fallible. That no more follows than the fact that the Bereans' "examin[ing] [*anakrino*] the Scriptures every day to see if what Paul said was true" (Acts 17:11; Luke implies commendation for their doing so) means that what Paul taught them did not have full, infallible, apostolic authority.[67]

It is difficult to see how 1 Corinthians 14:36a provides convincing evidence of lower authority prophecy. Paul's question there ("Did the word of God originate with you?") is almost certainly addressed not to the prophets specifically but to the whole church at Corinth, in relation to other churches (see v. 33b). Together with the question in the latter part of the verse, it is "biting rhetoric";[68] it has the force of something like, "Does the truth begin and end with you? Do you have a corner on the gospel and its implications?"

Nor does Paul's peremptory command to the prophets in 1 Corinthians 14:37–38 establish their lower authority—any more than his sharp rebuke of Peter in Galatians 2:11–14 means that the latter did not teach with full, infallible authority when he properly exercised his apostolic office. At issue here (and throughout this passage) is not the *content* of prophecy (and its relative authority), but the *conduct* of those who prophesy.

---

[67]Note the substantial semantic overlap between *anakrino* and *diakrino*. That overlap (an overlap that also includes the use of *dokimazo* in 1 Thess. 5:21) can be seen most conveniently in the semantic domain analysis of J. P. Louw and E. A. Nida, *Greek-English Lexicon of the New Testament Based on Semantic Domains* (New York: United Bible Societies, 1988), 331–32, 363–64 (esp. sec. 27.44–45, 30.108–9).

[68]G. D. Fee, *The First Epistle to the Corinthians*, NICNT (Grand Rapids: Eerdmans, 1987), 710.

Of itself 1 Thessalonians 5:20 ("Do not treat prophecies with contempt") does not seem to carry much weight, if for no other reason than that in 2 Corinthians 10:10 Paul uses the same verb to describe his opponents' derogatory assessment of *his* preaching as "beneath contempt" (NEB). True, this applies to the formal side of his speaking (i.e., his "style") in distinction from that of his letters, but a disparaging reflection on *content* can hardly be eliminated.

(d) One other text should not go unnoticed here, one that presents low view continuationists with a monumental predicament. First Corinthians 12:28 expresses the order: "first of all apostles, second prophets, third teachers. . . ." There is general agreement that this ranking has to do with value or usefulness.[69] If so, then their view is left with the following conclusion: In the church prophecy, always subject to evaluation as fallible and therefore never binding on anyone, is more useful and edifying than teaching based on God's clear, authoritative, and inerrant word! Prophecy takes precedence over such teaching! An obviously unwanted and unacceptable conclusion, I would hope. But how can they avoid this conclusion?

(e) Finally, virtually all, especially fallible view, continuationists insist that prophecy is always subordinate to Scripture and must be tested by it, so that its unimpaired sufficiency and authority is not only not threatened but maintained. But how will such testing take place? Prophecy in the New Testament (e.g., Agabus), and as it allegedly takes place today, sometimes has a specificity that simply cannot be evaluated by existing Scripture. For instance, a particular course of action urged upon an individual or group on the basis, say, of a dream cannot be judged by the Bible other than whether the proposed action might involve violating a biblical commandment.[70] For the rest, it is a matter of trying to judge "apples" by "oranges." Scripture

---

[69]E.g., Fee, *Empowering Presence*, 190; Grudem, *Gift of Prophecy*, 69.

[70]Williams (*Renewal Theology*, 2:384) is emphatic that prophecy today "may confirm but never by itself direct. . . . Predictive prophecy—prophecy as essentially foretelling—is to be strongly guarded against." But why this exclusion, if it is the New Testament gift? On what basis, especially since (apart from the book of Revelation) the only other concrete examples in the New Testament (Agabus) are clearly such "directional prophecy"?

by its very nature is silent precisely on those details that give the dream its specific and distinct (and sought-after) "revelatory" significance and appeal. Furthermore, unlike the Scriptures (and general revelation), which are always accessible and open to interrogation apart from their interpretations, on this view there is no access to the underlying revelation or any way to distinguish it from its fallible report/interpretation by the one prophesying.[71]

This view, I cannot see otherwise, opens the door to revelation in the life of the church today that is neither (inscripturated) special, redemptive revelation nor general revelation (from ourselves, as created in God's image, and the world about us). What is affirmed is a *third kind of revelation* that goes beyond both. It is more than "revelation" in the sense of the Spirit's illumination for today of already revealed truth (Eph. 1:17; Phil. 3:15),[72] more than thoughtful reflection and prayerful wrestling, prompted by the Spirit, about contemporary circumstances and problems in the light of Scripture. In view is additional, immediate revelation that functions, especially where guidance is concerned, beyond Scripture and so unavoidably implies a certain insufficiency in Scripture that needs to be compensated for.[73] The tendency of this view, no matter how carefully it is qualified, is to divert attention from Scripture, particularly in practical and pressing life issues.

To put my concern here another way, this view blurs the essential difference between the truths of Romans 8:14 and

---

[71]This poses a question (which, unless I have missed it, is not really addressed by advocates of this view): Why would God reveal himself in such an ambiguous, not to say "inefficient" way? The answer cannot be the biblical one of revelation through human weakness (cf. 2 Cor. 4:7), because here, in the outcome (what is actually prophesied), weakness (human fallibility) *prevails over* revelation.

[72]The issue, then, is not whether God can be said to "reveal" himself today; of course he does. But in what sense? In this respect Carson's criticism of Vos (*Showing the Spirit*, 161–64) is largely beside the point (though Vos could perhaps have expressed himself more clearly at points).

[73]That seems clear, for example, in what Turner writes (though I appreciate the care with which he is concerned to formulate): In addition to the need for the illumination and application of inscripturated truth today, "there is need, too, for deep spiritual diagnosis of individuals and congregations, and of specific leading on a host of practical issues"—a need met, beyond Scripture, by the revelatory gifts of 1 Cor. 12:8–10 ("Spiritual Gifts," 55).

2 Peter 1:21. That is, obscured is the difference between being "led" by the Spirit (the privilege, note, of *all*, not just some, believers) and being "carried along" by the Spirit (the special, revelatory, redemptive-historical role of some, long since over). To use Calvin's classic figure of the Bible as the eyeglasses indispensable for understanding ourselves and the rest of creation,[74] prophecy is an additional lens that enhances vision; it temporarily augments or, on occasion, may even replace the lens of Scripture. That seems a fair assessment, especially in the light of how prophecy is usually understood to function today.

But God does not reveal himself, as this view would have it, along two tracks—one public, canonical, and completed (for the whole people of God), the other private and continuing (to individual persons and groups). The complaint has been made that this is an assertion without evidence.[75] But the fabric of Scripture from beginning to end, as a covenant-historical record, massively supports it.

The Bible, as inscripturated revelation, faithfully documents (in its true contours and scope, though not in its actual, full extent, e.g., John 21:25; 1 Cor. 5:9) a completed historical organism, a finished redemptive-revelatory process. It records the history that has reached its consummation in Christ's ascension and his sending of the Spirit—a history that, since then, is on hold, "between the times," until he returns. To be sure, throughout this history, God reveals himself to individuals in a variety of personal, highly intimate ways. But that revelation does not introduce or provide the precedent for a second track of private revelation intended to supplement corporate, "institutional" revelation, which is focused on the movement of redemptive history toward its consummation in Christ. Such revelation to individuals is itself an integral part of that once-for-all, Christ-centered revelation.

Continuationist positions, whether prophetic gifts or signs and wonders are in view, misconstrue their occurrence in Scripture (that is, throughout redemptive history) and so take the unwarranted step of extrapolating from what belongs to the

---

[74]Calvin, *Institutes of the Christian Religion* (Philadelphia: Westminster, 1960), e.g., 1:6:1; 1:14:1.

[75]Grudem, *Gift of Prophecy*, 316, n. 27.

ongoing process into the situation beyond its completion.[76] With that the risk is great of at least blurring, perhaps even denying, the all-important distinction between redemption/revelation in its completed accomplishment and in its subsequent, continuing application.

During this century especially we have become increasingly aware that the Bible is a redemptive- or covenant-historical record, not a systematic-theological textbook or a manual of ethics (as it has long tended to be treated, at least in practice); it is "not a dogmatic handbook but a historical book full of dramatic interest."[77] But there is need as well to recognize, much more frequently than has so far happened, the redemptive-historical rationale not only for the *content* but also for the *giving* of revelation. Revelatory word is tethered to redemptive deed.[78] With the completion of the latter comes the cessation of the former.

An ironic turnabout comes to light here. Contrary to the frequent charge, it is the continuationist view, not the cessationist position, that turns out to have an intellectualistic and overly notional understanding of Scripture. According to one representative continuationist, the Bible provides "major doctrines for the entire Christian world," "major doctrinal teachings"— revelation, accordingly, that is insufficient in that it then needs to be supplemented with "specific, localized information," supplied by ongoing prophecy.[79] On this view, the *revelatory* "lamp to my feet" and "light for my path" (Ps. 119:105) is only relatively the completed biblical canon, and Scripture is only relatively sufficient.

---

[76]This misunderstanding is massively at work, in my judgment, in Deere's *Power of the Spirit*, controlling his exegetical and theological reasoning virtually from beginning to end.

[77]G. Vos, *Biblical Theology: Old and New Testaments* (Grand Rapids: Eerdmans, 1948), 26; "The circle of revelation is not a school, but a 'covenant'" (17).

[78]See esp. Vos's comments in ibid., 14–17; also, "revelation is so interwoven with redemption that, unless allowed to consider the latter, it would be suspended in air" (24).

[79]Grudem, *Gift of Prophecy*, 85, 169, 245; cf. Turner, "Spiritual Gifts Then and Now," 54–56: Scripture provides "the fundamental structures of theology," "gospel truth and apostolic praxis," but is inadequate when it comes to "deep spiritual diagnosis of individuals and congregations" and "specific leading on a host of practical issues" (55).

6. Continuationists feel most secure in their view at 1 Corinthians 13:8–12. Here I can do little more than point out that the passage is not so unambiguous as they believe.[80] Paul's primary emphasis here is on the partial, obscured quality of the believer's present knowledge brought by prophetic gifts, in comparison with faith, hope, and especially love that have what we might call an eschatological "reach" or "grasp" (vv. 12–13). Such knowledge will not cease until the arrival of "perfection" (v. 10), at Christ's return;[81] only then, in contrast, will full "face to face" knowledge be ours (v. 12).

With this accent on the partial *quality* of the believer's present knowledge, the particular *media* of that revealed knowledge are, strictly speaking, incidental. Paul mentions prophecy and tongues because of his pastoral concern in the wider context (chaps. 12–14) about the proper exercise of these two gifts. But the time of their cessation is not a point he is concerned with, and it is gratuitous to insist on the contrary from verse 10. Rather, his interest is in showing the duration of our present, opaque knowledge—by whatever revelatory means it may come (and that would even include inscripturation[82]) and whenever they may cease.

This reading is reinforced in Ephesians 4:11–13, which emphasizes that the exalted Christ "gave some to be apostles, some to be prophets, some to be evangelists, and some to be pastors and teachers ... until we all reach unity in the faith ... attaining to the whole measure of the fullness of Christ." Almost certainly the "unity/fullness" of verse 13 has in view the same state of affairs as the "perfection" in 1 Corinthians 13:10 (echoed perhaps as well in the use of *teleios*, "perfect" or "mature," in Eph. 4:13), namely, the situation brought by Christ's return.

---

[80]For a fuller discussion, see my *Perspectives on Pentecost*, 109–12, and R. F. White, "Richard Gaffin and Wayne Grudem on 1 Corinthians 13:10: A Comparison of Cessationist and Noncessationist Argumentation," *JETS*, 35 (1992): 173–81, who expresses more adequately what I intend to say.

[81]To argue, as some cessationists do, that "the perfect" has in view the completion of the New Testament canon or some other state of affairs prior to the Parousia is just not credible exegetically.

[82]"In the state of glory there shall be 'no more temple in the city,' but also no more Bible in the oratory. A Bible in the oratory is a sign that you yourself are still a sinner in a sinful world" (A. Kuyper, *Principles of Sacred Theology* [New York: Scribner's, 1898], 358).

On that assumption, Ephesians 4, read as continuationists insist 1 Corinthians 13 must be read, leaves us with an unavoidable conclusion: There will be apostles in addition to prophets until the Parousia—a conclusion, as noted earlier, many (though not all) continuationists reject. But how can they do so consistently? In terms of gifts related to ultimate goal, how is the structure of this passage any different from 1 Corinthians 13:8–12?[83] Continuationists cannot have it both ways: If these passages teach that prophecy/prophets continue until the Parousia, then so also do apostles.

A sounder reading of both passages is to recognize that they do not address whether prophecy or any other gift will cease before the Parousia; this particular question is left open.

7. Jon Ruthven advances the thesis: *"The Specifically Eschatological Dimension of the Doctrines of Pneumatology and the Kingdom of God is Inimical to Cessationism."*[84] This perception has become a commonplace among continuationist writers; spiritual gifts, including the miraculous gifts, belong to realized eschatology.[85] This thesis, however, is questionable from several angles.

(a) Signs and wonders, healing, and prophetic gifts are hardly unique to the arrival of the eschatological kingdom. Such phenomena, for instance, are amply attested throughout the Old Testament.[86] The most that might be plausibly argued is that with the coming of Christ and Pentecost they are even more copiously present, but that does not make the phenomena as such distinctively eschatological.

(b) A basic point of 1 Corinthians 13:8–13 is the temporary, that is, less than eschatological significance of prophetic gifts like prophecy and tongues. Continuationists will deny this, insisting that Paul wants to make clear that these gifts belong to the

---

[83]Grudem's view (*Systematic Theology*, 911, n. 9) that Eph. 4:11 describes "a one-time event" and "initial giftings," leaving room for subsequent giftings of one or more but not necessarily all of the gifts mentioned, draws more from the aorist tense "he gave," as well as from the context, than either will support.

[84]Ruthven, *On the Cessation*, 196 (italics original); cf. 115–23.

[85]E.g., Carson, *Showing the Spirit*, 151 (more cautiously); Deere, *Power of the Spirit*, 225–26, 285, n. 6; Fee, *Empowering Presence*, 893; Grudem, *Systematic Theology*, 1019, 1063–64; Turner, "Spiritual Gifts Then and Now," 61–62 (n. 175).

[86]See, e.g., the cataloging provided by Deere (*Power of the Spirit*, 253ff.).

"already" of eschatology, but not to the "not yet."[87] But that explanation will hardly suffice. Can the realities of realized *eschatology* really be said to "cease" and "pass away" (v. 8)?! Furthermore, the continuationist rejoinder obscures, if not entirely misses, Paul's primary concern in this passage: For the present, until Jesus returns, our faith, hope, and love—not our knowledge (along with the prophetic gifts that provide that knowledge)—have abiding, that is, eschatological meaning. These qualities (and other elements among the "fruit" of the Spirit, Gal. 5:22–23), in contrast to particular gifts, are eschatology presently being realized. In terms of the metaphors Paul uses elsewhere, this fruit, preeminently love, not the gifts, embody the eschatological "firstfruits" and "deposit" of the Spirit (Rom. 8:23; 2 Cor. 1:22; 5:5; Eph. 1:14).[88]

(c) Like word gifts, healing is simply not an eschatological phenomenon. That can be seen, for instance, in the miracles of Jesus. In Mark 2:1–12 (Matt. 9:1–8; Luke 5:17–26), for instance, the eschatological reality is the gospel word, "Son, your sins are forgiven" (v. 5); the healing of the paralytic points to the authority of Jesus, the Son of Man, to render such final, eschatological judgment now, in the present ("on earth," v. 10). But the healing is not itself eschatological. It brings genuine and merciful, but still no more than temporary and eventually ineffective, alleviation; that is, the healed paralytic, we have no reason to doubt, is eventually overtaken by the ultimate paralysis of death.

The resurrection of Lazarus points out Jesus' claim, "I am the resurrection and the life" (John 11:25). Moreover, it shows, as do the other healing miracles, that the salvation Christ brings

---

[87]E.g., Fee and Grudem as cited in n. 85.

[88]In support of this reading of the passage, note that it removes the perennial problem that exegesis has wrestled with in verse 13: How can faith and hope be said to continue after the Parousia, especially in the light of such passages as 2 Corinthians 5:7 ("we live by faith, not by sight") and Romans 8:24 ("hope that is seen is not hope")? This question misses the point. The "abiding" in view is not beyond the Parousia, but concerns the present, eschatological significance of faith and hope (as well as love), in contrast to the nonenduring, subeschatological quality of our present knowledge (including the word gifts that bring that knowledge). Note, too, tying in with our earlier comments on this passage, that this perspective on verse 13 shows how questionable it is to insist that verse 10 demands that prophecy and tongues will continue until the Parousia.

is not merely forgiveness as some bloodless abstraction but involves the restoration of sinners as whole persons. But—and this is the issue—the miracle experienced by Lazarus points to resurrection in a no more than temporary and insubstantial way. He does not receive a glorified, eschatological body, the "spiritual" body (1 Cor. 15:44), at this time. Together with all other dead believers he awaits that resurrection at Christ's return, along with the profound psychophysical[89] transformation it will bring.

On balance, we may say, the miracles of the New Testament are more than merely external parables of internal realities. They appropriately disclose "the essence of the kingdom and its blessings," but they do so "without at the same time constituting or embodying that essence."[90] Turner states that he is "not entirely happy" with this "qualification" and offers exorcisms as evidence to the contrary.[91] But here too the distinction in view has to be maintained. To take the most vivid and climactic instance in the Gospel records (Matt. 12:22–28; cf. Luke 11:14–22), the eschatological substance of what transpired (parallel to the raising of Lazarus) is not that the once demon-possessed man is now able to talk and see but that he has been "rescued ... from the dominion of darkness and brought ... into the kingdom of the Son [God] loves" (Col. 1:13). The latter is essential, it must take place; that is not true of the former.

"Though outwardly we are wasting away, yet inwardly we are being renewed day by day" (2 Cor. 4:16). This expresses a categorical distinction that is basic to Paul's anthropology and his understanding of the Christian life, a distinction that the church blurs to its peril.[92] In terms of bodily existence (i.e., "outwardly"), along with the entire creation (Rom. 8:20–21), believers are subject to unremitting decay leading to death (1 Cor. 15:42–44); that mortality may be temporarily alleviated but not removed. Only at the core of our being (i.e., "inwardly") do

[89]That the resurrection of the body will be more than physical in the narrow sense (it will certainly include that) is clear from 1 Cor. 15:51: "We will not all sleep, but we will all be changed."

[90]Gaffin, *Perspectives on Pentecost*, 45.

[91]Turner, "Spiritual Gifts Then and Now," 61–62 (n. 175).

[92]Where that blurring occurs, some form of distorting triumphalism inevitably intrudes into the life of the church.

believers presently experience the Spirit's eschatological power. No physical exam or psychological test will ever enable us to tell the difference between believers and unbelievers (though, in general, faith in Christ and obedience to God's commands promote health in mind and body). Balance here is not only requisite but critical; it may be captured by saying (of believers) that what is true *in* the body[93] is not yet true *for* the body.

Is there healing in the cross? Yes, nothing less than the "healing" that will come as the resurrection of the body. In the meantime, until Jesus returns, anything less is nothing more than an insubstantial, subeschatological pointer.

All told, the New Testament writers would not have us miss the distinction between the gift (singular) and the gifts (plural) of the Spirit—between the eschatological gift, the indwelling Spirit himself, in which all believers share, and his subeschatological giftings, none of which is received by every believer (by divine design, by the way, not lack of faith, 1 Cor. 12:28–30).

8. I close these observations on cessationism by noting a state of affairs that is both puzzling and worth pondering. Among continuationists none is so confident as Fee. To the question of the duration of the *charismata*, "[Paul's] answer is plain: 'Of course they will continue as long as we await the final consummation.'" The issue is not even discussible. Even to raise the question and the possibility of the cessation of some gifts is alien to Paul; it betrays that one is trapped in a hermeneutical loop that the apostle "could not have understood."[94]

Earlier, however, we find Fee taking note of the difficulty in distinguishing between "the word of wisdom" and "the word of knowledge," particularly their content, and concluding that the difference "is perhaps forever lost to us."[95] I find this admission remarkable. If the New Testament teaches with such certainty that these gifts, along with all the others listed in 1 Corinthians 12, continue in the church today, why the difficulty and uncertainty in distinguishing them and knowing what they are?

---

[93]Certainly it is true only there (in the body), not as an abstraction.

[94]Fee, *Empowering Presence*, 893, including n. 20; cf. G. Fee, *Gospel and Spirit: Issues in New Testament Hermeneutics* (Peabody, Mass.: Hendrickson, 1991), 75–77.

[95]Ibid., p. 167–68. This difficulty is expressed by other continuationists; e.g., Grudem, *Systematic Theology* (1080): "Our conclusions will probably be somewhat tentative in any case."

Moreover, at the conclusion of a discussion of glossolalia, Fee appends a footnote in which he says that the question whether contemporary tongues-speaking "is the *same* in kind as that in the Pauline churches is moot—and probably irrelevant. There is simply no way to know." As an experience, he continues, "it is *analogous* to theirs . . . a supernatural activity of the Spirit which functions in many of the same ways, and for many of its practitioners has value similar to that described by Paul."[96]

This apparent afterthought is even more startling. Now it appears, unless I am mistaken, that measured by the instance of tongues, it is after all not a simple "of course all the gifts continue until the consummation." Rather, what we have today are no more than analogues displaying certain similarities with their presumed New Testament counterparts.

These concessions (that word does not seem unfair) concerning tongues, the word of wisdom, and the word of knowledge, coupled with the fact, already noted, that continuationists cannot agree among themselves what prophecy is, prompt this question: If the Spirit of God, the Spirit of truth and order, is really restoring these prophetic gifts to the church today in a widespread way, would there be, as there in fact is, such widespread ambiguity and confusion, not to mention division, about them? Does the Spirit, who gives gifts to unify and edify, work in this ambivalent and uncertain way?

These questions prompt a final observation about our contemporary situation. At work here as much as anything, I suspect—especially in the context of the church in the West, where the secularized exercise of reason and the deistic autonomy of the Enlightenment have held baleful sway for so long—is the desire for a compensating experience of the supernatural that accents the intuitive and nonrational capacities of our humanity.[97] That desire may well have legitimate concerns that need to be explored. But *that* agenda, as such, is an agenda alien to the New Testament. Particularly when it is imposed on passages about prophetic gifts, the resulting confusion about them (including their cessation) is inevitable.

---

[96]Fee, *Empowering Presence*, 890, n. 17 (italics original).

[97]That desire is particularly evident in Lederle's essay, "Life in the Spirit and Worldview."

C. CHURCH LIFE TODAY

Obviously I cannot comment on the contemporary exercise of gifts that I do not believe are present in the church today. But some brief remarks on spiritual gifts in general may be in order, if for no other reason than to dispel certain misconceptions about the cessationist position I (and others) hold.

1. Not all the gifts have ceased. To assert that may seem to involve arbitrarily picking and choosing what continues. But the New Testament, as I have tried to show, provides guidelines. Some gifts, such as the prophetic gifts, functioned as part of the "canonical" principle for the church during the foundational time in which the New Testament documents were being written. With its completion, the closing of the canon, such gifts have ceased. The same conclusion may be reached for sign-gifts tied to the apostolic founding of the church. For the rest, the gifts continue more or less as we find them in the New Testament.

Furthermore, within the overall profile of the New Testament, the Pastoral Letters as a whole can be seen as making apostolic provision for the postapostolic future of the church, so that they aid in identifying continuities and discontinuities. Specifically as to revelation, God's word for the church today, the only provision they make is for teaching and preaching (e.g., 2 Tim. 1:13; 2:2), under the oversight of elders (1 Tim. 3:2; 5:17; Tit. 1:9) and focused on the apostolic "deposit" (1 Tim. 6:20; 2 Tim. 1:14; cf. Jude 3: "the faith . . . once for all entrusted to the saints").

2. We should recognize the great breadth of spiritual gifts. When the lists most often discussed (Rom. 12; 1 Cor. 12; Eph. 4) are compared, we see a certain amount of overlap and yet differences among them. This pattern shows that, whether individually or taken together, they are not exhaustive but provide a representative sampling of gifts. To confine our attention to these lists, as so often happens, is unduly limiting.

Paul himself, in addressing a series of marital issues, provides an indication of the dimensions of the breadth involved: "Each [person] has his own gift from God; one has this gift, another has that" (1 Cor. 7:7; the next occurrence of the Greek word *charisma* is its multiple use in chaps. 12–14). For the believer, Paul is saying, the question of whether or not to marry has to be answered in terms of one's (spiritual) "gift"; spirituality and sexuality cannot be separated.

This is as we should expect it to be, because the Spirit of God is the wind of nothing less than a new creation. When the Spirit takes hold of us, he claims us from top to bottom. We may fairly say, then, that whatever about me is taken over in the service of Christ and his church—and that even includes aptitudes and capacities I had before I became a believer—is a spiritual gift.

3. In 1 Peter 4:10, the sole New Testament occurrence of *charisma* outside of Paul, Peter summarizes important aspects of its teaching on spiritual gifts. "Whatever gift [one] has received" points to the full range and wide distribution of gifts in the church. "To serve others" captures the ministerial dimension essential to their exercise (cf. 1 Cor. 12:4–6); the gifts are for what they enable us to do for others, for the overall edification of the church (cf. 1 Cor. 12:7; 14:12). "Faithfully administering God's grace in its various forms" again accents both the diversity of the gifts and their ministerial purpose, with the important reminder that they flow from God's grace revealed in Christ (cf. v. 11b).

The next verse advances our understanding with a valuable two-part profile on the entire range of spiritual gifts: "If anyone speaks ... if anyone serves. ..." All the gifts, in their full diversity, Peter is saying, reduce to one of two basic kinds: word gifts and deed gifts. Spiritual gifts, to put it another way, are all the ways in which the gospel is ministered in word or deed.

4. How do I determine my spiritual gift(s)? This is a practical and multifaceted question, to which at least this much may be said here in reply. One way *not* to proceed is to take the "spiritual inventory" approach and ask: What is it that I would like for my spiritual specialty? What is "my thing" spiritually that sets me apart from other believers? The New Testament would have us take a more functional or situational approach to identifying spiritual gifts. The key question to ask is this: What needs are there in the situation where God has placed me? What in the circumstances where I find myself are the particular opportunities for serving others? In light of the dual profile of 1 Peter 4:11, what are the specific ways in which I can minister the gospel of Jesus Christ in word or deed?

Asking the question that way (with prayer and reflection, and in consultation with other believers, especially the elders of the church) will take us a long way, not only toward identifying our spiritual gifts but also, and more importantly, toward actually exercising them.

D. DANGERS

As I look back over all I have written here, I am aware that I may have unintentionally misrepresented the views of others or am guilty of talking by them. Where that has happened, I apologize and look to be corrected.

An even greater danger is that in situations of controversy among believers, we lose perspective, especially on our common bond in Christ. It is all too easy for cessationists to overlook or depreciate the genuine work of God's Spirit in and among believers who identify themselves as charismatic or Pentecostal (although we may continue to disagree on all the respects in which that is happening!).

A particular danger for cessationists, I suspect, is that in our concern about the perceived excesses and unhealthy tendencies of other positions, we forget the commitment, expressed at the outset, to the incalculability of the Spirit's activity. Much talk *about* the Spirit carries the risk of diminishing, perhaps even losing, a sense of how awesome our salvation in Christ, including the work of the Spirit, really is. Ultimately, we struggle to speak of matters that are "beyond words," just "too great for words" (2 Cor. 9:15; 1 Peter 1:7, NEB). Theology that ceases being swept up more or less spontaneously in doxology, like that of Romans 11:33–36, needs to reexamine itself. That sort of "cessationism" the church needs to avoid like the plague.

But the greatest danger for my position is the same one faced by the other views in this symposium. It is that we violate "Do not go beyond what is written" (1 Cor. 4:6), as that principle applies in the church today.

At the heart of the Protestant Reformation is the rediscovery of the self-interpreting clarity of Scripture. That rediscovery was so liberating and precious to those who experienced it that they had no higher priority than to preserve it, whatever the cost. Inexorably—against the tradition principle of Rome on the one side, and against the Radical Reformation with its claims of extrabiblical revelations on the other—they were forced to contend for the inseparability of word and Spirit (*Spiritus cum verbo*), the unbreakable bond between the Spirit's working and the inscripturated Word. The Reformers were resolved to hear nothing but "the Holy Spirit speaking in the Scripture" (Westminster Confession of Faith, 1:10). On that contemporary, ever-fresh speaking, on that always timely and relevant voice, in its full, all-sufficient, unmitigated (though not isolated) exclusiveness (*sola*), they staked everything.

That struggle is not over; it is perennial and carries the potential for undermining the power of the Reformation today. In the name of the Spirit, some continue to place church tradition on a virtual par with Scripture, while others claim new revelations and guidance apart from Scripture. But, nothing on *a par* with Scripture and nothing *apart* from Scripture—that issue remains as critical as any for the church today.

AN OPEN BUT CAUTIOUS RESPONSE TO RICHARD B. GAFFIN, JR.

Robert L. Saucy — Baptist

Gaffin's happy blend of theological thought and exegesis of specific passages have combined to set forth a very able cessationist position. Specifically, the emphasis placing the coming of the Spirit at Pentecost within the overall framework of redemption history was excellent, and in my opinion, highly significant for many of the questions involved in the entire discussion. The fact that he made his case without finding an explicit cessationism in relation to the coming of the "perfect" in 1 Corinthians 13:8–10 was also a positive.

I found myself in basic agreement with many points made in the essay, including what I perceive as its primary thrusts. These are that the coming of the Spirit at Pentecost was an integral part of Christian salvation and therefore not a second dimension of the Spirit's work not attained by all believers, and that the apostolic era was a foundational period in the history of the church, which does not provide the model for all of church history.

With regard to the first, Dr. Gaffin's argument that the coming of the Spirit at Pentecost was in reality the completion of the saving act of Christ's first coming and therefore belongs to every participant in Christ's salvation was superb. Perhaps more should have been said in response to some who attempt to sharply divide the Spirit's ministry between regeneration and empowerment. This allows them to agree that the believer has received the Spirit's new covenant ministry of regeneration and union with Christ as distinct from the Pentecostal experience of empowerment. The central place of the "baptism with the Spirit" in the predictions of the Gospels (cf. Matt. 3:11 and para.) and just prior to Pentecost in Acts 1:5, and especially Peter's explanation of Pentecost as the fulfillment of the Old Testament's promised outpouring of Spirit, make this division impossible. The coming of the Spirit at Pentecost was *the* gift of the Spirit in fulfillment of the new covenant promise and as such is part and parcel of new covenant salvation, not a second blessing that some believers never attain. Dr. Gaffin's presentation of Pentecost as a forward movement in the history of God's salvation program rather than a paradigm for individual believers throughout this age demonstrates that only believers living through this transition could experience what might be termed a two-stage relationship to the Spirit.

The cessationist's emphasis on the uniqueness of the apostles and their ministry as foundational to the church also seems biblical to me. This clearly raises questions for those who argue that all the gifts remain essentially the same throughout church history. I also agree that while miracles surely served other purposes, such as expressions of mercy and encouragement, the prominent scriptural use of the term "signs" in relation to Christ's ministry in the Gospels and the ministry of the apostles and others in Acts is intended to lead us to the conclusion that the primary function of miracles was as "signs" attesting to the validity of the apostles as inspired witnesses to the saving action of Christ.

I also agree wholeheartedly with Gaffin's presentation of biblical prophecy as inspired speech and his rejection of a lower form of prophecy that includes fallible human thoughts. Although "prophecy" has been used for preaching, as in the case of the Reformers, and unusual wisdom and insight has casually been referred to as "prophetic," the attempt to find a biblical gradation of revelatory prophecy from partial inspiration and fallibility to total inspiration and infallibility, to my knowledge, is of recent origin and is difficult to sustain from biblical evidence.

The emphasis on the Spirit's work in relation to the believer that is truly part of our eschatological salvation, namely, his sanctifying presence in ordinary life that promotes the fruit belonging to eternal life, also seems to be in harmony with apostolic teaching. That miraculous spiritual gifts will cease with this age demonstrates, as Gaffin aptly notes, that while they are manifestations of the essence of the kingdom, they do not constitute that kingdom itself.

Although I cannot draw all of the conclusions reached by Gaffin, his focus on the primary teaching of Scripture with regard to the ministry of the Spirit in the life of the believer, along with his recognition that God does still work miraculously on behalf of his people, leads me to agree that the cessationist position espoused is not putting the Spirit "in a box." Rather, it is an attempt to understand the power of God in relation to the truth of God, a combination clearly taught in Scripture.

While agreeing with many of the emphases in the cessationist position, some of the conclusions that demand the complete cessation of miraculous gifts in my opinion go beyond the express teaching of Scripture or necessary deductions from theological principles of Scripture. In various ways the position is expressed that the closing of the apostolic era demands the cessation of all manifestations of the gift of prophecy. The "cessation of the revelatory word gift of apostleship" (p. 45), the completion of the foundational revelation, and the closing of the canon (p. 44–45) are said to demand the cessation of prophecy, so that there can only be either inscripturated or general revelation today (pp. 52–53).

But does Scripture clearly draw this conclusion? Gaffin himself acknowledges that it would be wrong to argue that Luke intended to show that "miraculous gifts and power experiences ceased with the history he documented" (p. 38–39). If such is the case, then how can we believe that any continuation of gifts beyond the time of the apostles "pulls apart what for Luke belongs together" (p. 39)? I totally agree that Scripture shows that the preponderance of miraculous activity is linked to the apostles and a few others who with them bear inspired witness to Christ's saving work. But does it tie *all* miraculous gifts to this foundational revelatory period?

The cessationist is certainly correct, however, in pointing out that Scripture nowhere expressly says that miraculous gifts will continue. This lack of explicit teaching makes it difficult to affirm either cessationism or continuationism as the teaching of Scripture. Gaffin's attempt to link miraculous gifts to the apostles by arguing that all prophecy was related to the foundation of the church also seems to go beyond Scripture. Again, while I agree that prophets were involved in the foundation ministry of making known the mystery of Christ, the question is: Was *all* prophecy "tethered to redemptive deed" (p. 54) in such a way that when the foundational revelation was complete, all revelatory word gifts ceased (p. 44)?

Consideration of the various manifestations of prophecy in the scriptural record makes this hard to assert with confidence. In the first instance, it is not at all evident that some prophecies are witness to Christ's redemptive deed. Agabus's prophecy of a famine resulted in aid for those at Jerusalem, an act that no doubt helped to bind the Gentile believers at Antioch with the Jews at Jerusalem. But how is his prophecy revelatory of the mystery of Christ?

I am sure that no cessationists desire to claim all prophecies as canonical. Yet the insistence on linking prophecy to the canon seems almost to say this. Clearly both the Old and New Testaments indicate that there were many prophecies that were never included in the canonical Scriptures. In some instances we are told that certain individuals prophesied (Acts 15:32; 21:9); in others it simply tells us that prophecy was taking place in the church (e.g., 1 Cor. 14; 1 Thess. 5:19). But the content of none of these prophecies are included in Scripture. No doubt some of them related to the mystery of Christ. Others probably revealed God's will for a particular situation (cf. the sending out of Paul and Barnabas, Acts 13:2). With the evidence of prophecies that are not canonical and with no explicit Scripture telling us that all prophecy ceased with the end of canonical revelation, the link of prophecy to canonical Scriptures does not seem as clear as the cessationist position affirms.

Moreover, if Scripture expressly asserts the cessation of prophecy with the close of the apostolic era and the canon, what are we to do with the prediction of prophets in the future? Whether the two witnesses of Revelation 11 are two individuals or symbolic of the witnessing church, they are described as "prophets" (v. 10), who exercise a ministry of "prophesying" (vv. 3, 6) that is accompanied by miraculous activity.

There seems to be clear evidence that prophecy ceased or at least changed radically after the closing of the Old Testament canon. But this conclusion was not drawn so much from the teaching of the Old Testament itself as from the experience of the lack of prophecy among God's people. Similarly, when prophecy was again recognized as present in relation to the new work of Christ, it was acknowledged as such by virtue of its valid manifestation.

Without attempting to draw a direct analogy, it seems that believers today are in a somewhat similar position. Scripture does not clearly teach the cessation of prophecy. While it links prophecy to the foundational period, it does not show that *all* prophecy is *foundational*. The history of the church plainly demonstrates that the manifestation of prophecy changed radically since the apostolic era. In light of these various factors and the knowledge that God is yet to bring prophets, it seems that we cannot assert the impossibility of prophecy occurring today. But neither can we say it occurs as it did in the New Testament times. We must be open to what God desires to do, but seek to evaluate all phenomena by biblical criteria.

I also have reservations about Gaffin's argument that the possibility of prophecy today necessarily threatens the canonicity of the New Testament and inevitably relativizes the sufficiency and authority of Scripture (pp. 44–47). I agree that all biblical prophecy is inspired and therefore infallible. We are therefore bound to obey any divine prophetic command. But it is difficult to see how all prophetic words and even commands challenge the canon. If we assume from Acts 13 that Paul and Barnabas were sent out in obedience to a revelatory word, how does that add to the canon or in any way compete with its authority?

Many prophecies in both Old and New Testament times were never inscripturated to become part of the canon: for example, specific directions such as the church at Antioch received regarding Paul and Barnabas; the prediction of a famine, as with Agabus; an appropriate application of canonical truth, like some of the prophetic preaching of the Old Testament prophets. In any case I cannot see how all prophetic utterances somehow relativize the canon or add to the canon. Gaffin uses Paul's statement to the Corinthians, "Do not go beyond what is written" (1 Cor. 4:6) in support of his argument that the notion of prophecy today threatens the canon. While we do not live in the same open canon period as the Corinthians, this Scripture actually demonstrates that one can hold to canonical Scripture where it has spoken and still receive prophecies as in the Corinthian church.

The cessationists are correct in upholding the biblical teaching that the Scriptures are all-sufficient for equipping us for all good works (2 Tim. 3:16). In emphasizing the teaching of the inscripturated Word, they are directly following the apostolic pattern, especially that of Paul in the Pastoral Letters. But what does it mean to say that the Spirit is bound to the inscripturated Word and that his voice today is simply an "ever-fresh speaking" through the Scriptures (p. 64)?

While Scripture is the canon of truth, does not the Spirit reveal his will in specific situations, both personally and corporately as a church, beyond what anyone can legitimately exegete from any Scripture passage? If such guidance by the Spirit does not compromise the sufficiency of Scripture, why would it do so if such directions were at times given through inspired revelation? Gaffin's point that such prophecies might "divert attention from Scripture, particularly in practical and pressing life issues" (p. 52) is well taken. Scripture's direction to itself as the truth that God uses to inaugurate and nourish life precludes any prophecy that would compete with it. Most prophecy in Scripture was given through those who loved and lived the previously given revelation of God. The fact that the prophets could prophesy in no way directed their attention away from the revelation of God given previously through Moses. So also most insights and directions of divine guidance come to those whose hearts are filled with the truth of Scripture. The possibility of God's granting prophetic revelation to his people for specific circumstances in accord with his will, therefore, need not lead the believer away from the Scripture as his source of spiritual life and canon of belief and practice.

Finally, Gaffin implies that prophecy cannot take place because it cannot be tested by Scripture. Some, like those of Agabus, are so specific that Scripture would not speak to them(p. 51). But if it is granted that the prophecies of Agabus could not be tested by Scripture (and this seems valid), how was it ascertained that these prophecies were from God? Without getting into all that might be involved in answering that question, it surely seems valid to conclude that the same means used to validate the prophecies of Agabus could be used for contemporary prophecies. Thus, the fact that all prophecies cannot be tested by Scripture does not appear to demand cessationism.

The strength of the cessationist's position lies in the evidence that shows that there was a foundational period in the church that is different from the following history. I concur that this has ramifications for the question of the continuation of miraculous gifts in the church, which raise some unanswerable arguments against those who fail to see the uniqueness of this period. I am not convinced, however, that one can say from Scripture that the recognition of this foundational period leads to the subsequent cessation of all manifestations of the miraculous spiritual gifts in the church.

A THIRD WAVE RESPONSE TO RICHARD B. GAFFIN, JR.

C. Samuel Storms

My response to Richard Gaffin's essay will be unavoidably selective. I have chosen to focus on ten key issues that I believe define the difference between cessationists and, to use Gaffin's term, *continuationists* such as myself and Oss. My disagreement with his arguments for cessationism, though vigorous, in no way diminishes my profound respect for him both as a scholar of the highest order and, more importantly, as a brother in Christ.

1. Gaffin rightly objects to the portrayal of cessationists as advocates of deistic rationalism. The fact remains, however, that cessationists generally display a skepticism regarding postapostolic claims to the supernatural that seems to be fueled by a belief that if a natural explanation of a phenomenon is possible, it is probable. Cessationists generally do not expect the Holy Spirit to operate in overtly supernatural and miraculous fashion and are generally not as inclined as others to find the cause of certain physical and spiritual phenomena in the dynamic interplay between spiritual beings (angels and demons) or the immediate agency of the third person of the Trinity.

This is partly because they believe the Spirit's charismatic activity is concentrated in a so-called "foundational" period in the first century of church life. But it may also be due to the combined, though often barely conscious, impact of several factors, such as concern for the dangers of what they perceive to be excessive subjectivism, a desire for restraint and calm, lack of personal experience of charismatic phenomena,[1] and an unspoken disdain for the often unsophisticated and anti-intellectual form of piety on the part of those who are sometimes too quick to find the supernatural in the routine incidents of daily life.

2. Gaffin appeals to the purpose of Pentecost in redemptive history as a basis for rejecting the traditional Pentecostal notion of a "second blessing." Whereas I agree with him regarding the place of Spirit baptism in the *ordo salutis*, his argument could easily be used to prove more than it should.

Gaffin argues that Pentecost belongs to the once-for-all accomplishment of our redemption, not to its continuing application or the ongoing appropriation of its benefits. This is why what happened on that day cannot be an enduring paradigm for subsequent Christian experience. But this is misleading. Whereas it is true that the *day* of Pentecost, on which the Spirit was poured out in an unprecedented way, was once for all, this in no way implies, far less requires, that Christians in subsequent ages do not experience the Spirit and his power as did the 120 who had gathered in the upper room (I have in mind the gift of tongues, prophecy, and the experience of dreams and visions in Acts 2:5–21, not the noise from heaven or the "tongues of fire" in vv. 2–3).

We must ask, "In what sense does Pentecost serve as a once-for-all event?" Pentecost is not simply the *final* stage in Christ's redemptive work; it is also the *first* stage of the Spirit's empowering work in the church. Those in the early church refer back to Pentecost less because it was unique and more because it was *inaugural*.

Gaffin says that the redemptive work of Christ Jesus "reaches its climax" (p. 32) in the Spirit baptism of Pentecost, the "culmination" of the Messiah's ministry. But such terminology should not obscure the fact that Pentecost is equally the *beginning* of a new and ongoing work of the Messiah in the lives of all who embrace it. No one denies that Pentecost is the culmination of Christ's work. After all, Christ promised that when he left this earth, he would send the Spirit. The question is: What did he send the Spirit *to do*? Luke's perspective is that Pentecost

---

[1]See Jack Deere's discussion of this in *Surprised by the Power of the Spirit* (Grand Rapids: Zondervan, 1993), 54–76.

is a redemptive-historical hinge, on which both the historical once-for-all accomplishment of Christ and the future available-to-all-who-believe application to Christians, swings.

Peter says of Pentecost, "This is what" (Acts 2:16) Joel prophesied would transpire in the "latter days"—that period in redemptive history that we know to be the church age (cf. 1 Cor. 10:11; 1 Tim. 4:1; 2 Tim. 3:1; Heb. 1:2; 1 Peter 1:20; 2 Peter 3:3), in which the Spirit's work of revelatory activity is democratized among God's people. Nothing in Peter's language suggests that he envisioned the experience and behavior of the 120 to be tem-porally restricted or unavailable to others. On the contrary, this "promise" of the gift of the Holy Spirit, who inspires prophetic ministry and revelatory experiences, "is for you and your chil-dren and for all who are far off—for all whom the Lord our God will call" (Acts 2:38–39).

I see no biblical reason to view Pentecost as merely the "cul-mination" of a series of once-for-all events. It is also the "inau-guration" of the experiential application of the spiritual blessings those events were designed to procure. Gaffin seems to acknowl-edge this when he speaks of the "enduring consequences" (p. 35) of Pentecost. Surely, though, Peter identifies these as the impar-tation of charismata such as tongues, prophecy, as well as other expressions of revelatory activity (dreams and visions, in par-ticular).

The essence of Pentecost, he sums up, is twofold: it points to (1) the permanent presence of the Holy Spirit and (2) his uni-versal outpouring ("all people"). Precisely. But to what end is the Spirit given? For what purpose is he present? The answer is in large measure salvific and Christological (cf. John 15:26; 16:14). But it is no less charismatic: to empower God's people for life and ministry.

3. Gaffin argues that "Acts intends to document a *completed* history, a unique epoch in the history of redemption—the once-for-all, *apostolic* spread of the gospel 'to the ends of the earth'" (pp. 37–38). But Luke nowhere says this. He never suggests that what the Holy Spirit did in that "history" (Acts) is not to be expected in subsequent "histories" (postapostolic). Neither does he assert that Acts was "unique." Whereas everyone concedes that there are unique and therefore unrepeatable elements in the book of Acts, Luke nowhere argues that the charismatic work of

the Spirit is among them. I am unaware of anything in Acts that either implies or asserts that the way God related to and was active among his people in that particular "history" is finished.

Gaffin has articulated a premise that may have a measure of truth, but lacks textual evidence on which to support the theological conclusion he draws from it. One searches in vain for a text in which the charismatic and supernatural work of the Holy Spirit that attended the expansion of the gospel, and subsequently characterized the life and ministry of the churches that were planted, is not meant by God to attend the expansion of the gospel into the rest of the world in subsequent centuries or is not meant to characterize the life of such churches.

Gaffin contends that "it is in terms of this controlling perspective that the miraculous experiences of those at Pentecost and elsewhere in Acts have their meaning" (p. 38). He then points to the signs, wonders, and miracles as attesting to the realization of this apostolic missionary program. But is that their only meaning and function? None of this has any negative bearing on the perpetuity of the gifts unless Gaffin can locate some text, any text, where the exclusive purpose of miracles and charismata is attestation of apostolic mission. Gaffin isolates *one* function of miraculous phenomena, ties it in with the period in which it occurs, and then concludes that they can have no *other* function in any *other* period of church history. And he does this without one biblical text that explicitly asserts it. This sort of reductionism is foreign to the New Testament.

Gaffin places emphasis on the inaugural breakthrough of the gospel into Samaria and to the Gentiles and insists that the miraculous phenomena that occurred on those occasions played an essential role of attesting to this expansion. I agree. But we must also focus on the churches that were planted and emerged and endured in the aftermath of these so-called "epochal stages" in redemptive history. The ministry of the Holy Spirit as portrayed in Acts, 1 Corinthians, Romans, Ephesians, 1 Thessalonians, and Galatians indicates that the miraculous phenomena that accompanied the beginning and founding of these churches are to *characterize* their upbuilding and growth as well. Gaffin seems to be asking us to believe that *because* miraculous gifts helped launch the church by attesting the original proclamation of the gospel, those phenomena have no additional or ongoing function to sustain and nurture the church itself. But this is a non sequitur that lacks biblical evidence.

Gaffin says that "Acts 2 and the subsequent miraculous events that Luke narrates are not intended to establish a pattern of 'repetitions' of Pentecost to continue on indefinitely in church history. Rather, together they constitute, as already intimated, an event-complex, complete with the finished apostolic program they accompany" (p. 38). But why cannot the miraculous events and charismata continue without thinking that this means a "repetition" of Pentecost? Again, the once-for-allness of Pentecost as a redemptive historical *event* does not require, or even suggest, the restriction of miraculous charismata to that period. What Gaffin persists in "concluding" by theological inference the Bible itself nowhere asserts.

Gaffin concludes that "it would certainly be wrong to argue ... that Luke intended to show that miraculous gifts and power experiences ceased with the history he documented" (pp. 38–39). I find this confusing in view of his affirmation, cited above, that the miraculous events in Acts subsequent to Pentecost are *not* intended by Luke to tell us what the rest of church history is to be like. These events (presumably, prophecy, tongues, and healing), according to Gaffin, were *"complete* with the *finished* apostolic program they accompany"(p. 38, emphasis mine).

He then asserts that "in this respect, to observe that in Acts others than apostles exercise miraculous gifts (e.g., 6:8) is beside the point. To offer that as evidence that such gifts continue beyond the time of the apostles pulls apart what for Luke belongs together" (p. 39). I disagree. I believe it is *precisely* the point—that the miraculous ministry of the Holy Spirit is designed not solely for the apostles or solely for the foundational work they performed. If, as Gaffin contends, miraculous phenomena and apostolic ministry belong together in Luke's mind, why then do others than the apostles perform miracles? It will not suffice for Gaffin simply to assert that nonapostolic miracles are beside the point. It is a vitally important point that cessationism cannot explain. Let us remember that it is, in fact, Luke himself who pulls apart the two. Perhaps he does so because that *was* his point!

Gaffin says that "others exercise such gifts *by virtue of the presence and activity of the apostles*; they do so under an 'apostolic umbrella,' so to speak" (p. 39, italics his). Where does Luke or any biblical author ever say this? And even if it should be granted, why would we conclude that God does not want the church to experience such gifts after the apostles are gone? Again, universally applicable conclusions have been deduced without textual warrant. In reflecting on the book of Acts, I find nothing in the perpetuity of miraculous gifts that threatens the integrity or uniqueness of the apostolic era. That uniqueness is that it was first and foundational, not that it was miraculous.

4. In a desire to retain a closed connection between apostolic ministry and miraculous gifts, Gaffin says it is a "disjunction foreign to Luke" (p. 39) to argue that the latter attest the message (gospel) and not necessarily the messenger. But such a distinction is hardly foreign to Luke, for he speaks of nonapostolic Christians performing miracles and nowhere explicitly attributes their power to any relationship or physical contact with the apostles. Neither Luke nor any other New Testament author says that God could not or would not attest the message with signs and wonders when it was proclaimed by ordinary believers. When this is combined with the fact that several ordinary, nonapostolic believers did exercise miraculous gifts, the distinction that Gaffin alleges is "foreign" to Luke appears quite familiar to him.

5. Gaffin provides two reasons for believing in the cessation of the gifts of healing and of working miracles.

First, he argues that the New Testament itself records these gifts in operation only in Acts. And these "accompany the unique and finished apostolic spread of the gospel" (p. 42). But nowhere does Acts or the New Testament ever say that what was unique about the apostles were the gifts or miracles they performed. How can it be argued that, because miraculous phenomena accompany the apostolic spread of the gospel, they cannot accompany the nonapostolic spread of the same gospel? The fact that the first-century apostles finished *their* work in spreading the gospel does not mean that others, in subsequent generations, are finished.

Also, I find it hard to understand how the exercise of miraculous gifts by average, nonapostolic Christian men and women in the church at Corinth, all for the purpose of edifying, encouraging, consoling, and helping one another to be more like Jesus, can in *any* sense be regarded as exclusively tied up with the alleged "unique and finished apostolic spread of the gospel." These people were not planting churches or extending the gospel across ethnic boundaries. They were just ordinary believers struggling with life and ministering to the daily needs, pains, and problems of other Christians. The same may be said of believers in Thessalonica (1 Thess. 5:19–22), Rome (Rom. 12:3–6), Galatia (Gal. 3:5), and elsewhere. How can one argue that such miraculous gifts lost their validity and practical value in accomplishing that for which God ordained them simply because at some point in the first century the apostles died?

Gaffin argues that because of the alleged exclusivistic link between apostolic ministry and miraculous gifts (a link nowhere asserted in Scripture), the continuation of the latter "into the postapostolic era may not simply be presupposed" (p. 42). To the contrary, when it is observed that Paul describes ordinary church life in 1 Corinthians 12:7–10 as involving miraculous gifts whose purpose is to edify believers and sanctify their souls, gifts that are nowhere exclusively (or even primarily) tied to the apostles or whose function is reduced to accompanying and attesting to their ministry, the continuation of such gifts is *precisely* what should be presupposed.

Second, Gaffin appeals to James 5, a passage I addressed in my essay, to which I would refer the reader.

6. Gaffin's principal concern is with the so-called revelatory gifts. His discussion focuses on Ephesians 2:11–21 (esp. v. 20) and the foundational ministry of apostles and prophets. He says that apostles and prophets belong to the period of the foundation, not the superstructure. But this ignores verses 21–22, where Paul refers to the superstructure as under construction, so to speak, *as he speaks/writes* (note the consistent use of the present tense in vv. 21–22). In other words, the apostles and prophets of verse 20, among whom was Paul, were also contributing to the superstructure, of which the Ephesians were a contemporary part, simultaneous with their laying the foundation on which it was being built. We must be careful not to push the metaphor beyond what Paul intended by it.

To use an analogy, once a man establishes a company, writes its bylaws, articulates its vision, hires employees, and does all the work essential in laying the foundation for its future work and productivity, he does not necessarily cease to exist or to serve the company in other capacities. As Deere points out, "the founding director of a company or corporation will always be unique in the sense that he or she was the founder, but that does not mean the company would not have future directors or presidents."[2]

On Gaffin's view, *all* New Testament prophets functioned foundationally. But there is nothing to suggest that "the prophets" in Ephesians 2:20 is an exhaustive reference to all possible prophets in the church. Why should we conclude that the only kind of prophetic activity is "foundational" in nature, especially in light of what the New Testament says about the extent and effect of prophetic ministry? It is simply not possible to believe that all prophetic utterances were part of the once-for-all foundation of the church. For one thing, the New Testament nowhere says they were. Furthermore, it portrays prophetic ministry in an entirely different light from the one Gaffin attempts to deduce from Ephesians 2:20. Surely not everyone who ministered prophetically was apostolic. Therefore, the cessation of the latter is no argument for the cessation of the former.

To suggest that Ephesians 2:20 has in view *all possible prophets* active in the early church does not measure up to what we read about this gift in the rest of the New Testament. It would require us to believe that all those who prophesied on the day of Pentecost and in the years following, "sons and daughters ... young men ... old men ... servants, both men and women," were laying the foundation of the church. The cessationist is asking us to believe that the long-awaited promise in Joel 2 of the unprecedented outpouring of the Holy Spirit on "all people" (Acts 2:17), with its resultant revelatory activity of dreams, visions, and prophecy, was exhaustively fulfilled in only a handful of individuals whose gifting functioned in an exclusively foundational, initiatory, and therefore temporary fashion! Does this theory adequately explain the text? The revelatory and charismatic experience of the Spirit, foretold by Joel and cited by Peter, can hardly be viewed as exhaustively fulfilled by a small minority of believers during a mere sixty-year span in only the first century of the church. It seems rather that Joel 2 and

---

[2]Ibid., 248.

Acts 2 are together describing normative Christian experience for the entire Christian community in the whole of the new covenant age, called "the last days."

Cessationism would also want us to believe that a group of anonymous disciples in Ephesus (Acts 19:1–7), who prophesied upon their conversion (none of which, be it noted, was ever recorded or mentioned again), did so with a view to laying the foundation of the church. It is no less a strain to think that the four daughters of Philip were a part of the once-for-all foundation of the church (21:9).

On Gaffin's thesis, all prophetic activity is foundation-laying activity. But if it were, would Paul have spoken of prophecy as a gift bestowed to common people for the "common good" of the body of Christ (1 Cor. 12:7–10)? Are we to believe that Paul exhorted all believers in every church to earnestly desire that they exercise foundational significance for the universal church (1 Cor. 14:1, 39)? On the contrary, prophecy is to be desired because its purpose is to communicate revelation from God that will "encourage" those who are discouraged, "comfort" those who are disconsolate, and "strengthen" those who are weak and untaught (1 Cor. 14:3).

Again, I must ask, how does the exposure of an unbeliever's secret sins in the churches at Corinth, Thessalonica, Rome, Laodicea, and throughout the inhabited earth—sins such as greed, lust, anger, selfishness—function in laying the once-for-all foundation of the universal church of Jesus Christ? Yet this is one of the primary purposes for the prophetic gift (1 Cor. 14:24–25).

Gaffin believes that tongues is also a revelatory, and therefore prophetic, gift. If this were true, we would have noncanonical revelation coming to individual Christians for their own personal edification, *not* to be shared with the church at large in the absence of an interpreter (1 Cor. 14:28). How could such private revelation in any way be conceived as contributing to the once-for-all foundation of the church at large?

Paul anticipated that every time Christians gathered for worship that, at least potentially, "each" believer would come with or contribute, among other things, a "revelation" (1 Cor. 14:26). He anticipated that a normal part of Christian experience was receiving revelatory data or insight from God. It is difficult to read his instruction for corporate worship and conclude that he viewed all revelatory, and thus prophetic, ministry as foundational for the universal church. There must have been thousands upon thousands of revelations and prophetic utterances throughout the hundreds of churches over the course of the years between Pentecost and the close of the New Testament canon. Are we to believe that this multitude of people and their even greater multitude of prophetic words constituted the once-for-all foundation of the church?

Gaffin seems to believe that once apostles and prophets ceased to function foundationally, they ceased to function altogether, as if the only purpose for apostles and prophets was to lay the foundation of the church. Nowhere does the New Testament say this, least of all in Ephesians 2:20. This text need say no more than that apostles and prophets laid the foundation once and for all and then ceased to function *in that capacity*. But nothing suggests that they ceased to function in other capacities, much less that they ceased to exist altogether. Certainly it is true that *only* apostles and prophets laid the foundation of the church, but it is anything but certain that such was the *only* thing they did.

In a word, the portrayal in Acts, 1 Corinthians, Romans, and 1 Thessalonians of who could prophesy and how it was to be exercised in the life of the church simply does not fit with the cessationist assertion that Ephesians 2:20 describes all possible prophets, every one of whom functioned as part of the once-for-all foundation of the church. Rather, Paul is there describing a limited group of prophets who were closely connected to the apostles, both of which groups spoke Scripture-quality words essential to the foundation of the church universal.

7. Gaffin objects to the possibility of postcanonical revelation on grounds that we would be "bound to attend and submit to" it (p. 47) no less than to Scripture. Aside from the fact that this wrongly presupposes that contemporary prophecy yields infallible, Scripture-quality words from God, the problem is one that the cessationist himself must face. For were not the Thessalonian Christians, for example, "bound to attend and submit to" (lit., "hold on to"; 1 Thess. 5:21) the prophetic words they received, no less than to the Scripture in which this very instruction is found? Evidently Paul did not fear that their response to the spoken, prophetic word would undermine the ultimate

authority or sufficiency of the written revelation (Scripture) that he was in process of sending them. The point is this: Non-canonical revelation was not inconsistent with the authority of Scripture *then*, nor need it be *now*. This is especially true if, as I argued in my essay, contemporary prophecy does not necessarily yield infallible words of God.

Someone might ask, "But how should we in the twentieth century, in a closed-canonical world, respond to noncanonical revelation?" The answer is, "In the same way as Christians responded to it in their first-century, open-canonical world, namely, by evaluating it in light of Scripture" (which was emerging, and therefore partial, for them, but is complete for us). Such revelation would carry for us today the same authority it carried then for them. Furthermore, we are in a much better position today than the early church, for we have the final form of the canon by which to evaluate claims to prophetic revelation. If they were capable of assessing prophetic revelation then (and Paul believed they were; witness his instruction in 1 Cor. 14 and 1 Thess. 5 to do precisely that), how much more are we today! If anything, contemporary claims of prophetic revelation should be easier to evaluate and respond to than were such claims in the first century.

Therefore, if noncanonical revelation was not a threat to the ultimate authority of Scripture in its emerging form, neither should it pose a threat to Scripture in its final form. If first-century Christians were obligated to believe and obey Scripture in the open-canonical period, simultaneous with and in the presence of noncanonical prophetic revelation, there is no reason to think noncanonical revelation in the closed-canonical period of church history would present any more of a problem.

In a related vein, Gaffin argues that contemporary prophecy cannot, in fact, be evaluated by Scripture because of the former's purported specificity. But this again is no more a problem for us today than it would have been for Christians in the first century. Did not *they* evaluate prophetic revelation in spite of its specificity and individuality? If they were obedient to Paul's instruction, they certainly did (1 Cor. 14:29; 1 Thess. 5:21–22). There is no reason to think that we cannot do the same today. In point of fact, we are better equipped than they were insofar as we hold in hand the final form of canonical revelation whereby to make that assessment.

8. Gaffin believes that to admit the possibility of revelation beyond Scripture "unavoidably implies a certain insufficiency in Scripture that needs to be compensated for" (p. 52). But one must ask, "What is Scripture sufficient *for*?" Certainly it is sufficient to provide us with those theological truths and principles essential for a life of godliness. Yet Gaffin himself concedes that "God reveals himself to individuals in a variety of personal, highly intimate ways" (p. 53). But there would be no need for him to do this if Scripture were as exhaustively sufficient as Gaffin elsewhere insists. That God should find it important and helpful to reveal himself to his children in personal and intimate ways bears witness to the fact that the sufficiency of the Bible is not meant to suggest that we need no longer hear from our heavenly Father or receive particular guidance in areas on which the Bible is silent. Scripture never claims to supply us with all possible information necessary to make every conceivable decision. Scripture may tell us to preach the gospel to all people, but it does not tell a new missionary in 1996 that God desires his service in Albania rather than Australia. The potential for God speaking beyond Scripture, whether for guidance, exhortation, encouragement, or conviction of sin, poses no threat to the sufficiency that Scripture claims for itself.

Permit me to cite an example from the ministry of Charles Spurgeon. While preaching at Exeter Hall, he once broke off his sermon and pointed in a certain direction, declaring: "Young man, those gloves you are wearing have not been paid for: you have stolen them from your employer." After the service, an obviously pale and agitated young man approached Spurgeon and begged to speak with him privately. He placed a pair of gloves on the table and said, "It's the first time I have robbed my master, and I will never do it again. You won't expose me, sir, will you? It would kill my mother if she heard that I had become a thief."[3] This information could not be found by Spurgeon from reading the Bible. But surely we do not undermine the latter's sufficiency by acknowledging that it was God who "revealed" this insight to him.

---

[3]Charles H. Spurgeon, *Autobiography: Volume 2, The Full Harvest, 1860–1892* (Edinburgh: Banner of Truth Trust, 1973), 60.

In his effort to deny postapostolic revelation, Gaffin asserts (without providing biblical evidence) that "revelatory word is tethered to redemptive deed. With the completion of the latter," he says, "comes the cessation of the former" (p. 54). I disagree. Whereas it may be said that "*Scripture* is tethered to redemptive deed," *revelation* is much broader than what ultimately made its way into the canon. I see nothing in Scripture that leads me to believe God became mute after the passing of the early church. If it was crucial in first-century Corinth for God to speak beyond Scripture in such a way that the sins of the unbeliever were exposed, leading him to repentance and eternal life, why should it be any less crucial in the twentieth century (cf. 1 Cor. 14:24–25)?

9. The debate over 1 Corinthians 13 continues. Space does not permit me to say much, and I doubt that I could improve on what others have already contributed. Be it noted, however, that Gaffin rightly rejects as not "credible exegetically" (p. 55, n. 81) the suggestion that the "perfection" of verse 10 has in view the completion of the New Testament canon or some other state of affairs prior to the Parousia. He does not believe that Paul even addresses the question of the continuation of the gifts in this passage and that it therefore remains an open question.

Let me say simply that it is a question that perhaps the larger context may go a long way in answering. For it is the nature, function, and comparative value of spiritual *gifts* that concerns Paul in 1 Corinthians 12 and 14. It certainly would not be out of line, then, to suggest that in 1 Corinthians 13 he again has in view the perpetuity of such gifts as he contrasts them with the eternal value of Christian love.

10. Finally, Gaffin is surprised by Gordon Fee's struggle in distinguishing between word of wisdom and word of knowledge, as well as the latter's apparent indifference toward the nature of contemporary tongues. In the first place, I cannot answer for Fee's uncertainty, but I am not ready to concede that we cannot know what word of wisdom, word of knowledge, and speaking in tongues were then (and now). Second, surely Gaffin does not mean to suggest that lack of clarity is an argument for cessation? If a criterion for believing and embracing a principle or practice is the complete lack of ambiguity, who knows how much in the Bible we would have to conclude was

not designed by God to retain validity beyond the death of the apostles!

I wonder if the Corinthians (and especially other churches in the first century to whom even less explicit instruction was given) might have faced the same struggle. Gaffin does not question the validity of such gifts then, yet they had no more special revelation on the distinction between the two than we do. If such lack of specificity did not hinder the exercise of those gifts in the first century, there is no reason to think it should in the twentieth.

A PENTECOSTAL/CHARISMATIC RESPONSE TO RICHARD B. GAFFIN, JR.

Douglas A. Oss

Professor Gaffin has written a thoughtful and charitable evaluation of Pentecostal/charismatic theology and defense of cessationism, for which all of us in the Pentecostal movement should be grateful. I myself am indebted to him as an esteemed professor whose influence both shaped my redemptive-historical approach to Pentecostalism and showed me the wisdom of "plundering the Egyptians." So it is with affection and admiration that I offer some reflections on his essay.

1. Professor Gaffin has made an important point to those Pentecostals who engage in the rhetorical condemnation of evangelicals, denying them any work of the Spirit and pejoratively casting dismissive aspersions at them as rationalists whose faith is restricted to arid doctrinal confessions (pp. 26–27). This divisive attitude is not accurate of most Pentecostals; we Pentecostals *are* evangelicals who have accepted a portion of the biblical witness as paradigmatic that some within our evangelical family do not accept in the same way. But we are a Bible-based movement, both historically and in the present, often using the label "full gospel" to describe the broader Pentecostal movement.

The same mentality that attempts to separate Pentecostalism from its evangelical roots also embraces many modernist presuppositions and rejects cardinal commitments of evangelicalism. Indeed, there is a pronounced trend among some in the Pentecostal academy to reject inerrancy and biblical authority. As Professor Gaffin has noted, instead of drinking from the wellspring of salvation in the Scriptures, they drink from the cistern of postmodernistic cynicism and nihilism, adopting radical forms of existentialism as their framework for understanding spirituality. For example, many have adopted a community-based, sociological view of autonomous authority that has supplanted the Pentecostal commitment to revelation-based (e.g., Scripture) authority. Professor Gaffin is thus accurate in his assessment of this shift within Pentecostalism when he warns, "Pentecostal power and postmodern pretensions have nothing to do with each other" (p. 28).

It would be easy to use my entire response to evaluate this departure from Pentecostalism's evangelical roots that is occurring within the Pentecostal academy, especially since it presents the single, most significant threat to the future of the Pentecostal movement. We find ourselves in the same shifting theological sand as those who endured through the Presbyterian controversy earlier in this century.[1] But Professor Gaffin has raised several other issues that demand our attention as well.

2. Both Gaffin and I have adopted the redemptive-historical approach in our essays. Gaffin uses the approach to argue *against* second experiences and *against* the continuation of selected charismatic manifestations of the Spirit (e.g., especially utterance gifts and personal guidance). My essay uses the same approach to argue *for* the validity of second experiences as well as *for* the continuation of the manifestations of the Spirit that define the "last days" phase of kingdom-fulfillment.

Professor Gaffin narrows the focus of the debate to the crucial question in pointing out that "what constitutes the eschatological essence of the Spirit's present work in the church serves to focus a pivotal difference between cessationists and noncessationists" (p. 29). He then restricts the redemptive-historical fulfillment of the Spirit's work to regeneration and sanctification. My essay presents biblical evidence that the redemptive-historical unfolding of the Spirit's work reveals *two* works: one inner-transforming; the other empowering. Gaffin's view omits a major thread of this evidence in the redemptive-historical record, focusing instead on only part of the picture.

---

[1]Those of us who have read Bradley J. Longfield's *The Presbyterian Controversy* (New York: Oxford, 1991) find its descriptions to be strikingly parallel to the contemporary crisis within Pentecostalism.

Plainly, the Old Testament anticipates, and the New Testament confirms through fulfillment, the prophetic/charismatic nature of the Spirit's work during the last days. But this truth does not exclude other evidence concerning the Spirit's inner-transforming work. The *eschatological* nature of the Spirit's work is both inner-transforming and empowering. Professor Gaffin is correct in emphasizing that Pentecost belongs to the history of salvation (*historia salutis*), not to the order of salvation (*ordo salutis*). As such, Acts records both the eschatological fulfillment of the Spirit's empowering work and his inner-transforming work.

Probably the most fundamental error Professor Gaffin makes is his confusion of the *ordo salutis* and the *historia salutis*. He purports to demonstrate his view based on the latter, but consistently imports categories from the former to squeeze his way out of the obvious dilemma he faces in the eschatological fulfillment of the "last days" expectations in the New Testament. That is, he does not consistently apply his own "history of salvation" principles. Examples of this are spelled out below.

3. In linking Acts 2 with the Baptist's prophecy in Luke 3:16 and with Acts 1:6–8 (pp. 31–32), Gaffin again omits a major share of the evidence. He asserts that John's prophecy refers to the Messiah's activity in its *entirety* (pp. 31–32), but *restricts* this activity to the Spirit's inner-transforming work. This is not what Luke, in fact, portrays in Acts. Luke describes the fulfillment of the prophecy in terms of empowerment as well as salvation (see my essay, pp. 252–56), thus portraying the work of the risen Christ through his Spirit in its *entirety*.

Part of the hermeneutical problem evident in Gaffin's argument is that he reads Luke through a Pauline grid. Another way of putting it is this: He uses the order of salvation to flatten out differences that are obvious in the history of salvation. While I have argued in my own essay that Paul and Luke complement each other but have different emphases operating in their writings (which are not exclusive of each other), it is nevertheless simply inadequate to equate the two and assume they use language the same way. The Pauline center is apparent in Gaffin's description of Reformed theology, "Reformed theology, more importantly, the theology of Paul that it seeks to reflect, does not view either Christ's death or his resurrection as being 'symbolic' or providing 'analogies' for particular experiences, whether subsequent to conversion or distinct from the initial experience of salvation" (p. 33).

We will leave aside the question of whether Paul in passages such as Romans 6:1–14 is explaining union with Christ analogically on the basis of Christ's death and resurrection, and whether this is the historical understanding of the Reformed faith.[2] The point to be made here is Gaffin's explicit assertion of a Pauline starting point by which other canonical writings are interpreted. And his essay immediately applies this principle to the question of Pentecost in interpreting Acts through the grid of 1 Corinthians 12:13. He brings out the "redemptive-historical, Christological significance of Pentecost" from 1 Corinthians 12:13, arguing further that the significance of Pentecost is not unique to Luke–Acts but emerges elsewhere in the New Testament (the other texts he cites are from John 14–16, p. 34). While certainly the implications of Pentecost are broader than just the prophetic/charismatic theology of Luke, it is nonetheless invalid to read Paul and John into Luke–Acts, under the assumption that Luke's writing must carry essentially the same meaning as Paul.

4. Professor Gaffin argues that Pentecost is not a repeatable paradigm (pp. 30–34). However, the *essential experience of the Spirit's power* is repeated even *within* the book of Acts (e.g., 4:30–31), not to mention elsewhere in the New Testament (e.g., the worship at Corinth, although abusive, was not essentially askew of the New Testament pattern). To argue that Pentecost is not a repeatable event because it was the once-for-all giving of the Spirit to the church misses the essence of the Pentecostal position and shifts the debate off of the real issue. No Pentecostal would argue that the *day* of Pentecost, as the once-for-all, historical day on which Christ gave his Spirit to the church, is repeatable in that sense.

Rather, Pentecostals argue that since Christ has indeed poured out his Spirit, and since the Spirit does indeed dwell in the church, the Spirit is available to all believers in the same experiential manner as it was available to all the believers on that first day: in power. In that sense Pentecost is repeatable.

---

[2]Cf. John Murray, *The Epistle to the Romans* (Grand Rapids: Eerdmans, 1968), 213–29.

Why would any believer want to experience the Spirit in a manner that is inconsistent with, or that falls short of, the biblical witness concerning that experience? Why would any believer want sanctification devoid of expressions of the fruit of the Spirit? Likewise, why would any believer want to be endued with power by the Spirit in a manner devoid of all, or even selected, biblically definitive charismatic expressions?

If the Bible mandated or described a change in the expression of the Spirit's power subsequent to the foundational period, that would be binding on Pentecostals. But the Bible does not even hint at a change in the way the Spirit's power is manifested. Rather, it speaks only of *individuals* (not manifestations or gifts) whose role was foundational (e.g., Eph. 2:20–22). Again the point is simply this: The Spirit's eschatological work is both inner-transforming and empowering, and each experience has a distinctive nature and expression.

5. Professor Gaffin argues that "the history that interests Luke is *finished*" (p. 38, his italics). In response, while Acts records the *fulfillment* of redemptive history, it records only the *beginning* of the "last days" fulfillment. While some events are once-for-all, other aspects of the message of Acts reveal what is characteristic of the entire period known as "the last days," which continue until the Lord's return. Thus Acts, along with the rest of the New Testament, serves as the foundation for the life of the church throughout these last days. Part of the characteristic life for the church is life in the power of the Spirit as the Bible describes and explains it.

6. With regard to Gaffin's cessationist argument, he secures his argument with two linchpins: the "apostolic umbrella," and inscripturation (canon). Miraculous gifts are inextricably bound up, he asserts, with the authority of the apostles and the process of inscripturation. Before addressing these two foundational elements of his argument, however, one brief point is in order with reference to his view that Pentecost (the account in Acts) has little to say about "individual Christian experience, postconversion or otherwise" (p. 41). First, the emphasis in Acts is indeed upon the expansion of the kingdom, through the Spirit, to various groups of people. Pentecostals have never questioned this. At the same time, however, there is no corporate experience without individual experience.

Furthermore, the emphasis of Pentecostal theology is not on individual experience in opposition to corporate experience, any more than Luke's is. Peter himself, on that day, said, "The promise is for you and your children and for all who are far off—for all whom the Lord our God will call" (Acts 2:39). Pentecostals believe the empowering work of the Spirit is for the corporate body of Christ, but in a real, concrete sense. That is, the Spirit's empowering work among people groups will be expressed by individuals within those groups in the same ways that his empowerment has always been expressed—by bold preaching, miraculous gifts, utterance manifestations, healings, and so on. This characteristic "last days" life is for everyone in the body of Christ.

Professor Gaffin's main concern is with the cessation of all revelatory or word gifts (what I have called "utterance gifts"; Paul uses the word "manifestation" (*phanerosis*) in 1 Cor. 12:7ff.). He mentions specifically prophecy and its evaluation, tongues and interpretation of tongues, the word of wisdom, and the word of knowledge. Basing his remarks on the foundational function of the "apostles and prophets" in Ephesians 2:19–22, he links utterance gifts exclusively to the role of these people because these gifts communicated the apostolic and prophetic "inspired, revelatory witness" (p. 44). To Gaffin, utterance gifts functioned only in this capacity, resulting eventually in inscripturation.

In response to this portion of his argument, which is the main thrust of his cessationist position, it is important to note first of all that Ephesians 2 is not about miraculous gifts. The subject of miraculous gifts must be imported from other texts by implication. While legitimate implications are certainly within the framework of our discussion, in my opinion, it cannot even be demonstrated that this passage would have *implied* to an original readership that certain spiritual manifestations ceased when the apostles passed off the scene.

Second, it has been well documented elsewhere that the utterance manifestations are not exclusively linked either to the apostles or to inscripturation.[3] What is the purpose of the utterance manifestations, then? Paul cites the edification of the body

---

[3]See Grudem, *Prophecy in the New Testament*, 228–43; *Systematic Theology*, 361–72; and not as thoroughly my own contribution to this symposium.

as their purpose (1 Cor. 12:7; 14:1–19, 26–33). But the apostle provides insight into the specific content of utterances as well, for example, that tongues may give expression to prayer (14:14), singing (14:15b), or praise and thanksgiving (14:16–17); or that prophecy calls the sinner to repent and be saved (14:24–25; cf. also Acts 2:11; 10:46). But all are ways to edify the body (tongues, of course, require an interpretation in order to accomplish this task [1 Cor. 14:5]).

Inasmuch as 1 Corinthians provides explicit teachings on the purpose of utterance gifts (cf. also Rom. 12:3–8), and since there is no explicit teaching in the New Testament that says the function of these gifts was restricted to the apostolic office or to inscripturation, it appears that the view of absolute cessation with regard to utterance manifestations is untenable. When the gifts are discussed in the Scriptures, the biblical authors do not even raise the issue of cessation. It seems that such an important doctrine would have been mentioned in propositional form somewhere, or else at least be part of an analogical pattern in a biblical narrative.

Of course the concomitant question of the authority of the content of these utterances always arises next. Professor Gaffin, having defined them as revelatory in a canonical sense (pp. 44–45), next raises the problem of an open canon. However, Pentecostals do not vest canonical authority in these utterances, but rather submit them to the authority of Scripture (see my essay, pp. 278–79). Nevertheless, are Pentecostals inconsistent at this point? Can something that is inspired of God be less than canon? Yes it can. These utterances are coming through fallible human speakers, just as at Corinth, who may be out of order or even incorrect at times (cf. 1 Cor. 12–14). This is much different from our understanding of the inspiration of an infallible biblical author. If these utterances are confirmed by the Scriptures, then they edify the body. But even then, they are not in and of themselves "canon"; rather, these utterances are judged by canon.[4] Inscripturation is simply not the focus of these chapters.

Professor Gaffin also does not accept the notion of Spirit-to-spirit communication in personal guidance, arguing instead that only the Bible gives personal guidance. To him, it seems that

---

[4]Cf. Grudem, *Systematic Theology*, 1049–61.

any communication from God is a threat to "canon" (pp. 52–54). Yet we have clear biblical precedent for this kind of guidance, both in the letters (1 Cor 12:7–8) and in narrative (e.g., Acts 13:1–3). Certainly these impressions of the Spirit's voice are subjective, can be flawed, and so must be evaluated by the Scriptures. But that does not mean they should be dismissed as a phenomenon that undermines the authority of Scripture. The believer's perceptions of the Spirit's voice must be subjected for evaluation to the only infallible and inerrant rule of faith and practice, the Scriptures. Spirit-to-spirit communication is not infallible or inerrant and is certainly not equivalent to canon. Furthermore, this form of spiritual communion with Christ through the Spirit is a *blessing* of the covenant; it is not an extra-covenantal curse.

In sum, the cessation of the function of individuals who were part of the foundation of the church does not imply that utterance gifts ceased. Likewise, the closing of the canon does not imply that utterance gifts ceased. The utterance manifestations are nowhere in Scripture linked in this manner to individuals who had once-for-all functions. Furthermore, it is inaccurate of mainstream Pentecostalism to say that at work within it,

> as much as anything, I suspect—especially ... where the secularized exercise of reason and the deistic autonomy of the Enlightenment have held baleful sway for so long— is the desire for a compensating experience of the supernatural that accents the intuitive and nonrational capacities of our humanity. That desire may well have legitimate concerns that need to be explored. But *that* agenda, as such, is an agenda alien to the New Testament (p. 60).

That agenda is also alien to mainstream Pentecostalism. But hearing the voice of the Spirit, whether audibly in a manifestation intended by God to bring edification to the body of Christ, or through the still, small voice of the Spirit within, is a *biblical* agenda.

Chapter Two

AN OPEN BUT CAUTIOUS VIEW

Robert L. Saucy

AN OPEN BUT CAUTIOUS VIEW

Robert L. Saucy

Good summary of problem

All evangelical believers worship a God of supernatural power. This power is manifest in every instance of spiritual redemption from the bondage of sin. It is also displayed in overtly miraculous actions, some of which are associated with "miraculous spiritual gifts" exercised by God's people. How and even whether these gifts are to be used in the ministry of the church today is for many (including myself) problematic. Since Scripture does not provide explicit teaching on all the issues involved, we must seek answers from a broad consideration of biblical teachings that impinge on various related topics as well as from the experience of the church.

A. THE EXPERIENCE OF GOD SUBSEQUENT TO SALVATION

(following)

The exercise of miraculous gifts in the church is often associated with the teaching of a second definite spiritual experience, subsequent to the initial experience of salvation. This experience, sometimes described as baptism *in* or *with* the Spirit, is said to be the time when the believer receives power for ministry. While this power is necessary for the exercise of all spiritual gifts, it is most evident in those gifts that require the supernatural for their explanation, that is, the miraculous gifts. Those who hold to a second definite experience commonly consider speaking in tongues as its initial evidence. All of this provides an obvious experience of the supernatural that is said to be essential to true Christianity. While I totally agree that believers should experience the supernatural (not necessarily the miraculous), the model of a two-stage experience for the believer in the church is in my mind not sustained by Scripture.

The experiences of the believers at Pentecost (Acts 2) and Samaria (Acts 8), usually cited as evidence of a two-stage Christian experience, represent the inaugural coming of the Spirit on different groups of believers (Jews and Samaritans) who lived during the transition from the old covenant to that of the new age of the Spirit. They are not therefore normative for all believers of this age. Note that this second experience came to these believers without anything said about their meeting any added spiritual requirements generally held necessary for this occurrence. The fact that it came on all and not some of the believers in these instances adds support to this.

But the greatest objection to the concept of the reception of or baptism with the Spirit as taking place some time following saving faith is the scriptural teaching that a relationship to the Spirit belongs to *all* believers. In various ways, Scripture reveals that the *only* condition for receiving the Spirit or experiencing Spirit baptism is the faith in Christ, which brings initial salvation. Such faith is the only condition associated explicitly with a "baptism" passage (Acts 11:17). It is also the only condition for being joined to Christ and becoming part of his body, which takes place through the baptism with the Spirit (1 Cor. 12:13).[1] Finally, faith is the only condition stated for receiving the Spirit (John 7:38–39; Gal. 3:2, 13–14). Nowhere can the argument be sustained that this reception of the Spirit through saving faith brings only an initial level of relationship to the Spirit. Jesus' teaching that the reception of the Spirit through faith in him would cause rivers of living water to flow out of the believer surely teaches nothing less than a fullness of spiritual life and not simply a basis for a further experience.

That all believers through faith in Christ have come into the final relationship with the Spirit is confirmed by the fact that Scripture contains no command for believers to seek a new relationship with the Spirit. No commands exist to be "baptized with the Spirit" or to receive the Spirit in a new and different way. The only two positive commands stated in relationship to the Spirit

---

[1]See also Galatians 3:26–28; Colossians 2:12.

are "live [lit., walk] by the Spirit" (Gal. 5:16, 25) and "be filled with the Spirit" (Eph. 5:18). Being expressed in the Greek present tense, these commands suggest an ongoing growth in the relationship to the Spirit that the believer already has, not a definitive new relationship. There may be decisive spurts in the believer's spiritual growth, which brings him or her into a deeper relationship with the Spirit. But these are deeper or fuller experiences of the Spirit who already lives in all believers.

The belief, crucial to most second-step theology, that the Christian should experience a supernatural power of the Spirit is a valid challenge to those for whom Christianity is more doctrine than life. The very concept of the term *spirit* has the idea of vitality and power. But Scripture places more emphasis on the experience of this power in the regular experience of daily life than in the miraculous.

Instructive in this regard are Paul's prayers for believers. The apostle expresses no concern for believers to experience the miraculous. Instead, his desire is that they experience the "power" of God in order to attain steadfastness and patience (Col. 1:11), to grow in the faith that makes Christ at home in their hearts and gives them experience in love (Eph. 3:16–19), and to maintain their hope (1:18; cf. Rom. 15:13). In other words, his prayers are for the experience of God's power in the three key areas of the present Christian life—faith, hope, and love. Peter likewise refers to power protecting the believer unto final salvation (1 Peter. 1:5).

Beyond these concerns for the experience of God's power for the inner spiritual life is the thrust of apostolic teaching that the presence of the Spirit in a believer's life will produce results in the realm of practical ethics (e.g., Gal. 5:22–23; Eph. 5:18ff.; cf. also the practical portions of all New Testament letters). Without denying the presence of the miraculous in the New Testament church, the clear emphasis of apostolic teaching is for believers to experience supernatural power in order to live as Christ in the world. To hope when all seems hopeless, to wait in faith when all human means are exhausted, to persevere in the midst of trials (a common theme in the New Testament), and, most of all, to love others (including our enemies) involves the experience of the supernatural as much as performing the miraculous does.

B. CESSATIONISM

Any discussion of miraculous gifts must deal with the question of whether all of the gifts listed in the New Testament are normal for the church. Since there is no explicit biblical teaching on the issue (at least that all accept), a conclusion can be reached only by considering many passages and the experience of the church. Before delving into the question, however, two points of clarification are necessary. (a) By "miraculous" spiritual gifts, I mean those gifts whose operation truly yields miraculous phenomena. Considerable confusion often surrounds the contemporary discussion because different concepts of gifts are held.[2] (b) It is important that the question of the cessation of miraculous spiritual gifts not be confused with the issue of whether miracles take place today. Contrary to the impression sometimes given that cessationists deny that God still works miracles, I personally know of no cessationist who denies that God can and does work miracles throughout the church age. The issue of cessationism, therefore, is not whether God still works miracles, but whether all of the same phenomena of miraculous spiritual gifts seen in the early church of the New Testament are *normal* for the entire church age.

To state my opinion up front, the New Testament does not explicitly teach the cessation of certain gifts at a particular point in the experience of the church. It is, therefore, impossible to say, on the basis of biblical teaching, that certain gifts cannot occur at any given time according to God's sovereign purpose. On the other hand, there are several lines of evidence that demonstrate that the miraculous phenomena experienced in the early biblical church are not standard for the life of the church throughout all time.

1. The Uniqueness of the Apostolic Era

Insofar as Scripture provides the normative teaching for the theology and practice of the church for all of its history, it is sometimes reasoned that everything in the biblical picture of the

---

[2]For my understanding of the nature of the different miraculous spiritual gifts, see below, pp. 126–37.

church remains the same throughout history. Since the mission of the church is unchangeable, the spiritual gifts to accomplish that mission must also be the same. But this rationale founders on the special role of the apostles in the church.

Even those who hold a present church ministry as successors of the apostles agree that the original biblical apostles were in some sense unique. While the exact number of apostles in the sense of which we are speaking is not clear in Scripture (this word is also used for "representatives of the church," e.g., 2 Cor. 8:23), there was clearly a relatively small group known as "apostles," who represented Christ as uniquely authoritative ministers in the early church. They laid the foundation of "apostolic tradition," which became the normative canon for the church throughout history. In limiting the canon of Scripture to certain books that contained "apostolic tradition," the later church explicitly marked the first apostles as distinctive, setting them apart from the later ministry of the church with its "church tradition."

Since no gift of "apostleship" is listed among the spiritual gifts, some have argued that the apostles did not have any special "spiritual gift." They simply exercised a combination of other listed gifts, such as prophecy and teaching. If such is the case, then, the cessation of apostles did not involve the termination of any spiritual gifts. The manner in which the apostles are mentioned in the discussion of spiritual gifts, however, suggests that their ministry was something more than simply a combination of other gifts. They are listed along with "prophets" and "teachers," who all agree were individuals who regularly exercised the corresponding gifts of prophecy and teaching (cf. 1 Cor. 12:28–29; Eph. 4:11). Even as prophets and teachers were such by corresponding spiritual gifts that they exercised, so were apostles.

This thought is verified by Paul's discussion of gifted ministers in Ephesians 4:7–11. Although the common term for spiritual gifts, *charisma*, is not directly applied to these gifted individuals, it is clearly implied. Paul begins his discussion of spiritual gifts given by Christ to the church by saying, "To each one of us grace [*charis*] has been given as Christ apportioned it" (v. 7). Since a *charisma* is by definition a gift that is the result of grace (*charis*), the fact that these individuals are each given a measure of grace in this discussion of gifts surely leads to the conclusion that each one has his own spiritual gift (*charisma*) for ministry. The same apostle makes a direct connection between *charis* given for ministry and its expression in a *charisma* in his letter to the Romans: "We have different gifts [*charismata*], according to the grace [*charis*] given to us" (12:6; cf. v. 3).

Thus, in Ephesians 4, although different terms are used in speaking of "Christ's gift [*dorea*]" (v. 7, NASB) and his giving "gifts [*domata*] to men" (v. 8), it is evident that the "apostles" (v. 11) as one of these gifts are those individuals who received a particular grace (*charis*) for ministry—a grace expressed in a particular spiritual gift (*charisma*). Thus, while the apostles exercised various gifts common to others (such as prophecy and teaching), they were also endowed with a unique spiritual gift that enabled them to minister as apostles.

If the *charisma* of being an apostle did not continue in the church, then we must acknowledge that not all of the spiritual gifts operative in the New Testament church have continued throughout history. Furthermore, this fact creates the possibility that other *charismata* have also ceased or changed. In particular, the mention of "the things that mark an apostle—signs, wonders and miracles" (2 Cor. 12:12) at least suggests that certain miraculous works were related specifically to apostles. With the absence of apostles, some change in the manifestation of such signs could be expected. The disappearance of apostles in the church thus argues rather clearly that not all has remained the same in the church with regard to miraculous gifts.

Moreover, the record of Acts reveals miraculous phenomena that few would claim as normal for all ages. Along with the gift of tongues at Pentecost, there was the miraculous sound like rushing wind and the appearance of tongues of fire on each one gathered in the upper room (Acts 2:2–3). Ananias and Sapphira (apparently believers) were instantaneously killed for lying (5:1–11), and an obstructer of the gospel was blinded (13:6–12). Chains fell off and prison doors were miraculously opened (cf. 5:17–22; 12:1–11; 16:23–26). On several occasions *all* who came to be healed were in fact healed (cf. 5:16; 28:9). Even the "shadow" of Peter was effective in healing (5:15), as were "handkerchiefs and aprons" that had touched Paul (19:11–12).

If, therefore, it is impossible to say that certain phenomena of the early church continued throughout church history and are present today, the question of the presence of contemporary miraculous spiritual gifts cannot be solved by simply looking at what occurred in the biblical picture of the early church and by asserting that the same is intended for the church today. Rather, our investigation requires a much broader consideration of the phenomena of the miraculous and their purpose throughout Scripture.

2. The Unevenness of Miracles in Biblical History

a. The Biblical Evidence of Special Periods of Miracles

Scripture records miraculous activity throughout all of biblical history, much of which involved the gift of prophecy. But other miracles also occurred, such as God's supernatural destruction of the Assyrian army (2 Kings 19:35), the feats of Samson (Judg. 14–16), and the reversing of the shadow on the stairway of Ahaz (2 Kings 20:9–11). However, it is also apparent that miraculous activity was particularly concentrated at certain times. There were three prominent periods of miracles: that of Moses and the Exodus, the ministries of Elijah and Elisha, and Christ and the apostles.[3] We have already noted something of the miraculous activity during the time of the apostles, and the special miracle working of Jesus has always been recognized.

The significance of the time of Moses and the Exodus in relation to miraculous activity is seen in that the phrase "signs and wonders" in the Old Testament is by and large reserved for texts dealing with this period.[4] "Signs" and "wonders" (usually used separately) are occasionally used for other miracles (e.g., 2 Chron. 32:24, 31), but it was God's activity in redeeming his people from Egypt and bringing them into the Promised Land that saw the preeminent miracles in Israel's remembrance.

Clusters of miraculous activity are also associated with the ministries of Elijah and Elisha.[5] The extraordinary status of these

---

[3]Some add the times of Daniel and the end of this age. Regarding the latter, the special miraculous activity of "signs and wonders" is especially linked to those opposed to Christ (e.g., Matt. 24:24; 2 Thess. 2:9; Rev. 13:13; 16:14; 19:20).

[4]See Exodus 7:3; Deuteronomy 4:34; 6:22; 7:19; 26:8; 29:3; 34:11; Nehemiah 9:10; Psalms 78:43; 105:27; 135:9; Jeremiah 32:20–21.

[5]Elijah raised the dead (1 Kings 17:17–24), called down fire from heaven (ch. 18), and outran Ahab's horse drawn chariot (18:46). In addition to working miracles, Elijah also experienced miraculous sustenance on two occasions (17:4–6; 19:6–7),

prophets (particularly the former) is evident in later Scripture. In his first sermon at Nazareth, Jesus compares his own prophetic ministry to both of these Old Testament prophets. As they both worked miracles and, perhaps even more significantly, were rejected by their own people and thus turned to help those outside Israel, so it would happen in Jesus' own ministry (Luke 4:24–27).[6] The miracles of Jesus recorded in the Gospels are generally recognized as similar to both those of Elijah and Elisha.[7] Moreover, the total ministry of Jesus as a great miracle-working prophet evoked the popular thought that he was the expected Elijah of the last days (Matt. 16:14; Mark 6:15: Luke 9:8).[8]

The biblical picture of both Moses and the prophets Elijah and Elisha thus reveals that their extraordinary ministries were accompanied by special miraculous activity. Again, miracles were not limited to these two eras; Jeremiah suggests that miracles continued throughout Israel's history (Jer. 32:20). But miracles were not a daily or even a weekly occurrence, and some times of history far eclipsed others in the magnitude of miraculous activity. The very fact that miraculous phenomena were not constant throughout the history of God's people in the Old Testament should caution us against assuming that the level of miracles in the early church of the apostles is constant for all of subsequent church history.

God appeared to him (19:11–13), and he was finally caught up to heaven in a fiery chariot (2 Kings 2). Similar miraculous activity surrounds his successor Elisha (see 2 Kings 2–13).

[6]For a discussion of this comparison, see I. Howard Marshall, *The Gospel of Luke*, NIGTC (Grand Rapids: Eerdmans, 1978), 178, 188–89.

[7]Darrell L. Bock, "Elijah and Elisha," in *Dictionary of Jesus and the Gospels*, ed. Joel B. Green and Scot McKnight (Downers Grove, Ill.: InterVarsity, 1992), 206.

[8]Further evidence of the special place of Elijah in Old Testament history is found in his being placed alongside Moses by the prophet Malachi. At the same time as Malachi commands the people to obey the law given through Moses, he predicts the coming of the prophet Elijah (Mal. 4:4–6). Just as the historical Elijah preached repentance when Israel had turned away from God's covenant to worship other gods, so the eschatological Elijah would minister to bring the people back to God (v. 6). Elijah, therefore, stands with Moses as God's prophets at crucial turning points in the history of his people. Moses represents the initial establishment of the covenant while Elijah, "pictured very much in Mosaic guise," seeks to reestablish the covenant at a crucial point of apostasy in Israel's later history (William J. Dumbrell, *Covenant and Creation* [Nashville: Thomas Nelson, 1984], 167; cf. also Hans Bietenhard, "Elijah," in *NIDNTT*, ed. Colin Brown [Grand Rapids: Zondervan, 1975], 1:543).

b. The Explanation for the Special Periods of Miracles

Seeing that miracles did not regularly occur among God's people, equipping them to live for him and to accomplish their mission in the world, the key to understanding the purpose of miracles is seen in the term *sign*. Whereas the other common biblical terms used for miracles, *power* and *wonder*, describe aspects of their nature or effect, *sign* designates their purpose. A sign is that which points to something else.[9] What is crucial in a sign is not the sign itself but its functional character, which is designed to give credibility to something.[10]

This *sign* purpose of miracles is evident in Scripture even when the word is not used. Moses was given certain "signs" to perform so that the people "may believe that the LORD . . . has appeared to you" (Ex. 4:5; cf. v. 31). When Elijah raised the son of the widow of Zarephath from the dead, she exclaimed, "Now I know that you are a man of God and that the word of the LORD from your mouth is truth" (1 Kings 17:24). Note that a miracle pointed to the validity both of the messenger and of his message; it also pointed to God. In his contest with the prophets of Baal, Elijah prayed, "Let it be known today that you are God in Israel and that I am your servant and have done all these things at your command" (1 Kings 18:36; cf. Ex. 10:2; Deut. 4:34–35).

The miracles of Jesus were likewise explained as "signs" that verified who he was and validated his claims. Nicodemus acknowledged that Jesus had come from God, explaining that "no one could perform the miraculous signs you are doing if God were not with him" (John 3:2). When John the Baptist sent his disciples to question Jesus as to whether he was the Promised One, Jesus replied by pointing to his miracles: "Go back and report to John what you have seen and heard: The blind receive sight, the lame walk, those who have leprosy are cured, the deaf hear, the dead are raised, and the good news is preached to the poor" (Luke 7:22). At Pentecost Peter described Jesus as "a man accredited by God to you by miracles, wonders and signs" (Acts

---

[9]Hofius defines a "sign" as that "by which one recognizes a particular person or thing, a confirmatory, corroborative, authenticating mark or token" (O. Hofius, "Miracle," *NIDNTT*, 2:626).

[10]F. J. Helfmeyer, "אוֹת," *TDOT*, ed. G. Johannes Botterweck and Helmer Ringgren (Grand Rapids: Eerdmans, 1977), 1:170.

2:22; cf. John 20:30). Similarly, miracles are accrediting signs related to the apostles (2 Cor. 12:12) and to the first proclamation of the gospel by Jesus and those that heard him (Heb. 2:3–4).

I do not deny that these same miracles frequently expressed the compassion of the Lord. They also provided glimpses into the nature of God's kingdom as manifestations of the divine power that is able to overcome the effects of sin. But the *primary purpose* of the miracles was as signs of authentication pointing to God, his messengers or spokesmen, and their message, which was the word of God.

It is important to note that these "signs" did not accompany every individual who spoke or taught God's word. There were always teachers among God's people who spoke the word of God (cf. 2 Chron. 17:7–9; Mal. 2:4–9), but whose proclamation of the word was not authenticated by signs. When we examine the nature of those messengers of God who were accredited by signs, we find that they spoke God's word not simply as teachers but as prophets. That is, they claimed to speak words directly from God, not simply teach the word previously revealed. Clearly Moses, Elijah, and Elisha had such prophetic ministries. In the New Testament, those who were authenticated by miraculous signs were likewise those who exercised a prophetic ministry.[11] Jesus, for example, spoke inspired words and was widely acknowledged by the people to be a prophet (e.g., Matt. 21:11; John 4:19). The apostles who worked signs likewise claimed that their preaching was nothing less than the authoritative word of God (e.g., 1 Thess. 2:13).

While Stephen and Philip, who also performed miraculous signs (cf. Acts 6:8; 8:6), are not specifically designated as "prophets," there is considerable evidence that their ministry was in fact prophetic. Stephen's speech before the Jewish council, the longest of any recorded in Acts, was clearly inspired by the Spirit (cf. 6:10). Its content, asserting the temporary character of the Mosaic Law and temple worship, was new as far as we know from the record of the preaching of the early church, pro-

---

[11]For a good discussion of the truth that miraculous signs were for the attestation of prophetic ministries especially in the book of Acts, see Leo O'Reilly, *Word and Sign in the Acts of the Apostles* (Roma: Editrice Pontificia Universita Gregoriana, 1987).

viding a link with the later universalized gospel of Paul. The similarity of Stephen's message with the book of Hebrews has caused many to see him as the spiritual father of the writer of that later book. Stephen was thus not just a preacher of previously received revelation, but rather received his message through prophetic inspiration.

Furthermore, the experiences of Stephen—namely, the bitter antagonism of the Jews, the false witnesses brought against him, the language about the Son of Man at the right hand of God, and the prayer of forgiveness for his opponents—all suggest a similarity to Jesus' prophetic ministry. Stephen shows his own awareness of his prophetic ministry in his accusing attack on his opponents at the end of his speech. According to F. F. Bruce, by attacking the people at this point and pointing to Israel's traditional hostility to the prophets, Stephen was placing himself in "the prophetic succession."[12]

The ministry of Philip also exhibits prophetic characteristics, although he himself is termed "the evangelist" (Acts 21:8).[13] His miracles are called "signs," a term that throughout biblical history typically served to confirm prophetic roles, notably Moses and Elijah.[14] The description of his activity as "preaching the good news of [evangelizing] the kingdom of God" (Acts 8:12), reminiscent of the ministry of John the Baptist and Jesus (cf. Luke 3:18; 4:43), probably also denotes inspired speech. As Friedrich explains, evangelizing (*euangelizō*) "is not just speaking and preaching; it is proclamation with full authority and power."[15] The fact that God used Mark, Luke, James, and Jude

---

[12]F. F. Bruce, *Commentary on the Book of Acts*, NICNT (Grand Rapids: Eerdmans, 1954), 162.

[13]F. Scott Spencer, *The Portrait of Philip in Acts*, JSNTSup 67 (Sheffield: Sheffield Academic Press, 1992).

[14]Howard Kee says, "In the OT and the intertestamental writings the deeds performed by miracle workers or in their behalf (by direct divine intervention) serve to confirm them as chosen instruments of God. The prototype is Moses, through whom 'signs and wonders' accomplish the deliverance of Israel from bondage. The divine sanction of the prophetic roles of Elijah and Elisha is likewise provided through miracles performed by them or at their word" ("Miracle Workers," *IDBS* [Nashville: Abingdon, 1976], 598).

[15]Gerhard Friedrich, "εὐαγγελίζομαι, κτλ.," *TDNT*, ed. Gerhard Kittel et al. (Grand Rapids: Eerdmans, 1964ff.), 2:720.

to write inspired Scripture shows that prophetic ministries could be exercised by those who, like Philip and Stephen, are not specifically identified in Scripture as apostles or prophets.

Scripture thus reveals clusters of miraculous activity that functioned as signs to authenticate particular individuals who had a prophetic ministry. But such miraculous signs are not associated evenly with all prophets. There were numerous prophets throughout Israel's history, but (as already noted) "signs and wonders" accompany only Moses, Elijah, and Elisha in the Old Testament. Similarly in the New Testament, certain prophets mentioned in Acts (e.g., Agabus, 11:28; 21:10; the daughters of Philip, 21:9; Judas and Silas, 15:32; cf. also 13:1) are not credited with performing "signs and wonders" or proclaiming the new gospel like the apostles and Stephen and Philip.

What, in fact, we find in the Scripture is that "signs and wonders" accompany those whose prophetic ministries occur at certain crucial turning points in the history of salvation. The period of the giving of the Law with Moses and its reaffirmation during the time of Elijah and Elisha have already been noted. The inauguration of the eschatological salvation in Christ brought the climactic time when Christ and those with him first proclaimed the new "good news" of the promised salvation (cf. Luke 4:18; 9:6; Acts 5:42; 8:12). Even during the spread of this new gospel in the early church, Acts appears to relate the presence of "signs and wonders" with certain turning points as the gospel moved out from Jerusalem to the rest of the world—that is, at the initial entrance of the gospel into each new area.[16]

The fact that in these inaugural steps the ministries of some people other than the apostles were also accompanied with miraculous signs must not lead us to the conclusion that such miraculous authenticating "signs" were widely distributed

---

[16]After looking at the overall plan of Acts, O'Reilly concisely summarizes these phases of the first missionary proclamation of the gospel. "The apostles collectively represent the initial preaching in Jerusalem in continuity with Judaism; Stephen marks the decisive break with Judaism and the temple and the beginning of the movement out of Jerusalem; Philip is the representative of the mission in Judea [and Samaria], and finally, Paul ... represents the mission to the pagans" (*Word and Sign in the Acts of the Apostles*, 210; see esp. 208–11; cf. also G. W. H. Lampe, "Miracles in the Acts of the Apostles," in *Miracles: Cambridge Studies in Their Philosophy and History*, ed. C. F. D. Moule [London: A. R. Mowbray, 1965]).

among all members of the early church and were regular happenings among them. The references to miracles in the book of Acts are rather clearly restricted to the apostles and those few individuals noted above.

One might counter that the lack of reference to general miracles working through ordinary church members was in accord with Luke's purpose to highlight the ministry of the apostles and that, in fact, miracles were a regular part of the church. While some measure of this may be true and some miracles may have taken place in the church that are not mentioned, it should be noted that we find believers bringing their sick *to the apostles* for healing (Acts 5:12–16; esp. 9:36–42). If healing miracles were a regular part of church ministry, one has to wonder why the believers were compelled to bring their sick to this group of people. The picture of the early church in Acts makes it all but impossible to deny a special miraculous activity limited to the apostles and a few others with them who shared in the first prophetic proclamation of the gospel of Christ.

The writer to the Hebrews confirms this picture of Acts by asserting that the message of salvation "first spoken through the Lord . . . was confirmed to us by those who heard him, God also bearing witness with them, both by signs and wonders and by various miracles and by gifts of the Holy Spirit" (Heb. 2:3–4, NASB). The thrust of this statement is clearly on the absolute reliability and therefore the validity and importance of this initial word of salvation, not about the continual preaching and teaching of God's word throughout all generations. Just as the revelation at Sinai, "spoken by angels, was binding [*bebaios*, i.e., valid, guaranteed, certain]" (v. 2), so, the writer asserts, the new Christian revelation was "confirmed" or "guaranteed" (*bebaios*, v. 3) to us by the first witness of Christ, to which God also "testified" with miraculous activity.[17] Although this text does not identify these first witnesses as apostles ("apostle" being

---

[17]What the writer to the Hebrews is saying in 2:3–4 about the confirmation of the gospel through miraculous activity has been aptly summarized by Moffatt. This new gospel cannot be neglected because "it reached us, accurate and trustworthy. No wonder, when we realize the channel along which it flowed. It was authenticated by the double testimony of men who had actually heard Jesus, and of God who attested and inspired them in their mission" (James Moffatt, *A Critical and Exegetical Commentary on the Epistle to the Hebrews*, ICC [Edinburgh: T. & T. Clark, 1924], 19).

reserved by the writer for Christ, 3:1), it does speak of those who heard Christ directly. It therefore certainly includes the apostles, but perhaps others also who with them, as in Acts, were used by God to proclaim the message with guaranteed certainty as inspired prophets.

This text does not limit the actual miracle-working to those who heard Christ. The mention of the "gifts [lit., distributions] of the Holy Spirit" (v. 4) may well include the gifting of some to work miracles among those that heard the original witnesses. But whether such is the case or not, it is important to note that the purpose of all miraculous activity is to "testify to" the original proclamation of the new message of salvation. Nothing in this text suggests that this miraculous witness would accompany all subsequent proclamation of salvation, nor does it suggest that miracles were for the general life of the church in its struggle against evil.

Paul's question in Galatians 3:5, "Does God give you his Spirit and work miracles among you because you observe the law, or because you believe what you heard?" is best understood as parallel to the Hebrews passage. This entire section (3:1–5) focuses on the initial reception of the Spirit by the Galatian believers.[18] Paul's joining of the giving of the Spirit with the working of miracles, therefore, suggests that these miracles among the Galatians were closely connected with their initial reception of the Spirit, which in turn accompanied the initial proclamation of the gospel by the apostle (and perhaps others with him). Thus the text, while not limiting miracles to the apostles or other missionaries who proclaimed the gospel,[19] does associate the miraculous activity to this ministry of the first witnesses.

The picture does not necessarily mean that miracles happened only at the very first preaching. The description of God

---

[18]The question of verse 5 is essentially a repetition of the earlier question in verse 2: "Did you receive the Spirit by observing the law, or by believing what you heard?" See Richard N. Longenecker, *Galatians*, WBC (Dallas: Word, 1990), 105; also Ernest De Witt Burton, *A Critical and Exegetical Commentary on the Epistle to the Galatians*, ICC (Edinburgh: T. & T. Clark, 1921), 152.

[19]While it is possible to interpret the working of miracles as being done only by the apostles "among" the Galatians, it is best to understand that the miracles were also performed by the Galatians themselves as a result of gifts endowed on them through the reception of the Spirit.

in the verse as the one who "works [present tense participle] miracles" suggests that the miraculous activity may well have continued among the believers in Galatia, similar to the miracle-producing gifts in the church at Corinth (cf. 1 Cor. 12:10), although how long the activity continued is not specified.[20] But even if such is the case, it still does not divorce the miraculous activity from its connection with the initial inspired proclamation of the gospel.

F. F. Bruce also places this miracle-working among the Galatians in its proper context. While limiting it to the apostle, he nevertheless sees Paul's reference to the "marks of an apostle" (2 Cor. 12:12) as related to this text, concluding that "the introduction of the gospel to new territories was regularly accompanied by miraculous healing and other 'signs and wonders' is attested throughout the NT not only in Paul's writings but in Hebrews (2:4) and in Acts (2:43 *et passim*)."[21] We should also add that in each of these instances in the New Testament where miracles occur, the preaching is the inspired proclamation of those with the gift of prophecy, not just the witness of believers who spread the gospel wherever they traveled (cf. Acts 8:4). The direct application of Galatians 3:5 to the church when such prophetic proclamation is no longer normal, therefore, is highly questionable.

Further evidence for the special nature of the apostolic period of the church is found in Paul's teaching that the church

---

[20]The question of the continuity of miracles is not entirely clear in the language of the verse. While most interpreters see the present tense of the participles as indicating some continuity in both participles, i.e., in the supplying of the Spirit and working of miracles, the verbs of the sentence are unexpressed and therefore have to be supplied from the context. Seeing that the question in verse 5 seems to repeat the earlier question of verse 2, which uses the aorist tense (usually translated as a past tense), Longenecker says that the verbs supplied in verse 5 should also be aorist, which would result in his translation, "Did God, then, give you his Spirit and work miracles among you on the basis of the works of the law?" (Longenecker, *Galatians*, 99, 105); see also the discussion of the present tenses in Burton, whose conclusion must be considered: "The choice of the present tense rather than the aorist shows that the apostle has in mind an experience extended enough to be thought of as in progress, but not that it is in progress at the time of writing" (Burton, *Commentary on Galatians*, 152).

[21]F. F. Bruce, *The Epistle to the Galatians*, NIGTC (Grand Rapids: Eerdmans, 1982), 151.

is "built on the foundation of the apostles and prophets" (Eph. 2:20), which plainly refers to those first apostles who, like Paul, proclaimed the new message of the gospel with full authority or divine inspiration. The "prophets" mentioned with them are no doubt the same New Testament prophets who along with the apostles (as in Acts) are given the revelation of the mystery of Christ and the gospel to be proclaimed among the Gentiles (Eph. 3:5; cf. also 4:11).[22]

These apostles and prophets form "the foundation" of the church, no doubt a reference to their functional role of revealing the authoritative interpretation of God's saving action in Christ. But in calling them "the foundation," the apostle also indicates that they belonged to the initial period of the church when the authoritative teaching, which was to be the foundation for the church of all time, was divinely given through prophetic revelation. If such a *foundational* period of *special* prophetic revelation can be distinguished from later church history, it follows that the accompanying miraculous signs also have *particular* reference to this period.

The witness of Scripture thus leads to the following three conclusions: (i) miraculous activity was clustered around certain crucial points in the biblical record of salvation history; (ii) these clusters of miracles had the primary purpose of "signs" authenticating God's revelation and his prophetic spokespersons at crucial steps; and (iii) the era of Christ and the apostles was one such era of extraordinary miraculous signs.

3. The Witness of Church History Regarding Miracles

The conclusion that the era of Christ and the early apostolic church was a particular time of miracles that did not continue at the same level in the later church is strongly confirmed by the witness of church history. The use of such historical evidence is sometimes challenged on the basis that it is an argument from experience and not Scripture. While this charge cannot be ignored, two things must be kept in mind here. (a) According to Scripture, experience often serves as the criterion for recognizing God's work. For example, how did the Israelites know that

---

[22]Andrew T. Lincoln, *Ephesians*, WBC (Dallas: Word, 1990), 153.

Moses was sent from God and brought his law if not from hearing Moses and observing his activity? In this instance and numerous others like it throughout Scripture, there was no prior biblical teaching that made this identification to which the people could look. To be sure, prior revelation provided some criteria that could be used to evaluate the experience. But it was not the prior revelation alone that led to the conclusion; it was also that which they saw and heard. In other words, experience has always played a valid part in the interpretation and recognition of God's activity.

(b) We find that experience with regard to miracles has been used by proponents on both sides of the debate over the issue of miraculous gifts. Those who argue for their continued presence in the church refer to the experience of miracles in church history as proof. Similarly, those who deny the continuation of the miraculous activity of Christ and the apostles today use the same history to support their understanding. The fact that historical evidence has been used for both positions points to the difficulty of its interpretation. Even as today, so in the past it is difficult to distinguish a genuine divine miracle from a spurious or even a demonic one. This, however, does not make the historical record of no value. While the evaluations of many reported miracles may differ, it seems impossible to deny that miraculous activity of the *quality* and *extent* associated with the era of Christ and the apostles is not found as a continuing phenomenon in the later church.

A brief survey of the evidence demonstrates this. The writings immediately following the apostolic age contain little evidence of the miraculous when compared with the picture of the apostles and others in the biblical record. With few exceptions, the references to miraculous activity in the writings of the second and third centuries are confined to the gifts of prophecy and healing, which included exorcism.[23] Without denying any valid expressions of these miraculous gifts during this time, these two

---

[23]J. H. Bernard, "The Miraculous in Early Christian Literature," in *The Literature of the Second Century*, ed. F. R. Wynne, J. H. Bernard, and S. Hemphill (New York: James Pott & Co., 1891), 147. Irenaeus, for example, refers to prophecy and healing as present in his time, but resurrections from the dead are placed in the past tense (163–64).

are the most difficult to evaluate.[24] The association of healing with the effects of exorcism also makes it difficult to determine the extent of the miraculous healing of genuine organic diseases.[25]

Furthermore, healings during this period appear to have occurred primarily through prayer, presumably following the instructions of James 5:14–16. How healing in such instances is related to "miraculous spiritual gifts" is not clear. In addition, according to Amundsen and Ferngren, the healing reports of the second and third centuries "were usually somewhat vague. . . . The majority of writers did not claim to have seen the events related; [and] those through whom the healings or exorcisms were accomplished were not usually named."[26]

Beyond the limitedness and the character of the reports of miracles from this early period, we also find evidence of "the growing suspicion that miracles are dying out," and that the miracles of this time were "different in kind from those of the apostolic age."[27] Origen, for example, writes, "Miracles began with the preaching of Jesus, were multiplied after His ascension, and then decreased; but even now some traces of them remain with a few, whose souls are cleansed by the word."[28]

We find little during this period about miracles authenticating the contemporary preachers as was true in the apostolic era. Rather, the emphasis was on the miracles of Scripture. Although the church fathers of the second and third centuries did not say it directly, there is considerable evidence in their writings for the opinion later explicitly taught by Chrysostom and others that the age of miracles was essentially over. The pur-

---

[24]Thus we find in the writings of the early church great concern for false prophets and instructions for discerning them, cf. ibid., 148.

[25]For a discussion of the reports of healing in the early centuries, especially as it relates to the exorcism of that time, see, J. S. McEwen, "The Ministry of Healing," *SJT*, 7 (1954): 133–52.

[26]Darrel W. Amundsen and Gary B. Ferngren, "Medicine and Religion: Early Christianity Through the Middle Ages," in *Health/Medicine and the Faith Traditions*, ed. Martin E. Marty and Kenneth L. Vaux (Philadelphia: Fortress, 1982), 103; on the miracles of this early period, see also, G. W. H. Lampe, "Miracles and Early Christian Apologetic," in *Miracles: Cambridge Studies in Their Philosophy and History*, 205–18.

[27]Bernard, "The Miraculous in Early Christian Literature," 156.

[28]Origen, *Contra Celsum*, 1.2; cited by Bernard, ibid., 155–56. Along the same line as Origen, Tertullian recognized that the apostles had a special spiritual power (155).

Conversion is a miracle

pose of the miraculous activity of Christ and the apostles had been for the inauguration of the gospel and the church and was not intended for all subsequent time.[29] Origen and especially the later writers began to refer more to conversions and the transformation of lives by the gospel as evidence of continuing miracles in their times.[30]

Reports of miracles became noticeably different from the fourth century on, both in number and sensationalism. In these later accounts "a wide variety of people, both alive and dead, are credited with miracles that in many instances must be labeled bizarre even by the most sympathetic reader."[31] A brief sketch of the first ten of a much longer list of miracles recorded by Augustine in his *City of God* provides an example of what was deemed miraculous in his time:

> In the first, a blind man was cured by saint's relics. In the second, painful surgical intervention was made unnecessary by fervent prayer. In the third, a woman was cured of breast cancer by following advice received in a dream to have a newly baptized woman make the sign of the cross on the affected breast. In the fourth, a physician was healed of gout by baptism. In the fifth, a man suffering from paralysis and hernia was healed by the same sacrament. The sixth instance recorded that demons, who were causing sickness among both cattle and slaves on a farm, were driven out by a priest who celebrated the Eucharist there and offered prayers. In the seventh, a paralytic was healed at a shrine built over a deposit of "holy soil" brought from the vicinity of Christ's tomb. The eighth involved two miracles: a demon was driven from a youth at a shrine, and the injury done to the youth's eye by the departing demon was miraculously healed. In the ninth, a young female demoniac was freed from possession when she anointed herself with some oil into which had fallen the tears of a priest who was praying for her. In the tenth, a demon was driven out of a young man by the assertion that "even today miracles are being wrought

---

[29]Lampe, "Miracles and Early Christian Apologetic," 214–15.
[30]Ibid., 212; M. F. Wiles, "Miracles in the Early Church," in *Miracles: Cambridge Studies in Their Philosophy and History*, 223–25.
[31]Amundsen and Ferngren, "Medicine and Religion," 103.

in the name of Christ, sometimes through His sacraments and sometimes through the intercession of the relics of His saints."[32]

Although Augustine is frequently mentioned as affirming the continuation of miracles in the church, it is safe to say that none today would acknowledge all of these reports as genuine biblical miracles. The greatness of many of the church leaders of this period and throughout the Middle Ages cannot be denied. But many nonbiblical elements that affected their understanding and practice of the miraculous had been accepted into Christianity by this time, including "the veneration of saints and martyrs, the traffic in relics, Christian magic, an excessive preoccupation with demonism, and miracle-mongering."[33]

The evidence by which many miracles were substantiated also raises doubts about their validity. In marked contrast to someone like the apostle Paul, who claimed to work miracles, none of the writers reporting these later miracles ever claimed to have miraculous power themselves. Since by this time the saintliness of a person was measured to some extent by the amount of miraculous power he had, we frequently find miracles attributed to saints by their biographers. Interestingly, the farther a biographer was removed in time from the saint of whom he wrote, the more the life of the saint was glorified with miracles.[34]

The limited reports of miracles during the first two centuries immediately following the New Testament and the questionableness of many of the reported miracles especially from the fourth century on make it impossible to say that the level of miraculous activity seen in the era of Jesus and the apostolic church continued as the norm of church history. The church not only recognized a change regarding miracles, but, as already noted, this change was explained by seeing the miracles of the New Testament era as intended to attest to the first proclamation of the gospel and thus not to continue throughout all history.

---

[32]Ibid., 106.

[33]Ibid., 105; for further evaluation of the alleged miracles of this later period and the evidence for them, see Bernard, "The Miraculous in Early Christian Literature," 166–80.

[34]Bernard, "The Miraculous in Early Christian Literature," 172–76.

What happened with regard to miracles in the history of the church is also true about prophecy. Though there have been general and widespread reports of prophecy in the church throughout history, Robeck's assessment that the gift of prophecy as seen in Scripture lost some of its "spontaneity as time progressed" is generally accepted. Moreover, the manifestations of prophecy that did occur were primarily "among a variety of sects and cults."[35] Various reasons have been proposed for this decrease in prophecy, including its suppression by the church.[36] But it is difficult to see how the church through ecclesiastical authority or any other means could actually cause the cessation of prophecy. No religious authority could stop God from sending true prophets to his people in the Old Testament and at the inauguration of the Christian era. And such prophets were eventually recognized by his people.

The cumulative evidence we have examined—the limitation of the apostolic gift to the first generation, the clusters of miracles in the biblical record, and the evidence from church history—points unmistakably to the fact that there were special times of miraculous activities in which the miracles functioned primarily as signs. Since the time of Christ and the apostles was such a time of extraordinary miracles, the same level of activity cannot be seen as the norm of all church history. This evidence, therefore, leads to several conclusions about the presence of the miraculous gifts today.

(a) The primary purpose of miraculous activities during these special periods was not for the general needs of God's

---

[35]C. M. Robeck, Jr., "Prophecy, Gift of," in *Dictionary of Pentecostal and Charismatic Movements*, ed. Stanley M. Burgess and Gary B. McGee (Grand Rapids: Zondervan, 1988), 740 (see esp. 735–40 for a good summary of prophecy in church history). In this connection it should also be noted that some, like Origen and the later Reformers, actually modified the meaning of prophecy to mean the divine illumination of Scripture behind the expository preaching of Scripture. When they refer to the gift of prophecy, therefore, it is not evidence for prophecy in its biblical meaning of proclamation by direct inspiration.

[36]Some have associated the decrease of prophecy with the development of the canon of Scripture. Others attribute it to the disrepute brought upon prophecy by its association with such sects as the Montanists, or to the taking over of the gifts of prophecy by the organized church, which led ultimately to the doctrine of papal infallibility.

people. To be sure, people benefited from the miraculous activity (e.g., healings), but the fact that they are called "signs" points to their primary purpose as authentication of God's spokesmen and their prophetic message.

(b) The "sign" purpose of the miracles suggests that such miracles are not a part of the kingdom blessing available to all believers during this age. The miracles of Jesus and the disciples as signs point beyond themselves to the power of God and the nature of the kingdom (i.e., the reversal of the effects of sin). They are not a part of an already inaugurated kingdom.[37]

(c) The recognition of the apostolic era as a special time of miraculous activity leads further to the conclusion that Jesus' charge to his disciples during his earthly ministry does not belong to the church of all time. In sending out his disciples, Jesus gave them "authority to ... cure every kind of disease and sickness" and commanded them to "heal the sick, raise the dead, [and] cleanse those who have leprosy," which they did (Matt. 10:1, 7; cf. Mark 6:12–13 and the record of Acts).[38] Significantly, these commands were not part of the final commission that the resurrected Christ gave to the disciples. In this so-called Great Commission we find only the command to make disciples (including baptism) by preaching the gospel of the forgiveness of

---

[37]That miraculous signs are not part of the inaugurated kingdom may be demonstrated by comparing miracles with those realities that, according to Scripture, clearly belong to the presence of the kingdom today. These kingdom realities focus on the *spiritual* blessings of the new covenant, i.e., forgiveness of sins and the gift of the Spirit with its resultant new life. While the presence of the Spirit today is a "deposit guaranteeing" our full kingdom inheritance (Eph. 1:14), it is never said to be a "sign." Instead the Spirit and the blessing of forgiveness *are* the presence of the kingdom itself and as such are available to anyone and everyone who receives them through faith in Christ. Only those blessings of the kingdom that are promised to *every* believer through saving faith in Christ may be said to belong to the "already" aspect of the kingdom during this age. A further indication that miracles of healing and even raising the dead are not the actual beginning of kingdom blessings is that they are all temporary. The healed, for example, eventually die. Insofar as the kingdom belongs to the new age, its provisions are eternal. On miracles as signs of the kingdom and not the kingdom itself, see Herman Ridderbos, *The Coming of the Kingdom* (Philadelphia: Presbyterian and Reformed, 1962), 115ff.

[38]Frequently when these commands are taken for the church, the additional imperatives in Matthew 10 limiting money and clothing, etc., and especially the limitation of preaching to Israel are ignored.

sins and teaching the commandments of Jesus (cf. Matt. 28:19–20; Mark 16:15; Luke 24:47).[39]

(d) Finally, the presence of extraordinary "sign" miracles at certain times in biblical history denies the explanation, sometimes put forward, that the lack of comparable miracles at other times was due to sin or unbelief. God sent miracle workers among his people whenever he desired, *even in times of great unbelief*. The depth of the faith of the people of Israel at the time of the Exodus is questionable, especially during the desert wanderings. Yet God worked miracles in their midst through his servant Moses. Elijah and Elisha clearly worked miracles and prophesied in the midst of an apostate people. The same could be said for Jews among whom both Jesus and the apostles ministered. The record of Israel's history is sadly one of a tendency away from obedient belief in God. Nevertheless, God gave them prophets and worked miracles on their behalf according to his will.

That Jesus "did not do many miracles [in Nazareth] because of their lack of faith" (Matt. 13:58; cf. Mark 6:5–6) cannot be used as a general explanation for the lack of miracles among God's people. Note that it is not said that Jesus attempted to heal them but was unable to do so because the lack of faith of his townspeople made it impossible. Rather, to work miracles in this situation would have been contrary to the purpose of his ministry. The people of his hometown "took offense at him" (Matt. 13:57; Mark 6:3), meaning more than that they did not believe in his miracle-working ability. They were offended by his claims, with the result that their offense and unbelief actually became hatred (cf. Luke 4:28–30). Since he did heal some even in this situation, most likely the lack of more healing resulted from the fact that in their unbelief, they simply did not bring many sick to him for healing. Moreover, to heal in the face of such opposition could have had the result of compounding their guilt and further hardening their hearts.

Scripture reveals that the level of God's working of miracles was not primarily dependent on human faith, but on his sovereign plan and purpose. Nowhere in the New Testament are

---

[39]While the commission found in the disputed long ending of Mark's Gospel does refer to the presence of signs accompanying those who believe, these are not commanded as part of the commission itself.

believers encouraged to have faith so that they can become the recipients of miraculous works.[40]

The teaching of Scripture thus leads to the conclusion that there were special times of God's miraculous activity, the apostolic era being one such time. But this acknowledgment still leaves open to some extent the question of the continuation of miraculous spiritual gifts that were endowed on ordinary members of the church (cf. 1 Cor. 12:7–11).

4. The Possibility of the Continuation of Spiritual Gifts in the Church

Scripture does not provide us with a clear answer to the question of whether all of the spiritual gifts listed in Romans 12:3–8, 1 Corinthians 12, and Ephesians 4:11 were intended to continue on in the church. It does, however, provide us with some truths related to this question that can at least guard us from too hasty a conclusion.

The Bible does not present a picture of church life following the apostles. Those Scriptures that tell us about miraculous spiritual gifts in the church include the apostles and prophets. In 1 Corinthians 12, Paul refers both to spiritual gifts and to those who exercised them. At the time he wrote, the body of Christ included the "apostles" and "prophets" as gifted individuals, right alongside "teachers ... workers of miracles, also those having gifts of healing, those able to help others, those with gifts of administration, and those speaking in different kinds of tongues" (1 Cor. 12:27–29). In other words, those who formed the foundational ministry of the church (apostles and prophets), which did not continue, are listed right along with the other gifts, including the miraculous.

---

[40]While the ability to work miracles is related to faith (cf. Mark 9:23), the amount of faith is not emphasized. The reference to the inability of the disciples to cast out a demon because of "so little faith" is best understood not as a rebuke of a small quantity of faith, but of a misdirected faith (Matt. 17:17–20). Jesus immediately adds that "faith as small as a mustard seed" is sufficient to move mountains (v. 20). The disciples were apparently treating the power given to them as magical power rather than true faith, which depends totally on God. Mark's additional comment that prayer is required supports this understanding.

The question of how those special manifestations of miraculous gifts that did not remain permanent in the church are related to the miraculous gifts distributed among the other members of the church is not at all clear. Can we simply take away the foundational ministry of the apostles and prophets and say that the rest of the gifts continued to function among the members of the church? Or did the fact that these churches of the New Testament were recipients of the ministry of the apostles and those with a special prophetic ministry have anything to do with the presence of miraculous gifts among them?

We have previously noted scriptural evidence that miraculous gifts were bestowed on the first hearers of the gospel as confirmation of its reliability.[41] Paul's statement that his "testimony about Christ" was confirmed among the Corinthians by their rich endowment of spiritual gifts may well refer to this same thing (cf. 1 Cor. 1:5–7). It may be argued, of course, that the testimony to Christ given by preachers of all ages is confirmed by the same marvelous gifts of the Spirit. But it must be acknowledged that this conclusion is only an application of those biblical texts that explicitly refer *only* to the apostles and others of the first generation. In other words, the question of the operation of miraculous gifts in the church is not as simple as taking away the gifts that were limited to the first period (e.g., apostleship) and affirming the remainder as intended for the church in the same way as they are seen in Scripture.

A second truth in relation to the question of the continuation of the nonapostolic gifts is that we really have little evidence of how these gifts functioned in the biblical church. We are given a glimpse of what happened in the church at Corinth when they met together. There were apparently manifestations of some supernatural gifts, including tongues and prophecy among the ordinary believers (cf. 1 Cor. 14:26). But were these gifts intended to continue? The important role of prophecy at this time, for example, had some relation to the fact that the revelation intended as canonical for the church was only in the process of being given. The presence in the later church of the complete canonical Scriptures suggests a decrease in the need of this

---

[41]See our discussion of Galatians 3:5 and Hebrews 2:3–4, pp. 109–12.

prophetic activity in favor of the teaching of the canonical apostolic doctrine. This, as history indicates, is exactly what did occur.

With regard to the operation of other miraculous gifts, there is no evidence even within the New Testament. We do not see the average church members performing miracles of healing. Anyone who wanted healing brought their sick to the apostles. James's instructions for elders to pray for the sick says nothing about any of them having the gift of healing (James 5:14–16). No one in the church seems to have had a special healing ministry. In fact, a check of a concordance reveals that apart from the mention of the gift of healing in 1 Corinthians 12:9 and praying for healing in James 5, the word "heal" is never used in the letters.[42] This is most instructive when compared to the numerous references to healing in the Gospel records and the book of Acts, depicting the ministries of Jesus and the first witnesses of the gospel.

The same can be said with regard to other miraculous activity. Outside of the discussion of spiritual gifts in 1 Corinthians 12 and the working of miracles associated with the apostles and others with them, the New Testament letters contain no mention of "miracles," "signs," or "wonders," except for Galatians 3:5 and Hebrews 2:4 (discussed above). While these included miracle-working among the members of the church, these miracles were related to the initial ministry of the apostles.

Thus, it must be acknowledged that the New Testament simply does not give us a picture of the normal operation of gifts in the church following the apostolic era. The teaching of the letters is probably the closest that we come. Whereas Acts (as the name "Acts of the Apostles" indicates) focuses on the activity of the apostles, the letters are directed to believers and their lives in the church. Thus the distinction in frequency of reference to miraculous gifts between Acts and the letters is important. But even with this distinction, the letters are still descriptions of the church during the apostolic era and therefore cannot be used as descriptions of the postapostolic church. We thus have no

---

[42]*The NIV Exhaustive Concordance*, ed. Edward W. Goodrick and John R. Kohlenberger III (Grand Rapids: Zondervan, 1990). The only other use of "heal" is in Hebrews 12:13, where it refers to spiritual healing. The recovery of Epaphroditus from grave sickness is also noted, but no mention is made of its being miraculous or accomplished through the gift of healing (cf. Phil. 2:25–27).

explicit biblical teaching or portrait on what miraculous activity was divinely intended for the church after the ministry of Christ and the apostles.

5. The Issue of Specific Teaching on the Cessation of Certain Spiritual Gifts

It seems clear that there was something different about the apostolic era of the church in relation to miraculous spiritual gifts. But we must also acknowledge that Scripture nowhere explicitly teaches that some spiritual gifts were destined to cease with that age. Although most would agree that apostles did not continue beyond the first generation, there is no explicit teaching to this effect. This conclusion has been reached by consideration of various biblical data as well as the closing of the canon by the later church.

Paul's reference to the ceasing of tongues and doing away of knowledge and prophecy when "perfection" comes also, in my opinion, does not expressly teach the cessation of these gifts during the church age (cf. 1 Cor. 13:8–10). The statements in the context about seeing "face to face," suggesting a complete direct knowledge as opposed to the indirect vision of a mirror, and of coming to "know fully, even as I am fully known" (v. 12), clearly speak of the state of glorification (v. 13). These statements refer to the coming of Christ, when perfection arrives.[43] This text, therefore, does not indicate that certain gifts will cease before that state comes.

But neither does this text affirm the continuation of these gifts until the coming of Christ. Paul does not say that prophecy or tongues will continue until the perfect comes. The "in part" of knowledge and prophecy has to do with the content, not the function, of these gifts. The contrast between the "in part" and the "perfection" that will come is thus the fragmentary nature of the former in comparison to the completeness of the perfect. The translation of the RSV makes this clear: "For our knowledge is imperfect and our prophecy is imperfect; but when the perfect comes, the imperfect will pass away" (vv. 9–10). What

---

[43]The time of "perfection" may also refer to the personal glorification of the believer at death.

passes away at the coming of the perfect is not the functioning of these gifts themselves, but rather the incompleteness (or imperfection) of the knowledge that is obtained through them.[44] There is, therefore, nothing in this text that precludes these gifts from ceasing before the arrival of the perfect.

The reference to the apostles and prophets as foundational to the church (Eph. 2:20), while pertinent to the discussion of the continuation of spiritual gifts, also does not clearly teach the cessation of miraculous gifts. The reference to the "foundation" does point to a particular ministry of some that was not continued in the same way throughout later times. But it does not indicate, for example, that the gift of prophecy, to say nothing of other miraculous gifts, ceased functioning entirely when that foundation was laid.

The lack of specific biblical teaching of the cessation of miraculous gifts is frequently used as a strong argument for their continuation. But this does not necessarily follow either. If the New Testament does not explicitly teach that certain miraculous gifts will cease, neither does it explicitly teach that they will continue throughout this entire age. As mentioned above, the New Testament writers nowhere speak clearly of what we now call postapostolic times nor of the time of the closing of the canon.

This lack is understandable when we realize that the early Christians believed that Christ could (not necessarily would) return during their lifetime. If Paul, for example, believed it was possible for Christ to come during his lifetime, would one expect him to explain to the church what would happen after he and the other apostles were no longer present? Apparently God did not reveal to the New Testament writers the entire course of this church age; such a revelation would have made it impossible for them also to teach the possibility of his imminent return. It should not be expected, therefore, that they would explicitly teach the closing of the apostolic age and the canon. This same reasoning applies to the teaching of cessation with regard to gifts.

But the apostolic age did cease and the New Testament canon was recognized by the later church. If these things could

---

[44]For a good discussion of this position, see R. Fowler White, "Richard Gaffin and Wayne Grudem on 1 Cor. 13:10: A Comparison of Cessationist and Noncessationist Argumentation," *JETS*, 35 (1992): 173–81.

happen by divine providence without the Bible anywhere saying that they would, then it is surely possible that changes in
spiritual gifts could also occur without any explicit biblical
teaching to that effect.

That such change in the manifestation of spiritual gifts did,
in fact, occur without prior biblical teaching is plain in the experience following the completion of the Old Testament. According to the Jews, Malachi was "the seal of the Prophets" and "the
last among them." The manifestation of prophecy among God's
people ceased with Malachi because it had accomplished its purpose for that time.[45] While the question of the total cessation of
prophecy at this time is debated, that some change occurred is
generally accepted.[46] The flurry of references to prophecy found
at the beginning of the Gospel records points to the renewal of
this gift that was to attend the promised messianic age.[47]

Although a few Old Testament texts are sometimes seen as
pointing to the demise of prophecy (e.g., Ps. 74:9), most do not

---

[45]According to Verhoef, the prophecy of Malachi "contains the last words of a
whole generation, a generation of prophets through whom God had revealed himself to his people in a unique way. With Malachi these instruments of God's revelation concluded their task and were dismissed from office until the time of the
fulfillment not only of the Law but also of the Prophets (Matt. 5:17), in the advent
of the great Prophet, our Lord Jesus Christ" (Peter A. Verhoef, *The Books of Haggai
and Malachi*, NICOT [Grand Rapids: Eerdmans, 1987], 153).

[46]Napier's opinion seems generally accepted: "Long before the time of Jesus
prophecy had ceased to appear in Israel (Ps. 74:9; 1 Macc. 4:46; 9:27; 14:41), although
a special form of it continued to flourish in the writing of apocalyptic visions. The
Jews, however, fully expected its revival in the coming age of the Messiah (cf. Joel
2:28–29; Zech. 13:4–6; Mal. 4:5–6; Test. Levi 8:14; Test. Benj. 9:2). It is in the light of
this expectation that one must understand the claim, recorded by Josephus (War
1.68–69), that John Hyrcanus had the 'gift of prophecy.' Josephus also states that such
messianic pretenders as Theudas (*Antiq.* 20.97; cf. Acts 5:36) and 'the Egyptians'
(*Antiq.* 20.168–69; *War* 2.261; cf. Acts 21:38) claimed that they were prophets" (B. D.
Napier, "Prophet in the NT," *IDB*, ed. George A. Buttrick [Nashville: Abingdon,
1962], 3:919).

[47]E.g., Luke 1:67ff.; 2:26–33; 3:3ff.; 4:17ff. G. F. Hawthorne writes, "Luke in particular (though the other Gospel writers concur) seems to be saying that the longed-
for universal age of the Spirit (cf. Joel 2:28, 29) had at last arrived (Lk 4:18, 19; cf. Is
61:1–3) and that the age of prophets and prophecy, if it had indeed died out, was
now being re-born" ("Prophets, Prophecy," *Dictionary of Jesus and the Gospels*, ed. Joel
B. Green, Scot McKnight, I. Howard Marshall [Downers Grove, Ill.: InterVarsity,
1992], 637).

see any explicit teaching in the Old Testament to the effect that the gift of prophecy would be withdrawn. Nevertheless, it did cease or at least was radically changed. This example provides legitimate precedent that God can, if he so desires, withdraw the manifestations of any gifts at any time without expressly mentioning it in Scripture.

6. Conclusion

The evidence considered both from Scripture and the experience of the church thus leads to two facts concerning the manifestation of miraculous spiritual gifts in the church today. (a) There is no explicit biblical teaching that some spiritual gifts seen in the New Testament church did in fact cease at some point in church history. (b) But neither does Scripture explicitly teach that all of the miraculous activity seen in the record of the New Testament church is intended to be normal throughout church history. There is, in fact, strong biblical evidence that certain gifts and miraculous activity, associated with the apostles and other prophets, were meant to be foundational for the church and thus not continue as a regular expression of church life. Subsequent church history supports this conclusion by clearly testifying that miraculous activity in the postapostolic church, both in extent and quality, was not the same as that of the time of Christ and the apostles.

C. SPECIFIC GIFTS AND MINISTRIES

The above evidences from Scripture and church history make the ministry of miraculous spiritual gifts in the contemporary church more complex than simply claiming that Scripture teaches their presence or their absence. The specialness of the apostolic era, along with the lack of any explicit teaching on the cessation of certain gifts, suggests that we must be open at all times to what God desires to do.

This openness, however, must be joined with obedience to the apostle's exhortation to "test everything" (1 Thess. 5:21). Practices purporting to be manifestations of miraculous gifts must be carefully evaluated on the basis of what Scripture says about these gifts, particularly their true nature, their proper use, and the purpose they serve. The issue of purpose is particularly important for those who believe that there was something special with regard to miraculous activity in the church. Is its purpose somehow fulfilled in another way today, or was there something about it that related only to the needs of the foundational period of the church?

1. Prophecy

It is important to the question of the manifestation of the gift of prophecy that we have a common understanding of this gift. Scholarly studies on this subject have traditionally viewed all biblical prophecy as "inspired utterances" that came through direct revelation from God, and I see no reason to change this definition.[48] The attempt to see prophecy as having different levels, ranging from that which is totally God's Word and therefore inerrant to that which is mixed with varying degrees of human thought including error, is difficult to support biblically.[49]

Prophecy as revelatory speech directly inspired by God should also be distinguished from the ordinary preaching of the Scriptures.[50] Perhaps more significantly in the contemporary climate, prophecy should be distinguished from divinely given personal guidance. Scripture does speak of "revelation" in connection with the Spirit's work of illuminating one's

---

[48]Gordon D. Fee, *The First Epistle to the Corinthian*, NICNT (Grand Rapids: Eerdmans, 1987), 595; see also Gerhard Friedrich, "προφήτης," *TDNT*, 6:828–30; David E. Aune, *Prophecy in Early Christianity and the Ancient Mediterranean World* (Grand Rapids: Eerdmans, 1983), 195; G. F. Hawthorne, "Prophets, Prophecy," *Dictionary of Jesus and the Gospels*, 636; C. M. Robeck, Jr., "Prophecy, Prophesying," *Dictionary of Paul and his Letters*, ed. by Gerald F. Hawthorne, Ralph P. Martin, and Daniel G. Reid (Downers Grove, Ill.: InterVarsity, 1993), 755.

[49]For attempts to support different levels of prophecy, see Wayne A. Grudem, *The Gift of Prophecy in the New Testament Today* (Westchester, Ill.: Crossway Books, 1988); Graham Houston, *Prophecy: A Gift for Today?* (Downers Grove, Ill.: InterVarsity, 1989); Donald Gee, *Spiritual Gifts in the Work of Ministry Today* (Springfield, Mo.: Gospel Publishing House, 1963). It is beyond our scope to deal with all the arguments given to support this position. On the critical matter of evaluating prophecy and its relationship to this issue, see the Appendix to this chapter.

[50]James D. G. Dunn, *Jesus and the Spirit*, 228; Gordon Fee, *The First Epistle to the Corinthian*, 595; C. M. Robeck, Jr., "Prophecy, Prophesying," 761.

understanding of Scripture and giving personal insight (Matt. 16:17; Eph. 1:17; Phil. 3:15), but this use of revelation is not to be equated with prophecy.

Genuine manifestations of prophecy are predicted for the future (e.g., Rev. 11:3, 10), and Scripture does not explicitly deny the possibility today. Any purported expression of this gift, however, must meet the biblical pattern: (a) It must be totally harmonious with canonical revelation. (b) It must be judged carefully by the community (1 Cor. 14:29). Whether "the others" who pass judgment were those with the prophetic gift or those having the "gift of distinguishing between spirits," there was to be serious evaluation of the prophecies. People could not simply claim to be giving a word of prophecy without being evaluated. (c) The content of the prophecy should be edifying to the community (1 Cor. 14:3–4). It must not be something simply to demonstrate supernatural power or so trite or commonly known from Scripture that it adds essentially nothing to the community save for a purported display of a miraculous gift. (d) Prophecy must also be done in an orderly manner in accord with the apostle's instructions to the Corinthians (1 Cor. 14:19–33).

While prophecy meeting these biblical criteria may occur in the church today, present experience and church history do not give much evidence of it. It is certainly valid, as the church has largely done throughout history, to see the need for such prophecy decrease when the explanation of the saving activity of Christ as given in Scripture became accessible to all believers. The ministry of the early prophets who brought edification, exhortation, and consolation to the church on the basis of the gospel of Christ is now accomplished through other spiritual gifts that depend on the prophecy recorded in Scripture. It is significant that in the last letters of Paul, there is no reference to prophecy save to remind Timothy of the prophecy made at his ordination (1 Tim. 1:18; 4:14). The focus of these letters, which are termed the "Pastorals" because they give instructions for ministry in the church, is on teaching, exhorting, and commanding the Scriptures.[51]

---

[51]Cf. 1 Timothy 4:11, 13, 16; 5:17; 2 Timothy 2:2; 3:14–17; 4:2; Titus 1:9.

2. Healing

The close association of the spiritual gift of healing with other supernatural manifestations of the Spirit suggests that this gift also refers to that which was clearly miraculous. The reports of such healings in Scripture reveal that they were instantaneous. Whether we understand that certain people were permanently endowed with this gift or that the Spirit manifested his power of healing through different people at different times (1 Cor. 12:9, 30), the healing was associated with an individual and was not simply the result of the prayers of the church or a group of believers. These marks of the miraculous gift of healing in Scripture make it questionable as to how many reports of healing today truly manifest this gift.

We must also remember, before we identify a supposed supernatural healing as the result of the gift of healing, that extraordinary healings can have other explanations. Some illnesses, including blindness, deafness, and paralysis, may be symptoms of psychological trauma or hysteria, not genuine organic diseases. Emotional healing campaigns with their powerful suggestions can produce at least temporary spectacular results in such cases. But these are not genuine miracles. Nothing short of "miraculous" cures have been recorded that were produced by the power of faith and hope even when these had nothing to do with God.[52]

Scripture clearly teaches the psychosomatic union of the human spirit and body, whereby the state of the spirit has a powerful effect on the health of the body, both positive and negative (cf. Ps. 38:3; Prov. 17:22). If faith and hope even apart from God can produce bodily healing, how much more faith in God.[53]

---

[52]For an example of such, see Bernie S. Siegel, *Love, Medicine & Miracles* (New York: Harper & Row, 1986), 33ff.; see also Norman Cousins, *Head First, the Biology of Hope* (New York: E. P. Dutton, 1989).

[53]McCasland's comment on the power of faith in healing, therefore, must be kept in mind when evaluating healing in the church. "It is well known that real faith contributes to good health and the healing of disease. Faith is an aid even in organic disease, but medical science would say that it has limits in this respect. So far as we know, faith cannot restore missing eyeballs or amputated limbs. On the other hand, in the area of diseases which are psychogenic in origin the healing value of faith can scarcely be overemphasized" (S. V. McCasland, "Miracle," *IDB*, 3:400).

The healing of a twisted spirit through the invasion of God's peace and joy associated with conversion or a believer's repentance from sin can produce a dramatic turnaround in physical ailments. While such bodily healings are truly from God, it does not seem to be a manifestation of the biblical gift of healing.

The issue of the operation of this gift in the church today must be based on a thoughtful examination of just what this gift is as well as a total biblical theology of physical healing. Such a theology makes it plain that God normally brings healing to the body through the means he has created. God has equipped the body with various healing systems. In addition, there are favorable connotations attached to the occupation of the physician and the use of medicines.[54] God, who revealed himself as Israel's healer and performed miracles for their health (cf. Ex. 15:25–26), also included numerous natural health regulations in the statutes of Israel's laws. Finally, as we have noted, God has so constituted us that spiritual healing can have a powerful effect on the body. Not all sickness is the result of sin (cf. Job 2:1–8; Dan. 8:27), though some clearly is (e.g., 1 Cor. 11:30). Healing that results from confession of sin may simply be the result of the natural spirit-body symbiosis.

A theology of healing must recognize that bodily health is nowhere promised as a provision of salvation for this age. The body is presently doomed to death because of sin (Rom. 8:10). In contrast to our being "inwardly" renewed through the grace of salvation, "outwardly we are wasting away" (2 Cor. 4:16). The body must still be redeemed, leaving the believer in a state of groaning with the rest of creation (Rom. 8:23), no doubt partially because of physical pains.[55] Thus little is said about the ministry of healing in the church. Only one passage refers to healing as a gift (1 Cor. 12:9, 30). Nowhere else are the saints to minister to each other through healing, nor is it listed in the ministries of

---

[54]Cf. Isaiah 1:6; Jeremiah 8:22; Matthew 9:12; Luke 10:34; Colossians 4:14; 1 Timothy 5:23.

[55]Something similar might be said about psychological pain during this age, although it could be argued that this is more closely related to the spirit than the body and therefore more affected by the change of spirit that occurs in regeneration. It is interesting, however, that at the same time that interest has increased in miraculous healing of the body, cure of the psyche is more and more relegated to the natural laws of psychology.

the gathered community in 1 Corinthians 14:26. For the church to place an emphasis on miraculous physical healing or to hold special healing campaigns, therefore, seems foreign to the New Testament picture of the church community.

As with all infirmities of this age, however, God desires to be gracious with his people. He may choose to grant miraculous healing either through the prayers of his people or the manifestation of the gift of healing as defined above. Such healing may even be a "sign" in the spread of the gospel, as has been reported in the rapid growth of the church in China.[56] On the other hand, God may grant his supernatural power to a person to persevere in the trial of bodily infirmity (cf. 2 Cor. 12:7–10). In both situations he does so for his own glory and our ultimate good.

3. Tongues

The nature and function of the gift of tongues are not easily determined from Scripture. However, there are certain biblical principles that do provide some guidelines for the practice of this gift within the church.

First, whether tongues referred to in Scripture were the miraculous speaking of foreign languages unknown to the speaker or the language of glory (i.e., "tongues of angels," 1 Cor. 13:1) or both,[57] the important point is that they were all language,

---

[56]For an interesting account of miraculous activities associated primarily with the first generation of the recent phenomenal church growth in China, see Alan Cole, "The Spread of Christianity in China Today," in *God the Evangelist*, ed. David Wells (Grand Rapids: Eerdmans, 1987), 101–6.

[57]Because the first occurrence of tongues at Pentecost (Acts 2) appears to be the miraculous speaking of foreign languages unknown to the speaker, many conclude that this is the nature of all biblical glossalalia. Several things, however, make it difficult to see the tongues of 1 Corinthians as human languages. They require the equally supernatural gift of interpretation for their understanding. In cosmopolitan cities such as Corinth there were undoubtedly many languages present, but the possibility of someone present who could understand the language naturally is not considered. Most importantly, Paul uses foreign "languages" (a different word than used for "tongues") as an analogy for tongues (1 Cor. 14:10–13). Something is not usually identical to that with which it is said to be analogous (cf. the other analogies used in vv. 7–9). Mark's use of the word "new" (*kainos*) in Mark 16:17 to describe tongues, a term that is commonly used to refer to the "wholly different and miraculous" things that belong to the new age, also suggests that tongues are not simply other

i.e., they conveyed conceptual thought. The gift of tongues could be interpreted with understanding. This biblical truth is particularly important in light of the fact that some studies have shown that many expressions of contemporary tongues have no linguistic characteristics.[58]

Beyond the nature of tongues, the manifestation of this gift must be evaluated by its biblical function. Admittedly, this is difficult to determine with precision, but some general principles can be ascertained. Negatively, tongues were not for the proclamation of the gospel to foreigners,[59] nor were they the normal evidence of the baptism with the Spirit. Scripture, as we have noted earlier, makes it clear that all believers have received the gift of the Spirit or, in other terminology, have been baptized with the Spirit; but not all have the gift of tongues (1 Cor. 12:10, 30). The view that sees tongues in Acts as evidence of the baptism with the Spirit and therefore different from the gift of tongues as taught by Paul is difficult to sustain. Note that there are only three specific instances where tongues are mentioned in Acts (2:4ff.; 10:46; 19:6).[60] In each of these instances the gift was bestowed on an entire group and was given without any request for it. Both of these facts are contrary to the usual teaching of certain groups as to the requirements for the reception of the baptism with the Spirit beyond saving faith.

---

human languages (Johannes Behm, "καινός, κτλ.," *TDNT*, 3:449). A full discussion of the nature of tongues is beyond our purview, but there are good reasons to believe that even the tongues of Acts 2 were more than human languages. In addition to Behm, advocates of this position include George T. Montague, *The Holy Spirit: Growth of a Biblical Tradition* (New York: Paulist, 1976); Richard Belward Rackham, *The Acts of the Apostles* (London: Methuen, 1901); Christian Friedrich Kling, "The First Epistle to the Corinthians," in *Lange's Commentary on the Holy Scriptures*, ed. John Peter Lange, vol. 10 (Grand Rapids: Zondervan, 1960 rpt); Dale Moody, *Spirit of the Living God* (Philadelphia: Westminster, 1968); Abraham Kuyper, *The Work of the Holy Spirit* (Grand Rapids: Eerdmans, 1956).

[58]William Samarin, *Tongues of Men and Angels: The Religious Language of Pentecostalism* (New York: Macmillan, 1972).

[59]At Pentecost tongues brought the crowd, but Peter preached to them in a common ordinary language. No instances of tongues being used in foreign missionary service is seen in Scripture.

[60]It is possible that tongues also occurred at Samaria as there was apparently some manifestation of the Spirit. But the nature of this manifestation is not stated (cf. 8:18).

More significantly, Acts contains numerous accounts of salvation that do not mention tongues.[61] Not only is the number of such accounts impressive, but nowhere do we see a single individual speaking in tongues in connection with his or her salvation. This includes the apostle Paul, who not only experienced the miracle of regaining his sight, but was also said to be "filled with the Holy Spirit" (Acts 9:17–18). The three accounts in Acts where tongues accompanies salvation cannot be made the standard for all believers at all times. These instances are much better understood as evidence of the reception of the Spirit in relation to the inauguration of the new age of the Spirit and its spread to various people. As Carson says, "The way Luke tells the story, Acts provides not a paradigm for individual Christian experience, but the account of the gospel's outward movement geographically, racially, and above all theologically."[62]

In the positive sense, the only explicit statement of the purpose of tongues is Paul's teaching that "tongues ... are a sign, not for believers but for unbelievers" (1 Cor. 14:22). The various interpretations of this passage notwithstanding, the central thrust is that tongues have a basic purpose in relation to unbelievers. True, the church can receive edification through tongues, but only if they are interpreted. The phenomenon of tongues has "sign" value toward those who do not believe (probably as a sign of God's judgment on them, as the context indicates). What edifies the church in tongues is their intelligible content. This is why prophecy is more valuable in the church; it communicates intelligibly immediately (1 Cor. 14:1–12).

---

[61]The following list Hoekema developed of instances of salvation without any mention of tongues is: "2:42 (the 3,000 converted on Pentecost Day), 3:7–9 (the lame man who was healed), 4:4 (those converted after the healing of the lame man, when the number of the men came to be about 5,000), 5:14 (the many who became believers after the death of Ananias and Sapphira), 6:7 (a great company of priests), 8:36 (the Ethiopian eunuch), 9:42 (the many who believed after Dorcas was raised), 13:12 (those who turned to the Lord in Syrian Antioch), 13:12 (the procounsul at Cyprus), 13:43 and 48 (believers in Pisidian Antioch), 14:1 (believers in Iconium), 14:21 (disciples at Derbe), 16:14 (Lydia), 16:34 (the Philippian jailer), 17:4 (the believers in Thessalonica), 17:11–12 (the Bereans), 17:34 (the Athenians), 18:4 (those at Corinth), 18:8 (Crispus and other Corinthians), 28:24 (some of the Jews at Rome)" (Anthony A. Hoekema, *What About Tongue-Speaking?* [Grand Rapids: Eerdmans, 1966], 80).

[62]D. A. Carson, *Showing the Spirit: A Theological Exposition of 1 Corinthians 12–14* (Grand Rapids: Baker, 1987), 150.

Scripture, therefore, places clear restrictions on the manifestation of the gift of tongues in the assembly. It is to be done only if it is interpreted and then only to a limited extent (1 Cor. 12:5, 27–28). Group praying or singing in tongues is beyond scriptural grounds.

The biblical limitations on the expression of tongues in the church has led many to see its greatest value in the individual believer's prayer life. While Paul does allow individuals to speak in tongues that are not interpreted and even indicates that this edifies the speaker, it is not at all evident that he considers this a key purpose of tongues. The apostle's discussion of spiritual gifts emphasizes that they are given "for the common good," that is, for the edification of the community (cf. 1 Cor. 12:7; 14:3, 5–6, 12, 26).[63] It may be argued that tongues build a person up privately so that he or she may be more useful in ministry to the body perhaps through other gifts. Aside from the fact that this is nowhere expressed, this makes tongues a benefit to one's spiritual life—that is, in personal sanctification. But is it biblical that some receive gifts for *personal* growth, even if it enables them to minister more effectively? Are not the means of sanctification, even as in salvation, equally available to all?

In recognition of the personal edification that comes through speaking in tongues, the apostle may simply be acknowledging the truth that to experience the manifestation of the Spirit in the operation of a gift does bring some personal blessing, just as a teacher receives blessing in his teaching. It is no doubt true that the proper ministry of any gift helps the minister of that gift to grow personally, but this is never taught as the primary function of "spiritual gifts." In other words, Paul's allowance for a person to speak privately to God in the community and his recognition of some personal edification in

---

[63]See also, Ephesians 4:11–13, 16; 1 Peter 4:10. Beyond even rejecting this personal edification as the primary point of the gift, many interpreters deny that positive edification is in view at all in this reference. J. Goetzmann, for example, asserts that "the positive use of the word always refers to the community" (*NIDNTT*, ed. Colin Brown [Grand Rapids: Zondervan, 1976], 2:253). On the mark of a spiritual gift as that which serves others, see also Ronald Y. K. Fung, "Ministry, Community and Spiritual Gifts," *EvQ* 56 (January 1981): 9–10; Hans Küng, *The Church* (New York: Sheed and Ward, 1967), 182, 190, 394; Frederick Dale Bruner, *A Theology of the Holy Spirit* (Grand Rapids: Eerdmans, 1970), 296ff.

speaking in tongues do not provide a strong basis for making the private use of tongues its primary function. To say the least, tongues are never seen in Scripture as a crucial factor in the spiritual life. In fact, nothing is said about the exercise of any spiritual gift in passages that deal with personal spiritual life.[64]

The exercise of the gift of tongues in our day is not precluded by Scripture. However, there is much in Scripture that describes its nature, function, and operation that can and should be used to condition its manifestation.

4. Casting Out Demons

Scripture says nothing directly about the ministry of casting out demons in the New Testament church.[65] This stands in marked contrast to the prominence of exorcism in the postapostolic church.[66] On the other hand, Scripture clearly reveals that believers in the church are constantly at war with Satan and his demons. Recognition of this truth and the nature of the battle, often ignored by the church in the Western world, must be a part of the church's ministry.

According to biblical teaching, unbelievers are in bondage not only to their own sinful nature but also to evil powers (cf. Eph. 2:1–3). This bondage can lead to them actually having spirits within them that exercise various degrees of direct control over their bodily functions. While there are no examples of this phenomenon with regard to believers, it is not at all certain that this silence can be turned into a clear positive teaching that such cannot take place in any sense.[67] Both Scripture and experience

---

[64]For example, Romans 6–8; Ephesians 5–6; Colossians 3–4.

[65]The two instances related to the apostle Paul probably refer to his evangelistic ministry and concern unbelievers (Acts 16:16–18; 19:11–12).

[66]See McEwen, "The Ministry of Healing," 140–45.

[67]In suggesting that believers can have demons in them, I am not talking about "possession" in the sense of ownership. Nor is it necessary to see the evil spirit's presence in the believer like that of the Spirit of God. Whereas the Spirit is said to be in the "heart" and thus at the core of the person, an evil spirit may intrude at a more superficial level, where he can exert control over the bodily system. Delitzsch describes such demonic invasions: "demons intrude themselves between the corporeity—more strictly, the nervous body—and the soul of man, and forcibly fetter the soul together with the spirit, but make the bodily organs a means of their own self-attestation full of torment to men" (Franz Delitzsch, *A System of Biblical Psychol-*

show believers giving themselves to the influence and even servitude of sin (e.g., John 8:34; Rom. 6:12–13, 17) and evil powers (cf. Gal. 4:3, 8–9; 1 Tim. 3:7; poss. 2 Tim. 2:25–26[68]). Referring to Paul's warning about continual wrath giving place to the devil (Eph. 4:26–27), Charles Hodge says, "Anger when cherished gives the Tempter great power over us. . . ."[69]

The primary teaching of Scripture is on the believer's ability and responsibility to resist the attacks of Satan and the demonic (Eph. 6:13; James 4:7; 1 Peter 4:10). The spiritual warfare of the believer and the corresponding ministry of the church may be compared to the warfare that goes on in the realm of bodily health. Our physical systems are under continual attack by a variety of germs and viruses. If we have maintained good health, these attacks are for the most part resisted without our even being aware of them. At times these invaders make us aware of their presence and we take steps to strengthen our resistance, perhaps through better nutrition and rest. If the enemies of our health get beyond our ability to resist and gain control, we seek the help of others to aid us in the battle.

Applying this to spiritual warfare, we must be aware of the constant presence of the demonic and its attack. But as in the physical realm, where normally we are not constantly looking for germs, our emphasis cannot be on the demonic but on that which produces health. Spiritual warfare begins with strengthening our spiritual health through the incorporation of the health-producing and liberating truth of the gospel. But as with the physical, the enemy does sometimes gain a foothold, from which it requires the help of others to gain freedom.

---

ogy [Grand Rapids: Baker, 1966, rpt], 354; see 351–60 for more). The testimony of casting out demons from believers is widespread throughout postbiblical Christianity. See T. K. Oesterreich, *Possession Demonical and Other* (London: Kegan Paul, Trench, Trubnen & Co., 1930), 147–235.

[68]On 2 Timothy 2:25–26 Kelly says, "Paul has in mind the constructive re-education of misguided Christian brethren" (J. N. D. Kelly, *A Commentary on The Pastoral Epistles* [London: Adam & Charles Black, 1963], 190; cf. also Patrick Fairbairn, *Commentary on the Pastoral Epistles* [Grand Rapids: Zondervan, 1874, 1956 rpt], 358).

[69]Charles Hodge, *An Exposition of Ephesians* (Wilmington, Delaware: Associated Publishers and Authors, Inc., n.d.), p. 94. Even more forcefully Barth comments, "The warning . . . can be summed up this way: the Devil will take possession of your heart if your wrath endures" (Markus Barth, *Ephesians 4–6*, The Anchor Bible, vol. 34A [Garden City, NY: Doubleday, 1974], p. 515).

This help can best be given by aiding the one in bondage to resist the enemy through the application of God's truth. As Satan's primary attack is through deceit (cf. Gen. 3; Rev. 20:3, 8), the primary medicine to gain freedom is truth (cf. 2 Cor. 11:4–5). Rather than casting a demon out, far more valuable and longer lasting results are obtained by helping the person to resist the demonic through renouncing the lie of Satan and affirming the corresponding truth of the gospel.

The believer has every provision in Christ to gain spiritual victory over the enemy. But there will be times when he or she needs the aid of others to do so. In some instances the bondage may become so severe that seemingly Satan blocks the believer's ability to use his or her own faculties to lay hold of God's truth. At these points it can become necessary for other believers to exert control over the demon by the power of Christ so that the one in bondage may have the freedom to claim God's truth. I do not see any biblical teaching that would preclude the casting out of the demons when necessary in order to free their victims. But as in the physical realm, the more one can do to gain health, the more he or she will be able to deal with future threats to health, so in the spiritual realm. A ministry of summarily casting out demons not only runs the risk of frequent misdiagnosis, but fails in the primary goal of all ministry, namely, to do all that can be done to build up the spiritual strength of the person involved.

5. The Implementation of Gifts

Acknowledging the possibility of miraculous gifts in the church, what should be our attitude and practice concerning their expression? The general teaching of Scripture is that the manifestation of gifts is in God's control. He distributes the gifts according to his own will and places each member of the body into the place that he desires (cf. 1 Cor. 12:7).[70] While it may be argued that God chooses to give gifts according to the desire of the person, the Bible says nothing about individuals having a responsibility of choosing a particular gift for themselves. The exhortation to "desire the greater gifts," expressed in the plural

---

[70]See also Romans 12:3, 6; 1 Corinthians 12:11, 18, 28; Ephesians 4:11; 1 Peter 4:10.

(12:31), is best understood as encouraging the community to value and utilize those gifts that provide the greater edification for all (cf. 1 Cor. 14:1ff.).[71] This does not preclude a person from having a natural propensity toward a certain ministry that would provide a starting point for that individual in the ministry of gifts. God usually takes up what he has created in an individual and uses it in the spiritual ministry of the church. It is difficult, however, to understand how one can have a natural propensity in relation to the miraculous gifts.

Significantly, Scripture provides little, if any, exhortation for individuals to seek their gifts. The encouragement is rather to have the proper attitude (especially humility, cf. Rom. 12:3) that makes a gift usable, and then to get busy in serving others. In this activity of serving and loving others, the gifts that God has given will become manifest through the edification given to others and the joyful satisfaction experienced by the individual.

D. THE GIFTS AND THE LIFE OF THE CHURCH

According to Scripture, the exercise of spiritual gifts is indispensable to the life and growth of the church. Thanks somewhat to the so-called charismatic movement, the church is becoming increasingly aware of this biblical truth. But what shape should the manifestation of gifts take in the church today?

1. Gifts That Are Preeminent

Thus far, I have sought to show that Scripture nowhere gives us a model of church life after the close of the apostolic era. I have argued on both biblical and historical grounds that the miraculous activity of the apostolic era is not normal for the later church. The understanding of the operation of spiritual gifts today, therefore, must come from the broad biblical teaching on the life and growth of the church and the ministries involved in producing these.

Without question, the Bible reveals that coming to spiritual life and increasing in that life are by means of hearing and

---

[71]This text may also be an encouragement to the person who has more than one gift to focus on the one that brings greater edification to the community.

appropriating by faith the divine truth of the Word.[72] In accordance with this truth Scripture emphasizes those ministries that in one way or another communicate understandable truth. While prophecy was present and played an important role during the foundational period before the complete canon was available, the dominant emphasis of Scripture with regard to church life is on those gifts that the entire church has recognized as present throughout its history. Prominent among these is teaching, which we have already noted in relation to Paul's letters of pastoral instruction but which is present in other writings as well.[73] Other forms of ministering the truth of the gospel are also present in the church, including exhortation, admonishing, encouraging, counseling, and even singing.[74]

With the awareness that the word of God is what brings life, is there also a need for miracles to accomplish that end? The definition of "power evangelism" as proclamation supported by miracles is in my mind somewhat of a misnomer. Scripture attributes power to the word of God itself (e.g., Isa. 55:11; Heb. 4:12). Jesus spoke of his words as "spirit" (living power) and "life" (John 6:63). The gospel, according to Paul, has the power to save (Rom. 1:16; 2 Tim. 3:15). The many references to the efficacy of the word of God show that it has power to produce life. Thus the proclamation of the gospel in the power of the Spirit, backed up by the life of the preacher, is already "power evangelism" (cf. 1 Thess. 1:5; 2:13).

True, God has used miracles throughout history and continues to do so in the service of evangelism. As we have already noted in connection with the church in China, the reports of miracles seem more prevalent within emerging rather than well-established churches. Another situation where one could reasonably expect the physical manifestation of God's supernatural power is in an environment where Satan expresses his power in like manner. Even as God can display his superior power in the casting out of demons, so it is logical to think that God would demonstrate his power in some way triumphing

---

[72]Cf. John 8:32; 17:17; Romans 1:16; 10:17; 1 Thessalonians 2:13; James 1:21; 1 Peter 1:23, etc.

[73]Cf. Galatians 6:6; Colossians 3:16; Hebrews 5:12; James 3:1; 1 John 2:27.

[74]Cf. Romans 14:17; Ephesians 5:19; Colossians 3:16; 1 Thessalonians 4:18; 5:11; 2 Thessalonians 3:15; Hebrews 10:24–25.

over the overt manifestations of the demonic realm. But to acknowledge that God in his sovereign will does work miracles in some instances is far from suggesting that Scripture teaches that overt supernatural works are the normal complement to the proclamation of the gospel in evangelism.

What should accompany the verbal proclamation wherever possible is the manifestation of supernatural love in practical action. Scripture not only commends the power of love and good works to persuade (e.g., Matt. 5:16),[75] but many church historians see these as a key to the evangelistic success of the early church. According to Henry Chadwick, "The practical application of charity was probably the most potent single cause of Christian success."[76]

This leads to the second major area of gifts that should be normative in today's church: gifts of service, that is, those that do not predominately involve speaking (cf. 1 Peter 4:10–11, where gifts are divided between speaking and serving). The operation of gifts related to loving service in the contemporary church is considerably weak compared to that revealed in the history of the early church. I suggest that we would gain more power and blessing through an increase in the practical working of supernatural love both inside and outside the church than through more miraculous activity.

2. The Development and Training of Gifts

Little is said in Scripture about the training and development of the ministry of spiritual gifts. It would seem, however, that those gifts in which the Spirit utilizes our personal abilities in their function would be capable of developing greater effectiveness through training. To be "able to teach" (1 Tim. 3:2) surely is also "able to study." The same could be said especially of all gifts that in some way communicate God's truth based on Scripture. Thus we find Paul's encouragement to study the

---

[75]Cf. also John 13:35; 1 Peter 2:12.

[76]Henry Chadwick, *The Early Church* (Baltimore: Penguin Books, 1968), 56; see also G. W. Lampe, "Diakonia in the Early Church," in *Service in Christ*, ed. James I. McCord and T. H. L. Parker (Grand Rapids: Eerdmans, 1966), 49–50; Rowan A. Greer, *Broken Lights and Mended Lives* (University Park, Pa.: Pennsylvania State Univ. Press, 1986), 122–23.

Scripture (2 Tim. 2:15) and to receive teaching in order to teach (2:2). The many biblical pictures of discipling by example likewise apply to the development of ministry gifts (e.g., 2:10; cf. Phil. 2:22). Ministry, like the Christian life in general, may be likened to a skill that is furthered both by cognitive information and training, through which the student learns by practice to follow the example of a master craftsman.

It is difficult to see how such training and development would apply to the so-called miraculous gifts. As the name suggests, they transcend one's natural abilities with overtly supernatural manifestation. Surely there was no training involved in the manifestation of tongues in any of the recorded instances in Acts. It is hard to see how human skills and training are involved in such gifts as tongues, interpretation of tongues, miracles, and even prophecy.

3. The Corporate and Personal Ministry of Gifts

Since the church is the church whether members are gathered for corporate meeting or scattered in their homes and communities, the ministry of gifts can take place in all situations. The crucial factor in New Testament ministry is that all of God's people have gifts and not just certain professionals. The body grows through the ministry of every member (Eph. 4:16). Much ministry of gifts takes place as believers fulfill the many exhortations to teach, admonish, and comfort "one another" personally outside of the corporate meetings. Every glimpse that Scripture gives us of the corporate worship shows this same mutual ministry of gifts. The ministry of the Word was no doubt central, but it was done through a variety of gifts.[77] In biblical worship, the Spirit manifested himself to minister God's grace to the needs and edification of the community through many gifts. Some gifts, such as teaching, no doubt involved the Spirit's ministry in preparation prior to the actual teaching in the meeting as a person sought divine guidance. On the other hand, some ministry was also no doubt spontaneous.

The viewpoint on miraculous spiritual gifts that I have espoused means that we should be open to the manifestation of

---

[77]Cf. 1 Corinthians 14:26; Ephesians 5:19; Colossians 3:16.

miraculous gifts, but these gifts should not be seen as normal along with those gifts that focused on applying the truth of Scripture and loving acts of service. We should also be open to the miracles that God desires to perform simply through the prayers of his people (e.g., healing), which are not evident manifestations of a spiritual gift.

The ministry of spiritual gifts is the encounter of God with his people. For a person open to God, the reception of gifted ministry is the experience of his supernatural work. Too often this is primarily seen and therefore sought in the miraculous. But the edifying experiences of rebuke, conviction, encouragement, comfort, etc., brought through the nonmiraculous gifts, are as much supernatural and the experience of God as are miracles.

Finally, nowhere in Scripture does the ministry of gifts (publicly or privately) produce any supernatural physical manifestation, such as shaking or falling down. Because we are psychosomatic beings, spiritual experiences directed toward the heart will always, if they truly reach the heart, impact the physical dimension. The effect at times could be very obvious, e.g., weeping or various bodily expressions of joy. But these manifestations are not the direct work of the Spirit on the body, any more than the leaping of the man healed by Peter (Acts 3:8). I do, of course, allow for the possibility that the Spirit may affect the body directly. Certainly this is the case in miraculous healing. But the Bible does not portray bodily manifestations as demonstrations of the immediate supernatural power of the Spirit of God. The Spirit brings self-control (Gal. 5:23; cf. Acts 24:25). Moreover, the most Spirit-filled of all human beings, Jesus, showed no evidence of physical manifestation as a result of his being controlled by the Spirit.

4. Personal Guidance from God

The question of how God guides the individual believer in personal decisions of life is frequently framed in terms of whether we can expect "new revelation" or whether revelation ceased with the closing of the canon of Scripture. Those holding to the continuation of revelation speak of God's guidance through the gift of prophecy or the words of knowledge and wisdom. Those denying new revelation see God's guidance as limited to the application of Scripture and various other means considered nonrevelatory, such as the counsel of others and circumstances.

While God uses a variety of means to guide an individual, in my opinion, the result is often new revelation. It is difficult to see how the thought in my mind that I believe to be God's direction and the answer to my prayer, if it is truly guidance from God, is not revelatory. Moreover, if it concerns an issue that is not revealed in Scripture—and there are many, both personal (e.g., marriage, career) and corporate (for the church)—then it is new or fresh.

Without attempting a full discussion of God's guidance, I do not believe that what we have just referred to as guidance by God's revelation should be related to miraculous gifts. Rather, this is what might be called new covenant guidance, the guidance that in its perfected reality belongs to glorification. Scripture says that God has written his law on the heart of every believer. Along with the truth that every believer has received the Holy Spirit as Comforter and Teacher, this fact means that God is at work in us to fulfill his promise to guide us.[78] The present work of God in us surely uses all of the external means of guidance mentioned, especially the truth of Scripture. But the final product is the thought in our mind that emanates from the heart, with all of its feeling and impulse. If we believe the Spirit of God is at work in this process, then we must acknowledge that the thought within us is in some way produced by him and is not simply the product of our own minds.

In practical terms, as we use all of the means of guidance at our disposal, especially meditation on Scripture, we should carefully probe our hearts and minds for God's voice. But we should also remember that this voice of God is in *our* hearts and minds, which are still a mixture of the new work of God and our old sinful egos. Thus the thought of our hearts may be the word of self rather than of God. In this age of an imperfect heart, one cannot confidently assert, "God told me. ..." The voice from the heart must be submitted to other tests of divine guidance, especially

---

[78]Two helpful works in this respect are Klaus Bockmuehl, *Listening to the God Who Speaks* (Colorado Springs, Colo.: Helmers & Howard, 1990), and Dallas Willard, *In Search of Guidance* (San Francisco: Harper and Row, 1993).

to the counsel of other believers to whom God also speaks. In summary, people should be encouraged to listen for the voice of God's guidance with an open and humble heart, and especially one that is prepared by the knowledge of the truth of Scripture.

5. Relating with Those Who Differ on Miraculous Gifts

Among the many theological issues over which Christians differ, some hinder practical fellowship far more than others, especially those that immediately impact the life of the church. People may live together happily while differing on theological interpretations that do not directly or significantly impact behavior (e.g., eschatology or creation issues) or on those that are practiced individually (e.g., particular practices of spiritual growth). Such is not the case with the topics of this book. Many of these issues directly affect behavior within the corporate church, making it difficult for people of differing positions to fellowship together.

In my opinion the greatest problem to unity comes from those views that create (perhaps unintentionally) distinct spiritual levels among believers or cast aspersions on another person's spirituality. Insisting that a particular relationship to the Spirit be evidenced by a particular miraculous manifestation clearly draws a line marking off some from others spiritually. So also does advocating the manifestation of a particular gift as providing a significant key to fellowship with God. Even teaching that the failure of the church to manifest gifts equal to the apostolic era is a sign of sin or lack of faith can imply a spiritual differentiation. At least those who believe this recognize their failure, while others are not even repentant over their unbelief.

At the same time, perhaps more subtly, those who advocate that no miraculous gifts are available today may disparage others who do believe, for example, that they are using the biblical gift of tongues in their prayer life. They imply (or even teach outright) that such tongue speakers are deceived at best and involved with other spirits at worst. In all such instances, it is hard to see how those who hold the contrary positions could maintain fellowship in the church.

Unity in fellowship is based on similarity of belief and practice. Unity grows as divergent beliefs become less or are held as less significant, thereby providing more toleration of those who differ. History demonstrates that full unity on all things is probably not possible. But it also reveals that discussion among those of goodwill can do much to dissolve some differences and bring greater love and respect when difference remains. The recent history of miraculous gifts, while it has engendered some confusion in the church, has also brought helpful dialogue among opposing positions and some blurring of the traditional lines. Believers who seek Christ's goal of unity for the church must continue to make these issues a matter of study. Where the positions sincerely held allow for coexistence in church life, such fellowship should be pursued. Where issues sincerely held make regular church fellowship impossible, respect, love, and cooperation in the things of Christ must still flow across the lines to those who hold the same precious faith in the other areas of vital Christian doctrine.

E. DANGERS IN THE VARIOUS POSITIONS

To consider the dangers of one's own position is often a difficult task. The ideal is, of course, to hold a theological position that promotes spiritual health without presenting hazards along the way. While I am sure that my colleagues in this book will help me find others, the only possible danger that comes to mind for one holding the position presented here is that while avowing openness to God's miracle working, one might in reality be closed. The denial that the same phenomena of the apostolic era are normal for today naturally reduces the expectation of miracles, which may end up being no expectation at all.

As for the dangers of the other positions, I suggest that cessationism also leads to an excessive closure with regard to the miracle working of God and possibly produces an undue skepticism of the reports of miracles from around the world. As noted above, those who hold this position also can mark themselves as having superior theological and spiritual maturity over those who need and therefore seek physical manifestations of the Spirit to support their faith.

My greatest concern is with those who advocate miraculous spiritual gifts as normal for the Christian life during this age. As noted above, this position has the potential of categorizing believers with regard to spirituality, leading to the danger of elitism on the one side and feelings of inferiority on the other. The assurance given by some that God's healing is available to all has also raised false hope and subsequent disappointment for those to whom healing has never come despite earnestly seeking it.

This position can also produce havoc by pronouncing false prophecies over others. Moreover, the teaching of miraculous gifts as normal may place so much emphasis there that some believers lose the biblical emphasis that spirituality is evidenced primarily by the fruit of the Spirit and loving service to others. Finally, the advocates of continuationism may promote what might be called a triumphant Christianity of overt power, which in reality awaits the next age. According to Scripture, the present age is far more characterized by the power of suffering and persevering love than by the overt power of miraculous triumph over all of the effects of evil.

APPENDIX: ON EVALUATING PROPHECY

One of the key evidences for seeing a form of prophecy that is less than fully inspired and authoritative is Paul's call for the "weigh[ing] carefully [*diakrinō*] what is said" in the church (1 Cor. 14:29). The Greek word involved has the basic meaning of distinguishing between different things. The same word is used for the gift of "distinguish[ing] between spirits" (12:10), which is listed immediately following the gift of prophecy and is understood by many as operative in the evaluation of prophecy (see James D. G. Dunn, *Jesus and the Spirit* [Philadelphia: Westminster Press, 1975], 233ff.; Gordon Fee, *The First Epistle to the Corinthians*, 693).

The more widespread manifestation of prophecy in the New Testament church compared to the Old Testament no doubt made the matter of evaluation more important. But evaluation of prophecy was always necessary, to determine true from false prophets (Deut. 13:1–5; 18:22) and the validity of a purported prophecy from someone known as a true prophet (1 Kings 13:18). Paul's caution to the

Romans that one exercising this gift must do so "in proportion to his faith" (Rom. 12:6) suggests not only the possibility of false prophecies (in reality not divine prophecies
at all), but also that true prophecy might be, as Cranfield
says, "adulterated by additions derived from some source
other than the Holy Spirit's inspiration" (C. E. B. Cranfield,
*A Critical and Exegetical Commentary on the Epistle to the
Romans*, ICC [Edinburgh: T. & T. Clark, 1979], 2:620).

The distinguishing of prophecies, therefore, might be
between true and false prophets or between a prophecy
that truly comes from God and one that does not. Nothing
here suggests a change in the meaning of prophecy itself
from the Old Testament. The discrimination in all cases
does not deal with levels of prophecy, but with the separation of that which is prophecy from that which is not.

Paul's assertion of authority over the church prophets
is also seen as evidence that the prophecy of the latter has
less authority. But if prophets can submit to the discernment of the church, they can surely submit to the discernment of the apostle who, in his apostleship, represents
Christ's authority over the church. In both instances the
issue is not degrees of authority but discernment of what
is authoritative. Though it may be reasoned that the one
who evaluates the other exercised greater authority, such
is not really the case. People frequently had to determine
whether the ones who claimed to speak for God were genuine—including Moses. But when the determination was
made that God was truly speaking, the message was
received as authoritative and the people submitted to it. In
all such instances of evaluation, some criterion deemed
authoritative by the evaluators had to be used. This generally included prior revelation from God. The apostle himself happily submits his authoritative teaching to the
Berean believers, who used the Scripture to see if what he
was saying was true (Acts 17:11).

What we have, then, in the case of the apostle and the
prophets at Corinth is simply that Paul uses the criterion
of what he knows to be the command of the Lord as the
authority by which these prophets and their prophecies are
to be judged. It does not indicate that Paul claimed his

words were more authoritative than genuine prophecy that came through the church prophets at Corinth. Anyone who spoke contrary to the Lord's command should not consider himself or herself a prophet. If prophecy is truly an inspired revelation from God, it is authoritative no matter who is the vehicle through whom it is received. The biblical question that is still pertinent today is not that of levels of authority, but rather whether it is genuine prophecy.

A CESSATIONIST RESPONSE TO ROBERT L. SAUCY

Richard B. Gaffin, Jr.

1. The reader will have noted the substantial agreement there is between our two positions. I particularly appreciate the survey Saucy provides, especially of the Old Testament, in the section, "The Unevenness of Miracles in Biblical History." This section (which makes up for one of the gaps in my own presentation) brings to light an important point for this symposium: the *epochal* (or in Saucy's words, "uneven") movement or flow of biblical history as a whole, that is, of the history of redemption that the Bible records.

The truth of the matter lies somewhere between the position of Jack Deere, for instance, and the view he opposes.[1] While it is no doubt too restrictive to limit miracles in the Old Testament to the times of Moses/Joshua and Elijah/Elisha, Deere overstates, even on the basis of the evidence he marshals (see his table), in drawing the conclusion that from Samuel on miracles are "constant" and "regular," and that "supernatural events are a *normal* part of life in the Old Testament."[2] He does qualify his statement by saying that they were not "everyday events." But, surveying the period from Noah on, or even from Abraham on, the biblical record hardly shows that miracles "occur with some regularity in virtually every generation of Old Testament believers."[3] Psalm 74:9 and 77:11 (which Deere cites for the abnormal

---

[1]Jack Deere, *Power of the Spirit* (Grand Rapids: Zondervan, 1993), 253–66 ("Appendix C: Were There Only Three Periods of Miracles?").

[2]Ibid., 255–61.

[3]Ibid., 264.

exception), for instance, point to a rather different conclusion; to take another example, what about the experience of those numerous generations of God's people, except for the last one, during the long four hundred-year period of bondage in Egypt?

Miracles in Scripture are not free-standing phenomena, primarily for the benefit (or destruction) of those individuals most directly involved. What Deere and others miss—and this is the key insight reflected in the view he rejects—is that the occurrence of miracles is tethered to the contours of the unfolding history of salvation, the history of God's saving acts that begins already in the Garden of Eden at the time of the Fall, and ends in the finished work of Christ. That tethering happens as miracles are tied throughout this history to God's giving of his revelatory word, with the focus of that word, in turn, on his redemptive acts; word revelation either attests or explains redemption (see my discussion on p. 54).

But the history of redemption is anything but a smoothly-flowing, unbroken progression; rather than *Heilsgeschichte* ("salvation history") it often seems to be exactly the opposite, *Unheilsgeschichte*, a history of judgment and destruction, not of grace and blessing. At any rate, it is a history of starts and stops, ups and downs, marked by climactic moments and epochal surges separated by (sometimes long) periods of (relative) inactivity.

So, too, despite what may be our initial impression in reading the Old Testament, revelation is not a steady constant in Israel's history, say from the Exodus to the Exile. In view of the correlation of revelatory word to redemptive deed, the history of revelation is not an even, uninterrupted flow. Revelation tends to come in epochal fashion. Together with those media and other miraculous phenomena that either mark or accompany it, revelation clusters about and is copiously given in connection with the climactic and decisive events of redemptive history.

Specifically, without having (or wanting) to deny that revelation/miracles can occur, sporadically, at other times throughout salvation history, those cluster points, in the main, are God's dealings with Noah, the call of Abraham and the other patriarchs, the Exodus, developments surrounding the monarchy, the beginning and end of the Exile, and, preeminently and consummately, the coming and work of Christ (including the founding of the church).[4] The observable negative corollary, then, is that periods of pause and inactivity in the history of redemption (such as the slavery in Egypt and the interval following the return from exile until the coming of Christ) are, correlatively, times of silence in the history of revelation. Saucy's comments help to reinforce this redemptive-historical, theocratic rationale for the occurrence of revelation and other accompanying miracles.

That rationale, it should also be noted, involves the fact that throughout redemptive history the power experiences of individuals were, as far as the individuals themselves were concerned, a strictly ancillary aspect. That is, the individuals involved had power experiences not for their own sake as individuals, but such experiences were bound up with their particular roles (as prophets, judges, kings, etc.) in salvation history.

In this section I also found helpful Saucy's treatment of Hebrews 2:3–4 and Galatians 3:5. What he says about these passages provides, I believe, an adequate rejoinder to the diverging conclusions drawn from one or both of these passages by the other two participants in this symposium (see Storms, p. 190, n. 21, and Oss, p. 276). In Hebrews 2:3, "those who heard" may not be intended as a formal designation for the apostles and is not necessarily restricted to them. But clearly the "confirming" activity ascribed to this ear-witness group, like the revelatory activity of the (old covenant) angels with which it is contrasted (v. 2), has, as the author says, a "binding" quality. And that quality stands or falls with belonging to the uniquely commissioned revelatory witness of the apostles to Christ (to "the salvation, which was first announced by the Lord"). And verse 4 permits no conclusion about "signs, wonders and various miracles, and gifts of the Holy Spirit" other than that they provided further testimony joined with and subservient to the actual giving of this new, apostolically mediated revelation to Christ.

2. Passing over other points of agreement that could be noted, I want to suggest that Saucy's position, in its basic thrust, is really more "cautious" and less "open" than it appears to be.

His primary hesitation about saying that any New Testament gift has ceased is that there is no *explicit* biblical teaching

---

[4]Note, too, that the revelation given at and focused on these critical junctures takes in as well, looking either backward or forward, the periods that intervene.

to that effect. But does this not place too restrictive a demand on the teaching authority of the Bible? The individual statements of Scripture, I'm sure he would agree, are not isolated units of meaning. Each is embedded in an expanding horizon of contexts and has its sense, ultimately, in terms of the divinely established "pattern [or standard] of sound teaching" (cf. 2 Tim. 1:13) provided by Scripture as a whole. The Bible, by its very nature, as a unified totality of truth, invites a process of comparing Scripture with Scripture that necessarily involves drawing consequences and noting implications. "The whole counsel of God concerning all things necessary for his own glory, man's salvation, faith and life, is either expressly set down in Scripture, or by good and necessary consequence may be deduced from Scripture ..." (Westminster Confession of Faith, 1:6).

Obviously, a great danger lurks here; care (including methodological controls) must be taken to insure that a given consequence is not drawn arbitrarily but is truly "good and necessary." Abuse, however, should not be allowed to nullify legitimate use; the fact that our capacity to reason and draw consequences is subject to error does not mean that the consequences themselves are inevitably false or uncertain.

I doubt that we disagree substantially on this. For instance, Saucy affirms repeatedly the uniqueness of the apostolic era as the foundational period of the church's history and that apostles do not continue beyond that time.[5] Also, and more importantly, he affirms that the New Testament canon is closed. Furthermore, he recognizes the inner connection there is between the cessation of the apostolate and the closing of the canon.

It is not clear to me, however, on what basis Saucy holds these positions. Certainly the New Testament nowhere states *explicitly* either the closure of the twenty-seven-book canon or the cessation of apostles like the Twelve and Paul. But are not these convictions "good and necessary consequences" of its teaching (confirmed by subsequent church history)? Do they

---

[5]Does that not mean, then—as he himself recognizes—that there is at least one spiritual gift, apostleship, which in fact is the "first" (1 Cor. 12:28; Eph. 4:11), that has ceased, at least in any sense continuous with those who were uniquely appointed and authorized by Christ?

not at least lie on the trajectory of truth fixed by that teaching?[6] If not, we dare not make any sort of *binding*, *theological* appeal to them.

But (1) if these convictions are binding, and (2) given Saucy's view, correct in my judgment, that prophecy and tongues (with their interpretation) are inspired, infallibly revelatory speech, does that not argue for their cessation? As far as I can see, biblical teaching for the closed canon is no more (or less) clear than for the cessation of tongues and prophecy; the completion of the canon and the ceasing of inspired, infallible revelation stand or fall together. On the assumption that such revelation continues today, even if it were possible to apply meaningfully the criterion Saucy proposes ("totally harmonious with canonical revelation"), which I doubt is possible (see my essay, pp. 46–47 and 51–54), the canon would still not be truly closed. As far as God's infallible word for today is concerned, Scripture would be incomplete or, at the most, only relatively complete. It seems to me that Saucy's basic commitments ought to make him more open to the cessation of prophecy and tongues and more resolutely cautious about their continuation than he apparently is. But perhaps, after all, we are not so far apart on this point.

This is an appropriate place to remind our readers that my cessationist position for its part is not as closed as it might appear. I do not deny that experiences may occur today, incalculably in the Spirit's sovereign working, that in some respects are similar to those associated with the revelatory word gifts present in the New Testament. What I do question is that the New Testament teaches that these gifts are to continue or are to be sought today, and that those individuals and groups that claim to have received them today are, in that respect, closer to New Testament Christianity than those who have not.

3. I appreciate Saucy's caution and concern for balance in discussing demon possession, especially his emphasis on "preventive medicine" (a good dose of biblical truth!) in maintaining spiritual health for carrying on spiritual warfare.

---

[6]For an effort to demonstrate this to be the case, see R. B. Gaffin, Jr., "The New Testament As Canon," in *Inerrancy and Hermeneutic*, ed. H. M. Conn (Grand Rapids: Baker, 1988).

I wonder, though, if the disease model is not even more appropriate in this area than he brings out. It is noteworthy that in Scripture demon possession is never viewed as sin. Jesus' "rebuke," for instance, is never for demon-possessed people but for the possessing demon (Mark 1:25; 9:25 and parallels; cf. Acts 16:18). Demon possession is "victimization" in the truest and deepest sense. In this respect I think Saucy needs to distinguish more clearly demon possession from exposure to the demonic seductions of Satan and his hosts. Capitulation to the latter is culpable; it is sin and ought not, as such, to be "demonized."

Also, I certainly do not wish to diminish the full reality and intensity of the spiritual warfare believers are involved in (e.g., Eph. 6:11–12) or the ferocity of the devil's devouring efforts directed at them (1 Peter 5:8). But I have difficulty squaring New Testament teaching with the scenario whereby a believer is rendered so incapacitated by Satan's domination that the efforts of other believers (exorcism?) are necessary to bring about deliverance. This scenario, it seems to me, misses the nothing less than eschatological nature of the believer's conversion. We ought to continue to petition, for instance in the words of the Lord's Prayer, "your kingdom come," and "lead us not into temptation, but deliver us from the evil one" (Matt. 6:10, 13). But for believers these prayer-imperatives are grounded in the indicative that the kingdom has already come, and that, irrevocably, they have already been "rescued ... from the dominion of darkness and brought ... into the kingdom of the Son [God] loves" (Col. 1:13).[7]

4. Saucy maintains the important distinction—denied or blurred in current discussions—between prophecy and personal guidance. But I am troubled when later on in discussing guidance, he says that it often results in "revelation" that is "new or fresh." My problem is not with this language as such, although I might question its usefulness, but with viewing such revelations as distinct from other means of guidance, including the application of Scripture, which Saucy calls "nonrevelatory."

The Spirit may and ought to be at work in the feelings, intuitions, or hunches that believers have about specific decisions and particular courses of action. That presence is *not* at issue

---

[7]For a helpful treatment of this entire question, see D. A. Powlison, *Power Encounters: Reclaiming Spiritual Warfare* (Grand Rapids: Baker, 1995).

here. It belongs to the process of sanctification and is to be assumed in those (*all* believers) who are "spiritual" (e.g., 1 Cor. 2:15; Gal. 6:1) and are "led" by the Spirit (Rom. 8:14). My concern, however, is with giving such (Spirit-prompted) impulses a revelatory character parallel to, and so *in addition to and apart from*, the (no less Spirit-worked) application of Scripture, especially when Saucy considers the latter to be nonrevelatory. That, it seems to me, at the very least loosens the bond in the believer's life between God's word and the Spirit's activity, with the harm that will inevitably result.

The whole matter of guidance deserves much more attention than I can give to it here. I refer the reader particularly to the brief but incisive comments of John Murray.[8]

---

[8]John Murray, "The Guidance of the Holy Spirit," *Collected Writings* (Edinburgh: Banner of Truth, 1976), 1:186–89.

A THIRD WAVE RESPONSE TO ROBERT L. SAUCY

C. Samuel Storms

Whereas Robert Saucy's essay expresses a perspective on gifts much closer to mine than does Gaffin's, there are a few issues that call for extensive comment.

1. In spite of the fact that the term *charisma* is never applied to apostleship, both Saucy and Gaffin insist that it is a spiritual gift that did not survive beyond the first century. This, they believe, may well open the door to acknowledging that other spiritual gifts were likewise temporary.

But is apostleship a spiritual gift? Saucy points out that apostles "are listed along with 'prophets' and 'teachers,' whom all agree were individuals who regularly exercised the corresponding gifts of prophecy and teaching (cf. 1 Cor. 12:28–29; Eph. 4:11). Even as prophets and teachers were such by corresponding spiritual gifts that they exercised, so were apostles" (p. 101).

It is easy to understand this with regard to prophets and teachers and other similar gifts. Exhorters exhort, teachers teach, healers heal, those who have the gift of faith exercise extraordinary faith, and so on. But how does an "apostle" (noun) "apostle" (verb)? Whereas both Saucy and Gaffin insist that apostleship is a spiritual gift, neither one defines it. Saucy comes close when he says that "while the apostles exercised various gifts common to others (such as prophecy and teaching), they were also endowed with a unique spiritual gift that enabled them to minister as apostles" (p. 102).

But what does it mean to minister as an apostle? One ministers as a discerner of spirits by discerning spirits. One ministers as a giver by giving. However, to say that one is enabled to minister as an apostle does not tell me what the gift of *apostle-ing* (to coin a term) is. As Deere explains,

> It is virtually impossible to define the "gift" of apostleship in the same way that the other gifts can be defined. We can easily conceive of someone exercising the gift of prophecy without being a prophet. The same is true for all the other gifts. But how could someone come to a meeting of a local assembly and exercise the gift of apostleship in that meeting without actually being an apostle? An apostle in an assembly might teach, or prophesy, or heal, or lead, or administrate. But what would it mean to exercise the gift of apostleship? We simply cannot think of apostleship apart from the historical apostles. In the New Testament an apostle is not a spiritual gift but a person who had a divinely given commission and ministry.[1]

Spiritual gifts, such as those described in 1 Corinthians 12:7–10, are divinely energized deeds that are performed. But how does one do *apostle-ing*? I have no problem with how one might do prophecy or show mercy or give encouragement. But apostleship, it would seem, is not an inner working of the Holy Spirit through a human vessel, but an office to which one is called by Christ Jesus himself.

This raises the question of criteria for apostleship, which inescapably set it apart from all spiritual gifts. If apostleship were a *charisma*, it would be the only one for which a person must meet certain qualifying criteria. Paul describes the *charismata* as if the potential always exists for any person to be the recipient of any gift, depending on the sovereign will of the Spirit (1 Cor. 12:11). Not so with apostleship. Virtually everyone acknowledges that to qualify as an apostle one must be both "an eye-and-ear-witness to the resurrection of Christ" and receive a personal commission from Jesus himself (Acts 1:22–26; 1 Cor. 9:1–2; 15:7–9; cf. also Rom. 1:1, 5; 1 Cor. 1:1; 2 Cor. 1:1; Gal. 1:1).

---

[1]Jack Deere, *Surprised by the Power of the Spirit* (Grand Rapids: Zondervan, 1993), 242.

Thus, unlike the *charismata*, only a select few who met specific conditions could even be considered as possible apostles.

There is another related reason why it is unlikely that Paul thought of apostleship as a spiritual gift. I have in mind his repeated exhortation to "eagerly desire the greater gifts" (1 Cor. 12:31; cf. 14:1, 12). The *charismata* are to be desired and prayed for (14:13). In fact, we are especially to desire those gifts that are most effective in edifying the church (in this regard, see especially 14:12). Most scholars believe the list in 12:28–29, at the top of which is apostleship, is prioritized according to this principle. But if apostleship is a gift like prophecy or teaching, Paul would be in the awkward position of encouraging all Christians to desire, above all else, that they might be apostles! Yet, as noted above, this is not something that could be prayed for or desired or in any sense sought after. Either you are an eye-and-ear-witness of Christ's resurrection or you are not. Either you have received a personal commission from Jesus or you have not.

In a word, whereas apostles themselves certainly received *charismata*, such as the ability to prophesy, heal, show mercy, etc., apostleship per se is not a *charisma*. Apostleship is not an enabling power; it is an ecclesiastical position.

The reason why many wish to classify apostleship as a spiritual gift is not hard to see. Saucy writes: "If the *charisma* of being an apostle did not continue in the church, then we must acknowledge that not all of the spiritual gifts operative in the New Testament church have continued throughout history. Furthermore, this fact creates the possibility that other *charismata* have also ceased or changed" (p. 102). I am happy to concede the *possibility* that *all* of the charismata have ceased. But it is a possibility I will entertain only if something in Scripture explicitly asserts them to be temporary or defines these gifts in such a way that necessarily excludes them from subsequent church life. There is, however, nothing inherent in any of the gifts that either suggests or implies that they were temporary.

This sort of argument is like saying the *potential* exists for *no* practice of the early church to be valid today simply because we acknowledge that *some* are not. But we all admit that such a hypothetical scenario has no ultimate theological or practical bearing on the continuing validity of any particular activity. Each practice must be evaluated for what it is and why God ordained it. Therefore, if the New Testament explicitly defines a

spiritual gift as exclusively tied to the first century and consequently invalid for Christians in any subsequent period of
church history, I will be the first to declare myself a "cessationist" (insofar as that *one* gift is concerned). However, nothing that
either Saucy or Gaffin has written leads me to believe that any
of the *charismata* fall into that category.

2. Saucy repeatedly makes the point that the extent and
intensity of apostolic signs, wonders, and miracles has not continued *unchanged* throughout church history (p. 102). I agree. But
this would prove only that the apostles operated at a level of
supernatural power unknown to other Christians, something
virtually everyone concedes. It has no bearing, however, on the
question of whether the miraculous gifts of 1 Corinthians 12:7–
10 are designed by God for the church in every age. Deere is
again helpful:

> It is simply not reasonable to insist that all miracu-
> lous spiritual gifts equal those of the apostles in their
> intensity or strength in order to be perceived as legitimate
> gifts of the Holy Spirit. No one would insist on this for
> the nonmiraculous gifts like teaching or evangelism. . . .
> We should, of course, expect the healing ministry of
> the apostles to be greater than that of others in the body
> of Christ. They were specially chosen by the Lord to be
> his handpicked representatives, and they were given
> authority and power over all demons and over all dis-
> ease. . . . They possessed an authority that no one else in
> the body of Christ possessed. . . .
> If we are going to say that the apostolic ministry sets
> the standard by which we should judge the gifts in
> Romans 12 and 1 Corinthians 12, we might be forced to
> conclude that no gifts, miraculous or nonmiraculous,
> have been given since the days of the apostles! For who
> has measured up to the apostles in any respect?[2]

Therefore, the most that we may conclude from our not seeing *apostolic* healing or *apostolic* miracles is that we are not seeing
healings and miracles at the level they occurred in the ministry
of the *apostles*. It does not mean that God has withdrawn gifts of
healing or the gift of working miracles (1 Cor. 12:9–10) from the
church at large.

---

[2]Ibid., 67.

3. Saucy's extensive discussion of the role of signs and wonders as signs, attesting the prophetic word, is one with which I would generally agree. Yet, I must also insist on the distinction between "signs and wonders" on the one hand, and "miraculous gifts of the Holy Spirit" on the other. The phrase "signs and wonders" is often used to describe an extraordinary outpouring of miraculous activity, especially, though not exclusively, associated with Jesus and the apostles. Miraculous gifts of the Spirit, however, such as we have seen in 1 Corinthians 12, are designed by God for the sanctification and edification of all believers in the church and are nowhere in the New Testament restricted to extraordinary people in unusual times. Max Turner put it this way:

> We need not doubt the apostles were marked by occasionally dramatic events of healing (Acts and 2 Cor. 12:12); but ... we need to remember that the descriptions in Acts are sometimes self-consciously of *extra*ordinary healings (cf. 19:11), not the "ordinary" ones. Even here, however, there is little evidence of frequent healing *independent* of seeking faith; quite the contrary. Nor do we know the apostles experienced no failures or relapses (2 Tim. 4:20; Mt. 12:45; Jn. 5:14). As for the "ordinary" gifts of healing (1 Cor. 12:10 etc.; cf. Jas. 5:15) they may well have been less immediate and spectacular. ...
>
> We merely insist, on the one hand, that the idealized picture of apostolic healing, drawn from some sections of Acts should not be taken necessarily as *representative* (certainly not of *charismata iamaton* operating *outside* the apostolic circle, 1 Cor. 12:28f.) and, on the other hand, that serious modern testimony points to phenomena so congruent with even some apostolic experiences that only *a priori* dogmatic considerations can exclude the possibility that New Testament *charismata iamaton* [gifts of healings] have significant parallels.[3]

4. There are other issues raised by Saucy that I address either in my essay (e.g., the nature and purpose of tongues) or in the longer response to Gaffin (such as the meaning of Eph. 2:20 and the foundational role of apostles and prophets). I can only comment briefly on a few additional matters.

---

[3]Max Turner, "Spiritual Gifts Then and Now," *VoxEv* 15 (1985): 48–50.

Saucy appears on several occasions to fall into the same reductionist mind-set as Gaffin. His assertion that the "primary purpose of miraculous activities during these special periods was not for the general needs of God's people" (pp. 117–18) runs directly counter to Paul's assertion that miraculous gifts, including the gift of "working miracles," are given to people "for the common good," that is, for the edification and sanctification of the body of Christ as a whole (1 Cor. 12:7; 14:3, 26).

Saucy also believes it is significant that the New Testament does not provide examples of the operation of such miraculous gifts as healing. He claims that "no one in the church seems to have had a special healing ministry" (p. 122). But neither does the New Testament provide explicit examples of the operation of such gifts as mercy or giving or faith or leading. People undoubtedly showed mercy and gave and led and the like, even as they prayed for the sick (James 5), but in none of these instances is the word *charisma* used. Surely Saucy would not, for that reason, deny the validity of the *gift* of mercy or the *gift* of giving or the *gift* of leading. Why then question the validity of the *gift* of healing or the *gift* of working miracles? We should be no more surprised by the lack of reference to people with a special healing ministry than by the lack of reference to people with a special evangelistic ministry or special encouraging ministry.

Saucy's treatment of the casting out of demons is quite good. My only major concern is his reluctance to find in the four Gospels a valid model for conducting spiritual warfare (e.g., Luke 10:17–20).

In his discussion of church history, Saucy points to the "bizarre" examples cited by Augustine, such as the use of relics for healing, instruction mediated through a dream, healing power and authority over demons as a result of the observance of baptism and the Lord's Supper, and healing through the use of oil into which the tears of a compassionate priest had fallen. As strange as such phenomena may seem, we would do well to remember "that strangeness is not a criterion for truth. Nor is it a criterion we would want to use in order to decide whether something is scriptural or unscriptural."[4] Notwithstanding my deep respect for Augustine, I am not prepared to defend every claim of miraculous healing in his writings.

---

[4]Deere, *Surprised by the Power of the Spirit*, 74–75.

But is it any less strange that a man should be raised from the dead after making contact with the decaying bones of Elisha (2 Kings 13:21)? I find it "bizarre" that a man should have to wash seven times in a river to be healed of leprosy (5:1–14)! That demons should be cast out of two men and enter into a whole herd of pigs, who proceed to run into the sea and drown, is a bit unusual (Matt. 8:28–32)! Using spit and mud (John 9:6–7), a man's "shadow" (Acts 5:14–15), and another's "aprons" to heal (19:12) all seem a bit out of the ordinary. I am not suggesting that such events are normative, but simply that God's ways are often "bizarre" by human standards. We must be neither naively gullible nor unduly skeptical when it comes to claims for the miraculous.

Saucy's intimation that the presence of the completed canon suggests "a decrease in the need" (pp. 121–22) for the prophetic gift is an assertion nowhere made in Scripture. It *might* be true only if New Testament prophetic revelation yielded Scripture quality words from God. Furthermore, the use of prophecy, for example, to expose the secret sins of an unbeliever, leading him to repentance (1 Cor. 14:24–25), could hardly be rendered obsolete or unnecessary by the canon.

Later on Saucy argues that "the ministry of the early prophets who brought edification, exhortation, and consolation to the church on the basis of the gospel of Christ is now accomplished through other spiritual gifts that depend on the prophecy recorded in Scripture" (p. 128). Again, Paul never says this. Would it not make better and more biblical sense to argue that the ministry of edification, exhortation, and consolation will be accomplished precisely in the way Paul explicitly says it will be accomplished, namely, through the exercise of the gift of prophecy? Furthermore, where does the New Testament say that the exercise of spiritual gifts other than prophecy depends on the prophecy recorded in Scripture? If that were true, then we must conclude that no spiritual gifts *other* than prophecy operated *prior* to the closing of the canon. No one, I trust, would want to assert any such thing.

It seems that Saucy would also have us believe that because Paul only twice mentions prophecy in his later letters, the gift is invalid for subsequent church life. But if Paul gave extensive, repeated instruction on the nature and role of prophecy in

1 Corinthians, a book he wrote in about A.D. 55, and again encouraged the use of the prophetic gift in Romans, a book he wrote in about 57, why should we demand that he repeat himself in those letters that were written for a different purpose a mere eight or nine years later? Saucy's appeal to the fact that Paul made preparations for his death by directing Timothy to the Scriptures and not to prophecy proves the very point for which I argued in my essay, namely, that New Testament congregational prophets spoke with less authority than either apostles or Scripture. It no more proves his belief that the gift of prophecy was to decrease than it proves the cessation of other practices or principles addressed in an earlier letter but omitted from the Pastorals (e.g., the Lord's Supper or the gift of faith).

Finally, Saucy appeals to the *plural* in the exhortation to "earnestly desire" spiritual gifts (1 Cor. 12:31; 14:1) as grounds for rejecting the idea that Christians should seek them. But of course the verb is plural, as are virtually all Paul's commands in letters other than those addressed to individuals (such as Philemon, Titus, and Timothy). Paul is writing to *everyone* in the church at Corinth, each of whom is responsible for individually responding to an exhortation that has validity for the entire church. In other words, what is the corporate church if not a collection of *individuals* on *each* of whom the obligation falls? The plural of this exhortation simply indicates that *all* believers in Corinth are to heed the apostolic admonition. It is a duty *common* to everyone.

In conclusion, I share Saucy's concern that "the greatest problem to unity comes from those views that create (perhaps unintentionally) distinct spiritual levels among believers or cast aspersions on another person's spirituality. Insisting that a particular relationship to the Spirit be evidenced by a particular miraculous manifestation clearly draws a line marking off some from others spiritually" (p. 144). An especially encouraging feature of this book is that none of the participants in this symposium have written anything that would contribute to this potential problem.

A PENTECOSTAL/CHARISMATIC RESPONSE TO ROBERT L. SAUCY

Douglas A. Oss

Dr. Saucy has penned a memorable essay, and the one that probably exhibits best the dramatic shift in evangelicalism with regard to miraculous gifts—a progressive dispensationalist who is not a cessationist. The entire evangelical community will be enriched by this essay.

1. Dr. Saucy's statement against the second experience doctrine of Pentecostalism (pp. 97–99) appeals primarily to Paul and only lists four non-Pauline texts (John 7:37–39; Acts 2; 8; 1 Peter 1:5). He does not consider the redemptive-historical evidence in any detail, making only the briefest reference to it (pp. 98, 124–25). This, I think, warrants further reflection, especially since the case for a distinct second experience rests primarily on redemptive-historical fulfillment.

Moreover, Dr. Saucy's essay exhibits some misunderstanding of Spirit baptism and hermeneutics in Pentecostal theology. Pentecostals would not describe Spirit baptism as a "definitive new relationship" (p. 99). Spirit baptism is an experience within an already existing new covenant relationship, since all believers receive the Spirit at conversion.[1] This new experience is an endowment with power that is different from regeneration and sanctification. Also, we would not argue that Spirit baptism is a once-for-all experience. We agree with Dr. Saucy that after the

---

[1] Although, as stated in my essay, sometimes subsequence is not discernible, as in Acts 10.

distinct, inaugural experience, there is continued growth in this area of Christian life, just as there is continued growth in holiness subsequent to regeneration. Dr. Saucy describes these periods of dramatic growth as "decisive spurts" (p. 99). Pentecostals would describe the inaugural Spirit baptism, and further fillings with the Spirit and power, more as decisive *gushers*.

As for his statement that the New Testament nowhere commands us to be baptized in the Spirit, my suggestion is for a closer look at what Pentecostals say about the interpretation of Luke–Acts and Paul. First, the narrative genre expresses imperatives differently than a letter. What is meant in Acts 1:6–8 when Jesus tells his disciples that the fulfillment of the Baptist's prophecy is looming on the horizon and that they should wait in Jerusalem until they receive power (*dynamis*) when the Holy Spirit comes upon them? And what theology is communicated through the fulfillment of this promise throughout the remainder of Acts? Is this not the narratological equivalent of an imperative? Remember Peter's sermon, "The promise is for you and your children and all who are far off—for all whom the Lord our God will call" (Acts 2:39). Second, Luke must be allowed to explain redemptive-historical fulfillment in his own terms; we should not import theology from Paul and unnaturally impose it on Luke-Acts. Harmonization must come after divinely ordained diversities are understood, and Luke's agenda emphasizes the Spirit's charismatic power.

2. The discussion of the cessation of miraculous gifts in this essay is more detailed. Here Dr. Saucy agrees that the New Testament does not teach cessation, but neither is he convinced that all the gifts are standard for the church throughout all time (p. 100). The concerns he raises are basically the same as those raised by Professor Gaffin, although he does not draw the same absolute conclusions. He discusses the apostolate (more broadly understood as the circle of "first witnesses" [p. 110]), the canon, and the purpose of gifts.

3. On the latter issue he draws the purpose too restrictively when he asserts that "the purpose of all miraculous activity is to 'testify to' the original proclamation of the new message of salvation" (p. 110). As we have seen elsewhere in this book, the purpose of gifts cannot be restricted to this function (e.g., edification is the purpose in the context of the church at worship).

4. Saucy's explanation of the "cluster" argument (pp. 103–12) fails upon closer analysis. The clusters of miracles are not nearly as clear as argued; many miracles occurred outside the clusters, thus casting this entire line of argumentation into serious doubt.[2]

5. The argument from church history (pp. 112–20, 126) has, in my opinion, always been irrelevant. Perhaps this seems too strong a statement, but it seems to me that the experience and/or traditions of the church are not the same as the teaching of Scripture, and at times are even in conflict with biblical doctrine. In any event, Dr. Saucy draws the picture here in terms that are too absolute.[3] For example, Ronald Kydd, in a reworked doctoral dissertation, covers the period up to about A.D. 320, and Stanley Burgess provides bibliographical resources for the medieval period.[4] Even a short survey of these works will indicate that the historical data do not support cessationist claims. The *Didache* spoke of prophets continuing into the second century,[5] and even the Reformers gave serious treatment to the matter of signs and wonders and prophetic claims.

Luther threw barbs at Carlstadt's claims of prophetic powers—"Oh the blindness and the mad fanaticism of such great heavenly prophets, who boast daily of speaking with God!"[6]—

---

[2]Cf., e.g., Deere, *Surprised by the Power of the Spirit* (Grand Rapids: Zondervan, 1993), 229–66.

[3]Much of what follows on church history is unpublished research originally done by Wayne Grudem and Dale Brueggemann, which was put in essay form by Brueggemann. It is used here with only minor revisions.

[4]Ronald Kydd, *Charismatic Gifts in the Early Church* (Peabody, Mass.: Hendrickson, 1984); Stanley M. Burgess, "Medieval Examples of Charismatic Piety in the Roman Catholic Church," in *Perspectives on the New Pentecostalism*, ed. Russel P. Spittler (Grand Rapids: Baker, 1976), 14–26.

[5]Charles E. Hummel, *Fire in the Fireplace: Contemporary Charismatic Renewal* (Downers Grove, Ill.: InterVarsity, 1978), 164–66, 192–93, 210–12; George H. Williams and Edith Waldvogel, "A History of Speaking in Tongues and Related Gifts," in *The Charismatic Movement*, ed. Michael Hamilton (Grand Rapids: Eerdmans, 1975), 64–70; Warfield, *Counterfeit Miracles* (Edinburgh: Banner of Truth Trust, 1983 [1918]), 3–69.

[6]Martin Luther, "Against the Heavenly Prophets," written to oppose Carlstadt's teaching on the Lord's Supper (*LW*, ed. Helmut T. Lehman, 40 vols. [Philadelphia: Fortress, 1958], 40.133). I am indebted to an unpublished paper by Ron Lutgens, "The Reformed Fathers and the Gift of Prophecy" (1987), for much of the following material from the Reformation.

but his polemical interactions with some who claimed dramatic gifts of the Spirit were tempered. For example, he wrote a note about this to Wittenberg from hiding in the Wartburg Castle, "Prove the spirits; and if you are not able to do so, then take the advice of Gamaliel and wait."[7]

Preaching on Mark 16 for Ascension Day, 1522,[8] Luther said, "Where there is a Christian, there is still the power to work these signs if it is necessary." He believed that even the apostles did not regularly perform miracles but "only made use of it to prove the Word of God." He said that since the gospel has now spread, there is less need for miraculous attestation, though if "need should arise, and men were to denounce and antagonize the Gospel, then we verily should have to employ wonder-working rather than permit the Gospel to be derided and suppressed." Because he identified miracles as attestation for the gospel rather than as the real presence of deliverance, he concluded, "But I hope such a course will not be necessary, and that such a contingency will never arise." On Ascension Day one year later he preached on Mark 16 and referred to John 14:12, saying,

> Therefore, we must allow these words to remain and not gloss them away, as some have done who said that these signs were manifestations of the Spirit in the beginning of the Christian era and that now they have ceased. That is not right; for the same power is in the church still. And though it is not exercised, that does not matter; we still have the power to do such signs.[9]

Calvin expressed an ambivalent attitude toward the gifts. On the one hand, he wrote a chapter entitled, "Fanatics, Abandoning Scripture and Flying Over to Revelation, Cast Down All the Principles of Godliness."[10] In commenting on Roman 12:6, he spoke of a twofold nature of New Testament prophecy, predictive and interpretive, indicating his view that *predictive* prophecy apparently flourished only while the Gospels were being written whereas *interpretive* prophecy continued in the church. In his

---

[7] Roland H. Bainton, *Here I Stand* (New York: Mentor, 1950), 209.
[8] Luther, *LW: Sermons*, Lenker edition, 12.207; preached on Ascension Day, 1522.
[9] Luther, *LW: Sermons*, Lenker edition, 12.190; preached on Ascension Day, 1523.
[10] Calvin, *Institutes of the Christian Religion*, 1.9.

commentary on 1 Corinthians 12–14, he vaguely allowed that "it is difficult to make up one's mind about gifts and offices, of which the church has been deprived for so long, except for mere traces or shades of them, which are still to be found."[11] Calvin allowed for the extraordinary gifts "as the need of the times demands" and wrote, "This class does not exist today or is less commonly seen."[12]

John Knox was even more open to prophecy, considering the Old Testament prophet as a model for his own vocation. Dale Johnson titles chapter 6 of his thesis, "Specific Prophecies of Knox."[13] Though the accuracy of these prophecies may be questioned, it is unquestionable that Knox thought God was once again giving prophetic gifts.[14]

The general opinion in the Reformed community is that the Westminster Confession affirms the cessation of "prophetic utterances"; however, Samuel Rutherford, a Scottish Presbyterian framer of the Westminster Confession, a Westminster divine, would not have agreed. He argued for a distinction between the objective external revelation inscripturated in the canon and the internal subjective revelation, which we would call "illumination." In addition, Rutherford also recognized two other subjective types of revelation: false prophecies—which are not prophecies at all—and predictive prophecy. He said he knew of men "who have foretold things to come even since the ceasing of the Canon of the word," mentioning Hus, Wycliff, and Luther as examples. In addition, he spoke of the following three occasions:

---

[11]Calvin, *1 Corinthians*, in *New Testament Commentaries* (Grand Rapids: Eerdmans), 9:211.

[12]Calvin, *Institutes*, 4.3.4.; Willem Balke says: "Calvin certainly had a feeling for the exceptional and charismatic. But he regarded every effort to make the exceptional and the charismatic regulatory for the life of the church to be destructive of the church. He insisted that the good order of the church is neither established nor maintained by that which is exceptional, but that the church moves forward only by the preaching and hearing the Word" (*Calvin and the Anabaptist Radicals* [Grand Rapids: Eerdmans, 1981], 245).

[13]Dale Johnson, "John Knox: Reformation Historian and Prophet" (M.A. thesis, Covenant Theological Seminary).

[14]Ibid.; Jasper Ridley, *John Knox* (New York: Oxford Univ. Press, 1968), esp. 517ff.

in our nation of Scotland, Mr. George Wisehart foretold that Cardinal Beaton should not come out alive at the Castle of St. Andrews, but that he should die a shameful death, and he was hanged over the window that did not look out at, when he saw the man of God burnt; Mr. [John] Knox prophesied of the hanging of the Lord of Grange; Mr. John Davidson uttered prophecies, known to many of the kingdom, diverse Holy and mortified preacher in England have done the like.[15]

Rutherford offered guidelines for differentiating between true and false prophecy: First, these postcanonical prophets "did tye no man to beleeve their prophecies as scriptures. Yea they never denounced Iudgement against those that beleeve not their predictions"; second, "the events reveled to Godly and sound witnesses of Christ are not contrary to the word"; and third, "they were men sound in the faith opposite to Popery, Prelacy, Socinianism, Papisme, Lawlesse Enthusiasme, Antinomianisme, Arminiansme, and what else is contrary to sound doctrine." Prophecies not meeting these criteria are false: "We cannot judge them but Satanicall. A lamed and maneked directory, of faith and manners, contrary to Scripture." Men who speak these things "doe and act all things from their owne spirit, and walke in the light of their own sparkes."[16]

The Westminster Confession of Faith says in 1.6:

> The whole counsel of God concerning all things neces-
> sary for his own glory, man's salvation, faith and life, is
> either expressly set down in Scripture, or by good and
> necessary consequence may be deduced from Scripture:
> unto which nothing at any time is to be added, whether
> by new revelations of the Spirit, or traditions of men.

In the light of Rutherford's belief about revelation, the line "new revelations of the Spirit" may be understood to refer to non-canonical but actual utterances that are subordinate to and judged by Scripture, and which may not be added to the canon. Canon, not prophecy, is the issue.

---

[15]Samuel Rutherford, *A Survey of the Spirituall Antichrist. Opening the Secrets of Familisme and Antinomianisme in the Antichristian Doctrine of John Saltmarsh (et al.)* (London, 1648), 42.

[16]Ibid., 43–45.

The Confession goes on to say (1.10):

> The supreme judge by which all controversies of religion
> are to be determined, and all decrees of councils, opinions
> of ancient writers, doctrines of men, and private spirits,
> are to be examined, and in whose sentences are to rest, can
> be no other but the Holy Spirit speaking in the Scriptures.

The mention of "private spirits" does not reject them out of hand;
it merely subjects them to the authority of Scripture along with
"all decrees of councils, opinions of ancient writers, doctrines of
men." Thus, when the Westminster Confession of Faith speaks of
"those former ways of God's revealing His will unto His people
now being ceased," it should not necessarily be interpreted to
indicate that God no longer reveals himself in any extraordinary
way but to indicate that the canon is closed and that it alone is
the rule of faith and practice. At least this is how Rutherford
understood it. When the Confession refers to "the direct communication which once was" and "the indirect communication
which now is," is this a distinction between "revelation" and
"illumination" or between canon and all other revelation? The
former was committed "wholly unto writing" (Confession 1.1),
but such prophecies as those given in Corinth were not all
deposited in the canon—though of the Spirit, they were not of
the deposit of faith. Rutherford's understanding as a framer certainly leaves open alternative interpretations of the Confession
than the prevailing cessationist interpretation of today.

6. On the role of 1 Corinthians 12–14, Dr. Saucy's essay does
not give this didactic material enough weight. He writes:

> Outside of the discussion of spiritual gifts in 1 Corinthi-
> ans 12 and the working of miracles associated with the
> apostles and others with them, the New Testament letters
> contain no mention of "miracles," "signs," or "wonders,"
> except for Galatians 3:5 and Hebrews 2:4. . . . While these
> included miracle-working among the members of the
> church, these miracles were related to the initial ministry
> of the apostles.
>
> Thus, it must be acknowledged that the New Testa-
> ment simply does not give us a picture of the normal
> operation of gifts in the church following the apostolic
> era (p. 122).

First, Saucy takes the infrequency of discussions of healing in New Testament letters as evidence that they diminished after the generation of first witnesses (p. 122). This is a non sequitur. Letters are task-specific writings, written to deal with specific problems in the churches. Healing was not a pastoral problem that needed to be addressed, except perhaps for the recipients of the letter of James, who were *not* praying that the sick would be healed and needed specific exhortation to correct that error. So we would not expect it to receive much attention; it was normal and healthy.

Second, the fact is that 1 Corinthians 12–14 *is* in the Bible. It tells us, along with Acts and the rest of the New Testament, what is characteristic and normal during *the last days*, not the apostolic era. This distinction between apostolic and subapostolic eras is foreign in the Bible and is only useful for describing the role of persons who founded the church (e.g., Eph. 2:20ff.), not for defining the nature of "the last days." To do the latter, one should search the New Testament with a view toward determining what is normal in the church during the period from Pentecost to the return of the Lord. There may be some differences in *how* the church applies the teaching of the New Testament, but there should be no difference in *what* the Bible teaches and *what* we believe.

Chapter Three

A THIRD WAVE VIEW

C. Samuel Storms

A THIRD WAVE VIEW

C. Samuel Storms

The church has not always been polite to the Holy Spirit. As Alister McGrath has said, "The Holy Spirit has long been the cinderella of the Trinity. The other two sisters may have gone to the theological ball; the Holy Spirit got left behind every time."[1] The very existence of this book indicates that a shift has occurred and that the third person of the Trinity is now receiving his proper due. Today a prayerful cry is being heard throughout the church: "Come, Holy Spirit!"

But what might the Holy Spirit do, should he choose to accept this invitation? It is my contention in this chapter that we should pray for his appearance with the expectation that he will minister *to* God's people *through* God's people by means of the full range of *charismata* listed in such passages as 1 Corinthians 12:7–10, 28–30.

This has not always been my belief. For over fifteen years I taught others that certain gifts of the Spirit, in particular, word of knowledge, healing, miracles, prophecy, discerning of spirits, tongues, and the interpretation of tongues died with the apostles and were interred with their bones. My task will be to account for this shift in thinking and to explain why I now embrace all of the aforementioned gifts and encourage their use in the life and ministry of the church. Before doing so, however, I need to address the issue of Spirit-baptism and the doctrine of subsequence.

---

[1]Alister E. McGrath, *Christian Theology: An Introduction* (Oxford: Blackwell, 1994), 240.

A. SECOND EXPERIENCES

Perhaps the principal distinction, theologically speaking, between classical Pentecostalism and the so-called Third Wave is the latter's rejection of the doctrine of subsequence. According to most Pentecostals and charismatics, baptism in the Holy Spirit is an event subsequent to and therefore separate from the reception of the Spirit at conversion, the initial evidence of which is speaking in tongues.[2]

The view for which I will contend is that Spirit-baptism is a metaphor that describes what happens when one becomes a Christian.[3] However, this does not preclude multiple, *subsequent* experiences of the Spirit's activity. After conversion the Spirit may yet "come" with varying degrees of intensity, wherein the Christian is "overwhelmed," "empowered," or in some sense "endued." This release of new power, this manifestation of the Spirit's intimate presence, is most likely to be identified with what the New Testament calls the "filling" of the Spirit. John Wimber is an advocate of this view:

> How do we experience Spirit-baptism? It comes at conversion. . . . Conversion and Holy Spirit-baptism are

---

[2]See Gary B. McGee, ed., *Initial Evidence: Historical and Biblical Perspectives on the Pentecostal Doctrine of Spirit-baptism* (Peabody, Mass.: Hendrickson, 1991). Gordon Fee is a notable exception to this rule. Although a member of the Assemblies of God, Fee has argued repeatedly against the doctrine of subsequence. See, for example, "Baptism in the Holy Spirit: The Issue of Separability and Subsequence," *Pneuma*, 7:2 (Fall 1985): 87–99; "Hermeneutics and Historical Precedent: A Major Problem in Pentecostal Hermeneutics," in *Gospel and Spirit: Issues in New Testament Hermeneutics* (Peabody, Mass.: Hendrickson, 1991), 83–104; and *God's Empowering Presence: The Holy Spirit in the Letters of Paul* (Peabody, Mass.: Hendrickson, 1994), 175–82. The most comprehensive treatment of Spirit-baptism is Henry I. Lederle's, *Treasures Old and New: Interpretations of "Spirit-Baptism" in the Charismatic Renewal Movement* (Peabody, Mass.: Hendrickson, 1988).

[3]The expression "baptism in the Holy Spirit" occurs seven times in the New Testament, six of which refer to Pentecost (Matt. 3:11; Mark 1:8; Luke 3:16; John 1:33; Acts 1:5; 11:16). The seventh is in 1 Corinthians 12:13. To be baptized in water is to be immersed or submerged. This provides us with an appropriate analogy for what happens when the Holy Spirit comes upon us. Just as one is deluged and engulfed by water in baptism, so also the believer is overwhelmed and engulfed and drenched by the Holy Spirit. In water baptism we get immersed in water; in Spirit-baptism we get immersed (soaked and saturated) in the Spirit.

simultaneous experiences. The born-again experience is the consummate charismatic experience.[4]

Key to this interpretation is 1 Corinthians 12:13, "For we were all baptized by one Spirit into one body—whether Jews or Greeks, slaves or free—and we were all given the one Spirit to drink." There are a number of reasons for understanding this text as descriptive of the conversion experience of all Christians. (1) If the text describes the experience of only some believers, those who lack this second blessing do not belong to the body of Christ.

(2) The context of 1 Corinthians 12 militates against the doctrine of subsequence. The apostle stresses that all, regardless of their gift, belong to the body as co-equal and interdependent members. The idea of a Spirit-baptized elite would have played directly into the hands of those who were causing division in Corinth. Paul emphasizes here the *common* experience of the Holy Spirit for everyone, not what one group has that another does not (note the emphatic "we all").

(3) Some insist that the preposition *eis* does not mean that Spirit-baptism incorporates one "into" the body of Christ. Rather, *eis* means something like "with a view to benefiting" or "for the sake of," the idea being that Spirit-baptism prepares them for service/ministry to the body in which they had *previously* been placed by faith in Christ. Grammatically speaking, had this been Paul's intent, he would probably have used another preposition that more clearly expresses the idea (e.g., *heneka*, "for the sake of," or *hyper* with the genitive, "in behalf of, for the sake of").[5]

(4) Still others argue that Paul is describing a baptism "by" the Holy Spirit into Christ for salvation (which all Christians experience at conversion), whereas elsewhere in the New Testament it is Jesus who baptizes "in" the Holy Spirit for power (which only some Christians receive, though it is available to all). Part of the motivation for this view is the seemingly awkward

---

[4]John Wimber, *Power Points* (San Francisco: Harper, 1991), 136.

[5]It should be noted that the preposition *eis* has two fundamental meanings: (1) a *local* sense, indicating that into which all were baptized, or (2) a reference to the *purpose or goal* of the baptizing action, i.e., "*so as to become* one body." See Murray J. Harris, "Prepositions and Theology in the Greek New Testament," *NIDNTT*, 3:1207–11.

phrase, "*in* one Spirit *into* one body"—hence the rendering, "*by* one Spirit *into* one body." But what sounds harsh in English is not so in Greek. As D. A. Carson points out, "the combination of Greek phrases nicely stresses exactly the point that Paul is trying to make: *all* Christians have been baptized in *one* Spirit; *all* Christians have been baptized into *one* body."[6]

We should note the same terminology in 1 Corinthians 10:2, where Paul says that "all were baptized *into* Moses *in* the cloud and *in* the sea." Here the "cloud" and the "sea" are the "elements" that surrounded or overwhelmed the people and "Moses" points to the new life of participation in the Mosaic covenant and the fellowship of God's people of which he was the leader.[7] In the other texts referring to Spirit-baptism (Matt. 3:11; Mark 1:8; Luke 3:16; John 1:33; Acts 1:5; 11:16), the preposition *en* means "in," describing the element in which one is, as it were, immersed. In no text is the Holy Spirit ever said to be the agent by which one is baptized. Jesus is the baptizer; the Holy Spirit is he in whom we are engulfed or the element with which we are saturated and deluged, resulting in our participation in the spiritual organism of the church, the body of Christ.[8]

(5) Another variation is to argue that whereas 1 Corinthians 12:13a refers to conversion, verse 13b describes a second, postconversion work of the Holy Spirit. But parallelism is a common literary device employed by the biblical authors. Here Paul employs two different metaphors (*baptism*, or immersion in the Holy Spirit, and *drinking* to the fill of the Holy Spirit) that describe the same reality. Whatever occurs to those in verse 13a occurs to those in verse 13b. That is, the same "we all" who were

---

[6]D. A. Carson, *Showing the Spirit: A Theological Exposition of 1 Corinthians 12–14* (Grand Rapids: Baker, 1987), 47.

[7]See Wayne Grudem, *Systematic Theology: An Introduction to Biblical Doctrine* (Grand Rapids: Zondervan, 1994), 768.

[8]In the New Testament to be baptized "by" someone is expressed by the preposition *hypo* plus the genitive. People were baptized "by" John the Baptist in the Jordan River (Matt. 3:6; Mark 1:5; Luke 3:7). Jesus was baptized "by" John (Matt. 3:13; Mark 1:9). The Pharisees had not been baptized "by" John (Luke 7:30), etc. Most likely, then, if Paul had wanted to say that the Corinthians had all been baptized "by" the Holy Spirit, he would have used *hypo* with the genitive, not *en* with the dative (see Harris, "Prepositions and Theology," 1207–11).

baptized in one Spirit into one body were also made to drink of the same Spirit. The activity in the two phrases is co-extensive.

Paul may be alluding in verse 13b to the Old Testament imagery of the golden age to come, in which the land of Israel and its people have the Spirit poured out on them (Isa. 32:15; 44:3; Ezek. 39:29). Thus, conversion is an experience of the Holy Spirit analogous to the outpouring of a sudden flood or rainstorm on parched ground, transforming dry and barren earth into a well-watered garden (cf. Jer. 31:12). Fee points out that

> such expressive metaphors (immersion in the Spirit and drinking to the fill of the Spirit) ... imply a much greater experiential and visibly manifest reception of the Spirit than many have tended to experience in subsequent church history. Paul may appeal to their common experience of Spirit as the presupposition for the unity of the body precisely because, as in Gal. 3:2–5, the Spirit was a dynamically experienced reality, which had happened to all.[9]

Whereas biblical usage suggests that we apply the terminology of Spirit-baptism to the conversion experience of all believers, this in no way restricts the activity of the Spirit to conversion. The New Testament endorses and encourages multiple subsequent experiences of the Spirit's power and presence. Therefore, evangelicals are *right* in affirming that all Christians have experienced Spirit-baptism at conversion, but they are *wrong* in denying the reality of subsequent, sensible, and often dramatic experiences of the Spirit in the course of the Christian life. Charismatics are *right* in affirming the reality and importance of postconversion encounters with the Spirit that empower, enlighten, and transform, but they are *wrong* in calling this experience "Spirit-baptism." The more appropriate terminology is that of being "filled with the Holy Spirit." Spirit-filling is itself a metaphor that describes our continuous, ongoing experience and appropriation of the Holy Spirit. *To be filled with the Spirit is to come under progressively more intense and intimate influence of the Spirit*.

There are two senses in which one may be filled with the Holy Spirit. (1) There are texts that describe people as being *"full*

---

[9]Fee, *God's Empowering Presence*, 181.

of the Holy Spirit," as if it were a *condition* or consistent *quality* of Christian character, a moral *disposition*, or a possession of a maturity in Christ (see Luke 4:1; Acts 6:3, 5; 7:55; 11:24; 13:52). This is the ideal condition of every Christian, emphasizing the *abiding state* of being filled.

(2) Other texts describe people as being *"filled with* the Holy Spirit,"* enabling them to fulfill or perform a special task or equipping them for service or ministry. This empowering may be lifelong, preparatory for an office or particular ministry (Luke 1:15–17; Acts 9:17), but there are also instances that call for an immediate and special endowment of power to fulfill an important and urgent need or spiritual emergency. Thus, someone who is already filled with the Holy Spirit may experience an additional filling. That is, no matter "how much" of the Holy Spirit one may have, there is always room for "more"! (See Luke 1:41, 67; Acts 4:8, 31; 13:9; cf. Old Testament instances: Ex. 31:3; 35:31; Num. 24:2; Judg. 6:34; 14:6, 19; 15:14; 1 Sam. 10:6; 16:13.) In Acts 7:55 Stephen, though "full of the Holy Spirit" (6:3, 5), is again "filled" with the Holy Spirit to empower him to endure persecution and eventual martyrdom (and perhaps to prepare him for the vision of Jesus).[10]

In summary, there is one Spirit-baptism, but multiple fillings. In no New Testament text is there an appeal or a command to be baptized in the Holy Spirit. On the other hand, we *are* commanded in Ephesians 5:18 to "be filled with the Spirit." This is not so much a dramatic or decisive experience that settles things for good but a daily appropriation. Thus it is possible to be baptized in the Spirit and to experience his permanent indwelling, and yet not be filled with the Spirit. Says Gaffin:

> This command ... is relevant to all believers throughout the whole of their lives. No believer may presume to have experienced a definitive filling of the Spirit so that the command of verse 18 no longer applies. Short of death or the Lord's return, it continues in effect for every believer.[11]

---

[10]Note especially the cause and effect relationship between being *filled with the Spirit* and *inspired speech* (see Luke 1:41 and its relation to 1:42–45; 1:67 and its relation to 1:68–79).

[11]Richard Gaffin, *Perspectives on Pentecost: Studies in New Testament Teaching on the Gifts of the Holy Spirit* (Phillipsburg, N.J.: Presbyterian and Reformed, 1979), 33.

There are several other texts that speak of postconversion encounters or experiences with the Holy Spirit that are related to but not identical with infilling.

(1) There is the impartation of revelatory insight and illumination into the blessings of salvation (Eph. 1:15–23; cf. Isa. 11:2). Paul prays that God will impart the Spirit to believers yet again, so that he may supply the wisdom to understand what he reveals to them about God and his ways. This is something for which we must pray (both for ourselves and for others). There are dimensions of the Spirit's ministry in our lives that are suspended, so to speak, on our asking.

It strikes some as odd that Paul would pray for the Spirit to be given to those who already have him. But this hardly differs from Paul's prayer in Ephesians 3:17, that Christ might "dwell" in the hearts of people in whom he already dwells! Paul is referring to an experiential enlargement of what is theologically true. He prays that, through the Spirit, Jesus might exert a progressively greater and more intense personal influence in the souls of believers. Thus, in both texts Paul is praying for an expanded and increased work of God in the believer's life.

(2) There is also the anointing of power for the performance of miracles, as seen in Galatians 3:1–5 (esp. v. 5). Paul clearly refers both to the Galatians' initial reception of the Spirit (v. 2) and to their present experience of the Spirit (v. 5). The unmistakable evidence that they had entered into new life was their reception of the Spirit (v. 2). Fee explains:

> The entire argument runs aground if this appeal is not also to a reception of the Spirit that was dynamically experienced. Even though Paul seldom mentions any of the visible evidences of the Spirit in such contexts as these, here is the demonstration that the experience of the Spirit in the Pauline churches was very much as that described and understood by Luke—as visibly and experientially accompanied by phenomena that gave certain evidence of the presence of the Spirit of God.[12]

---

[12]Fee, *God's Empowering Presence*, 384. When God "comes near" (James 4:8) to people either to reveal his glory and power or to flood the soul with an experiential awareness of his love (Rom. 5:5), unusual physical and emotional phenomena may occur. What might be called the *manifest presence* of God often provokes such reactions as trembling (Hab. 3:16; cf. Isa. 66:2), awestruck reverence (Isa. 6:1–5; Matt.

Paul speaks of God as the one who continually and liberally supplies the Spirit to men and women who in another sense have already received him. This is especially evident when one takes note of Paul's use of the present tense (i.e., "He who *is supplying* you with the Spirit"). Evidently there is a close, even causal, relationship between the supply of the Spirit and the resultant working of miracles. That is to say,

God is present among them by his Spirit, and the fresh supply of the Spirit finds expression in miraculous deeds of various kinds. Thus Paul is appealing once more to the visible and experiential nature of the Spirit *in their midst* as the ongoing evidence that life in the Spirit, predicated on faith in Christ Jesus, has no place at all for "works of law."[13]

17:2–8), the inability to stand (1 Kings 8:10–11; 2 Chron. 7:1–3; Dan. 8:17; 10:7–19; John 18:6; Rev. 1:17), overwhelming joy (Ps. 16:11), and other related manifestations. This is especially true in those times of the extraordinary outpouring of God's Spirit that we call *revival* and *renewal*. For an evaluation of such occurrences in the contemporary church (in particular, the so-called "Toronto Blessing"), I recommend Guy Chevreau, *Catch the Fire* (London: Marshall Pickering, 1994), and *Pray with Fire* (Toronto: HarperCollins, 1995); Rob Warner, *Prepare for Revival* (London: Hodder & Stoughton, 1995); Patrick Dixon, *Signs of Revival* (Eastbourne: Kingsway, 1994); Dave Roberts, *The Toronto Blessing* (Eastbourne: Kingsway, 1994); Don Williams, *Revival: The Real Thing* (LaJolla: published by the author, 1995); Derek Morphew, *Renewal Apologetics* (A Position Paper of the Association of Vineyard Churches in South Africa, 1995); John White, *When the Spirit Comes With Power* (Downers Grove, Ill.: InterVarsity, 1988); John Arnott, *The Father's Blessing* (Orlando: Creation House, 1995); Wallace Boulton, ed., *The Impact of Toronto* (Crowborough: Monarch, 1995); Mike Fearon, *A Breath of Fresh Air* (Guildford: Eagle, 1994); Mark Stibbe, *Times of Refreshing: A Practical Theology of Revival for Today* (London: Marshall Pickering, 1995); David Pawson, *Is the Blessing Biblical? Thinking Through the Toronto Phenomenon* (London: Hodder & Stoughton, 1995); Ken and Lois Gott, *The Sunderland Refreshing* (London: Hodder & Stoughton, 1995); Andy and Jane Fitz-Gibbon, *Something Extraordinary Is Happening: The Sunderland Experience of the Holy Spirit* (Crowborough: Monarch, 1995). For a more critical assessment, see James A. Beverley, *Holy Laughter and the Toronto Blessing* (Grand Rapids: Zondervan, 1995); B. J. Oropeza, *A Time to Laugh* (Peabody, Mass.: Hendrickson, 1995); Stanley E. Porter and Philip J. Richter, eds., *The Toronto Blessing—or Is It?* (London: Darton, Longman, & Todd, 1995); Clifford Hill, ed., *Blessing the Church?* (Guildford: Eagle, 1995); Leigh Belcham, *Toronto: The Baby or the Bathwater?* (Bromley, Kent: Day One Publications, 1995); and Stanley Jebb, *No Laughing Matter: The "Toronto" Phenomenon and its Implications* (Bromley, Kent: Day One Publications, 1995).

[13]Fee, *God's Empowering Presence*, 388–89.

(3) Paul also speaks about the provision of the Spirit to face hardship with hope (Phil. 1:19). I do not believe he is thinking so much of the Spirit's "help" but of the gift of the Spirit himself, whom God continually supplies to him. In other words, the phrase "the provision of the Spirit" is an objective genitive. The Spirit is himself being given or supplied anew to Paul by God to assist him during the course of his imprisonment.

(4) In 1 Thessalonians 4:8 the apostle speaks of the continuous exertion of strength from the Holy Spirit necessary for purity. He states specifically the Holy Spirit is given "into" (eis) you, not simply "to" you. The point is that God puts his Spirit inside us (cf. 1 Cor. 6:19). The use of the present tense emphasizes the ongoing and continuous work of the Spirit in our lives. If Paul had in mind the Thessalonians' conversion and thus their initial, past reception of the Spirit, he would probably have used the aorist of the verb (cf. 1:5–6). In context, Paul's point is that the call to sexual purity and holiness comes with the continuous provision of the Spirit to enable obedience. Thus the Spirit is portrayed as the ongoing divine companion, by whose power the believer lives in purity and holiness.

(5) The Spirit is also responsible for our deepened awareness of adoption as sons and daughters and for increased confidence and assurance of salvation. It is the work of the Spirit to intensify our sense of the abiding and loving presence of the Father and Son (see John 14:15–23; Rom. 5:5; 8:15–17). There are times in the Christian life when believers find themselves more than ordinarily conscious of God's love, presence, and power (see Eph. 3:16–19; 1 Peter 1:8). In other words, there is a heightened, increased, or accelerated experience of the Spirit's otherwise ordinary and routine operations. Why? J. I. Packer explains:

> Why should there be this intensifying—which, so far from being a once-for-all thing, a "second [and last!] blessing," does (thank God!) recur from time to time? We cannot always give reasons for God's choice of times and seasons for drawing near to his children and bringing home to them in this vivid and transporting way, as he does, the reality of his love. After it has happened, we may sometimes be able to see that it was preparation for pain, perplexity, loss, or for some specially demanding or discouraging piece of ministry, but in other cases we may only ever be able to say: "God chose to show his child his

love simply because he loves his child." But there are also times when it seems clear that God draws near to men because they draw near to him (see James 4:8; Jeremiah 29:13,14; Luke 11:9–13, where "give the Holy Spirit" means "give experience of the ministry, influence, and blessings of the Holy Spirit"); and that is the situation with which we are dealing here.[14]

It comes as no surprise, therefore, that Jesus encourages us to ask the Father for more of the Spirit's ministry in our lives. In Luke 11:13 he says, "If you then, though you are evil, know how to give good gifts to your children, how much more will your Father in heaven give the Holy Spirit to those who ask him!" Could it be that this exhortation to pray for the Holy Spirit flows from his own experience of the Spirit? Could it be that he himself prayed for continued, repeated anointings, infillings, or fresh waves of the Spirit's presence and power to sustain him for ministry, so that he here encourages his followers to do the same?[15] Where Luke says the Father will give the "Holy Spirit" to us, Matthew says he will give "good things." Why the difference? John Nolland suggests:

> It will be best to see that, since from a post-Pentecost early church perspective, the greatest gift that God can bestow is the Spirit, Luke wants it to be seen that God's parental bounty applies not just to everyday needs (already well represented in the text in [the] Lord's Prayer) but even reaches so far as to this his greatest possible gift.[16]

Since this exhortation in Luke 11:13 is addressed to believers, the "children" of the "Father," the giving of the Spirit in response to prayer cannot refer to one's initial experience of sal-

---

[14]James I. Packer, *Keep in Step With the Spirit* (Old Tappan, N.J.: Revell, 1984), 227.

[15]The best treatment of the Holy Spirit in the life of Jesus is Gerald Hawthorne's, *The Presence and the Power: The Significance of the Holy Spirit in the Life and Ministry of Jesus* (Dallas: Word, 1991). See also James D. G. Dunn, *Jesus and the Spirit: A Study of the Religious and Charismatic Experience of Jesus and the First Christians as Reflected in the New Testament* (Philadelphia: Westminster, 1975); Robert P. Menzies, *The Development of Early Christian Pneumatology with Special Reference to Luke–Acts* (Sheffield: Sheffield Academic Press, 1991).

[16]John Nolland, *Luke 9:21–18:34*, WBC (Dallas: Word, 1993), 632.

vation. *The prayer for the Holy Spirit is not by a lost person needing a first-time indwelling of the Spirit but by people who already have the Spirit and who also stand in need of a greater fullness, a more powerful anointing to equip and empower them for ministry.* In fact, this petition is part of the instruction on persistence and perseverance in prayer that began in 11:1. In other words, *we are repeatedly and persistently and on every needful occasion to keep on asking, seeking, and knocking for fresh impartations of the Spirit's power.*

Such texts dispel the concept of a singular, once-for-all deposit of the Spirit that supposedly renders superfluous the need for subsequent, postconversion anointings. The Spirit, who was once given and now indwells each believer, is continually given to enhance and intensify our relationship with Christ and to empower our efforts in ministry. But we need not label any one such experience as Spirit-baptism.

B. THE CEASING OF CESSATIONISM

It is now time to address the issue of the perpetuity of the so-called miraculous gifts. It is important to point out at the outset that not all cessationists (or even the majority) deny the possibility of miraculous phenomena occurring subsequent to the death of the apostles. What most do deny is the postapostolic operation of what they call "revelatory gifts" (prophecy, tongues, interpretation of tongues) and in particular the *charisma* of "miracles" mentioned by Paul in 1 Corinthians 12:10 (lit., "workings of powers").[17] Whereas the potential for miracles is affirmed by

---

[17]See Norman Geisler, *Signs and Wonders* (Wheaton: Tyndale, 1988), 127–45. One would be hard-pressed to find a more explicit affirmation of cessationism than that provided by Richard Mayhue in his book, *The Healing Promise* (Eugene, Ore.: Harvest House, 1994): "*The Scriptures teach that miracles through human agents served a very specific purpose.* That purpose focused on authenticating the prophets and apostles of God as certified messengers with a sure word from heaven. When the canon of Scripture closed with John's Revelation, there no longer existed a divine reason for performing miracles through men. Therefore, such kinds of miracles ceased according to the Scriptures" (184). I will respond at length to this argument later in this essay. Be it noted here that it is unwise to draw too much of a distinction between what God does through gifted people and what he does independently of them. According to the apostle Paul, it is God who (lit.) "works all things [i.e., all the *charismata*, v. 4] in all persons" (1 Cor. 12:6). Even when people perform miracles (or utilize any spiritual gift), the energizing source is always God.

most cessationists (but with minimal expectancy), the presence of the gift itself in contemporary church life is denied.

Similarly, most cessationists believe God can and occasionally does supernaturally heal people today. But the *gift* of healing is no longer available to the church. One of the principal reasons for this doctrine is a misconception about miraculous gifts. Many cessationists erroneously believe that to be the recipient of "the gift of healing" or "the gift of miracles" means that one invariably can exercise supernatural power at will, anytime, for any occasion, with the same degree of effectiveness as did the apostles. When they measure this against what they perceive to be the infrequency and inefficiency of modern claims to the miraculous, it seems only reasonable to conclude that such *charismata* are no longer operative in the church. This, however, is not what the New Testament teaches concerning the nature of these gifts. I will address this point later on, but for now I refer the reader to the relevant portions of Jack Deere's book, *Surprised by the Power of the Spirit*.[18]

Be it noted, then, that when I speak of signs, wonders, and miraculous phenomena available to the church today, I have in mind not the mere potential for rare supernatural activity or surprising acts of providence, but the actual operation of those miraculous gifts listed in 1 Corinthians 12:7–10.

(1) An argument that I at one time cited frequently in defense of cessationism was that signs, wonders, and miracles were not customary phenomena even in biblical times. Rather, they were clustered or concentrated at critical moments of revelatory activity in redemptive history. John MacArthur is today an outspoken advocate of this argument:

> Most biblical miracles happened in three relatively brief periods of Bible history: in the days of Moses and Joshua, during the ministries of Elijah and Elisha, and in the time of Christ and the apostles. None of those periods lasted much more than a hundred years. Each of them saw a proliferation of miracles unheard of in other eras. ... Aside from those three intervals, the only super-

---

[18]Jack Deere, *Surprised by the Power of the Spirit* (Grand Rapids: Zondervan, 1992), 58–71, 229–52.

natural events recorded in Scripture were isolated incidents.[19]

Several things may be said in response to this argument. (a) At most this might suggest that in three periods of redemptive history, miraculous phenomena were *more* prevalent than at other times. This fact does *not* prove that miraculous phenomena in other times were nonexistent, nor does it prove that an increase in the frequency of miraculous phenomena could not appear in subsequent phases of redemptive history.

(b) For this to be a substantive argument one must explain not only why miraculous phenomena were prevalent in these three periods but also why they were, allegedly, infrequent or, to use MacArthur's term, "isolated," in all other periods. If miraculous phenomena were infrequent in other periods, a point I concede here only for the sake of argument, one would need to ascertain why. Could it be that the relative infrequency of the miraculous was due to the rebellion, unbelief, and apostasy rampant in Israel throughout much of her history (cf. Pss. 74:9–11; 77:7–14)? Let us not forget that even Jesus "could not do any miracles there [in Nazareth], except lay his hands on a few sick people and heal them" (Mark 6:5), all because of their unbelief (at which, we are told, Jesus "was amazed," v. 6). The point is that the comparative isolation of the miraculous in certain periods of Old Testament history could be due more to the recalcitrance of God's people than to any supposed theological principle that dictates as normative a paucity of supernatural manifestations.

(c) *There were no cessationists in the Old Testament.* No one in the Old Testament is ever found to argue that since miraculous phenomena were "clustered" at selected points in redemptive history, we should not expect God to display his power in some other day. Moreover, *at no point in Old Testament history did miracles cease.* They may have *subsided,* but this proves only that in some periods God was pleased to work miraculously with greater frequency than he did in others.

---

[19]John F. MacArthur, *Charismatic Chaos* (Grand Rapids: Zondervan, 1992), 112. One of the most thorough critiques of MacArthur's work is Rich Nathan, *A Response to Charismatic Chaos* (Anaheim: Association of Vineyard Churches, 1993).

The fact that miracles do appear throughout the course of redemptive history, whether sporadically or otherwise, proves that miracles never ceased. How, then, can the prevalence of miracles in three periods of history be an argument for cessationism? And how does the existence of miracles in every age of redemptive history serve to argue against the existence of miracles in our age? The occurrence of miraculous phenomena throughout biblical history, however infrequent and isolated, cannot prove the *nonoccurrence* of miraculous phenomena in postbiblical times. The *continuation* of miraculous phenomena *then* is *not* an argument for the *cessation* of miraculous phenomena *now*. The fact that in certain periods of redemptive history few miracles are recorded proves only two things: that miracles *did* occur, and that few of them were recorded. It does not prove that only a few actually occurred.

(d) The assertion that miraculous phenomena outside these three special periods were isolated is not altogether accurate. One can make this argument only by defining the miraculous so narrowly as to eliminate a vast number of recorded supernatural phenomena that otherwise might qualify. MacArthur insists that to qualify as a miracle the extraordinary event must occur "through human agency" and must serve to "authenticate" the messenger through whom God is revealing some truth. In this way one is able to exclude as miraculous any supernatural phenomenon that occurs apart from human agency and any such phenomenon unrelated to the revelatory activity of God. Thus, if no revelation is occurring in that period of redemptive history under consideration, no supernatural phenomena recorded in that era can possibly meet the criteria for what constitutes a miracle. On such a narrow definition of a miracle, it thus becomes easy to say they were isolated or infrequent.

But if "human agency" or a "gifted" individual is required before an event can be called miraculous, what becomes of the Virgin Birth and the resurrection of Jesus? What about the resurrection of the saints mentioned in Matthew 27:52–53, or Peter's deliverance from jail in Acts 12? Was the instantaneous death of Herod in Acts 12:23 not a miracle because the agency was angelic? Was the earthquake that opened the prison in which Paul and Silas were housed not a miracle because God did it himself directly? Was Paul's deliverance from the venom of a viper (Acts 28) not a miracle simply because no human agency was utilized in his preservation? To define as a miracle only those supernatural phenomena involving human agency is arbitrary. It is a case of special pleading, conceived principally because it provides a way of reducing the frequency of the miraculous in the biblical record.

And did miracles always accompany divine revelation as a means of attestation? That miracles confirmed and authenticated the divine message is certainly true. But to *reduce* the purpose of miracles to this one function is to ignore other reasons for which God ordained them. The association of the miraculous with divine revelation becomes an argument for cessationism *only* if the Bible *restricts* the function of a miracle to attestation. And the Bible does not do that. More on this later.

My reading of the Old Testament reveals a consistent pattern of supernatural manifestations in the affairs of humanity. In addition to the multitude of miracles during the lifetime of Moses, Joshua, Elijah, and Elisha, we see numerous instances of angelic activity, supernatural visitations and revelatory activity, healings, dreams, visions, and the like. Once the arbitrary restrictions on the definition of a miracle are removed, a different picture of Old Testament religious life emerges.[20]

(e) Note the assertion of Jeremiah 32:20, in which the prophet addresses his God, who "performed miraculous signs and wonders in Egypt, and *have continued them to this day*, both in Israel and among all mankind, and have gained renown that is still yours" (italics added). This text alerts us to the danger of arguing from silence. The fact that from the time of the Exodus to the Exile fewer instances of signs and wonders are recorded does not mean they did not occur, for Jeremiah insists they did. One might compare this with the danger of asserting that Jesus did not perform a particular miracle or do so with any degree

---

[20]For an extensive listing of miraculous phenomena in the Old Testament, see Deere, *Surprised by the Power of the Spirit*, 255–61. One thinks especially of Daniel, who ministered in the first half of the sixth century B.C., well beyond the time of Elijah and Elisha. Yet, as Deere points out, "proportionately Daniel's book contains more supernatural events than the books of Exodus through Joshua (the books dealing with the ministries of Moses and Joshua) and 1 Kings through 2 Kings 13 (the books dealing with the ministries of Elijah and Elisha)" (263).

of frequency simply because the Gospels fail to record it. John tells us explicitly that Jesus performed "many other miraculous signs in the presence of the disciples, which are not recorded in this book" (John 20:30), as well as "many other things" that were impossible to record in detail (21:25).

(f) Most cessationists insist that both New and Old Testament prophecy are the same. They also readily acknowledge that New Testament prophecy was a "miracle" gift. If Old Testament prophecy was of the same nature, then we have an example of a miraculous phenomenon recurring throughout the course of Israel's history. In every age of Israel's existence in which there was prophetic activity, there was miraculous activity. What then becomes of the assertion that miracles, even on the narrow definition, were infrequent and isolated?

It would appear, then, that the argument for cesssationism that appeals to the notion of miraculous phenomena as being clustered and therefore isolated in redemptive history is neither biblically defensible nor logically persuasive.

(2) A second argument to which I often used to appeal is this: Signs, wonders, and miraculous gifts of the Holy Spirit (such as tongues, interpretation, healing, and the discerning of spirits) were designed to confirm, attest, and authenticate the apostolic message. It seemed to me only reasonable to conclude, therefore, as Norman Geisler has said, that "the 'signs of an apostle' passed away with the times of an apostle."[21] It is true

---

[21]Geisler, *Signs and Wonders*, 118. Often Hebrews 2:3–4 is cited in this regard: "How shall we escape if we ignore such a great salvation? This salvation, which was first announced by the Lord, was confirmed to us by those who heard him. God also testified to it by signs, wonders and various miracles, and gifts of the Holy Spirit distributed according to his will." But let us note several factors: (a) The author does not limit this text to the apostles, nor does the word "apostle" even appear in the passage. Although I am happy to grant that the apostolic company are included in the phrase "those who heard," there is no reason to limit it to them. Many more than the Twelve heard Jesus, did miracles, and exercised spiritual gifts. (b) The text does not explicitly identify to *what* or to *whom* God bore witness by signs and wonders ("to it" in the NIV translation is not represented by anything in the Greek text), though the message of salvation (v. 3) is the likely candidate. Jesus first proclaimed the message. Those who heard him confirmed it to those who did not have the privilege of hearing it firsthand. God in turn confirmed the veracity of this gospel by signs, wonders, various miracles, and gifts of the Spirit. (c) Were the miracles that confirmed the message performed *only* by those who originally heard the Lord? The text allows

that signs, wonders, and miracles often attested to the divine origin of the apostolic message. But this is a persuasive argument against the contemporary validity of such phenomena only if you can demonstrate two things.

(a) You must demonstrate that authentication or attestation was the *sole and exclusive purpose* of such displays of divine power. However, there is not one text of inspired Scripture that does so. *Nowhere in the New Testament is the purpose or function of the miraculous or the charismata reduced to that of attestation.* The miraculous, in whatever form in which it appeared, served several other distinct purposes. For example, there was a *doxological* purpose. Such was the primary reason for the resurrection of Lazarus, as Jesus himself makes clear in John 11:4 (cf. v. 40; cf. also 2:11; 9:3; Matt. 15:29–31). Miracles also served an *evangelistic* purpose (see Acts 9:32–43). Much of our Lord's miraculous ministry served to express his *compassion* and *love* for the hurting multitudes. He healed the sick and fed the five thousand because he felt compassion for the people (Matt. 14:14; Mark 1:40–41).

There are several texts that indicate that one primary purpose of miraculous phenomena was to *edify* and *build up* the body of Christ. At one point in his book MacArthur says that

---

for the possibility that when God testified to the message of salvation, he did it among and through the author of Hebrews and his audience as well. The fact that this is a *present* participle ("God also bearing witness," NASB) at least suggests (though it does not require) "that the corroborative evidence was not confined to the initial act of preaching, but continued to be displayed within the life of the community" (William Lane, *Hebrews 1–8*, WBC [Dallas: Word, 1991], 39). (d) Nothing in the text asserts that such miraculous phenomena must be restricted either to those who personally heard the Lord or to those who heard the message of salvation secondhand. Why would not God continue to testify to the message when it is preached by others in subsequent generations? (e) The use of *merismois* ("gifts ... distributed") rather than the dative plural of *charisma* is curious. Perhaps the author is not even describing "gifts" per se, in which case *pneumatos hagiou* may be an objective genitive referring to the Spirit himself as the one whom God distributed or supplied to (cf. Gal. 3:5) his people. If, on the other hand, "gifts" are in view, note that he distinguishes between "various miracles" (lit., "powers," *dynamesin*) and "gifts" of the Spirit. This would suggest that by "gifts" he intends more than what we would call miraculous *charismata*. Is anyone prepared to restrict *all* spiritual gifts to the first century simply because they served to authenticate and attest to the gospel message? In view of these factors, I am not persuaded that this passage supports cessationism.

noncessationists "believe that the spectacular miraculous gifts were given for the edification of believers. Does God's Word support such a conclusion? No. In fact, the truth is quite the contrary."[22] What, then, will one do with 1 Corinthians 12:7–10, the list of what all agree are miraculous gifts (such as prophecy, tongues, healing, and interpretation of tongues)? These gifts, says Paul, were distributed to the body of Christ *"for the common good"* (v. 7), that is, for the edification and benefit of the church! These are primarily, though not exclusively, the very gifts that served as the background against which Paul then encouraged (in vv. 14–27) all members of the body to minister one to another for mutual edification, insisting that no one gift (whether tongues or prophecy or healing) was any less important than another.

One must also explain 1 Corinthians 14:3, where Paul asserts that prophecy, one of the miraculous gifts listed in 12:7–10, functions to edify, exhort, and console others in the church. The one who prophesies, says Paul in verse 4, "edifies the church." We find a similar emphasis in verse 5, where Paul says that speaking in tongues, when interpreted, also edifies the church. And what will one do with verse 26, in which Paul exhorts believers, when they assemble, to be prepared to minister with a psalm, a teaching, a revelation, a tongue, an interpretation—all of which are designed, he says, for "the strengthening of the church"?

If tongues never were intended to edify believers, why did God provide the gift of interpretation so that tongues might be used in the gathered assembly of believers? If tongues never were intended to edify believers, why did Paul himself exercise that gift in the privacy of his own devotions (cf. 1 Cor. 14:18–19, where he suggests in a somewhat exaggerated way that he almost never speaks in tongues in church). If in church Paul virtually never exercised this gift, yet spoke in tongues more frequently, fluently, and fervently than anyone, even more so than the tongue-happy Corinthians, where did he do it? Surely it must have been in private.

My point is this: *All* the gifts of the Spirit, whether tongues or teaching, whether prophecy or mercy, whether healing or

---

[22]MacArthur, *Charismatic Chaos*, 117.

helps, were given, among other reasons, for the edification, building up, encouraging, instructing, consoling, and sanctifying of the body of Christ. Therefore, even if the ministry of the miraculous gifts to attest to and authenticate the apostles and their message has ceased—a point I concede only for the sake of argument—such gifts would continue to function in the church for the other reasons cited.

(b) One must demonstrate that *only the apostles* performed signs, wonders, or exercised so-called miraculous *charismata*. But this is contrary to the evidence of the New Testament. Others who exercised miraculous gifts include (i) the seventy who were commissioned in Luke 10:9, 19–20; (ii) at least 108 people among the 120 who were gathered in the upper room on the day of Pentecost; (iii) Stephen (Acts 6–7); (iv) Philip (ch. 8); (v) Ananias (ch. 9); (vi) church members in Antioch (13:1); (vii) new converts in Ephesus (19:6); (viii) women at Caesarea (21:8–9); (ix) the unnamed brethren of Galatians 3:5; (x) believers in Rome (Rom. 12:6–8); (xi) believers in Corinth (1 Cor. 12–14); and (xii) Christians in Thessalonica (1 Thess. 5:19–20).

Furthermore, when one reads 1 Corinthians 12:7–10, it does not sound as if Paul is saying that only apostles were endowed with the *charismata*. On the contrary, gifts of healings, tongues, miracles, and so on, were given by the sovereign Spirit to ordinary Christians in the church at Corinth, for the daily, routine building up of the body. Farmers, shopkeepers, housewives, along with apostles, elders, and deacons, received the manifestation of the Spirit, all "for the common good" of the church.

A counterargument is often made to the effect that signs, wonders, and miraculous gifts in Acts were closely connected with the apostles or with those who were themselves associated with the apostolic company. But remember that the book of Acts is, after all, the Acts of the *Apostles*. We title it this way because we recognize that the activity of the apostles is the principal focus of the book. We should hardly be surprised or try to build a theological case on the fact that a book *designed* to report the acts of the apostles describes the signs and wonders they performed.

Furthermore, to say that Stephen, Philip, and Ananias do not count because they are closely associated with the apostles proves nothing. Virtually *everyone* in Acts has some degree of association with the apostolic company. It is difficult to think of one person who figures to any degree of prominence in the book of Acts who is *not* associated with at least one of the apostles. But was there not a remarkable concentration of miraculous phenomena characteristic of the apostles as special representatives of Christ? There was indeed (cf. Acts 5:12). But the prevalence of miracles performed by the apostles in no way proves that no miracles were performed by or through others.

At this point 2 Corinthians 12:12 comes to mind. Does not this text refer to miracles as "signs" of the apostles? No, in point of fact, it does not. The NIV contributes to the confusion by translating as follows: "The things that mark an apostle—signs, wonders and miracles—were done among you with great perseverance." This rendering leads one to believe that Paul is identifying the "signs/marks" of an apostle with the miraculous phenomena performed among the Corinthians. But the "signs/marks" of an apostle is in the nominative case, whereas "signs, wonders and miracles" are in the dative. Contrary to what many think, Paul does *not* say the insignia of an apostle *are* signs, wonders, and miracles. Rather, as the NASB more accurately translates, he asserts that "the signs of a true apostle were performed among you with all perseverance, *by* [or better still, *accompanied by*] signs and wonders and miracles."

Paul's point is that signs, wonders, and miracles accompanied his ministry in Corinth; they were attendant elements in his apostolic work.[23] But they were not themselves the "signs of an apostle." For Paul, the distinguishing marks of his apostolic ministry were, among other things: (a) the fruit of his preaching, that is, the salvation of the Corinthians themselves (cf. 1 Cor. 9:1b–2, "Are not you the result of my work in the Lord? Even though I may not be an apostle to others, surely I am to you! For you are the seal of my apostleship in the Lord"; cf. 2 Cor. 3:1–3); (b) his Christlike life of holiness, humility, etc. (cf. 2 Cor. 1:12; 2:17; 3:4–

---

[23]The instrumental dative is grammatically possible but conceptually unlikely. What could it possibly mean to say that suffering, holiness, and Christlike humility were done "*by means of* signs and wonders"? The associative dative, which designates accompanying circumstances, seems more fitting (cf. F. Blass and A. Debrunner, *A Greek Grammar of the New Testament* [Chicago: Univ. of Chicago Press, 1961], 195, 198). The important point is that Paul does not equate the marks of apostleship with miracles as if to suggest that *only* the former do the latter.

6; 4:2; 5:11; 6:3–13; 7:2; 10:13–18; 11:6, 23–28); and (c) his sufferings, hardship, persecution, etc. (cf. 4:7–15; 5:4–10; 11:21–33;
13:4). Paul patiently displayed these "things that mark[ed]" his
apostolic authority. And this was accompanied by the signs,
wonders, and miracles he performed.

Let us also remember that Paul does not refer to the "signs"
of an apostle or to the miraculous phenomena that accompanied
his ministry as a way of differentiating himself from other, nonapostolic Christians, but from the false apostles who were leading the Corinthians astray (2 Cor. 11:14–15, 33). "In short," writes
Wayne Grudem, "the contrast is not between apostles who could
work miracles and ordinary Christians who could not, but
between genuine *Christian* apostles through whom the Holy
Spirit worked and *non-Christian* pretenders to the apostolic
office, through whom the Holy Spirit did not work at all."[24]

Nowhere does Paul suggest that signs and wonders were
exclusively or uniquely apostolic. My daughter takes dance
lessons and especially enjoys ballet. Although only seventeen
years old, she has incredibly strong and well-developed calf
muscles. Indeed, it might even be said that the "sign" of a ballet dancer is strong calf muscles. But I would never argue that
only ballet dancers display this physical characteristic. I simply
mean to say that when taken in conjunction with other factors,
her lower leg development helps you identify her as one who
dances on her toes. Likewise, Paul is not saying that signs, wonders, and miracles are performed only through apostles, but that
such phenomena, together with other evidences, should help the
Corinthians know that he is a true apostle of Jesus Christ.

Therefore, the fact that miraculous phenomena and certain
of the *charismata* served to attest and authenticate the message
of the gospel in no way proves that such activities are invalid for
the church subsequent to the death of the apostolic company.

(3) The third argument for cessationism pertains to the
alleged negative assessment many give to the nature, purpose,
and impact of signs, wonders, and miracles in the New Testament. I had been taught and believed that it was an indication

---

[24]Wayne Grudem, "Should Christians Expect Miracles Today? Objections and
Answers From the Bible," in *The Kingdom and the Power*, ed. Gary S. Greig and Kevin
N. Springer (Ventura, Calif.: Regal, 1993), 67.

of spiritual immaturity to seek signs, that it was a weak faith, born of theological ignorance, that prayed for healing or a demonstration of divine power. Some are even more pointed in their opinion. James Boice, in his contribution to the book *Power Religion*, quotes with approval the sentiment of John Wood-house, to the effect that "a desire for further signs and wonders is sinful and unbelieving."[25]

But consider Acts 4:29–31, which records this prayer of the church in Jerusalem:

> "Now, Lord, consider their threats and enable your ser-vants to speak your word with great boldness. Stretch out your hand to heal and perform miraculous signs and wonders through the name of your holy servant Jesus."
>
> After they prayed, the place where they were meet-ing was shaken. And they were all filled with the Holy Spirit and spoke the word of God boldly.

This text is important for at least two reasons: It shows that it is good to pray for signs and wonders and that it is not evil or a sign of emotional and mental imbalance to petition God for demonstrations of his power; it also shows that there is no nec-essary or inherent conflict between miracles and the message, between wonders and the word of the cross. Let me take each of these points in turn.

(a) It is good, helpful, and honoring to the Lord Jesus Christ to seek and pray for the demonstration of his power in healing, signs, and wonders. But what about Matthew 12:39 and 16:4? Did not Jesus denounce as wicked and adulterous those who "ask[ed] for" and "look[ed] for" signs (cf. 1 Cor. 1:22)? Yes, but note whom he was addressing and why he denounced them. These were *unbelieving* scribes and Pharisees, not children of God. Those who made such demands of Christ had no intention of following him. "Seeking signs from God is 'wicked and adul-terous' when the demand for more and more evidence comes from a resistant heart and simply covers up an unwillingness to believe."[26] Seeking signs as a pretext for criticizing Jesus or from

---

[25]James Montgomery Boice, "A Better Way: The Power of Word and Spirit," in *Power Religion*, ed. Michael Scott Horton (Chicago: Moody, 1992), 126.

[26]John Piper, "Signs and Wonders: Another View," *The Standard* (October 1991), 23.

a hankering to see the sensational is rightly rebuked. But that certainly was not the motivation of the early church, nor need it be ours. Perhaps an illustration will help:

> If we are carrying on a love affair with the world, and our husband, Jesus, after a long separation comes to us and says, "I love you and I want you back," one of the best ways to protect our adulterous relationship with the world is to say, "You're not really my husband; you don't really love me. Prove it. Give me some sign." If that's the way we demand a sign, we are a wicked and adulterous generation. But if we come to God with a heart aching with longing for vindication of his glory and the salvation of sinners, then we are not wicked and adulterous. We are a faithful wife, only wanting to honor our husband.[27]

Do you come to God insistent on a miracle, being prompted by an unbelieving heart that demands he put on a show before you will obey him? Or do you come humbly, in prayer, with a desire to glorify God in the display of his power, and with an equal desire to minister his mercy, compassion, and love to those in need? The former attitude God condemns; the latter he commends.

(b) The power of signs and wonders does not dilute the power of the gospel, nor is there any inherent inconsistency or unavoidable conflict between wonders and the word. Still, there are those who appeal to Romans 1:16 and 1 Corinthians 1:18, 22–23, texts that assert the centrality of the cross and the power of the gospel to save (theological truths to which all of us, I am sure, wholeheartedly subscribe). But the author of these passages is Paul, the same man who described his evangelistic ministry as one characterized "by the power of signs and miracles, through the power of the Spirit" (Rom. 15:19), the same man who wrote 1 Corinthians 12–14 and about whom most of Acts, with all its miraculous phenomena, is concerned. It is none other than Paul whose message and preaching came "not with wise and persuasive words, but with a demonstration of the Spirit's power" (2:4). And it was Paul who reminded the Thessalonians that the gospel did not come to them "simply with words, but also with power, with the Holy Spirit and with deep conviction" (1 Thess. 1:5).

---

[27]Ibid.

If there is an inherent inconsistency or conflict between miracles and the message, then why was God himself confirming "the message of his grace by enabling [the apostles] to do miraculous signs and wonders" (Acts 14:3)? *If signs and wonders dilute the word of God's grace, if signs and wonders detract from the centrality of the cross, if signs and wonders reflect a loss of confidence in the power of the gospel, then God cannot escape the charge of undermining his own activity.* If there is a conflict between wonders and the word, it is in *our* minds that the problem exists. It was not in Paul's mind, and it certainly is not in God's either.

Signs, wonders, and miraculous phenomena could not save a soul then, nor can they do so now. The power unto salvation is in the Holy Spirit working through the gospel of the cross of Christ. But such miraculous phenomena

> can, if God pleases, shatter the shell of disinterest; they can shatter the shell of cynicism; they can shatter the shell of false religion. Like every other good witness to the word of grace, they can help the fallen heart to fix its gaze on the gospel where the soul-saving, self-authenticating glory of the Lord shines.[28]

---

[28]Ibid. In his book *The Final Word: A Biblical Response to the Case for Tongues and Prophecy Today* (Carlisle: Banner of Truth, 1993), O. Palmer Robertson creates an unnecessary dichotomy between wonders and the word when he says that "a strong faith in the power of the gospel's truth will go much further toward the salvation of sinners than a reliance on the miraculously dazzling. The established pattern and the explicit teaching of Scripture is that the clear proclamation of the truth rather than the working of wonders is the most effective method for spreading the gospel" (83). As stated earlier, no one claims that miracles are more soteriologically effective than the message of the cross. But a comment such as Robertson's calls into question both the theology and wisdom of virtually every evangelist in the New Testament, including Jesus (John 5:36; 10:25, 37–38; 12:9–11; 14:11; 20:30–31), Philip (Acts 8:4–8), Peter (9:32–43), and Paul (Rom. 15:18–19). Whereas it would be wrong to suggest that evangelism unaccompanied by the miraculous is substandard, one cannot escape the close biblical interrelation between wonders and the word of the cross. See especially "Power Evangelism and the New Testament Evidence," in *The Kingdom and the Power*, ed. Gary S. Greig and Kevin Springer, 359–92; Wayne Grudem, *Power and Truth: A Response to the Critiques of Vineyard Teaching and Practice by D. A. Carson, James Montgomery Boice, and John H. Armstrong in "Power Religion"* (Anaheim: Association of Vineyard Churches, 1993), 19–28, 38–47.

We should note that if any generation was least in need of supernatural authentication, it was that of the early church. Yet they prayed earnestly for signs and wonders.

> This was the generation whose preaching (of Peter and Stephen and Philip and Paul) was more anointed than the preaching of any generation following. If any preaching was the power of God unto salvation and did not need accompanying signs and wonders, it was this preaching. Moreover, this was the generation with more immediate and compelling evidence of the truth of the resurrection than any generation since. Hundreds of eye-witnesses to the risen Lord were alive in Jerusalem. If any generation in the history of the church knew the power of preaching and the authentication of the gospel from first-hand evidence of the resurrection, it was this one. Yet it was they who prayed passionately for God to stretch forth His hand in signs and wonders.[29]

Others have argued that signs, wonders, and miracles breed a spirit of triumphalism inconsistent with the call to suffer for the sake of the gospel. Those who desire and pray for the miraculous, so goes the charge, do not take seriously the painful realities of living in a fallen world. Weakness, afflictions, persecution, and suffering are an inevitable part of living in the "not yet" of the kingdom. But when I read the New Testament, I see *no inherent conflict between signs and suffering*, and it *is* the New Testament, not the posturing or glitz of certain TV evangelists, that must be allowed to decide the issue. Paul certainly sensed no incompatibility between the two, for they were both characteristic of his life and ministry. As C. K. Barrett put it, "Miracles were no contradiction of the *theologia crucis* [Paul] proclaimed and practised, since they were performed not in a context of triumphant success and prosperity, but in the midst of the distress and vilification he was obliged to endure."[30]

John Piper has said, "Paul's 'thorn' [in the flesh] no doubt pressed deeper with every healing he performed."[31] Yet personal

---

[29]Piper, "Signs and Wonders," 23.

[30]C. K. Barrett, *A Commentary on the Second Epistle to the Corinthians* (New York: Harper & Row, 1973), 321.

[31]John Piper, "The Signs of the Apostle," *The Standard* (November 1991), 28.

trials and afflictions did not lead him to renounce the miraculous in his ministry. Nor did the supernatural displays of God's power lead him into a naive, "Pollyanna" outlook on the human condition. Again, if signs and suffering are incompatible, one must look somewhere other than in the Bible to prove it.

(4) A fourth argument for cessationism pertains to the closing, completion, and sufficiency of the canon of Scripture. Signs, wonders, and miraculous gifts accompanied and attested to the truth of the gospel until such time as the last word of canonical Scripture was written. The need for such manifestations of divine power, so it is claimed, then ceased. The Bible itself has replaced miraculous phenomena in the life of the church.

There are several problems with this argument. (a) The Bible itself never says any such thing. No biblical author ever claims that written Scripture has replaced or in some sense supplanted the reality of signs, wonders, and the like.

(b) Why would the presence of the completed canon preclude the need for miraculous phenomena? If signs, wonders, and the power of the Holy Spirit were essential in bearing witness to the truth of the gospel *then*, why not *now*? In other words, it seems reasonable to assume that the miracles that confirmed the gospel in the first century, wherever it was preached, would serve no less to confirm the gospel in subsequent centuries, even our own.

(c) If signs, wonders, and miracles were essential in the physical presence of the Son of God, how much more so now in his absence! Surely we are not prepared to suggest that the Bible, for all its glory, is sufficient to do what Jesus could not. Jesus thought it necessary to utilize the miraculous phenomena of the Holy Spirit to attest and confirm his own ministry. If it was essential for him, how much more for us. In other words, if the glorious presence of the Son of God himself did not preclude the need for miraculous phenomena, how can we suggest that our possession of the Bible does?

(5) Yet another argument surfaces from church history: "If the so-called miracle or sign gifts of the Holy Spirit are valid for Christians beyond the death of the apostles, why were they absent from church history until their alleged reappearance in the twentieth century?"

(a) To argue that all such gifts were nonexistent is to ignore a significant body of evidence. After studying the documentation for claims to the presence of these gifts, D. A. Carson concludes that "there is enough evidence that some form of 'charismatic' gifts continued sporadically across the centuries of church history that it is futile to insist on doctrinaire grounds that every report is spurious or the fruit of demonic activity or psychological aberration."[32]

(b) If the gifts were sporadic, there may be an explanation other than the theory that they were restricted to the first century. We must remember that prior to the Protestant Reformation in the sixteenth century, the average Christian did not have access to the Bible in his or her own language. Biblical ignorance was rampant. That is hardly the sort of atmosphere in which people would be aware of spiritual gifts (their name, nature, and function) and thus hardly the sort of atmosphere in which we would expect them to seek and pray for such phenomena or to recognize them were they to be manifest. If the gifts were sparse (a point, in itself, still up for debate), it could have been due as much to ignorance and the spiritual lethargy it breeds as to any theological principle that limits the gifts to the lifetime of the apostles.

(c) I think it entirely possible that numerous churches that advocated cessationism experienced these gifts but dismissed them as something less than the miraculous manifestation of the Holy Spirit. The ministry of Charles Spurgeon is a case in point. Consider the following account taken from his autobiography:

> While preaching in the hall, on one occasion, I deliberately pointed to a man in the midst of the crowd, and said, "There is a man sitting there, who is a shoemaker;

---

[32]Carson, *Showing the Spirit*, 166. Especially helpful in this regard is the series of articles by Richard Riss, "Tongues and Other Miraculous Gifts in the Second Through Nineteenth Centuries," *Basileia* (1985). See also Ronald Kydd, *Charismatic Gifts in the Early Church* (Peabody, Mass.: Hendrickson, 1984); Kilian McDonnell and George T. Montague, *Christian Initiation and Baptism in the Holy Spirit: Evidence from the First Eight Centuries* (Collegeville, Minn.: Liturgical Press, 1991); Cecil Robeck, *Prophecy in Carthage: Perpetua, Tertullian, and Cyprian* (Cleveland: Pilgrim Press, 1992); Stanley M. Burgess, "Proclaiming the Gospel With Miraculous Gifts in the Postbiblical Early Church," in *The Kingdom and the Power*, eds. Greig and Springer, 277–88; idem, *The Holy Spirit: Eastern Christian Traditions* (Peabody, Mass.: Hendrickson, 1989); idem, *The Spirit and the Church: Antiquity* (Peabody, Mass.: Hendrickson, 1984); Paul Thigpen, "Did the Power of the Spirit Ever Leave the Church?" *Charisma*, (September 1992), 20–29.

he keeps his shop open on Sundays, it was open last Sabbath morning, he took ninepence, and there was
fourpence profit out of it; his soul is sold to Satan for
fourpence!" A city missionary, when going his rounds,
met with this man, and seeing that he was reading one of
my sermons, he asked the question, "Do you know Mr.
Spurgeon?" "Yes," replied the man, "I have every reason
to know him, I have been to hear him; and, under his
preaching, by God's grace I have become a new creature
in Christ Jesus. Shall I tell you how it happened? I went
to the Music Hall, and took my seat in the middle of the
place; Mr. Spurgeon looked at me as if he knew me, and
in his sermon he pointed to me, and told the congregation that I was a shoemaker, and that I kept my shop
open on Sundays; and I did, sir. I should not have
minded that; but he also said that I took ninepence the
Sunday before, and that there was fourpence profit out
of it. I did take ninepence that day, and fourpence was
just the profit; but how he should know that, I could not
tell. Then it struck me that it was God who had spoken
to my soul through him, so I shut up my shop the next
Sunday. At first, I was afraid to go again to hear him, lest
he should tell the people more about me; but afterwards
I went, and the Lord met with me, and saved my soul.[33]

Spurgeon then adds this comment:

I could tell as many as a *dozen* similar cases in which
I pointed at somebody in the hall without having the
slightest knowledge of the person, or any idea that what
I said was right, except that I believed I was moved by the
Spirit to say it; and so striking has been my description,
that the persons have gone away, and said to their friends,
"Come, see a man that told me all things that ever I did;
beyond a doubt, he must have been sent of God to my
soul, or else he could not have described me so exactly."
And not only so, but I have known many instances in
which the thoughts of men have been revealed from the
pulpit. I have sometimes seen persons nudge their neigh-

---

[33]Charles H. Spurgeon, *The Autobiography of Charles H. Spurgeon* (London: Curts
& Jennings, 1899), 2:226–27.

bours with their elbow, because they had got a smart hit, and they have been heard to say, when they were going out, "The preacher told us just what we said to one another when we went in at the door."[34]

I believe that this is a not uncommon example of what the apostle Paul described in 1 Corinthians 14:24–25. Spurgeon exercised the gift of *prophecy* (or some might say the *word of knowledge*, 12:8), but he did not label it as such. Yet that does not alter the reality of what the Holy Spirit accomplished through him. If one were to examine Spurgeon's theology and ministry as well as recorded accounts of it by his contemporaries and subsequent biographers, most would conclude from the absence of explicit reference to miraculous *charismata* such as prophecy and the word of knowledge that these gifts had been withdrawn from church life. But Spurgeon's own testimony inadvertently says otherwise!

(d) If we concede that certain spiritual gifts were less prevalent than others in the history of the church, their absence may well be due to unbelief, apostasy, and other sins that serve only to quench and grieve the Holy Spirit. We should not be surprised at the infrequency of miraculous gifts in periods of church history marked by theological ignorance and personal immorality.

No one concludes from the corruption of soteriological truth in the first 1,400 years of church history that it was God's intention for the Holy Spirit to cease teaching and illuminating people concerning this vital doctrine. The same might be said of the concept of the priesthood of all believers. Why did Christians suffer from the absence of those experiential blessings that these critical verities might otherwise have brought to their church life? Those who believe in a pretribulational rapture must also explain the absence of their cherished doctrine from the collective knowledge of the church for almost 1,900 years!

Undoubtedly the response will be that none of this proves that God ceased to want his people to understand such doctrinal principles. Precisely! And the relative infrequency or absence of certain spiritual gifts during the same period of church history does not prove that God was opposed to their use or had

---

[34]Ibid., 227.

negated their validity for the remainder of the present age. *Both theological ignorance of certain biblical truths and a loss of experiential blessings provided by spiritual gifts can be, and should be, attributed to factors other than the suggestion that God intended such knowledge and power only for believers in the early church.*

(e) Finally, what has or has not occurred in church history is not the ultimate standard by which to judge what *we* should pursue, pray for, and expect in the life of our churches today. The final criterion for deciding whether God wants to bestow certain spiritual gifts on his people today is his Word. It is unwise to cite the alleged absence of a particular experience in the life of an admired saint from the church's past as reason for doubting its present validity. Neither the failure nor the success of Christians in days past is the ultimate standard by which we determine what God wants for us today. We can learn from their mistakes as well as their achievements. The only question of ultimate relevance for us and for this issue is: "What saith the Scripture?"

(6) There is one more reason why I remained for years committed to the doctrine of cessationism. This one is not based on any particular text or theological principle; yet it exercised no less an influence on my life and thinking than did the other five. In mentioning this fact, I am in no way suggesting that others are guilty of this error. This is not an accusation; it is a confession. I am talking about *fear*: the fear of emotionalism, the fear of fanaticism, the fear of the unfamiliar, the fear of rejection by those whose respect I cherished and whose friendship I did not want to forfeit, the fear of what might occur were I fully to relinquish control of my life and mind and emotions to the Holy Spirit, the fear of losing what little status in the evangelical community that I had worked so hard to attain.

I am talking about the kind of fear that energized a personal agenda to distance myself from anything that had the potential to link me with people I believed were an embarrassment to the cause of Christ. I was faithful to the eleventh commandment of Bible-church evangelicalism: *"Thou shalt not do at all what others do poorly."* In my pride I had allowed certain extremists to exercise more of an influence on the shape of my ministry than I did the text of Scripture. Fear of being labeled or linked or in some way associated with the "unlearned" and "unattractive" elements in contemporary Christendom exercised an insidious power on my ability and willingness to be objective in the reading of Holy Scripture. I am not so naive as to think that my understanding of Scripture is now free from subjective influences! But I am confident that at least fear, in this form, no longer plays a part.

In conclusion, I believe all the gifts of the Holy Spirit are valid for the contemporary church for these reasons. (1) The Bible gives no evidence indicating they are *not* valid. Such was the principal focus of what has preceded. This is not, however, a mere argument from silence, because the New Testament is *anything but silent* concerning the *presence* of these gifts in the church. Beginning with Pentecost and continuing throughout the book of Acts, whenever the Spirit was poured out on new believers, they experienced the manifestation of his *charismata*. There is nothing to indicate this phenomenon was restricted to them and then. Rather, it appears to be both widespread and common in the New Testament church. Christians in Rome (Rom. 12), Corinth (1 Cor. 12–14), Samaria (Acts 8), Caesarea (Acts 10), Ephesus (Acts 19), Thessalonica (1 Thess. 5), and Galatia (Gal. 3) all experienced the miraculous and revelatory gifts. It is difficult to imagine how the New Testament authors could have said any more clearly than *this* what new covenant Christianity was supposed to look like. In other words, the burden of proof rests with cessationists. If certain gifts of a special class have ceased, the responsibility is theirs to prove it.

(2) The ultimate purpose of each gift is to build up the body of Christ (1 Cor. 12:7; 14:3, 26). Nothing that I read in the New Testament or see in the condition of the church in any age, past or present, leads me to believe we have progressed beyond the need for edification and therefore beyond the need for the contribution of the *charismata*. I freely admit that spiritual gifts were essential for the birth of the church, but why should they be any less important or needful for its continued growth and maturation?

(3) Three texts come to mind. First Corinthians 1:4–9 implies that the gifts of the Spirit are operative until "our Lord Jesus Christ [is] revealed" (v. 7). Ephesians 4:11–13 explicitly dates the duration of the gifts: They are required "until we all reach the unity in the faith and in the knowledge of the Son of God and become mature, attaining to the whole measure of the fullness of Christ" (v. 13). The end or goal for which the gifts are

bestowed is that level of spiritual and moral maturity that the individual Christian and the church corporately will attain only at the end of the present age. And despite the controversy that still surrounds it, I remain convinced that 1 Corinthians 13:8–13 dates the cessation of the *charismata* at the perfection of the eternal state, consequent upon Christ's return.

(4) I believe that these gifts have been designed by God to characterize the life of the church *today* for much the same reason I believe in church discipline for today, in rule by a plurality of elders for today, in the observance of the Lord's Supper for today, and in a host of other biblical practices and patterns explicitly ordained in the New Testament and nowhere explicitly designated as temporary or restricted to the first century.

(5) I do not believe the Holy Spirit simply inaugurates the new age and then disappears. He, together with his gifts and fruit, *characterizes* the new age. As D. A. Carson has said, "the coming of the Spirit is not associated merely with the *dawning* of the new age but with its *presence*, not merely with Pentecost but with the entire period from Pentecost to the return of Jesus the Messiah."[35]

C. SPECIFIC GIFTS AND CHURCH LIFE

I now want to move beyond gifts in general to three in particular and use them as a case in point of how they are to function in the church. For years now the focus of debate between cessationists and charismatics has most often been on the gifts of prophecy, tongues, and healing. If these are indeed gifts for today, as I have argued, how should they function in the life of the individual believer and in the congregation as a whole?[36]

---

[35]Carson, *Showing the Spirit*, 155. See also Max Turner, "Spiritual Gifts Then and Now," *VoxEv* 15 (1985): 7–64 (esp. 39–41).

[36]I emphasize these three gifts only because they are central to the ongoing debate. Contrary to widespread perception, neither the Vineyard, of which I am a part, nor others who identify themselves with what has been called the Third Wave focus on prophecy, tongues, and healing to the exclusion of other *charismata*. Helps, administration, service, teaching, giving, exhorting, and showing mercy, among others, are no less essential to the proper functioning of the local church. An excellent treatment of the distinctives of the Third Wave is provided by Rich Nathan and Ken Wilson in their book, *Empowered Evangelicals: Bringing Together the Best of the Evangelical and Charismatic Worlds* (Ann Arbor: Servant, 1995).

1. The Gift of Prophecy

A few comments are in order concerning the gift of prophecy, its place in the church, and whether it has a primary role in providing subjective guidance to the believer in the routine decisions of life. I want to begin with several basic observations concerning this gift.[37]

Prophecy is always rooted in revelation (1 Cor. 14:30). It is not based on a hunch, a supposition, an inference, an educated guess, or even on sanctified wisdom. Prophecy is not based on personal insight, intuition, or illumination. Prophecy is the human *report* of a divine *revelation*. It is this that distinguishes prophecy from teaching. Teaching is always based on an inscripturated text; prophecy is always based on a spontaneous revelation.

However, although rooted in revelation, prophecy is occasionally fallible. This sounds contradictory and poses the greatest obstacle to the acceptance of the prophetic gift in the church today. "How can God reveal something that contains error? How can God, who is *infallible*, reveal something that is *fallible*?" The answer is simple: He cannot. He does not.

The key is in recognizing that with every prophecy there are four elements, only one of which is assuredly of God: There is the *revelation* itself; there is the *perception* or *reception* of that revelation by the believer; there is the *interpretation* of what has been disclosed or the attempt to ascertain its meaning; and there is the *application* of that interpretation. God is alone responsible for the revelation. Whatever he discloses to the human mind is altogether free from error. It is as infallible as he is. It contains no falsehoods; it is wholly true in all its parts. Indeed, the revelation, which is the root of every genuine prophetic utterance, is as inerrant and infallible as the written Word of God itself (the Bible). In terms of the *revelation* alone, the New Testament prophetic gift does not differ from the Old Testament prophetic gift.

---

[37]Helpful discussions of the prophetic gift may be found in Wayne Grudem, *The Gift of Prophecy in the New Testament and Today* (Westchester: Crossway, 1988); Graham Houston, *Prophecy: A Gift for Today?* (Downers Grove, Ill.: InterVarsity, 1989); Bruce Yocum, *Prophecy* (Ann Arbor: Servant, 1976); David Pytches, *Prophecy in the Local Church* (London: Hodder & Stoughton, 1993). For a survey of the variety of perspectives among noncessationists, see Mark J. Cartledge, "Charismatic Prophecy: A Definition and Description," *JPT* 5 (1994): 79–120.

Error enters in when the human recipient of a revelation *mis*perceives, *mis*interprets and/or *mis*applies what God has disclosed. The fact that God has *spoken* perfectly does not mean that human beings have *heard* perfectly. They *may* interpret and apply, without error, what God has revealed. But the mere existence of a divine revelation does not in itself guarantee that the interpretation or application of God's revealed truth will share in its perfection.

This may be the case in Acts 21, where the Holy Spirit evidently revealed to some disciples at Tyre that Paul would suffer should he go to Jerusalem. Their misguided but sincere application of this revelation was to tell Paul ("through the Spirit," v. 4) not to go, counsel that he directly disobeyed (cf. 20:22). I should also briefly mention the oft-argued case of Agabus and his prophecy concerning the manner of Paul's arrest (21:11), two elements of which proved inaccurate (it was the Romans who bound Paul, not the Jews [21:33; 22:29]; and far from the Jews delivering Paul into the hands of the Gentiles, he had to be forcibly rescued from them [21:31–36]). Those who insist that the New Testament gift is no less infallible than its Old Testament counterpart are faced with accounting for this mixture of truth and error. To this point I have only heard that we noncessationists are being "overly pedantic"[38] or are guilty of "precisionism."[39] Yet it appears that the strict standards applied under the Old Testament are now conveniently stretched in the New Testament under the pressure of a passage that does not fit the cessationist theory. Might it not rather be that New Testament

[38]Gaffin, *Perspectives*, 66.

[39]Robertson, *The Final Word*, 114. Brian Rapske (*The Book of Acts and Paul in Roman Custody*, vol. 3 of The Book of Acts in Its First Century Setting [Grand Rapids: Eerdmans, 1994], 409–10) asks us to believe that the arrest report in Acts 21:27–33 is condensed, the purported fuller version of which would have included those details pertaining to the manner in which Paul fell into Roman hands. But is it wise to base one's view by conjecturing what Luke did *not* say? Surely Luke was aware of the discrepancy in his written report between the prophecy and its "fulfillment." Are we to believe that he could easily have eliminated this confusion but declined to do so? Also, the suggestion that 28:17 refers to the fulfillment of Agabus's prophecy fails to note that Paul is describing his transfer "out of" (*ek*) Jerusalem into the Roman judicial system at Caesarea (23:12–35), not the events associated with the mob scene in 21:27–36.

prophecy is occasionally fallible and therefore has to be carefully judged (1 Cor. 14:29; 1 Thess. 5:19–22)?

Although New Testament prophecy does not carry intrinsic divine authority, it is eminently profitable and to be prized (1 Cor. 14:1, 39; 1 Thess. 5:20). To many people, the fact that New Testament prophetic utterances do not possess the same intrinsic divine authority as do Old Testament prophecy and holy Scripture renders the former insignificant and unedifying. The answer to this is found in comparing the gift of prophecy with the gift of teaching.

When people exercise the spiritual gift of teaching, their ministry is rooted in a divine revelation (the Bible) and is sustained by the Holy Spirit. All admit that such teaching edifies the church, *even though what the teacher says is occasionally wrong or tainted with error*. What the teacher says has divine authority only in a secondary, derivative sense. Teaching has no intrinsic divine authority; only the Bible does. As with the gift of prophecy, there is in all teaching the revelation (the biblical text), the interpretation, and the application. Only the revelation is infallible. The teacher may misinterpret or misapply the infallible and error-free Word of God. But we do not dismiss the spiritual gift of teaching simply because the teacher occasionally (or even frequently) communicates error.

Prophecy, no less than teaching, is prompted by the Spirit and based on a revelation from God. In some way beyond ordinary sense perception, God *reveals* something to the mind of the prophet not found in Scripture (but never contrary to Scripture). Since God never makes a mistake, we know that this revelation is true and free from error. But the gift of prophecy does not guarantee the infallible *transmission* of that revelation. The prophet may *perceive* the revelation imperfectly, he may *understand* it imperfectly, and consequently he may *deliver* it imperfectly. That is why Paul says we see in a mirror dimly (1 Cor. 13:12). The gift of prophecy may result in *fallible* prophecy, just as the gift of teaching may result in *fallible* teaching. Therefore, if teaching (a gift prone to fallibility) can edify and build up the church, why cannot prophecy be good for edifying as well (see 1 Cor. 14:3, 12, 26)—even though both gifts suffer from human imperfection and stand in need of testing?

The accuracy of any prophetic utterance will vary in proportion to the intensity of the gift and the faith of the one speaking. In Romans 12:6 (one is to prophesy "in proportion to his faith"), Paul seems to be saying that "some who had the gift of prophecy had a greater measure of faith (that is, a trust or confidence that the Holy Spirit would work or was working in them to bring a revelation which would be the basis of a prophecy)."[40] In other words, there will always be greater and lesser degrees of prophetic ability and consequently greater and lesser degrees of prophetic accuracy (which, it seems reasonable to assume, may increase or decrease, depending on the circumstances of that person's life). Thus, the prophet is to speak in proportion to the confidence and assurance he or she has that what is spoken is truly from God. Prophets are not to speak beyond what God has revealed; they must be careful never to speak on their own authority or from their own resources.

The principal content of most prophetic utterances is defined by the effects they produce. Prophetic utterances may *edify*, *exhort*, and *console* (1 Cor. 14:3). They may bring *conviction* as the secrets of the sinner's heart are *exposed* (14:24–25). They may *teach* (14:31). They may on occasion give *direction for ministry* (Acts 13:1–3), contain *warnings* (21:4, 10–14), or present *opportunities*. They may even *identify and impart spiritual gifts* (1 Tim. 4:14).

All prophetic ministry should be subject to the oversight and direction of pastoral leadership. Frequently, a prophetically gifted person will receive revelation with such pristine clarity and spiritual power that his or her passion to prophesy overrides the call to patience. A prophet may be tempted to conclude that the supernatural dynamic of the revelatory experience, in which he or she hears the unmediated voice of God, is for that

---

[40]Wayne Grudem, *The Gift of Prophecy in the New Testament and Today*, 208. See also David Hill, *New Testament Prophecy* (Atlanta: John Knox, 1979), 119; James D. G. Dunn, *Jesus and the Spirit* (Philadelphia: Westminster, 1975), 211–12. A case can be made for interpreting *he pistis* ("the faith") as those objective truths embodied in the gospel tradition. Thomas Gillespie (*The First Theologians: A Study in Early Christian Prophecy* [Grand Rapids: Eerdmans, 1994]) appeals to three other Pauline texts in which he believes *pistis* with the definite article points to the content of faith (although Rom. 10:8 is questionable). He concludes that "together Galatians 1:23, Romans 10:8, and Philippians 1:27 suggest that when Paul uses *he pistis* to denote the content of Christian belief, he has in mind the substance and structure of the gospel. This means that in Romans 12:6b prophecy is (1) drawn into the orbit of gospel proclamation, and (2) subjected to the standard provided by the content of this message" (61). However, if this were Paul's meaning, it would be an exceptionally rare usage of *pistis*.

reason exempt from the otherwise important biblical guidelines for communication and ministry in the body of Christ. This belief is a prescription for disaster.

Related to this principle is the fact that in no New Testament text are prophets portrayed as bearing ecclesiastical authority. Church leadership is the responsibility of the elders. The New Testament never says, "Be subject to the prophets"; rather, "Be subject to your elders" (1 Peter 5:5, NASB; cf. Heb. 13:17). Paul did not go from city to city to ordain or appoint prophets, but elders (Acts 14:23; 20:17; 1 Tim. 5:17; Titus 1:5; cf. 1 Peter 5:2). Whereas it is good that some elders/pastors be prophetically gifted, such is not a qualification for office. Elders are to be "able to *teach*" (1 Tim. 3:2), not able to prophesy.

Finally, one should avoid looking to or depending on the gift of prophecy for making routine daily decisions in life.[41] God does not intend for the gift of prophecy to be used as the *usual* way we make decisions regarding his will. How does the apostle Paul envision himself and us making decisions regarding God's will? Consider the following declarations by Paul: "But I *think it necessary* [i.e., I have *reckoned*] to send back to you Epaphroditus" (Phil. 2:25). Paul did not appeal to a revelation from God but *reckoned* with the situation, its circumstances, the principles of Scripture, the needs of both Epaphroditus and the Philippian believers, and so on, and made his decision.

Or again, Paul writes: "I say this to shame you. Is it possible that there is nobody among you *wise enough to judge a dispute* between believers?" (1 Cor. 6:5). To the Corinthians, among whom there was no shortage of prophetically gifted people, Paul gives this advice: Find someone with *sanctified wisdom* who can settle your disputes.

Concerning his travel plans, Paul writes, "If it *seems advisable* for me to go also, they will accompany me" (1 Cor. 16:4). It is not prophetic revelation that Paul anticipates will inform his decision but a sober evaluation of what is *fitting* or *advisable* in view of the circumstances and what he feels would please God.[42]

---

[41]I am indebted to John Piper for these observations on prophecy and guidance. All italics in the biblical texts quoted in the next few paragraphs have been added.

[42]This is not to say, however, that Paul was never guided in his travels by divine revelation (see Acts 16:6–10), nor is it to say that God would never do so with us.

And consider also these words of counsel from the apostle: "And this is my prayer: that your love may abound more and more in *knowledge and depth of insight,* so that you may *be able to discern what is best*" (Phil. 1:9–10a). "We have not stopped praying for you and asking God to fill you with the *knowledge of his will through all spiritual wisdom and understanding*" (Col. 1:9). If we want to know God's will, we need to be filled with spiritual wisdom and understanding. Finally, "Do not conform any longer to the pattern of this world, but be transformed by *the renewing of your mind. Then you will be able to test and approve what God's will is*—his good, pleasing and perfect will" (Rom. 12:2). Paul envisioned *proving* the will of God by the use of our minds to examine, verify, and embrace what he wants.

2. Gifts of Healings

The above title reflects the fact that both words are plural and lack the definite article in Greek (*charismata iamaton*).[43] Evidently Paul did not envision that a person would be endowed with one healing gift operative at all times for all diseases. His language suggests either many different gifts or powers of healing, each appropriate to and effective for its related illness, or each occurrence of healing constituting a distinct gift in its own right.

One of the principal obstacles to a proper understanding of healing is the erroneous assumption that *if anyone could ever heal, he could always heal.* But in view of the lingering illness of Epaphroditus (Phil. 2:25–30), Timothy (1 Tim. 5:23), Trophimus (2 Tim. 4:20), and perhaps Paul himself (2 Cor. 12:7–10; Gal. 4:13), it is better to view this gift as subject to the will of God, not the will of humankind. A person may be gifted to heal many people, but not all. Another may be gifted to heal only one person at one particular time of one particular disease. When asked to pray for the sick, people are often heard to respond: "I can't. I don't have the gift of healing." But if my reading of Paul is cor-

---

[43]Although I rejected cessationism before writing *Healing and Holiness* (Phillipsburg, N.J.: Presbyterian and Reformed, 1990), the regrettable effect of that volume was to discourage people from praying for healing with any degree of expectancy. Whereas I stand by much of what I wrote in that book, I am no longer comfortable recommending it to those interested in this subject. My views today are better represented in Jack Deere's book, *Surprised by the Power of the Spirit.*

rect, the Spirit may sovereignly distribute a *charisma* of healing for that one occasion, even though previous prayers for physical restoration under similar circumstances were not answered. "Gifts of healings," therefore, are occasional and subject to the purposes of God.

There may well be a close connection between gifts of healings and the gift of faith that immediately precedes it in Paul's list of the *charismata*. The *gift* of faith does not refer to the faith of justification (which all Christians have) or to that ongoing trust that serves as the basis for our daily relationship to God. Rather, this is a special faith that "enables a believer to trust God to bring about certain things for which he or she cannot claim some divine promise recorded in Scripture, or some state of affairs grounded in the very structure of the gospel."[44] In other words, it is the "God-given ability, without fakery or platitudinous exhortations, to believe what you do not really believe, to trust God for a certain blessing *not* promised in Scripture."[45] The gift of faith is that mysterious surge of confidence that rises within a person in a particular situation of need or challenge and that gives an extraordinary certainty and assurance that God is about to act through a word or an action.

A personal example will help illustrate what I am saying. One Sunday a couple came to me before the service and asked the elders of our church to anoint their infant son and pray for his healing. After the service we gathered in the back room and I anointed him with oil. I do not recall the precise medical name for his condition, but at six months of age he had a serious liver disorder that would require immediate surgery, possibly even a transplant, if something did not change. As we prayed, something unusual happened. As we laid hands on this young child and prayed, I found myself suddenly filled with an overwhelming and inescapable confidence that he would be healed. It was altogether unexpected. I recall actually trying to doubt, but could not. I prayed confidently, filled with a faith unshakable and undeniable. I said to myself, "Lord, you really are going to heal him." Although the family left the room unsure, I was absolutely *certain* God had healed him. The next morning the

---

[44]Carson, *Showing the Spirit*, 39.
[45]Ibid.

doctor agreed. He was totally healed and is a healthy, happy young boy today.

Perhaps, then, "the prayer of faith" to which James (James 5:15) refers is not just any prayer that may be prayed at will, but a uniquely and divinely motivated prayer prompted by the Spirit-wrought conviction that God intends to heal the one for whom prayer is being offered. The faith necessary for healing is itself a gift of God, sovereignly bestowed when he wills. When God chooses to heal, he produces in the hearts of those praying the faith or confidence that such is precisely his intent. The particular kind of faith to which James refers, in response to which God heals, is not the kind that we may exercise at our will. It is the kind of faith that we exercise only when God wills. Thus there is no reason to think that had I prayed for another afflicted infant boy that day, he would necessarily have been healed. The fact that I received a gift for healing on this one occasion is no guarantee that I may pray with equal success on some other occasion.

Many in the church today say they believe that God still heals, but live as functional deists who rarely, if ever, actually lay hands on the sick and pray with any degree of expectancy. Jesus laid his hands on the sick (Luke 4:40), as did the early church (Acts 9:17; 28:7–8; cf. Mark 16:18)—and so should we.

People often confuse praying *expectantly* with praying *presumptuously*. Prayer is *presumptuous* when the person *claims* healing without revelatory warrant[46] or on the unbiblical assumption that God *always* wills to heal. This, then, requires one to account for the absence of healing by an appeal either to moral failure or deficiency of faith (usually in the one for whom prayer is offered). On the other hand, people pray *expectantly* when they humbly petition a merciful God for something they do not deserve but know that he delights to give (Luke 11:9–13; cf. Matt. 9:27–31; 20:29–34; Luke 17:13–14). Expectant prayer flows from the recognition that Jesus healed people because he loved them and felt compassion for them (Matt. 14:13–14; 20:34; Mark 1:41–42; Luke 7:11–17), a disposition that nothing in Scripture indicates has changed. In other words,

---

[46]By "revelatory warrant" I mean either an explicit biblical assertion that provides objective assurance for an impending healing or revelatory insight via a word of knowledge (cf. Acts 14:8–10), prophecy, or through a dream or vision.

if the Lord healed in the first century because he was motivated by his compassion and mercy for the hurting, why would we think he has withdrawn that compassion after the death of the apostles? Why would we think he no longer feels compassion when he sees lepers or those dying from AIDS? Why would we think he is now content to demonstrate that compassion only by giving grace to endure the suffering rather than grace to heal the condition? If Jesus and the apostles healed in the first century to bring glory to God, why would we think God has discarded a major New Testament instrument for bringing glory to himself and his Son?[47]

3. The Gift of Tongues

a. The Purpose of Praying in the Spirit

First of all, speaking in tongues is a form of *prayer*. In 1 Corinthians 14:2 Paul says that speaking in tongues is speaking "to God" (see also v. 28). Again, in verses 14–15 he explicitly refers to "praying" in tongues or "praying" with (by) his spirit. Therefore, speaking in tongues is a means of communicating with God in supplication, petition, and intercession. According to 1 Corinthians 14:16, prayer in tongues is a perfectly legitimate way in which to express heartfelt gratitude to God. There is nothing in Scripture to indicate that people who speak in tongues lose self-control, become unaware of their surroundings, or lapse into a frenzied condition in which self-consciousness and the power for rational thinking are eclipsed. The person speaking in tongues can start and stop at will (1 Cor. 14:15–19, 27–28; cf. 14:32). There is a vast difference between an experience being "ecstatic" and being "emotional." Speaking in tongues is often (but not always) highly emotional, bringing peace and joy, but that does not mean it is ecstatic.

Speaking in tongues is also a means for *edifying* oneself (1 Cor. 14:4), which contrary to what some say, is not a bad thing.

---

[47]Deere, *Surprised by the Power of the Spirit*, 131. See also John Wimber, *Power Healing* (San Francisco: Harper & Row, 1987); David C. Lewis, *Healing: Fiction, Fantasy or Fact?* (London: Hodder & Stoughton, 1989); John Christopher Thomas, "The Devil, Disease and Deliverance: James 5:14–16," *JPT* 2 (1993): 25–50.

We study the Bible to edify ourselves. We pray to edify ourselves. Countless Christian activities are effective means of self-edification. And in Jude 20 we are commanded to edify ourselves by praying in the Spirit!

Every gift of the Spirit in some way or other edifies its user. This is not evil unless self-edification becomes an end in itself. If I am edified by my gift in such a way that I become more mature, sensitive, understanding, zealous, and holy, and thus better equipped to minister to others (1 Cor. 12:7), why should anyone complain? The fact that the ultimate purpose of gifts is the common good does not preclude other, secondary effects of each manifestation. Furthermore, self-edification from speaking in tongues cannot be wrong, or Paul would not have encouraged its use in 1 Corinthians 14:5a. And it *is* uninterpreted tongues that he has in mind, for he contrasts it with prophecy, insisting that the latter is better suited to edify others (unless, of course, the speaking in tongues is interpreted, v. 5b).[48]

Although one may wonder how something not understood even by the speaker can edify, the answer in part lies in 1 Corinthians 14:14–15 (also Rom. 8:26). As Gordon Fee has said,

> contrary to the opinion of many, spiritual edification can take place in ways other than through the cortex of the brain. Paul believed in an immediate communing with God by means of the S/spirit that sometimes bypassed the mind; and in vv. 14–15 he argues that for his own edification he will have both.[49]

---

[48]See Frank D. Macchia, "Sighs Too Deep for Words: Toward a Theology of Glossolalia," *JPT* 1 (1992): 66–67.

[49]Gordon D. Fee, *The First Epistle to the Corinthians* (Grand Rapids: Eerdmans, 1987), 657. Robertson (*The Final Word*) refuses to concede that someone can be edified apart from rational understanding. He therefore insists that God not only enables a person to speak in a language not previously learned, but also enables him to understand what he is speaking (contrary to 1 Cor. 14:14). But why, then, would there be a need for the distinct gift of interpretation? Each person speaking in tongues would already know what he is saying and could in turn communicate such to the congregation. Why forbid a person to speak in tongues in the absence of an interpreter (vv. 27–28) if every tongues-speaker is his *own* interpreter? And if the tongues-speaker can understand what he is saying, why encourage him to pray that he might interpret (v. 13)? It will not do for Robertson to say that the one gifted with interpretation has an exactness which goes "beyond the understanding of the sense

Speaking in tongues is a form of *blessing* the person and works of God (1 Cor. 14:16). Hence, such speech is a form of *praise* (esp. "singing in the Spirit"). There is no evidence that the speaking in tongues in Acts 2 (or elsewhere) served an evangelistic purpose. According to Acts 2:11, the content of the speech was "the wonders of God" (see the same phrase in 10:46; 19:17). The assembled people do not hear evangelism; they hear praise!—and it does not generate conversion but confusion. It is Peter's *preaching* that brings salvation.

I believe that praying in tongues may also be a way of conducting spiritual warfare. Paul describes tongues in 1 Corinthians 14:16 as praying or blessing "in (the) spirit" (*en pneumati*). In Ephesians 6:18 he encourages us to pray "in the Spirit" (*en pneumati*), using the same terminology. Thus, Paul's exhortation here that addresses our struggle with principalities and powers, although not limited to praying in tongues, most likely includes it. Finally, speaking in tongues is a way of compensating for our weakness and ignorance in praying for ourselves and others (cf. Rom. 8:26–27; this is true even if this text is determined not to refer to glossolalia).

b. The Place of Praying in the Spirit

I have already pointed to 1 Corinthians 14:14–19 as evidence that praying in tongues was a staple experience in Paul's private devotional life. This is confirmed by verse 28, where he gives instruction on what to do in the absence of an interpreter: "The speaker should ... speak to himself and to God." Where? Given the explicit prohibition of uninterpreted glossalalia "in the church," it seems likely Paul had in mind prayer in tongues in private, that is, in a context other than the corporate gathering.

Palmer Robertson disagrees and argues that Paul is instructing the tongues-speaker to pray silently to himself and to God while yet in the church gathering. But even if this is true

---

of the revelation possessed by the tongues-speaker" (33), because he believes that anytime God reveals truth to the human mind there is an a priori guarantee that *both* the *reception* of what is revealed and its *transmission* are perfectly accurate. In other words, for Robertson *all* revelation comes with a guarantee of perfection and divine exactness in both comprehension and communication.

(which I doubt), we would then have apostolic endorsement of *private* glossalalia. If, as Robertson contends, all speaking in tongues is revelatory and is designed only for rational communication, Paul's counsel makes no sense. Why would God impart infallible, revelatory knowledge only for the recipient to speak it to himself and back to God? Robertson envisions the tongues-speaker waiting patiently until an interpreter arrives, at which time he can then speak audibly. But this is reading into the text a scenario conspicuous by its absence. Paul's instruction is for a situation in which there is *no* interpreter; he says nothing about the tongues-speaker waiting until an interpreter is present.

Furthermore, is it consistent with Paul's emphasis in 1 Corinthians 14 on everyone working together for mutual edification that he would recommend that some (perhaps many) focus their spiritual energy inwardly (praying in tongues) while someone else is speaking outwardly, ostensibly to edify the very people who on Paul's advice are not paying attention?

c. Are Tongues a Sign?

According to 1 Corinthians 14:22, "tongues . . . are a sign." This follows Paul's quotation of Isaiah 28:11, the meaning of which is to be found in a prior warning of God to Israel in Deuteronomy 28:49. If Israel violated the covenant, God would chastise them by sending a foreign enemy, speaking a foreign tongue. Thus confusing and confounding speech was a sign of God's judgment against a rebellious people. This was the judgment that Isaiah said had come on Israel in the eighth century B.C., when the Assyrians invaded and conquered the northern kingdom (cf. also what happened in the sixth century B.C., Jer. 5:15).

Many cessationists argue that God was judging unbelieving Jews in the first century, the sign of which was language they could not understand (i.e., tongues). The purpose of tongues, therefore, was to signify God's judgment against Israel for rejecting the Messiah and thereby to shock them into repentance and faith. Tongues, so goes the argument, was an evangelistic sign gift. Since tongues ceased to function in this capacity when Israel was dispersed in A.D. 70, the gift was valid only for the first century.

There are numerous problems with this view. Even if tongues served as an evangelistic sign gift, nowhere in the New

Testament is it restricted or reduced to this one purpose. Tongues also serves the "common good" of the body of Christ (1 Cor. 12:7). In 14:4 tongues are said to edify the individual in private prayer. We must avoid the error of reductionism.

Furthermore, if tongues was not a spiritual gift *for the church,* why did Paul allow it to be exercised and used in the church at all? Yet he did; if interpreted, speaking in tongues was entirely permissible. But this seems difficult to explain if its only or even primary purpose was to declare judgment against unbelieving Jews. Also note that if uninterpreted tongues was designed for unbelievers, to stir them to repentance, it would not be necessary for God to provide the accompanying gift of interpretation. This latter gift makes sense only if speaking in tongues is profitable and beneficial to Christians in the assembly.

Moreover, if God intended tongues to serve as a sign for unbelieving Jews, Paul would not have counseled *against* its use when unbelievers were present (1 Cor. 14:23). And finally, the contrast in this context is between believer and unbeliever, not Jew and Gentile. Indeed, most commentators concur that the unbeliever (vv. 23–24) is probably a Gentile, not a Jew.

We may thus conclude that the view that says tongues is only (or even primarily) a sign of judgment on first-century unbelieving Jews is unconvincing. What, then, is the principle that Paul finds in Isaiah 28:11 that applies to Corinth (and to us)? It is this: When God speaks to people in a language they cannot understand, it is a form of punishment for unbelief. It signifies his anger. Incomprehensible speech will not guide, instruct, or lead to faith and repentance, but will only confuse and destroy. Thus, if outsiders or unbelievers come in and believers speak in a language they cannot understand, believers will simply drive them away. They are giving a "sign" to unbelievers that is entirely wrong, because their hardness of heart has not reached the point where they deserve that severe sign of judgment. So when believers come together (1 Cor. 14:26), if anyone speaks in a tongue, someone must interpret (v. 27). Otherwise the tongue-speaker should be quiet in the church (v. 29). Prophecy, on the other hand, is a sign of God's presence with believers (v. 22b), and so Paul encourages its use when unbelievers are present in order that they may see this sign and thereby come to Christian faith (vv. 24–25).

Therefore, Paul is *not* talking about the function of the gift of tongues in general, but only about the *negative* result of one particular *abuse* of tongues (namely, its use without interpretation in the public assembly). So uninterpreted speaking in tongues should not be permitted in church, for in doing so believers run the risk of communicating a negative sign to others that will only drive them away.

I should also mention the argument that speaking in tongues is explicitly mentioned in no New Testament letter aside from 1 Corinthians. The conclusion is then made that the gift of tongues was either infrequent or "on its way out." But the Lord's Supper is explicitly mentioned in the letters only in 1 Corinthians. Surely no one would conclude that it was infrequently observed or obsolete. And the silence of other New Testament letters can just as easily (and more sensibly) be explained as due to the fact that, unlike Corinth, tongues was not a problem in those other churches to whom Paul wrote and ministered.

d. Are Tongues Always Human Languages?

Acts 2 is the only text in the New Testament where speaking in tongues is explicitly said to consist of foreign languages not previously known by the speaker. But there is no reason to think Acts 2, rather than, say, 1 Corinthians 14, is the standard by which all occurrences of this phenomenon must be judged. Other factors suggest tongues could also be heavenly or angelic speech.

First of all, if tongues is always a foreign language intended as a sign for unbelievers, why are the tongues in Acts 10 and 19 spoken in the presence of only believers? Note also that Paul describes "different kinds of tongues" in 1 Corinthians 12:10. It is unlikely he means a variety of different human languages, for who would ever have argued that all tongues were only one human language, such as Greek or Hebrew or German? His words suggest that there are differing categories of glossalalia, perhaps at minimum human languages and heavenly languages.

We read in 1 Corinthians 14:2 that whoever speaks in a tongue "does not speak to men but to God." But if tongues are always human languages, Paul is in error, for "speaking to men" is precisely what human language does! Moreover, he says that when one speaks in a tongue "no one understands." But if tongues is always human language, many would understand, as they did on the day of Pentecost (Acts 2:8–11). This would especially be true in Corinth, a multilingual cosmopolitan port city that was frequented by people of numerous dialects.

If tongues is always human language, then the gift of interpretation would be one for which no special work or enablement or manifestation of the Spirit would be required. Anyone who was multilingual, such as Paul, could interpret the tongues by virtue of their talent.

In 1 Corinthians 13:1 Paul refers to "the tongues of men and of angels." Whereas he may be using hyperbole, it is just as likely that he is referring to heavenly or angelic dialects for which the Holy Spirit gives utterance. Gordon Fee[50] cites evidence in ancient Jewish sources that the angels were believed to have their own heavenly languages or dialects and that by means of the Spirit one could speak them.

Some say the reference in 1 Corinthians 14:10–11 to earthly, foreign languages proves that all glossalalia is also human languages. But the point of the analogy is that tongues function *like* foreign languages, *not* that tongues *are* foreign languages. His point is that the hearer cannot understand uninterpreted tongues any more than he can understand the one speaking a foreign language. If tongues *were* a foreign language, there would be no need for an *analogy*.

Paul's statement in 1 Corinthians 14:18 that he "speaks in tongues more than all of you" is evidence that tongues are not foreign languages. As Wayne Grudem notes, "If they were known foreign languages that foreigners could understand, as at Pentecost, why would Paul speak more than all the Corinthians in private, where no one would understand, rather than in church where foreign visitors could understand?"[51] Finally, if tongues is always human language, then Paul's statement in 14:23 would not always hold true. Any unbeliever who would know the language being spoken would more likely conclude the person speaking was highly educated rather than "out of [his] mind."

---

[50]Fee, *The First Epistle to the Corinthians*, 630–31.
[51]Grudem, *Systematic Theology*, 1072.

I want to conclude this discussion of tongues on a personal note by simply saying that I have found this gift to be profoundly helpful in my prayer life. It has served only to deepen my intimacy with the Lord Jesus Christ and to enhance my zeal and joy in worship. Caricatures notwithstanding, praying in the Spirit does not diminish one's capacity for rational thought or commitment to the authority of the written Word of God.

D. DANGERS

Wisdom dictates that I briefly mention three areas of concern for those who would embrace the view set forth in this chapter.

(1) There is often the danger of emotionalism in those who seek to minister in the miraculous *charismata* and who not only acknowledge but *expect* the often tangible and sensible operation of the Holy Spirit in their lives. However, this need not be the case. As Jack Hayford has said, if we are careful to create an environment where the Word of God is foundational and the person of Christ the focus, the Holy Spirit

> can be trusted to do *both*—enlighten the intelligence and ignite the emotions. I soon discovered that to allow Him that much space necessitates more a surrender of my senseless fears than a surrender of sensible control. God is not asking any of us to abandon reason or succumb to some euphoric feeling. He is, however, calling us to trust Him—enough to give *Him* control.[52]

(2) There is also the danger of measuring someone's personal value by their gifting. This was certainly a problem in ancient Corinth. Our tendency is to elevate the esteem of those whose gift(s) is characterized by a greater and more conspicuous supernatural display. Perhaps the most effective response to this is the constant reminder of Paul's rebuke of the Corinthians (1 Cor. 4:7) themselves: "For who makes you different from anyone else? What do you have that you did not

---

[52]Jack Hayford, *A Passion for Fulness* (Waco, Tex.: Word, 1991), 31. See my booklet *Emotions Versus Emotionalism: The Role of Feelings in Times of Refreshing* (Kansas City: Metro Vineyard Fellowship, 1995).

receive? And if you did receive it, why do you boast as though you did not?"[53]

(3) Finally, we must always be careful that the primary focus of our spiritual pursuit is the Giver, not the gifts. First and foremost we seek him, not them. Nevertheless, to those who are hungry for the power and gifts of the Holy Spirit, I say "Good! God bless you!" Let us never forget that to the very people guilty of abusing spiritual gifts Paul says that they should be eager and zealous for more! On the one hand he says, "Brothers, stop thinking like children. In regard to evil be infants, but in your thinking be adults" (1 Cor. 14:20). On the other hand, to these same people, he says, "Follow the way of love and *eagerly desire spiritual gifts*, especially the gift of prophecy" (14:1). And again, "I would like every one of you to speak in tongues, but I would rather have you prophesy" (14:5). And again, "Since you are eager to have spiritual gifts, try to excel in gifts that build up the church" (14:12). And yet once more, "Be eager to prophesy, and do not forbid speaking in tongues" (14:39).[54]

Not much of an OT analysis.
Just N.T. —

---

[53]Before we too quickly condemn the Corinthians, we would do well to take note of Packer's observation that "many churches today are orderly simply because they arc asleep, and with some one fears that it is the sleep of death. It is no great thing to have order in a cemetery! The real and deplorable carnality and immaturity of the Corinthian Christians, which Paul censures so strongly elsewhere in the letter, must not blind us to the fact that they were enjoying the ministry of the Holy Spirit in a way in which we today are not" (*Keep in Step with the Spirit*, 249).

[54]The verb *zēloute* ("eagerly desire") in 12:31 is grammatically ambiguous. A minority believe it to be an indicative and thus a statement characterizing the behavior of the Corinthians ("*you are eager* for the greater gifts"). But this view "suffers from the fact that in 14:1 and 39 *zēloute* is unambiguously imperative. It is difficult to believe that the same verb, in the same form, in the same context would represent such a dramatic difference of grammatical mood in this particular instance" (Gillespie, *The First Theologians*, 126). Therefore, it is thoroughly biblical for us to desire and pray for the impartation of additional spiritual gifts (14:13), all the while submitting to the sovereign purposes of the Holy Spirit (12:11).

A CESSATIONIST RESPONSE TO C. SAMUEL STORMS

Richard B. Gaffin, Jr.

Dr. Gaffin has combined his responses to Dr. Storms and Dr. Oss. The combined response can be found following Oss's essay (pp. 284–97).

AN OPEN BUT CAUTIOUS
RESPONSE TO C. SAMUEL STORMS

Robert L. Saucy

Storms's expression of the Third Wave position not only outlines the theology well, but breathes with the passion characteristic of this position, that is, the desire to know God and experience his supernatural power in life. This fervor for the Spirit and his ministry is to be commended. Its beneficial influence has seeped into much of the church where too often life has been lived by natural power and Christianity has been primarily a matter of doctrine rather than life.

Since the Third Wave represents a sort of go-between theology of the Spirit's ministry, combining aspects from traditional evangelicalism and classic Pentecostalism, it is natural that someone from the traditional evangelical position would find considerable agreement with many things in Storms's presentation. I especially appreciated his discussion of 1 Corinthians 12:13, showing that Spirit-baptism occurs at conversion and that the attempt to distinguish between a baptism "by" the Spirit experienced by all believers and a baptism "in" the Spirit administered by Christ (held by some Pentecostal positions) is impossible biblically. Storms rightly refers to any postconversion experience of the Spirit as the "filling" of the Spirit, which he notes correctly can have two senses: the consistent quality of life (i.e., being "full" of the Spirit) and a special equipping or empowering for a special task.

Some confusion is introduced, however, when he goes on to speak of "postconversion encounters or experiences with the Holy Spirit that are related to but not identical with infilling"

225

(p. 181). Referring to several verses that speak of the giving of the Spirit to believers, Storms seems to want to distinguish the reception of the Spirit himself by those who are already believers from the reception of his ministry. Referring to Paul's prayer in Ephesians 1:17, he says, "It strikes some as odd that Paul would pray for the Spirit to be given to those who already have him" (p. 181). Similarly, it is important for him that the genitive construction ("help of the Spirit," Phil. 1:19) be interpreted as an appositional genitive ("the help or provision that is the Spirit") rather than a subjective genitive ("the help the Spirit gives"). Commentators are divided with most taking the latter interpretation, but it is doubtful if Paul intended much of a difference between the two.

The references cited that speak of God as the one who gives the Spirit also cannot be made to assert a significant difference between the giving of the Spirit himself and his ministry. In some instances (e.g., Gal. 3:5) the present participle may be best understood not as a present supplying of the Spirit by God, but simply as a description of God as the Giver of the Spirit. In other instances the emphasis may be on the present supply of the Spirit for the needs of believers (e.g., 1 Thess. 4:8). But if the Spirit is a person who already indwells the believer, what does it mean to "supply anew" (p. 183) the Spirit to that person, if not to supply anew the ministry and power of the Spirit for the particular need? Storms himself tells us that praying for the Holy Spirit (Luke 11:13) is really asking the Father for more of the Spirit's ministry in our lives (p. 184).

These special receptions of the Spirit are apparently linked to "heightened, increased, or accelerated" experiences of the Spirit's ministry in the believer's life. Depending on exactly what is meant by these adjectives, I would concur that the normal believer will experience times of special awareness of God and his power through the Spirit. But I do not see how these experiences are different than the experience of the "filling" of the Spirit, especially when we consider its two aspects noted above.

My primary concern with the Third Wave position is the apparent assertion that the miraculous activity of the apostolic age should be normal for the church today. I say "apparent" because Storms seems to acknowledge that "a remarkable concentration of miraculous phenomena [was] characteristic of the apostles as special representatives of Christ." Yet he denies the idea of any "clusters" of miracles (p. 190) and claims that the picture of the gifts in the New Testament clearly tells us "what new covenant Christianity is supposed to look like" (p. 205). This sounds much like the statement of Jack Deere, another prominent advocate of the Third Wave (whom Storms frequently cites), that "the book of Acts is the *best* source that we have to demonstrate what normal church life is supposed to look like. . . ."[1] Moreover, many of the arguments presented in the essay appear to support this position, but I have problems with several of these arguments in light of Scripture.

1. Miracles are said to have multiple purposes, so that even if their purpose as "signs" (miracles designed to confirm or authenticate) did have particular reference to Christ and the apostles, their continuation is still valid for other reasons. I do not deny that God works miracles for purposes other than authentication, and even sign miracles served other purposes (e.g., the "signs" worked by Jesus and the apostles were usually works of compassion for hurting people). But it is questionable whether one can so easily argue for the same miraculous activity regardless of the "sign" purpose. In the first place one would expect a miracle that somehow points to God to express his nature of love. The fact that a "sign" is a work of compassion, therefore, does not mean that there are two purposes in the miracle. The very giving of a "sign" may be a work of compassion, but the ultimate purpose of the miracle is a "sign." The preeminent description of the miracles of Jesus and the apostles as "signs" shows that this was their ultimate purpose. Thus if "signs" are not permanently needed in the church, it seems reasonable to conclude that there would be fewer miracles.

2. Several times the thought is expressed that the church today has the same needs as the church in the New Testament and that therefore the same miraculous activity must continue. Storms suggests that we have an even greater need for signs to attest our ministry of Scripture today than Jesus did. In my opinion, he fails to distinguish between the ministry of Jesus and the apostles as bearers of new inspired revelation and the present

---

[1]Jack Deere, *Surprised by the Power of the Spirit* (Grand Rapids: Zondervan, 1993), 114.

ministry of teaching and preaching the revelation already given in the Scripture. The Bible nowhere associates "sign" miracles with the teaching of the Scripture, but rather with those who spoke inspired words directly from God. Since it is doubtful that any continuationists would assert that God is giving new revelation today to an *equal extent* as that which took place through the apostles and prophets in the first century, the need for signs is surely different. In relation to this, I do not think that the prayer for "signs" in Acts 4:29–31 can be used as an indication of the normal pattern for the church as Storms suggests. The following context suggests rather clearly that the "servants" (v. 29) through whom the signs and wonders would take place were the apostles (cf. 4:33; 5:12).[2]

The same argument from the needs of the church appears again in relation to the edification of the church. The continuationist argues that since all gifts were for the edification of the church and the church still needs edification, therefore all gifts must be present today. But everything today is not like it was then. We do not have apostles today like those in the foundational period of the church. Similarly, the closing of the canon indicates at least some change in the Spirit's ministry of revelation. Whether we say that some gifts ceased or simply changed, it is clear that the manifestation of spiritual gifts today is not identical to that in the New Testament. There have been changes by God's design, which make the question of the manifestation of gifts more complex than simply saying the needs are the same, therefore the gifts are the same.

3. A third argument for continuationism is made from the lack of biblical teaching that gifts would cease. Aside from being an argument from silence (the Bible does not explicitly teach the continuation of gifts either), some things, as we have just noted, have changed, and they have done so without any explicit teaching to this effect. There is no explicit teaching that canonical revelation would cease, but it did, even as canonical prophecy ceased in Old Testament times without any explicit words to that effect. The open possibility of the coming of Christ precluded

---

[2]C. K. Barrett, *A Critical and Exegetical Commentary on the Acts of the Apostles* (Edinburgh: T. & T. Clark, 1994), 1:243; F. F. Bruce, *Commentary on the Book of Acts* (Grand Rapids: Eerdmans, 1954), 105–7.

the biblical writers from specifying what would happen after they were gone. But the church of history has agreed that changes have occurred. The question of the continuation of spiritual gifts requires consideration of these changes.

4. A final comment on the general continuationist position concerns their explanation of why the miraculous activity of the apostolic era, seen primarily in Acts and 1 Corinthians, has not been the continual experience of the church. Instead of acknowledging that changes, such as those noted above, might have something to do with it, the continuationist points to the lack of spirituality or ignorance of biblical truth, especially that related to spiritual gifts. With regard to biblical ignorance, it is doubtful that history shows any relation to Bible knowledge and the reports of miracles. In fact, numerous reports of miracles come from times (such as the Middle Ages) when the average believer had little access to the Scriptures, since they were not available in the language of the people.

No doubt unbelief and apostasy can hinder the reception of God's miraculous power. God will surely do less if one never asks in faith. But as I noted in my essay, the sin of his people in biblical times did not preclude God from sending powerful prophets accompanied by miracles. If he could send Elijah and even the disciples of Jesus while he was on earth to work many miracles among people of little spirituality, surely he could do the same throughout church history. But there is little evidence of similar ministries in the church, which suggests that God's purpose and not the sin of his people accounts for the difference.

5. With regard to the use of specific gifts in church life, I appreciate what I consider the moderate position of the Third Wave on several issues related to the exercise of miraculous gifts. Storms's warning against depending on prophecy for routine daily decisions is well taken, as is his acknowledgment that healing is not God's will for every sickness. Likewise, the gift of tongues is not made the mark of a certain relationship to the Spirit or even suggested as possible for every believer's prayer life.

There are some aspects of the Third Wave position as presented by Storms, however, with which I have serious problems. Defining the gift of prophecy as "the human *report* of a divine *revelation*" (p. 207) so that the manifestation of the gift or the "prophecy" can include human error is in my mind contrary to the biblical portrayal of "prophecy." If this is the true meaning of prophecy in Scripture, then why is "prophecy" in the Old Testament more authoritative and apparently infallible than "prophecy" in the church as is popularly held by many advocates of this position, including Storms? This differentiation suggests this position holds two definitions of prophecy, which is difficult to substantiate in Scripture.

Aside from the difficulty in consistency, the real problem is the definition itself. Storms wants to separate "revelation" as being divine and therefore always infallible from the "perception or reception" of that revelation, which is human and therefore liable to error. Such a separation between the revelation and its reception leads one to believe that the revelation is not given in words, but is apparently more akin to the existentialist or neo-orthodox nonpropositional revelation. For if the revelation is given in words, then even if left to his own humanness, it is difficult to see how the prophet could fail to perceive or receive such revelation and speak it faithfully unless he deliberately wanted to change the words. I am not suggesting that the prophet is necessarily able to interpret the revelation. There are biblical prophets who apparently did not fully understand the words that they spoke (e.g., Dan. 12:8–9; Zech. 4:5; 1 Peter 1:10–11). But they conveyed the words of the prophecy accurately and infallibly.

Storms's definition of prophecy fails to see that the Spirit's work of inspiration in prophecy goes all the way to the actual prophecy, that is, the words spoken or written. As Peter says concerning prophecy, "men spoke from God as they were carried along by the Holy Spirit" (2 Peter 1:21). No matter what forms God's revelation to the prophet may entail (e.g., the visions of Ezekiel), the final revelation includes the verbal meaning. That is to say, the prophet's words are God's revelation and thus his words, not simply the human *report* of revelation (cf. 2 Sam. 23:2; Jer. 1:7, 9; 1 Cor. 2:13).

To suggest the possibility of fallibility in prophecy as there is in teaching fails to take into account an important distinction between these two ministries. Aside from the fact that Scripture never teaches the inspiration of the teacher as it does the prophet, the teacher's message can always be checked by others because we have the objective revelation in Scripture as the basis for the teaching. But in the case of prophecy, if we accept Storms's definition, it does not include an objective revelation available to others. Thus there is no way for others to get to the actual revelation in prophecy in order to correct the *report* of that revelation and come to a better understanding of it.

A further problem with the definition of prophecy allowing for human error is the attempted support of finding factual error in the prophecy of Agabus concerning Paul. Instead of the Jews binding him and delivering him into the hands of the Gentiles as the prophecy states (Acts 21:11), Paul was actually rescued by the Gentiles from the Jews, who wanted to kill him. While this might appear at first glance to represent a discrepancy in fact, such is really not the case. Paul himself recounts what took place in words essentially the same as the prophecy, "I was arrested in Jerusalem and handed over to the Romans" (28:17). It will not do to argue, as Storms does, that Paul was actually describing the time when he was secretly escorted out of Jerusalem by the Romans to Caesarea (23:12–35), for Paul was already "handed over to the Romans" before he left Jerusalem.

The apparent problem is easily solved when we understand the concept of "handing over to someone else" both in the prophecy and in Paul's statement. The Jews did not deliberately hand Paul over to the Romans, but they were in fact the cause of his arrest by the Romans. By their continual accusations they also prevented his release and caused him to finally appeal to Caesar. Paul's statement *and the prophecy* of Agabus are thus to be understood as a condensed statement of the event that "the Jews were responsible for his being in the hands of the Romans."[3] The prophecy is thus easily interpreted as without error, leaving no example of an errant prophecy to support the concept of fallible prophecy proposed by the Third Wave position.

Finally, I do not see how Paul's exhortation for the one prophesying to do so "in proportion to his faith" (Rom. 12:6) indicates that "there will always be greater and lesser degrees of prophetic ability and consequently greater and lesser degrees of prophetic accuracy" (p. 210). Paul's concern is for the prophet not to go beyond his dependence on God in his prophesying.

---

[3]A. T. Robertson, *Word Picture in the New Testament* (New York: Harper & Brothers, 1930), 3:486.

Nothing in his statement suggests that what one may say beyond that which is in accord with his faith is genuine "prophecy." Rather as Cranfield explains, "there was the possibility of false prophecy; there was also the possibility of true prophecy's being adulterated by additions derived from some source other than the Holy Spirit's inspiration. Hence the need also to exhort the prophets themselves to prophesy κατὰ τὴν ἀναλογίαν τῆς πίστεως [according to the analogy of faith]."[4]

In sum, I do not find any support in Scripture either for the definition of prophecy as the *report* of revelation or for prophecy with error. This does not necessarily preclude the manifestation of prophecy in the church today, but it does raise questions concerning much of what is purported to be prophecy by the continuationist today.

6. Turning to the discussion of the gift of healing, I agree with the general description that God can sovereignly grant to a person the ability to heal at a particular time. The discussion of James 5, however, raises some questions. First, there is no evidence for the manifestation of the gift of healings in this instance. Healing is the result of the praying of a group of elders, with no indication that one of them was granted the gift to heal. The suggestion that the gift of healing is linked to the gift of faith and that "the prayer of faith" in James is a manifestation of that gift is even more problematic. Assuming (in harmony with Storms's personal illustration) that all of the elders were not given the gift of healing, they also did not have the gift of faith. Does this, therefore, mean that only the prayer of one person was instrumental in the healing? Surely James intends us to understand that all of the elders were to pray "the prayer of faith" and that the concerted prayer would be effective.

The greatest problem with the continuationist's discussion of the gift of healing (and other miraculous gifts as well) is the unqualified use of Jesus' ministry of healing seen in the citation from Jack Deere. The suggestion that God would respond to our compassionate prayers and glorify himself through healings even as he did through Jesus is to completely disregard the significance of Jesus' healings as "sign" miracles. While the Gospels

---

[4]C. E. B. Cranfield, *A Critical and Exegetical Commentary on Romans*, ICC (Edinburgh: T. & T. Clark, 1979), 2:620.

do make frequent references to the compassion of Jesus in relation to his healing, the overriding biblical emphasis is on these miraculous acts as "signs" to authenticate him as a messenger from God (cf. John 20:30–31; Acts 2:22). If the primary purpose of God's healing is the expression of his compassion, what are we to make of the vast majority of times when God does not choose to miraculously heal? Is he less compassionate then? Or what about the fact, as even Storms acknowledges, that there was an extraordinary display of miraculous activity, including healings, connected with Jesus and the apostles? Is God more compassionate at certain points of history than at others?

God can and does work miraculous healings today. But to suggest that he wants to show compassion through the church by miraculous healings like that of Jesus fails to consider all of the biblical teaching related to Jesus' miracles. It also fails to provide a satisfactory explanation as to why the church has never experienced miraculous activity comparable to that of Jesus and why it is not healing those with AIDS today to the same extent that Jesus healed the lepers of his day (as is implied in the citation from Deere).

7. Finally, with regard to the gift of tongues, I do not see the apostle's statement that tongues are a sign to unbelievers as only talking about "the *negative* result of one particular *abuse* of tongues. ..." Precisely what Paul meant by his words, I acknowledge, is difficult to ascertain. But that it does teach something about the divine purpose of tongues and not simply the result of their abuse seems certain. Continuationists need somehow to encompass this statement more fully into their theology and practice of tongues.

This leads to my greatest concern with the discussion of the gift of tongues. In various ways the proposition is conveyed that the primary function of tongues is the edification of oneself, especially in private prayer and devotional life. The Spirit's intercessory work in Romans 8:26–27 is explained as involving tongues. As I explained more fully in my essay, it is difficult to see this focus of the purpose of tongues in Scripture. First, Paul's teaching of the Spirit's help in prayer in Romans 8 certainly applies to all believers. If this means speaking in tongues, then all believers should speak in tongues. Storms's entire thrust— that tongues bring "peace and joy" (p. 215), are "profoundly helpful ... in [our] prayer life," "deepen [our] intimacy with the Lord Jesus Christ," increase our zeal in worship (p. 222), and make us better equipped to minister to others (p. 216)—suggests that above all else tongues are for personal spiritual growth.

All of this is quite contrary to the nature of tongues as one of the "spiritual gifts" that, according to Scripture, are for the edification of the community and not primarily for self-edification, and are distributed among believers in the sense that not all have the same gift—that is, not all have the gift of tongues (1 Cor. 12:30). The latter point especially argues strongly against the personal-growth purpose of tongues, for surely the means of grace given by God to his people for growth in their relationship to him are available equally to all.

The continuationist's desire to experience all that God has for us as individuals and to see the manifestation of his glory in the present dark world is commendable. But the blanket approach so frequently found in their discussion of miraculous gifts today, in my opinion, cannot be fully sustained. Both Scripture and experience suggest that there was something different about the foundational era of the church, and this fact must be considered in relation to miraculous phenomena.

A PENTECOSTAL/CHARISMATIC RESPONSE TO C. SAMUEL STORMS

Douglas A. Oss

Dr. Storms has written a fine essay from the Third Wave framework that is for the most part in alignment with Pentecostalism. There are only a few areas where we disagree, and to these positions I offer here brief responses.

1. Terminology. Dr. Storms rejects the Pentecostal doctrine of Spirit-baptism more for its terminology than for its substance (p. 179). He suggests the alternative label of "filled with the Spirit" for this empowering work. Pentecostals already use "filled with the Spirit" as a synonym for Spirit-baptism, but hold that Luke's distinctive use of the phrase in Acts 1:6–8 as the program for the entire book justifies the use of the phrase "baptized in the Spirit" for the enduement with power.

2. Storms states there is no imperative in the New Testament for believers to be baptized in the Holy Spirit. My suggestion here is the same as that given in response to Dr. Saucy. Consider what Pentecostals say about the interpretation of Luke–Acts and Paul. First, the narrative genre expresses imperatives differently than a letter. What is meant in Acts 1:6–8 when Jesus tells the disciples that the fulfillment of the Baptist's prophecy is looming on the horizon, and that they should wait in Jerusalem until they receive *power* (*dynamis*) when the Holy Spirit comes upon them? And what theology is communicated through the fulfillment of this promise throughout the remainder of Acts? Is this not the narratological equivalent of an imperative? Remember Peter's sermon, "The promise is for you and your children and for all who are far off—for all whom the Lord our God will call" (Acts 2:39). Second, Luke must be allowed to

explain redemptive-historical fulfillment in his own terms without importing theology from Paul and unnaturally imposing it on Luke–Acts. Harmonization must come after divinely ordained diversities are understood, and Luke's agenda emphasizes the Spirit's charismatic power. To put an epistolary language test to a narrative is hermeneutically unsound.

3. Based in part on his view that the New Testament lacks any imperative for Pentecostal Spirit baptism, Storms asserts that the subsequent experience of "filling" is "this is not so much a dramatic or decisive experience that settles things for good but a daily appropriation" (p. 180). While Pentecostals do not argue that Spirit baptism is a once-for-all experience that settles things for good, neither would we settle for a description of the enduement with power, whether the inaugural experience or a further experience (e.g., Acts 2:4ff.; 4:31), that describes it as less than dramatic and decisive. Consider only a few statements from Acts: "These men are not drunk, as you suppose" (Acts 2:15); The crowd gathered was "utterly amazed," "bewildered," and "perplexed" (2:6–7, 12); "After they prayed, the place where they were meeting was shaken. And they were all filled with the Holy Spirit and spoke the word of God boldly" (4:31). This, along with the nature of the manifestations at Corinth, lead Pentecostals to define the enduement in more dramatic terms than Dr. Storms. Furthermore, the inaugural experience that first ushers one into the realm of the Holy Spirit's power is particularly intense, dramatic, and decisive. It opens the gate, but it does not settle things for good. Dr. Storms is correct in emphasizing the need for *daily*, fresh seeking of God and the presence and power of his Holy Spirit.

Based on the redemptive-historical evidence, there is solid biblical warrant to understand the enduement with power to be a work of the Spirit distinct from regeneration and sanctification. Dr. Storms's understanding of the New Testament brings him to agree with this in principle, even though his definitions are somewhat different from mine (pp. 180–85). Terminology aside, his argument is persuasive for the reality of regular experiences of spiritual power in the Christian life that are different than regeneration or sanctification.

4. On cessationism. I want only to say the "Amen" to what Dr. Storms has written about cessationism. It will encourage those who already agree and persuade many who do not.

Chapter Four

A PENTECOSTAL/ CHARISMATIC VIEW

Douglas A. Oss

A PENTECOSTAL/ CHARISMATIC VIEW

Douglas A. Oss

A. INTRODUCTION

The shift in the evangelical community with regard to miraculous gifts reached dramatic proportions by the late 1980s.[1] Although there were inklings during the previous two decades, many Pentecostals did not realize just how pervasive a shift it would prove to be. Even with the earlier publication of influential works such as Wayne Grudem's books on prophecy and D. A. Carson's *Showing the Spirit*, or developments such as Jack Deere's departure from Dallas Theological Seminary because of his own spiritual and theological paradigm shift (detailed in his published testimony, *Surprised By the Power of the Spirit*),[2] many Pentecostals were surprised at the extent of the change. With historical positions less entrenched, the realization dawned within most sectors of the Pentecostal community that there would now be increased opportunities for dialogue with noncharismatic

---

[1]For example, the topic of the 1989 annual meeting of the Evangelical Theology Group of the Society of Biblical Literature was spiritual gifts and miracles. A general abandonment of cessationism was evident in discussion from the floor.

[2]Wayne Grudem, *The Gift of Prophecy in 1 Corinthians* (Washington, D.C.: Univ. Press of America, 1982); *The Gift of Prophecy in the New Testament and Today* (Westchester: Crossway, 1988); D. A. Carson, *Showing the Spirit: A Theological Exposition of 1 Corinthians 12–14* (Grand Rapids: Baker, 1987); Jack Deere, *Surprised by the Power of the Spirit* (Grand Rapids: Zondervan, 1993).

evangelicals. The present work confirms the inclusiveness of broader evangelicalism on this issue—five evangelicals from different theological frameworks collaborating on a book the subject of which is miraculous gifts.

This chapter lays out a position that is representative of classical Pentecostalism.[3] True, Pentecostalism is not a theological monolith; indeed, there is much diversity under the Pentecostal umbrella. Yet inasmuch as my own framework is that of classical Pentecostalism, the conclusions of this chapter will by and large reflect its mainstream, although some of the methods may not be historically associated with it (e.g., the redemptive-historical approach). In addition, the charismatic position for some key areas of doctrine will be noted, especially where charismatics may hold a position different from classical Pentecostals. We begin now by discussing "second experiences" and whether there is a postconversion experience of the Spirit that Christians should seek.

B. ON SECOND EXPERIENCES

Some years ago during a private but formal roundtable discussion, a cessationist scholar asked me to justify the Pentecostal definition of the phrase "baptism in the Holy Spirit," since it had already been well defined as "conversion" in the history of theology. After my response a spirited exchange took place on a variety of related issues, many of which are also taken up in the present work. The initial question put to me in that forum, however, deserves special attention at the outset of this essay since it illustrates a point that is equally important to make in this context. Specifically, discussions about the validity of nonconversion experiences of the Spirit should not deteriorate into term-shifting debates concerning the definitions of technical theological terminology. The issue is too important to lose sight of by simply "talking through" the doctrinal grids and terminology of

---

[3]It would be impossible to footnote the thousands of discussions I have had with colleagues over the years. My views have been formed in a community of Pentecostal ministers and scholars, especially my esteemed comrades on the faculty of Central Bible College, past and present. Credit goes to them for whatever positive contributions my essay may make to this discussion. I myself am to blame for any shortcomings.

others. The theological label for such experiences notwithstanding, the question still remains: Are there experiences of the Spirit different from regeneration, and/or are they subsequent to it?

1. Is Pentecostalism Truly a Second-Blessing Movement?

The first objection that often arises with regard to Pentecostal theology is the emphasis it places on the empowering work of the Spirit in the life of the believer *subsequent to salvation*. This emphasis is often wrongly characterized by opponents as "second blessing" theology, without any qualification.[4] Those who raise this concern are defending the biblical teaching that the believer receives the Spirit at salvation, and they are rejecting what they perceive to be a misguided view of the efficacy of

---

[4]Here it is necessary to distinguish between Pentecostal and Pentecostal-holiness branches of the movement. The Pentecostal-holiness branches of Pentecostalism are classic second-blessing movements, being theological heirs of the holiness/Wesleyan revivals of the nineteenth century (cf. D. W. Dayton, *Theological Roots of Pentecostalism* [Grand Rapids: Zondervan, 1987], 35–60). In Pentecostal-holiness traditions sanctification is viewed as a postconversion, once-for-all experience, resulting in entire sanctification and the eradication of the sinful nature, which is followed by baptism in the Holy Spirit. These branches are smaller than other non-Wesleyan Pentecostal traditions. We will use the term "Pentecostal" in distinction to "Pentecostal-holiness" in our discussion. Pentecostal groups (e.g., The Church of God in Christ and The Assemblies of God), while strongly influenced in some respects by nineteenth-century holiness revivals, are theologically more akin to Reformed evangelical views of sanctification and "second blessings." Cf. E. L. Waldvogel, "The 'Overcoming Life': A Study of the Reformed Evangelical Origins of Pentecostalism" (Ph.D. diss., Harvard University, 1977), 1–7, 25, *passim*. Dayton's conclusions are too general with regard to both Pentecostalism and broader evangelicalism in adopting the view that the major influence in Pentecostalism across the board was second-blessing Methodism (e.g., Methodism was not uniquely second-blessing). Many of the earliest leaders of the Assemblies of God were from other traditions, chief among them Eudorus N. Bell, the first Chairman of the General Council of the Assemblies of God and a former Southern Baptist pastor. It is impossible to measure his influence, but it was certainly unsurpassed by any other individual at the time. In brief example, consider just two others, J. W. Welch (third Chairman of the General Council of the A/G from 1915–20) and D. W. Kerr (influential founder and pastor), both pastors from the Christian and Missionary Alliance who brought with them the Reformed traditions of A. B. Simpson and R. A. Torrey. Waldvogel is more precise in describing evangelical theological trends that influenced Pentecostalism and in identifying doctrines where those influences took root within the movement (cf., e.g., "The 'Overcoming Life,'" 22–43).

salvation. Indeed, it is a common misunderstanding of Pentecostalism to charge that it denies the Spirit to non-Pentecostal believers. To my knowledge no classical Pentecostal holds the view that the Spirit is not received at salvation (which would clearly contradict Scripture). Those who believe in Christ also have the Spirit living within; if anyone does not have the Spirit, he or she is not of Christ at all. Moreover, this is not a partial reception of the person of the Spirit; it is unqualified and complete (cf. Rom. 8:14, 9–17; Gal. 3:1–5; 4:6; Eph. 1:13–14).

When Pentecostals speak of "receiving" the Spirit as a postconversion experience, they are speaking of the work of the Spirit in which he empowers the believer in "charismatic" ways for witness and service. Several points of clarification are needed here. (1) To reiterate what was stated above, they do not mean that some believers are without the Spirit.[5]

(2) The emphasis of postconversion experience (or, within Pentecostalism, subsequence) is not on a *necessary* time lag between regeneration and "filling" (cf. Acts 8:12–16, where there was some delay between salvation and filling; 10:44–47, where everything happened as part of one complex of events), but rather theological separability of two works of the Spirit—one inner-transforming (regenerating/sanctifying, e.g., Rom. 8:1–11; Gal. 3:1–5; 4:6; 5:16–26) and the other empowering (empowering/charismatic, e.g., 1 Cor. 12–14).[6] The remission of sins must come first, but there is not always a discernible lapse of time between conversion and Spirit-baptism. In fact, Pentecostals historically have emphasized that this experience is available from the moment the Holy Spirit indwells the believer, and their testimonies often speak of being both saved and baptized in the Holy Spirit all at once, while responding to an invitation for salvation. Perhaps an apt expression of the Pentecostal view, then, is "extra-conversion experience."

---

[5]Myer Pearlman, *Knowing the Doctrines of the Bible* (Springfield: Gospel Publishing House, 1937), 305–8. Pearlman is representative of early Pentecostal theologians.

[6]Pentecostals are not alone in their view of an added conversion experience of empowerment. Martyn Lloyd-Jones believed there was an empowering experience, different from conversion, which he called a baptism in the Spirit. See Tony Sargent, *The Sacred Anointing: The Preaching of Martyn Lloyd-Jones* (Wheaton: Crossway, 1994), 39–101, esp. 40–42.

(3) Pentecostals do not believe that being baptized in the Holy Spirit is a once-for-all experience of empowerment. In fact, historically they have emphasized the necessity of being "refilled," a traditional expression to indicate that the empowering work of the Spirit, with diverse manifestations, is something that happens repeatedly in the life of a believer.[7]

In sum, then, whether Pentecostalism is truly a second-blessing movement depends on one's definition. Pentecostal pneumatology does not include the "second blessing" defined by nineteenth-century holiness revivalism as a once-for-all sanctifying or empowering work, but rather one that is closer to (but not identical with) the "many fillings" view.[8] Baptism in the Holy Spirit, as Pentecostals have defined it in their systematic theology, is the first experience of the Spirit's empowering work, which inaugurates a life characterized by continued anointings with the Spirit. It is not of the same once-for-all nature as regeneration. Moreover, the empowering work of the Spirit is available to the believer from the moment of faith, with no necessary delay and no prerequisite of attaining a certain level of sanctification first.[9]

However, if one defines second-blessing theology as the view that believers have experiences that are different from regeneration/sanctification and that these experiences are distinct works of the Spirit, empowering in nature, theologically separable from conversion, and inaugurated by a baptism in the Holy Spirit (as defined within Pentecostalism), then Pentecostalism is a second-blessing movement. As a Pentecostal, my own perception is that our pneumatology includes a first, a second, a third, a fourth, and so forth, anointings. In other words, being filled with the Spirit is as characteristic of the Christian life as sanctification.

In any event, the New Testament itself describes postconversion "fillings" and also commands the believer to be "filled" with the Spirit, subsequent to salvation. In Acts 4:31 the same

---

[7]Pearlman, *Knowing the Doctrine of the Bible*, 315–16.

[8]Probably because of the influence of A. B. Simpson, R. A. Torrey, and their associates.

[9]In the Pentecostal-holiness traditions, entire sanctification is the necessary prerequisite for baptism in the Holy Spirit.

group that was present on the day of Pentecost is once again "filled" (*eplesthesan*, the same verb and form as 2:4) with the Holy Spirit, after which they preached boldly and performed at least one miraculous sign (cf. also Acts 4:8; 6:3, 10; 7:55; 10:19, 38; 13:1–4, 9, 52).[10] And Paul exhorts the Ephesians to "be filled [continually] with the Spirit" (Eph. 5:18) and the Corinthians to prophesy, heal, speak in tongues, etc. (1 Cor. 12–14). The issue concerning the legitimacy of extra-conversion experiences boils down, then, not to whether there are experiences different from salvation, but to what kind of experiences these are. To construct a Pentecostal view of this issue, we turn now to a biblical-theological survey of the Spirit's work, including consideration of the differences between Pauline and Lukan presentations.[11]

---

[10]If the experiences of Acts 2 are unrepeatable for that particular people group, why do we have 4:31? Also, if the language of Acts 2 describes salvation, are then the believers of 4:31 being saved again? Another point to consider is this: 4:31 has the same verb and basically the same syntax as 2:4. It seems to me that if Luke were concerned about distinguishing between the nature of the two events, he would not have described them using identical language. But Luke is not concerned to distinguish between these events. Rather, in 4:31 he is presenting more of the same kind of work by the Spirit—his anointing for spiritual power.

[11]The two distinct works of the Spirit were a common aspect of early Pentecostal apologies, but no one worked out the methodology in a consistent and explicit manner in the early years of the movement (cf. Gary B. McGee, "Early Pentecostal Hermeneutics," in *Initial Evidence*, G. McGee, ed. [Peabody, Mass.: Hendrickson, 1991], 96–118). It was Dr. Anthony D. Palma who, as a graduate student during the 1960s and early 1970s, first developed the biblical-theological evidence in a systematic and thorough fashion (unfortunately for the scholarly world, his work has not yet been published). His careful and detailed scholarship demonstrated the Old Testament distinctions between the two fundamental works of the Spirit as well as the diversities in the pneumatologies of Paul and Luke. Indeed, his lectures on the differences between Paul's "inner-transforming" emphasis and Luke's "empowering" emphasis laid the foundation for later Pentecostal scholarship on the subject. My own course notes are from various courses from 1976 to 1979, taken at the Assemblies of God Theological Seminary in Springfield, Missouri: "The Holy Spirit in the New Testament Church"; "New Testament Theology"; and "Greek Exegesis: 1 Corinthians 12–14." Not since Dr. Palma's seminal work has anyone substantively advanced the discussion beyond his original insights. Some details have been filled in, such as more exhaustive analysis of the Septuagintal background of Lukan idiom (Roger Stronstad, *The Charismatic Theology of Luke* [Peabody, Mass.: Hendrickson, 1984]; Palma did include fairly substantial data from Septuagintal backgrounds in his lectures). New methods have more recently been used, such as literary

2. A Biblical-Theological Survey of the Spirit's Work

Although it may sound anachronistic, Pentecostal pneumatology is based on the redemptive-historical approach to biblical theology. While it is true that the redemptive-historical approach is not explicitly part of the history of Pentecostal hermeneutics, it was nevertheless the intuitive approach adopted by early Pentecostals as they worked through the implications of God's unfolding plan revealed in, for example, Joel 2:28–32 and its fulfillment in Acts. In contemporary Pentecostal hermeneutics, the redemptive-historical method has become explicit and will remain the foundational approach of the future because it organically demonstrates the validity of Pentecostal pneumatology. Thus our survey will proceed along redemptive-historical lines as we compare the empowering and inner-transforming works of the Spirit with a view toward answering the question of whether it is valid today to seek an "enduement with power" from the Spirit.[12]

a. The Spirit's Work Within the Old Testament Period

The first matter for our consideration is whether there is an empowering work of the Spirit within the Old Testament period itself that is different from his inner-transforming work. As a matter of fact, the empowering work of the Spirit is much more evident than the inner-transforming. For example, select individuals are anointed with the Spirit to prophesy (e.g., Num. 11:24–27; 1 Sam. 10:6, 10; 19:20; 2 Sam. 23:2; 1 Chron. 12:18; 2 Chron. 20:14–17; 24:20; and throughout the prophetic writings), perform miraculous feats (Judg. 14:6, 19; 15:14–17; 1 Kings 18:12), exercise spiritual power in leadership (Judg. 3:10; 6:34; 11:29;

---

approaches to Luke–Acts (e.g., Donald Johns, "Some New Directions in the Hermeneutics of Classical Pentecostalism's Doctrine of Initial Evidence," in *Initial Evidence*, 145–67).

[12]The phrase "enduement with power" was coined in early Pentecostalism as a synonym for baptism in the Holy Spirit and became a popular expression (cf. Pearlman, *Knowing the Doctrines of the Bible*, 308–13). We will hold in abeyance the issue of cessationism and the broader question of the continuity of miraculous gifts throughout the last days until the next section of our discussion, even though the biblical material itself overlaps with that topic.

1 Sam. 16:13), or simply carry out their appointed service within God's household (Ex. 35:30–35). Additionally, in numerous miracle narratives where the Spirit receives no explicit mention, the human agents are prophets whose definitive qualification is the Spirit's anointing (e.g., 1 Kings 17:17–24; 18:16–46; 2 Kings 2:19–22; 4:17). The Spirit's empowering work was limited to select individuals, and in most cases it "came upon" them for a relatively brief period of time for a specific purpose (e.g., prophecy, deliverance). The Old Testament anticipates that this work of the Spirit in the new age will be democratized in God's household, a point that we will explore below.

In addition to these incidents of the Spirit's charismatic activity, we also find in the Old Testament evidence of his inner-transforming work, which resulted in moral conformity to God's will. Whether the Old Testament explicitly presents the Spirit as the transformer of human nature within this period is a moot question. There are clear instances in which the inner-transforming work of the Spirit is implied. For example, God commands the Israelites to circumcise their hearts (Lev. 26:41; Deut. 10:16; cf. Rom. 2:28–29); the Israelites are said to have grieved God's Holy Spirit in the desert through their rebellion (Isa. 63:10–11); the Old Testament repeatedly asserts that God honors a humble and contrite spirit (e.g., 2 Sam. 22:28; 2 Kings 22:19; 2 Chron. 7:14; Pss. 25:9; 51:17; Isa. 57:15; 66:2); the Spirit gives both moral instruction and guidance (Neh. 9:20; Ps. 143:10).

Furthermore, God commands the members of the house of Israel to rid themselves of immorality and acquire a new heart and a new spirit (Ezek. 18:31). David expresses a similar desire for a new heart in his prayer of repentance for the Bathsheba affair (Ps. 51:10, 17; note the association of this request with David's Spirit-anointing in v. 11). But inner transformation, both required by God and desired by David, is not described as a universal experience among the people of God within this period. Rather, the Old Testament anticipates a future new age during which the transformative work of the Spirit will become a universal reality among God's people. We must therefore consider the Old Testament evidence also in the light of its preparatory nature as it expresses the hope of future fulfillment, a fulfillment that is realized with regard to both inner transformation and empowerment in the New Testament.

b. The Old Testament Anticipation of the Spirit's Future Work

With regard to the empowering work of the Spirit, the Old Testament clearly prepares the way for the "last days," when the Spirit's charismatic power will be universalized among God's people.[13] No longer restricted to a few select individuals, in the future age every member of the kingdom of God will receive the Spirit as prophetic anointer.[14]

This hope is first expressed by Moses in Numbers 11:29. Moses had become weary of bearing sole responsibility for leading the rebellious Israelites and appealed to the Lord for deliverance from this burden, even if it meant his own death (11:10–16). God told him to choose seventy from among Israel's elders and have them assemble in the Tent of Meeting where, the Lord promised, "I will come down and speak with you there, and I will take of the Spirit that is on you and put the Spirit on them. They will help you carry the burden of the people so that you will not have to carry it alone" (v. 17). After the designated elders had assembled, "the LORD came down in the cloud and spoke with [Moses], and he took of the Spirit that was on him and put the Spirit on the seventy elders. When the Spirit rested on them, they prophesied, but they did not do so again" (v. 25). The purpose of this anointing was to designate the seventy elders for, and initiate them into, leadership roles that would alleviate some of the burden on Moses. Prophecy functioned as a "sign" that they were indeed so designated and anointed.[15]

But the Spirit also rested on Eldad and Medad, two elders not selected among the seventy, and they prophesied in the

---

[13]There is general agreement that the hope of the Old Testament for this outpouring prepares the way for New Testament fulfillment. Cf. O. Palmer Robertson, "Tongues: Sign of Covenantal Curse and Blessing," WTJ 38 (1975): 43, 47. Robertson calls this relationship between Old Testament and New Testament the "preparation principle." Being a cessationist, he argues that the fulfillment was intended only for the foundational period of the church. Cf. also Wayne Grudem, "1 Corinthians 14:20–25: Prophecy and Tongues As Signs of God's Attitude," WTJ 41 (1979): 381–96. Grudem argues that the preparation in the Old Testament for the New Testament fulfillment lays the framework for the entire period of the last days, not just for a so-called "foundational period."

[14]This is true even of Messiah; cf. Isaiah 61:1–2a, quoted in Luke 4:18–19.

[15]Cf. S. B. Parker, "Possession Trance and Prophecy in Pre-Exilic Israel," VT 28 (1978): 271–85, esp. 276–77.

camp. In response to Joshua's plaintive request that they be stopped from prophesying, Moses said, "Are you jealous for my sake? I wish that all the LORD's people were prophets, and that the LORD would put his Spirit on them!" (v. 29). Thus the narrative expresses the hope of a universalized charismatic experience in which there is no mere human control over the Spirit's activity but rather freedom for the Spirit to come upon whomever he chooses.[16] Moses' wish also presages further canonical expansion in Joel's prediction that "all people" will someday prophesy.

The hope for the universalization of charismatic activity takes on more specific form in Joel 2:28–32. After a period of judgment (2:11) and repentance (2:12–17), Israel will be restored (2:18ff.). As part of this restoration God will "pour out" (Heb. *špk*; LXX *ekcheō*) his Spirit on all people (vv. 28a, 29b), resulting in universalized charismatic activity (vv. 28b–29; e.g., sons, daughters, old men, young men, even servants) and "wonders in the heavens and on the earth" (vv. 30–31a), prior to the "day of the LORD" (v. 31b).[17] During these times, everyone who calls on the name of the Lord and whom the Lord calls will be saved (v. 32). In contrast to the old era, when the Spirit's empowering work was restricted to select individuals, the outpouring of the Holy Spirit in this future age will extend to all of God's people and will be characterized by the Spirit's empowering work.[18]

The Old Testament also looks ahead to the Spirit's future inner-transforming work. The evidence we surveyed above regarding the circumcision of the heart and the work of the Spirit to transform human nature within the Old Testament

---

[16]Parker (ibid., 279–80) contends that the narrative represents attempts by the traditional leadership to control the prophetic activity of those who were not officially recognized as prophets. So also Martin Noth, *Numbers* (Philadelphia: Westminster, 1968), 90. The ideology of the narrative itself, as expressed in Moses' rebuke of Joshua, opposes any such control.

[17]Note the careful use of the LXX's *ekcheō* in Acts in both the quotation from Joel (Acts 2:17–18) and in later descriptions (2:33; 10:45).

[18]So also Douglas Stuart, *Hosea–Jonah*, WBC (Waco, Tex.: Word, 1987), 260–61. He explains: "In the new age *all* of God's people will have *all* they need of God's Spirit. The old era was characterized by the Spirit's selective, limited influence on *some* individuals: certain prophets, kings, etc. But through Joel the people are hearing of a new way of living, in which everybody can have the Spirit."

period (e.g., Lev. 26:41; Deut. 10:16; Neh. 9:20; Ps. 143:10; Isa. 63:10–11) is a harbinger of the canonical expansion of this aspect of the Spirit's work into the future hope expressed by the prophets. Jeremiah foresees the day when the Lord will make a new covenant with his people, at which time he will put his law in their minds and write it on their hearts (Jer. 31:31–34, esp. 33; cf. Heb. 8:7–13). Ezekiel specifically foresees this future transformation as the work of the Spirit. According to his description of the new age, it will be a time when God puts "a new spirit" in his people and gives them a new heart so that they will follow his law (Ezek. 11:19–20). This moral transformation will also be accomplished by God's own Spirit taking up residence in each individual (36:26–27; 37:14). The hope of regeneration was thus established through the promise of the indwelling Spirit.

In sum, the Old Testament contains two primary functions of the Holy Spirit, one empowering and the other inner-transforming. (i) The accounts that describe the Spirit's empowering work consistently portray his empowerment of select individuals to prophesy, perform miracles, deliver, or otherwise carry out their assigned service. The Old Testament also anticipates a new age when this operation of the Spirit will be universalized among God's people, no longer being restricted to the select few, and will continue to be characterized by charismatic manifestations. (ii) The Spirit transforms human nature, effecting circumcision of the heart and obedience to God's law. A new age of fulfillment for this work of the Spirit is also anticipated in the Old Testament, looking to an age in which God will put his Spirit in his people, giving them new hearts and minds on which his law is written.

We turn now to consider the New Testament, which reveals how the promised Spirit's work in the new age is fulfilled in Christ and his body, the church.

c. New Testament Fulfillment of the Spirit's Work

In the age of New Testament fulfillment, the two works of the Spirit continue but now in Christological fullness. We do not need to demonstrate the New Testament fulfillment of the Spirit's inner-transforming work; any standard introduction to theology covers this material thoroughly, and it is not an issue between Pentecostal and non-Pentecostal evangelicals. Both groups agree that the washing of regeneration is the transformative experience in salvation and that the indwelling Spirit is definitive of the Christian (e.g., Rom. 8:9; Titus 3:5–7). In fulfilling the Old Testament hope for the Spirit's indwelling work, Christ made the new birth by the Spirit available to all who have faith in him (e.g., John 3:5–8).

Rather, our purpose is to explore whether there is also an empowering experience of the Spirit, distinct from regeneration, that is presented in the New Testament as the fulfillment of the Old Testament hope for the new age of the Spirit. Discussions of this aspect of pneumatology inevitably revolve around the different emphases found within the Lukan corpus and parts of Paul's letters.

D. A. Carson wrote the following in evaluation of Roger Stronstad's approach to the distinction between Pauline and Lukan pneumatologies:

> If Luke and Paul develop complementary theologies, that is one thing (e.g., if Paul stresses only one conversion, but does not rule out some kind of post-conversion spiritual enduement, while Luke stresses the latter); but if Luke and Paul develop contradictory theologies, that is another (e.g., if Paul will not permit any form of second-blessing theology, while Luke insists upon it). The polarity may please that part of the modern mood that finds in the New Testament a diverse and even mutually contradictory array of theologies, with the canon providing the *range* of allowable options, but the price is high. One can no longer speak of canonical theology in any wholistic sense. Worse, mutually contradictory theologies cannot both be true, and one cannot even speak of the canon establishing the allowable range of theologies, since one or more must be false.[19]

Carson's warning concerning Stronstad's thesis is at the same time a warning about the historical Pentecostal approach to canonical differences between the two works of the Spirit, for

---

[19]D. A. Carson, *Showing the Spirit* (Grand Rapids: Baker, 1987), 151, commenting on Roger Stronstad's *The Charismatic Theology of Luke*.

Pentecostals have for decades included in their pneumatology the differences between Paul and Luke.[20]

In point of fact, Carson's first statement (about Luke and Paul developing complementary theologies) is accurate of classical Pentecostalism; that is, even though Paul and Luke have different emphases regarding the nature of the Spirit's work, neither one theologically excludes the other.[21] On the other hand, the antithetical approach Carson describes is characteristic of neither Stronstad nor historical Pentecostalism. Carson's warning concerning the authority and infallibility of Scripture, though, is still important for Pentecostals to heed lest there be

---

[20]See, for example, Pearlman, *Knowing the Doctrine of the Spirit*, 290–320; Palma, "Holy Spirit."

[21]Cf. Robert Menzies, "The Development of Early Christian Pneumatology with Special Reference to Luke–Acts," Ph.D. dissertation, University of Aberdeen, 1989 (since published: JSNTSup 54 [Sheffield: JSOT Press, 1991]; my citations are from the original dissertation). Menzies argues that Luke's pneumatology "excludes" any soteriological aspects of the Spirit's work, and thus theologically excludes Paul's view of the Spirit's work in salvation (309). In fact, he argues that Paul's soteriological pneumatology was unknown in other sectors of the early church until A.D. 70–80 (310) and that "neither Luke nor the primitive church attribute soteriological significance to the pneumatic gift in a manner analogous to Paul" (37; one wonders, then, about Jesus' own statement in John 3:5–8?). He also concludes that "Luke apparently was not acquainted with Paul's epistles" (310). Conversely, Paul's pneumatology excludes the Lukan perspective. Thus, with regard to Acts 19:1–6 Menzies argues that Paul would never and could never have asked the question of the Ephesian disciples that we find in this text, because Paul would never have conceived of someone being saved and not receiving the Spirit (262–68, esp. 268; here Menzies does not distinguish between receiving the Spirit as "regenerator" on the one hand, and as "anointer" on the other). Therefore, according to Menzies, the dialogue in Acts 19:1–6 is a "Lukan construction"; "Paul would undoubtedly have related the story differently" (268); and "Paul would not—indeed, I believe, could not—have interpreted and narrated" the events of Acts 19:1–6 as they are presented by Luke (this latter statement is in R. Menzies, "Coming to Terms with an Evangelical Heritage—Part 2: Pentecostals and Evidential Tongues," *Paraclete* 28 [1994]: 4). In writings subsequent to his dissertation Menzies continues to press the same history-of-religions reconstruction, but adds that Pauline and Lukan pneumatologies are ultimately "compatible" and "complementary" ("Coming to Terms with an Evangelical Heritage—Part 2," 1–10; "The Distinctive Character of Luke's Pneumatology," *Paraclete* 25 [1991]: 17–30). Although in the light of such an antithetical reconstruction of the Lukan–Pauline relationship his use of the term "complementary" is puzzling, still there is a formal commitment to the authority of Scripture; and perhaps the puzzling formulation will correct itself over time in order to agree with this commitment.

any departure from our roots in evangelicalism or from our unswerving commitment to the authority of God's Word. Carson is not calling on Pentecostals to abandon their view of distinctions between Paul and Luke; he is simply urging careful formulation in a manner that neither rejects biblical authority nor undermines it through dialectical conclusions.

Nevertheless, the differences between Paul and Luke are crucial to answering our question. After all, if there are no differences and Luke is simply using a different genre to express the same regenerative theology as Paul, then Pentecostal pneumatology is clearly askew. Pentecostals maintain that each biblical author should be allowed to speak for himself before integrating his perspective into the whole. The interpreter should not flatten out legitimate biblical diversities in the interest of traditional systematic-theological categories; the diversities in the New Testament are God-ordained diversities. And in the case of Luke's focus on the empowering work of the Spirit, incorporating his distinctive contribution is essential to a holistic understanding of the New Testament teaching on the Spirit. Thus, Pentecostals address the question by allowing Luke to carry out his own theological agenda; the focus of their interpretation is on Luke's own use of terminology and theological emphases.[22]

To illustrate this point we will take some examples from Luke's writings, beginning with elements of his Gospel.[23] Luke's account of Jesus' anointed life contains several pivotal descriptions that are unique to him; that is, they are not found in other Gospel accounts. His unique treatment of the Holy Spirit in the public ministry of Jesus begins with the baptism account (Luke 3:21–22). In all three Gospels the Holy Spirit descends on Jesus

---

[22]I. H. Marshall (*Luke: Historian and Theologian* [Grand Rapids: Eerdmans, 1970], 75) defines the issue in these same terms, arguing that Luke differs from Paul in some respects and must be allowed to speak as a theologian in his own right.

[23]Cf. R. F. O'Toole, *Unity of Luke's Theology* (Wilmington, Del.: Michael Glazier, 1984). He points out the many parallels between Jesus' life and ministry in Luke and the life and ministry of the early church in Acts. Stronstad ("The Influence of the Old Testament on the Charismatic Theology of St. Luke," *Pneuma* 2 [1980]: 46) likewise points out the similarities between Jesus and the church, arguing that the transfer of the Spirit from Jesus to the disciples is evocative of Old Testament prophetic transference.

after his baptism, but only Luke says the Spirit descended "as he was praying" (v. 21). This is an important part of the foundation Luke builds regarding the Spirit's work; his empowering work is closely linked to prayer (cf. Acts 4:31; 13:1–3).

Moreover, when Jesus is "led by the Spirit in the desert" to be tempted by Satan, only Luke says that he was "full of the Holy Spirit," clearly emphasizing that he defeated Satan by the power of the Spirit (Luke 4:1). Luke also uniquely attributes the power of Jesus' public ministry to the fact that he ministered "in the power of the Spirit" (4:14). In other words, Luke emphasizes the empowering work of the Spirit in the life of Jesus, clearly portraying the Spirit as the source of spiritual power that enabled him to defeat Satan and proclaim the gospel with authority (e.g., 4:15–30, 31–37; cf. Acts 10:38).[24] This same anointing with the Spirit for witness and service is given to the church in Acts.

Beginning with Jesus' command to the disciples in Acts 1:5 to wait for the baptism in the Holy Spirit (cf. Luke 3:16), we see that Luke's emphasis is on the empowering work of the Spirit for witness.[25] Spirit-baptism in Acts is not defined in terms of

---

[24]J. D. G. Dunn (*Baptism in the Holy Spirit* [Philadelphia: Westminster, 1970], 32) argues that the "empowering for service" of Jesus through the anointing with the Spirit is "only a corollary to it" and not its primary purpose. To Dunn, the primary purpose is to "initiate the individual into the new age and covenant, to 'Christ' (= anoint) him, and in so doing to equip him for life and service in that new age and covenant. In this Jesus' entry into the new age and covenant is the type of every initiate's entry into the new age and covenant." Two observations are in order. (1) Dunn states that empowerment is merely a corollary to the anointing, yet Luke's descriptions are cast exclusively in terms of empowerment rather than of regeneration. (2) Dunn observes that the anointing both initiates and equips for new age life. Here he is not necessarily at odds with Pentecostals, who hold that the anointing for service, in addition to regeneration, was the common experience of the initiate in the New Testament (thus, for example, we have Paul's question to the disciples in Acts 19:1–6). Moreover, equipping for service is not the same work of the Spirit as moral transformation. Dunn here appears to support the Pentecostal position even though he is explicitly rejecting it, in that he acknowledges that the empowering dimension of the Spirit's work is distinct from regeneration. Even Peter's own use of Jesus as an example is focused on empowerment (10:38). Cf. also Howard M. Ervin, *Conversion-Initiation and the Baptism in the Holy Spirit* (Peabody, Mass.: Hendrickson, 1984), 161.

[25]This is a reference to John's prophecy in Luke 3:16. The use of fire in the Old Testament (e.g., Mal. 3:24) and at Qumran (e.g., 1QS 4) as a symbol of purification has often been proffered as the background for Luke's usage. This background has

regeneration/sanctification but in terms of power for witness (Acts 1:8). When the fulfillment of the Old Testament expectation occurs (e.g., Num. 11:29; Joel 2:28–32) and the disciples are filled with the Holy Spirit (Acts 2:1–4), Luke describes the experience in a manner evocative of Old Testament prophetic anointings, accompanied by prophetic-type speech and other signs (e.g., strong winds, fire).[26] In point of fact, the crowd observing the events was bewildered and amazed (vv. 6, 7, 12), and some even said those being baptized were drunk (v. 13).

When Peter subsequently explains the events of the day, he appeals to Joel 2:28–32, a prophecy that describes the empowering work of the Spirit (e.g., prophecy, dreams, visions). Furthermore, the introductory phrase to this prophecy, "afterward" (Joel 2:28), is changed in Peter's sermon to "in the last days" (Acts 2:17), thus emphasizing the characteristic working of power by the Spirit during the "last days." The conclusion to Peter's sermon (2:38–39), then, must be understood in the light of this context, not through an imported Pauline context.[27] Repentance and

---

been used to argue that Luke is speaking of purification and thus salvation when he writes of the outpouring of the Spirit in Acts. But in the Old Testament fire was also associated with the divine sanction of prophetic activity (e.g., Ezek. 1:4–2:8), prophetic speech (e.g., Jer. 5:14; 23:29), and judgment (e.g., Ezek. 15:4–8; 19:12–14). During the intertestamental period the association of fire with prophetic activity continued. The prophetic word could be described as a torch and the prophet himself pictured as a fire arising to proclaim God's word (Sir. 48:1; cf. 1QH 3:28–36). During this time fire was also used as a symbol of God's presence and/or approval of certain individuals and their activities, including prophecy and teaching (e.g., 1 Enoch 14:17; 71:5; *Ber. Rab.* 59:4; *b., Hag* 15b; *Pesiq. Rab Kah.* 88b; *m.,'Abot* 2:10; *b., Ta'an.* 7a; *y., Hag.* 2.1.1). Thus, the conceptual background of baptism with fire is just as likely to have been this prophetic association. Luke is describing the beginning of the church as an anointed community in which prophetic speech as well as other empowering works of the Spirit (e.g., healing, exorcism, etc.) all witness to the gospel of Jesus Christ, and the "tongues of fire" in Acts 2:3 may very well have symbolized God's own sanctioning of the church's prophetic activity.

[26]Cf. Stronstad, "Influence," *passim*, esp. 46.

[27]Dunn (*Baptism*, 38–54) consistently interprets Acts 2 through Pauline spectacles (e.g., 47–48). He also does not adequately account for Luke's use of language identical to 2:4 to describe additional "fillings" of people who have already been baptized (e.g., 4:31; 13:52). Dunn concludes that in Acts Spirit baptism "is the gift of saving grace by which one enters into Christian experience and life, into the new covenant, into the church. It is, in the last analysis, that which makes a man a Chris-

baptism in the name of Jesus indeed bring salvation (2:38), but Luke is careful to emphasize the empowering work of the Spirit rather than inner transformation.[28]

That Pentecost is the beginning of the church's mission and the final stage in the inauguration of the new age hardly needs to be reiterated here. Anointing with the Spirit brought to fullness the early believer's experience of the gospel. But the one inauguration of the new age should not be confused with the distinct works of the Spirit that were anticipated for the new age. While anointing with the Spirit was the common experience of the initiate in the New Testament, it is different from regeneration and should not be theologically absorbed into it.

In the same regard, disassociation of the Spirit's empowering work from salvation is not necessary for Pentecostal pneumatology, nor is it warranted from the evidence in Luke–Acts. Peter's sermon explicitly links the outpouring to repentance and baptism in the name of Jesus (Acts 2:38), and as the kingdom advances according to the program of 1:8 (Jerusalem, Judea, Samaria, the ends of the earth), each pivot includes the salvation of yet another major people group (e.g., Samaritans in ch. 8; Gentiles in ch. 10). The common view imparted to me, as one raised in Pentecostalism, was that in the New Testament both salvation and baptism in the Holy Spirit often occurred as part of one conversion-initiation complex of events. Thus, the "ideal" paradigm for New Testament faith was for the new convert also to be baptized in the Holy Spirit at the very commencement of his or her Christian life. My Pentecostal elders usually lament the loss of that pattern, which has resulted in a contemporary environment in which the two works of the Spirit are often separated by significant passage of time. Their emphasis has always been on theological separability, not temporal subsequence.

Further evidence of the theological distinctiveness of the Spirit's empowering work is found in Acts 4:31. Here there can be no debate concerning the salvific status of the individuals; they were filled with the Holy Spirit on the day of Pentecost. Yet Luke uses precisely the same language here as we observed in

---

tian" (226). Acts does describe normal entrance into the kingdom, but it is not cast in terms of regeneration.

[28]Note, however, that regeneration is not absent from Acts (see 15:9).

2:4 to describe the initial "filling" (cf. also similar language in 4:8; 9:17; 13:9, 52). Luke consistently emphasizes the empowering experience of the Spirit rather than his inner-transforming work, even when the larger contexts of the accounts record the conversion-initiation of new people groups (e.g., 8:14–19; 10:44–46; 11:15–17; 19:1–7). His descriptions of these events portray anointings with the Spirit and power in keeping with the Old Testament's witness and its new age expectation.[29]

Thus, in fulfillment of the Old Testament hope, Luke portrays the church as a charismatic community, called by God to bear witness to the Lord Jesus Christ during the last days and empowered to accomplish this task by the Holy Spirit. Merely to equate Luke's presentation with Pauline regeneration is to lose a vital dimension of the New Testament witness to the work of the Spirit in the church.

Pentecostals, then, read Acts against the background of anointing for witness and service rather than regeneration. This background begins (as we have outlined above) with the Spirit's empowering work in the Old Testament and its expectation that in the new age this experience will be available to *all* God's people. Acts records the historical realization of the Old Testament hope in a way distinct from Paul's teaching on regeneration, even though Paul himself is well aware of the Spirit's empowering anointing (e.g., 1 Cor. 12–14). Specifically, Luke consistently describes the Spirit's work in a manner analogous to the Old Testament anointings associated with the theocratic offices (prophet, priest, and king) rather than exclusively in

---

[29]Over against his own misformulation of Pentecostal theology, Dunn (*Baptism* 62–63, 79–82) argues that Luke is presenting the Spirit as the sine qua non of what it means to be saved and incorporated into the body of Christ. He asserts that Pentecostals, like Catholics, allow for conversion without reception of the Spirit, which is impossible. Pentecostals do not hold this view, nor have any classical Pentecostals ever held this view. In traditional Pentecostal theology, the believer receives the Spirit at salvation as regenerator and indweller, but as anointer subsequent to salvation (cf. Pearlman, *Knowing the Doctrine of the Spirit*, 305–8; Ralph M. Riggs, *The Spirit Himself* [Springfield: Gospel Publishing House, 1949], 4246). Riggs (44) includes a major heading that reads, "ALL BELIEVERS HAVE THE HOLY SPIRIT," and explains, "They who are Christ's have the Spirit of Christ. The Holy Spirit baptizes them into the body of Christ, and the Holy Spirit resides in their hearts. Thus we see that all true born-again believers have the Holy Spirit."

terms of moral transformation, although the latter is probably assumed in fulfillment of the Old Testament hope for the Spirit's inner-transforming work (Acts 2:38; 10:9–16, 34–35, 43). Regeneration is most certainly *not* excluded in Luke's pneumatology; to argue that would be to argue from silence. Simply put, Luke's narrative expresses his own distinctive theological agenda—the Spirit's charismatic anointing.

In distinction to Pentecostalism, which holds that Spirit-baptism is a distinct experience of the Spirit that inaugurates an empowered life of witness, the charismatic movement includes a variety of positions on the issue of a second experience. Some within the charismatic movement hold a position that is virtually the same as Pentecostalism.[30] Others hold that everything the Spirit has for the Christian is received at conversion and from that point on the Christian life is a matter of actualizing what is potential within. But all within the charismatic movement agree that the Spirit empowers the believer and that this empowerment includes miraculous manifestations.

d. Excursus on 1 Corinthians 12:13

> For we were all baptized by one Spirit into one body—whether Jews or Greeks, slave or free—and we were all given the one Spirit to drink.

Frequent appeals to 1 Corinthians 12:13 have been made by those who disagree with the Pentecostal theology of Spirit-baptism, arguing that here Paul defines baptism "by one Spirit" as conversion, thus precluding the possibility that the phrase as it is used elsewhere in the New Testament can refer to an enduement with power subsequent to salvation. Likewise, Pentecostals have offered interpretations of the verse that emphasize the Spirit's agency in bringing the individual into the body of Christ, thus showing that Paul's theology does not preclude Spirit-baptism. We will consider briefly the meaning of this verse in its context and survey the main lines of suggested interpretation.

---

[30]Cf. J. Rodman Williams, *Renewal Theology* (Grand Rapids: Zondervan, 1990), 2:177–79, 198–200. For an overview of various issues and positions cf. Grudem, *Systematic Theology*, 763–87.

In the final analysis, the sense of this verse does not affect the conclusions we have already drawn because Paul is not specifically addressing here one's enduement with power. Granted, his language is similar to the language of Acts, but he is using the language to make a point concerning unity in the body of Christ.

Much of the discussion surrounding this verse centers on the meaning of the Greek phrase "by one Spirit" (*en heni pneumati*). One option is that it signifies the *sphere* or *element* into which the Corinthians have been baptized; in such a case it would be translated "in one Spirit."[31] The other option is that it shows the *Spirit's agency* in baptism into the body of Christ, with the concomitant translation of "by one Spirit."[32] There can be no doubt that Paul's emphasis in the context is on the baptism that all the Corinthians share, which provides the basis for their unity as members of one body. Moreover, the metaphors of the verse, baptism into one body and drinking of the one Spirit, must be understood in the light of the larger context's exclusive concern with unity among the members of Christ's body (e.g., v. 27).[33] Note that the emphasis of the context is on the unity of those who are baptized into the one body of Christ, not those who are baptized in the Spirit, a phrase that does not occur in any form elsewhere in Paul and not necessarily here.[34] In my opinion the

---

[31]So Gordon Fee, *God's Empowering Presence: The Holy Spirit in the Letters of Paul* (Peabody, Mass.: Hendrickson, 1994), 181; idem, *The First Epistle to the Corinthians* (Grand Rapids: Eerdmans, 1987), 6036; Wayne Grudem, *Systematic Theology: An Introduction to Biblical Doctrine* (Grand Rapids: Zondervan, 1994), 767–73; NRSV.

[32]So F. W. Grosheide (*Commentary on the First Epistle to the Corinthians* [Grand Rapids: Eerdmans, 1953], 292–93), who argues that the phrase refers to the work of the Spirit by which the individual is brought into the body of Christ and that *en* is used because the Spirit does not perform the actual rite of baptism; James Moffat, *The First Epistle of Paul to the Corinthians* (New York: Harper, 1938); O. Cullmann, *Baptism in the New Testament*, trans. J. Reid (London: SCM, 1950); NIV; NASB.

[33]Some Pentecostals have advanced the view that the metaphors refer to two different experiences of the Spirit: baptism into the body refers to conversion, while drinking of the one Spirit refers to Spirit baptism (e.g., Ervin, *Conversion-Initiation*, 98–102; R. E. Cottle, "All Were Baptized," *JETS* 17 [1974]: 75–80). There is no evidence in the context that Paul has two experiences in mind. Furthermore, his use of a closely related metaphor in 1 Corinthians 10:1–4 cannot be taken this way.

[34]In fact both NIV and NASB opt for the "agency" translation. Fee (*God's Empowering Presence*, 180–81) argues that Paul is emphasizing the common reception of the Spirit, the "most crucial element" in conversion. Certainly this is not arguable as a

NIV and NASB translators have captured the emphasis of the verse, which is on baptism into the body of Christ and the work of the Spirit as the means by which this is accomplished (see above).

Nevertheless, the specific sense of *en heni pneumati* remains a debatable point. Whichever view of verse 13 one adopts (sphere or agency), it does not change the argument for an empowering work of the Spirit that is distinct from salvation (based on biblical theology and Lukan pneumatology). Obviously, the "agency" view of 1 Corinthians 12:13 presents no problems for Pentecostal theology. But neither does the "sphere" view, since it is clear from the evidence previously presented that Luke and Paul use similar language to speak of different works of the Spirit. Even if Paul has in view here a "baptism in the Spirit" that brings one into the body of Christ (conversion), it does not change the fact that Luke presents an empowering work of the Spirit that is distinct from salvation.

Furthermore, Paul is not unaware of this empowering work of the Spirit (e.g., 1 Cor 12:4–11). The entire context of 1 Corinthians 12–14 addresses abuses that arose among the Corinthian believers, especially the proclivity to abuse tongues, because of misunderstandings about the Spirit's miraculous work apart from conversion. Paul was unapologetic and thankful to God concerning his own extensive experiences of speaking in tongues, which surpassed even the experience of the Corinthians (14:18). And the list of gifts in 12:4–11 exhibits broad knowledge of the varieties of manifestations that the Spirit works according to his own will. In sum, there is nothing in these chapters, and nothing in 12:13 in particular, that precludes the Pentecostal doctrine of Spirit-baptism.

Thus, the only case that could possibly be built from 1 Corinthians 12:13 against the Pentecostal view of the Spirit's empowering work (although not persuasively, in my opinion) is that Pentecostals have used the wrong label in adopting "baptism

---

part of Pauline theology more broadly. However, in this particular context, the primary concern of Paul is not on the order of salvation (call, faith, regeneration, justification, etc.) but on the nature of the body of Christ into which all believers have been baptized. Paul is stressing salvation understood from the perspective of the status it brings to the believer as a member of the body of Christ. Also, the syntax of the Greek construction demands that the prepositional phrase "into one body" function as the immediate referent of "we were all baptized," not "in one Spirit."

in the Holy Spirit" from among the options in the New Testament. But no case can be built based on this verse (nor, in my opinion, on any text of Scripture) against the substance of the Pentecostal doctrine of an enduement with the Spirit and power that is distinct from conversion. Many arguments against the Pentecostal doctrine of Spirit-baptism militate only against the label; they do not really address the substance of the issue. Non-Pentecostals who give serious consideration to this issue should resolve not to use the Pentecostal systematic-theological label for the experience as an excuse to shift the focus of the discussion off the *substance* of biblical teaching, focusing instead merely on the label itself as the rationale for dismissing the Pentecostal view.

e. Excursus on Initial Physical Evidence

Classical Pentecostals hold that the initial physical evidence (hereafter, IPE) of Spirit-baptism is speaking in tongues (if there is no manifestation of tongues, then there has been no Spirit-baptism). It is well known that the historic Pentecostal proof of this doctrine is based on the historical pattern of the book of Acts. That is, Acts consistently portrays speaking in tongues as the manifestation that accompanies Spirit-baptism. But in recent years other approaches have yielded further insight into this particular doctrine. The purpose of this excursus is simply to bring to the attention of the reader several of these recent approaches, though we cannot analyze them in depth. This brief survey will provide information to facilitate further investigation.

The traditional argument for IPE is based on the historical precedent in the book of Acts.[35] Pentecostals have long held that historical narrative is a legitimate mode of theological writing in its own right. And in contemporary scholarship there is no debate concerning the ideological purpose of biblical historiography. Biblical history is not positivist history; it is history with a theological agenda.[36] But this point still leaves two issues unresolved: the imitation of *positive* biblical precedent, and the demonstration of authorial intent.

---

[35]Cf. Roger Stronstad, "The Biblical Precedent for Historical Precedent," *Paraclete* 27/3 (1993): 1–10.

[36]See I. H. Marshall, *Luke: Historian and Theologian*, 22–28.

Acts clearly indicates that tongues was associated with Spirit-baptism and that tongues also functioned as evidence of this work of the Spirit (cf. Acts 2:4–11). Note how the circumcised believers at the house of Cornelius knew that the Spirit had been poured out on the Gentiles precisely because they heard them speaking in tongues (10:46). No other manifestation associated with Spirit-baptism in Acts is explicitly presented as evidence of the authenticity of the experience.

But the point of objection concerning tongues as IPE does not center on the function of tongues as presented in Acts, but on whether Luke intended the function of tongues in his book as a continuing, mandated paradigm for this experience.[37] Inasmuch as the historical account, carefully presented by the author (a claim he himself makes, cf. Luke 1:1–4; Acts 1:1–2), attaches an evidential function only to tongues, Pentecostals argue that Luke's intent is to mandate this relationship between the outpouring of the Spirit and tongues.

Beyond this traditional Pentecostal interpretation of Acts, two specific insights from narratology have proven helpful in more recent years in determining Luke intent: the idea of narrative as "narrative world" and narrative analogy.[38] Both of these aspects of narratological analysis are ways of looking at "patterns" as evidence of an author's intent in creating a narrative.

(i) Regarding the notion of "narrative world," in any historical narrative, the manner of retelling has a purpose: to inform a community about its heritage, identity, common experience, and essential qualities. The narrator at the same time is informing the community about the nature of its own world, how it ought to be structured, and in some instances how it ought not to be structured. Thus, in the case of biblical narrative, the accounts provide order to our "world" and are intended to tell

---

[37]There are many pieces to this puzzle and many intriguing questions that have no clear answer in the Scriptures. For example, what was the genesis of the Corinthians' misguided and abusive obsession with tongues? Is it possible that this abuse originated in the misappropriation of the evidentiary function of tongues? That is, having understood tongues to be evidence of the Spirit's empowering work, did they then begin to abuse the manifestation of tongues as a means to gain spiritual status in the congregation?

[38]On the analysis of Acts as "narrative world" see Johns, "Some New Directions," 153–56.

us how to live our lives, how we experience the Spirit's presence, etc.[39] The author uses the biblical "narrative world" to shape the believing community's world.

(ii) The second useful perspective on authorial intent is provided by what Meir Sternberg calls "narrative analogy."[40] This refers to a specific relationship among events in a narrative, inviting readers to read one story in terms of other similar stories. Thus one event provides "oblique commentary" on another. The narrator accomplishes this particular phenomenon through carefully developed patterns or "echoes." His repetition of similar or contrasting events establishes the points of comparison for the reader. Repeating themes, details, phrases, behaviors, etc., call the reader's attention to the analogy. The "echo effect" thus serves to control interpretation, adding emphasis and specifying communication of central meanings.[41]

The composition of Luke–Acts was surely not a haphazard process. The analogies, or echo effects, in the narrative are evident because of the careful crafting of the narrative by the author. He included details because they were central to his agenda. In the case of tongues and Spirit-baptism in Acts, it seems improbable that Luke was unaware of the echo he was creating. Rather, he intentionally created the relationship between tongues and Spirit-baptism in his narrative, along with the specific function of tongues as evidence, in order to communicate that relationship to his readership as a prescribed paradigm.

(iii) A redemptive-historical approach to the IPE doctrine is a third more recent development in Pentecostal hermeneutics. Simply stated, in the Old Testament when the Spirit came upon the prophets, prophetic speech always accompanied the Spirit's anointing. Likewise in Acts, when the Spirit comes upon an individual for the first time, Spirit-prompted speech occurs, except that in Acts the utterance is in tongues. Another dimension of this redemptive-historical development pertains specifically to Acts 10:44–46, where tongues is more than evidence of an individual experience (although it is that). There glossalalia also

---

[39]Ibid., 154.

[40]Meir Sternberg, *The Poetics of Biblical Narrative* (Bloomington: Indiana Univ. Press, 1985), 365.

[41]R. C. Tannehill, "The Composition of Acts 3–5: Narrative Development and Echo Effect," *SBLSemPap* 23 (1984): 229.

functions as evidence of the inclusion of Gentiles in the Spirit's anointing. Stated in principle, it is evidence that the Spirit's power is for *all* who come into the kingdom.

Charismatics for the most part diverge from Pentecostals on this issue. Among those who hold to a distinct anointing work of the Holy Spirit subsequent to salvation, few argue that tongues are the biblically mandated evidence of the experience. While speaking in tongues is normally associated with the experience, it is not necessarily manifested on every occasion of Spirit-baptism.[42]

3. Should Christians Seek the Empowering Work of the Spirit Today?

Pentecostals believe on the basis of their understanding of the New Testament fulfillment of the Old Testament that *both* works of the Spirit are for the contemporary believer, and therefore that every believer should desire both experiences. Indeed, every believer should desire all that the Lord has for her or him, which is demonstrably not restricted to conversion or even the inaugural Spirit-baptism of Pentecostalism. The Spirit's inner-transforming work continues in sanctification, and his empowering work continues after the initial filling with many more. Pentecostals today voice the same hope as Moses once voiced, "I wish that all the LORD's people were prophets and that the LORD would put his Spirit on them" (Num. 11:29).

Since there are two works of the Spirit clearly revealed in Scripture, it is equally clear that there are no injunctions found against either one. To the contrary, the exclusive view of Scripture points to both as desirable blessings from God; the narrative of Acts portrays for us a worldview in keeping with this, as do other portions of the New Testament (e.g., Rom. 6–8; 12; 1 Cor. 1:4–9; 12–14; Gal. 3:5; Eph. 1:1–14; 5:15–20; James 5:13–18). Moreover, with regard to the Spirit's empowering work, we are expressly commanded to seek such experiences (e.g., 1 Cor. 14:1–5) and not to forbid them or treat them with contempt (e.g., 14:39; 1 Thess. 5:19–21). Pentecostals believe Spirit-baptism, as presented in Acts, is the first in a sequence of similar empowering

---

[42]Cf. Williams, *Renewal Theology*, 2:211–12. He argues that tongues are the primary evidence, but not the only or the necessary evidence.

experiences of the Spirit that God provides to equip believers for witness and service—not disassociated from the regeneration that opens the door for spiritual power in the first place, but distinguished from it as a discrete working of power by God's Holy Spirit.[43]

By now it is obvious that this discussion inevitably veers toward the closely related question of cessationism. Thus we come on to the next section of our discussion.

C. ON THE CESSATION OF MIRACULOUS GIFTS

Jack Deere wrote concerning the origin of the doctrine of cessationism:

> No one ever just picked up the Bible, started reading, and then came to the conclusion that God was not doing signs and wonders anymore and that the gifts of the Holy Spirit had passed away. The doctrine of cessationism did not originate from a careful study of the Scriptures. The doctrine of cessationism originated in experience.[44]

Deere goes on to explain that the *lack* of miracles in Christian experience led to various attempts in church history to explain them as temporary endowments not to be expected anymore in the life of the church, and that a naive reader would never come to cessationist conclusions—in fact, quite the opposite.[45] This sec-

---

[43]Contra Dunn, *Baptism*, 226–27, passim. Pentecostal theology does not hold that Spirit baptism is an absolute prerequisite for empowering experience in the Christian life. Pentecostals do, however, understand Luke's theology of the Spirit's empowering work to be God's will for every believer. Thus, during New Testament times believers would have already experienced the enduement with power at the time any manifestations of the Spirit occurred. The combination of regeneration and anointing *should* still be the universal experience in Christian life. Furthermore, it should be noted that Pentecostals traditionally embrace a high view of God's sovereignty in these matters and accept the sovereign moving of his Spirit even when it does not necessarily align with their own distinctive aspects of faith and practice.

[44]Deere, *Surprised by the Power of the Spirit*, 99.

[45]Ibid., 99–103, 114. To the historical reasons for cessationist doctrine he adds the reaction of the Reformers to Rome, but this was not primary—lack of experience was the salient motivation. From my perspective it also seems that many cessationist arguments have been forged in response to the Pentecostal revival of this century.

tion presents evidence in support of Deere's observation concerning the natural reading of Scripture. The purpose in presenting such evidence is not to refute cessationist arguments that have been offered in church history but rather to present a biblical case for the continuing empowering work of the Spirit in the church throughout the "last days."[46]

In order to accomplish this, (1) we will proceed along redemptive-historical lines. Evidence from biblical theology points to three key issues that require our attention and on which the Pentecostal view rests: (a) the nature and duration of the "last days"; (b) the establishment of the Davidic kingdom, which forms the foundation for the outpouring of the Spirit during the last days; and (c) the biblical theology of the Spirit. (2) Having framed the issue within redemptive history, we will move to New Testament texts that teach specifically about miraculous gifts. (3) Finally, the broader issues of canon formation and the apostolate will be considered.

1. Continuity of Miraculous Gifts in Redemptive-Historical Perspective

The modern Pentecostal movement has from its inception emphasized Peter's "this is what is spoken" definition of the "last days" as the primary foundation for the empowering aspects of its pneumatology. Spurred on by this understanding of fulfillment, Pentecostals have steadfastly proclaimed the continuing charismatic nature of the church empowered by the Spirit. In my opinion, biblical theology not only supports such a reading, it prescribes it. Moreover, just as narrative provided the framework for the actualization of the old covenant (e.g., Deut. 6–11), so also narrative provides the framework for the actualization of the new. Luke's narration depicts the results of covenant fulfillment through the outpouring of the Spirit by Jesus.

---

[46]Deere points out (ibid., 101) that this whole debate is obtuse because there is not a single specific text of Scripture that teaches miracles and miraculous gifts were restricted to the New Testament period. At the same time, this was not an issue for the New Testament authors, so they did not defend continuity either.

a. The "Last Days"

Although Peter quotes from Joel 2:28–32 to explain the events of the day of Pentecost, the events themselves would probably have been understood more broadly as the fulfillment of the larger Old Testament expectation that anointing with the Spirit would be universalized in the new age (see above). Peter's citation of Joel follows the LXX with a few modifications, primarily the substitution of "in the last days" for Joel's "afterward" (LXX reads "after these things"; cf. Joel 2:28; Acts 2:17). With this modification Peter equates Pentecost with the emergence of the new age, specifically identifying this event with the Old Testament expectation of the "last days" as a time of messianic blessing (cf. Isa. 2:2ff.; Jer. 31:33–34; Ezek. 36:26–27; 39:29; Hos. 3:5; Mic. 4:1ff.).[47] Hence, with the outpouring of the Spirit the awaited age has come.[48]

Moreover, the last days are characterized by "wonders in the heavens above and *signs* on the earth below" (Acts 2:19). Peter modifies Joel's "wonders in the heavens and on the earth" (Joel 2:30), probably to bring attention to the miraculous activity (fire, wind, and particularly glossolalia) that signifies the realization of the Old Testament hope for the outpouring of the Spirit in the "last days." It is often pointed out in objection to this understanding of the text that the more cosmic events (Acts 2:19b–20) simply did not occur and therefore Acts 2 is not the fulfillment of Joel's prophecy.[49] But in the light of Peter's clear fulfillment language (e.g., "this is what is spoken"), it is better to understand the signs that occurred on the day of Pentecost as marking out the beginning of the last days and the more cosmic signs as belonging to the end of the last days, just prior to the day of the Lord.[50] In any event, to read Acts 2 in any manner that excludes its significance as the dawning of the age of the prophet-

---

[47]Note that in Isaiah 2:2ff. and Micah 4:1ff. people gather from all nations to Mount Zion (cf. Acts 2:5).

[48]So F. F. Bruce, *The Book of Acts* (Grand Rapids: Eerdmans, 1981), 68; I. H. Marshall, *The Acts of the Apostles* (Grand Rapids: Eerdmans, 1980), 73–74; and "Significance of Pentecost," *SJT* 30 (1977): 358.

[49]See, for example, T. R. Edgar, *Miraculous Gifts* (Neptune: Loizeaux Brothers, 1983), 75.

[50]So Marshall, *Acts of the Apostles*, in loc.

hood of all believers does violence to the redemptive-historical framework of Peter's sermon as well as the Lukan context.

This is also borne out by another modification in the citation. In Acts 2:18 Peter emphasizes the prophetic and universal nature of the outpouring by reiterating the prophecy theme from verse 17 with the addition of "and they will prophesy" (v. 18c; not found in Joel); in so doing, Peter expands the prophetic gift to an even greater variety of persons (e.g., male and female servants) than we find in Joel's original text. In the new age the gift of prophecy is no longer restricted to particular groups, such as institutional prophets, priests, and kings; rather, it is poured out on all of God's people, giving them the prophetic enduement.[51]

The presence and empowering activity of the Holy Spirit thus characterizes the life of God's people during the last days, a theological point Luke emphasizes (cf. Acts 4:8, 31; 6:3, 10; 7:55; 8:14–19; 10:19, 38, 44–46; 13:1–4, 9, 52; 19:16). This does not exclude the equally characteristic inner-transforming work of the Spirit in regeneration and sanctification, but it is clearly a different dimension. Failure to incorporate the empowering dimension of the Spirit's work into pneumatology results in an understanding of the Spirit that is not only less than fully orbed, but also deficient.

Finally, the last days do not conclude until the Lord's return (Acts 2:20b). There is not a scrap of biblical evidence that the last days are subdivided, postponed, or changed prior to the day of the Lord. Indeed, all evidence indicates that the last days continue in characteristic fashion *without* any pivotal changes until the Lord brings them to a close with his return (cf. 1 Tim. 4:1; 2 Tim. 3:1; Heb. 1:2; James 5:3; 1 Peter 1:20; 2 Peter 3:3; 1 John 2:18). And to sustain the church during the last days, the Lord has given her the Spirit as *both regenerator and anointer.*

b. The Davidic Kingdom

In Luke–Acts the Davidic reign is integrally related to the nature of the "last days," providing further redemptive-historical

---

[51]Cf. M. M. B. Turner, "Jesus and the Spirit in Lukan Perspective," *TynBul* 32 (1981): 38; Marshall, "Significance," 358; E. Haenchen, *The Acts of the Apostles* (Philadelphia: Westminster, 1971), 179.

perspective on those days as a phase of the kingdom (e.g., Luke 1:32–33, 68–79; Acts 2:25–39). In Acts 2:25–39 it is Christ who fulfills the Davidic promises and through whom the eternal Davidic reign is begun by pouring out the Spirit on all flesh. Indeed, the "last days" phase of the Davidic reign is *defined* by the outpoured Holy Spirit—Christ as Davidic king has accomplished what happened on the day of Pentecost, and this work will continue through the church over which he reigns (Acts 1:6–8; 2:25–39).[52] Not only is the Davidic reign central to Luke–Acts, it is central also to the New Testament concept of kingdom (e.g., Luke 1:32–33; Rom. 1:2ff; Rev. 22:16ff.). In other words, empowering activity by the Spirit, together with the diversity of the Spirit's work, characterizes the Davidic reign of Jesus.

To make his point on the day of Pentecost, Peter quotes Psalm 16:8–11, interpreting it as a statement about Messiah's resurrection in the light of David's death, burial, and decay (cf. Acts 13:32–37). Since David was not speaking of himself but about the Christ, he was speaking prophetically about a descendant of his who would sit eternally on his throne (2:30).[53] The reference to the eternal throne of David (v. 30b) reflects a series of Old Testament texts that are conceptually linked by this motif (e.g., 2 Sam. 7:11b–16; Pss. 89:3–4, 35–37; 132:11–18), the fulfillment of which Peter identifies with Jesus' resurrection and exaltation

---

[52]So also D. L. Bock ("The Reign of the Lord Christ," in *Dispensationalism, Israel, and the Church: The Search for Definition*, eds. C. Blaising and D. Bock [Grand Rapids: Zondervan, 1992], 37–67, esp. 47–55), who applies this Lukan perspective to the current discussion within dispensationalism. His point concerning miraculous occurrences (exorcisms, healings, etc.) is also worth noting for our purposes: These constitute the coming of the kingdom in nascent but powerful form (53–55). For similar views see J. Ruthven (*On the Cessation of the Charismata: The Protestant Polemic on Postbiblical Miracles* [Sheffield: Sheffield Academic, 1993], 115–23), who argues that a biblical theology of the kingdom is "inimical" to cessationism; R. E. Brown, *The Gospel According to John* (New York: Doubleday, 1980), 1:528–30; D. Williams, *Signs, Wonders and the Kingdom of God* (Ann Arbor: Servant, 1989), passim; G. E. Ladd, *A Theology of the New Testament* (Grand Rapids: Eerdmans, 1974), 67–69, 76–77.

[53]Bock ("The Reign of the Lord Christ," 49–53) argues that Jesus is the reigning Davidite sitting on David's throne, and that his present work is accomplished in his capacity as the eternal Davidite, a view I share. The last days usher in the spiritual blessings of the Davidic reign. Here our purpose is to apply this principle to the continuity of miraculous gifts, but it does have other implications (see Bock's excellent article).

to the "right hand of God" (Acts 2:33–35).[54] In quoting Psalm 110:1, Peter reinforces the present reign of Christ by coupling his position at the right hand of God with the Davidic "throne," an image of ruling authority. Thus, Christ's resurrection constituted his enthronement as the eternal Davidic king and inaugurated his eternal reign.[55]

With regard to the issue of cessationism, the significance of this fulfillment is found in Acts 2:30. In his capacity as the ruling Davidic king, Jesus has poured out the Holy Spirit. This is the central dimension of the present phase of the Davidic kingdom, which Luke continues to demonstrate throughout Acts by detailing the new life in the Spirit. For example, Jesus, the eternally reigning Davidite, continues to pour out the Holy Spirit on diverse people groups (chs. 8, 10, 19), whose experiences are similar or identical to those on whom the Spirit was poured out at the beginning (e.g., 10:44–46; 11:15; 19:1–6). Even in the case of the gentile outpouring in ch. 10 (Cornelius' household), Jesus' Davidic anointing is made explicit (10:36–38; cf. 1 Sam. 16:13). Thus, again we see that the outpoured Spirit defines the Davidic kingdom in the last days, and the manifestations of power wrought by the Holy Spirit in Jesus' name manifest the authority of his reign (e.g., Acts 3:12ff.; 4:7–12, 33; 6:8–15; 9:1–19; 10:1–48; 14:8–18; 19:1–22).

Moreover, the experiences of the early church are also similar to those of Jesus, particularly with regard to the empowerment of the Spirit for evangelism. There are too many parallels to detail all of them here, though detailed analyses have been done.[56] Here our purpose is to observe Jesus' transfer of the anointing-with-the-Spirit-and-power that he received at the Jordan to the church beginning at Pentecost. Having received the

---

[54]Cf. also Luke 1, which announces Jesus' birth primarily in terms of his Davidic identity, and 3:21–22 (a triple tradition found also in Matt. 3:13–17 and Mark 1:9–11), which links Jesus' baptism to his role as Davidite by using the conceptual thread of Psalm 2 and Isaiah 42:1.

[55]So also Bock, "The Reign of the Lord Christ," 49–51; Marshall, *Acts*, 76–80. Not every dimension of the Davidic reign is fulfilled at Pentecost (e.g., socio-political aspects), but the reign of the eternal Davidite has nonetheless commenced and the kingdom has been set in motion toward consummation.

[56]See O'Toole, *Unity of Luke's Theology*.

same anointing as David, the anointing with the Spirit and power (cf. 1 Sam. 16:13; Luke 3:21–22; 4:1, 14, 16–21, 31–32; Acts 10:38), Jesus passes that anointing on to the church to empower the believers for witness (Acts 1:6–8; 2:4ff., 33; 4:8, 31; etc.). The disciples' preaching of Christ's kingdom is characterized by the same boldness as Jesus' own preaching,[57] and they perform the same kinds of healings and exorcisms—and not in their ministries but by others as well.[58] In other words, the anointed Davidite, Jesus, passes on his own anointing to those who come under his reign.[59]

There can be no doubt that one of Luke's primary points is to demonstrate the inclusion of all people in the Davidic kingdom (e.g., Samaritans and Gentiles in Acts 8 and 10 respectively). And their inclusion in the kingdom is marked by the outpouring of the Spirit on them. But this does not collapse Luke's empowering understanding of the nature of the kingdom during the last days into a Pauline theology of regeneration. We know from other New Testament authors (e.g., Paul) that regeneration is the experience of the Spirit that *births one into* the body of Christ. We know from Luke (though not exclusively from him) that charismatic anointing with the Spirit *typifies life within* the body of Christ in fulfillment of the redemptive-historical expectation.[60] The traditional categories of systematic theology should not be applied in such a manner that they flatten out the legitimate perspectives of biblical theology.[61] Thus, with regard

---

[57]Consider the linkage in the Spirit-anointed proclamation of the kingdom by John the Baptist (Luke 1:41, 67, 80; 3:1–20), Jesus (e.g., 4:14, 16–21, 31–32), Peter (e.g., Acts 4:8; 10:34–46), Philip (6:3–6; 8:4–13, 26–40), Paul (e.g., 9:1–31; 13:1–3, 9; 19:1–7, 11–12), and Barnabas (e.g., Acts 11:22–26).

[58]These occur throughout Acts (e.g., Acts 8; 9:17; 11:27ff.; 13:3), and there is evidence elsewhere in the New Testament (e.g., 1 Cor. 12–14). In contemporary New Testament scholarship this point has become so axiomatic that it scarcely needs documentation.

[59]So also Craig L. Blomberg, "Healing," in *Dictionary of Jesus and the Gospels* (Downers Grove, Ill.: InterVarsity, 1992), 305–6.

[60]So also Grudem, *Gift of Prophecy in the New Testament*, 250–52; Deere, *Surprised by the Power of the Spirit*, 99–115, 229–52; Ruthven, *Charismata*, 115–23.

[61]Even a basic survey indicates that the majority of biblical references to the Spirit's presence and activity are broadly charismatic in nature (prophetic, empowering, etc.); references to his inner-transforming work are much less frequent. See Ruthven, *Charismata*, 114–15, n. 2. The phrase "history of salvation" refers to the his-

to fulfillment during the last days, Luke's pneumatology finds its basis in the Davidic covenant and its nature in the Old Testament prophetic tradition.

c. The Spirit in Redemptive History

As already noted, the Spirit in Scripture operates in charismatic fashion. This consistent activity provides yet another thread of redemptive-historical framework for the continuity position and calls into question contemporary pneumatological formulations that omit this predominant biblical expression of the Spirit's character. Here we will draw some conclusions for a biblical theology of the Spirit, based on the foundation we have already laid.

First, it strikes me as irreconcilable with the biblical record of the Spirit's person and work when contemporary theologians restrict and confine the evidence to such an extent that the resultant pneumatology bears little semblance to the Bible's powerful, *immutable*, God the Holy Spirit.[62] Indeed, to confine so narrowly the contemporary application of the Scripture's teaching on the Spirit denatures the third member of the Trinity. Given the dearth of explicit evidence, it strains credulity to postulate a point in time (whether the death of the last apostle, the end of New Testament canon formation, completion of the foundation of the church, or whatever) that effects a dramatic mutation in the Spirit's person and work so that he is no longer the power-anointing, charismatic being he once was, but is now restricted solely to his inner-transforming work. Not only is this scenario askew of the overwhelming biblical evidence concerning the Spirit's nature and work, but it also abjectly fails to account for the fulfillment of the redemptive-historical hope concerning life in the Spirit in the new covenant age.[63]

Second, cessationists commonly brandish the *ordo salutis* saber when slashing away those works of the Spirit that God did

---

torical unfolding of the central events in God's plan of salvation, e.g., creation, fall, history of Israel, incarnation, the cross, resurrection, ascension and exaltation, Pentecost, second coming, and new creation.

[62]So also, Deere, *Surprised by the Power of the Spirit*, 45–76, passim; Grudem, *Prophecy in the New Testament*, 250–52; Ruthven, *Charismata*, 114–15.

[63]So also Grudem, *Prophecy*, 250–52; Ruthven, *Charismata*, 114–15.

not intend for the contemporary church. Conditioned by traditional (e.g., Reformed, Baptist, dispensational) systematic theology, they ask only a limited set of questions concerning the Spirit's postapostolic work (e.g., the questions of nature, regeneration, and sanctification), and they fail to recognize that the lion's share of biblical evidence defines the Spirit as a charismatic being and points to the continuity of his empowering work during the new covenant epoch.[64] This argument is not intended to exclude moral transformation, which is central also to the Spirit's person and work, but simply to expand the discussion beyond those narrowly drawn boundaries of traditional *ordo salutis* language.

Third, as Jack Deere has aptly pointed out with respect to miraculous gifts, "pure biblical objectivity" is a myth.[65] Cornelius Van Til has argued that there are "no brute facts" because ultimate commitments (e.g., regenerate or unregenerate commitments) color everything the individual perceives.[66] In fact, at least since Rudolf Bultmann's well-known essay, "Is Presuppositionless Exegesis Possible?" there has been no significant debate concerning *whether* our ultimate commitments influence our understanding of biblical texts.[67] The discussion rather has centered on how, to what degree, and by what ultimate commitments (presuppositions) we are influenced. Applying this to miraculous gifts and the cessationism question, Deere makes the point that the *lack* of miraculous experience historically has led to the development of cessationist doctrine. To this should be added the theological conditioning of an approach that operates exclusively in terms of the traditional systematic-theological categories of salvation.

On the other hand, those whose commitments include charismatic experience should not ignore the objective propositional truth of Scripture. While it is inevitable that every

---

[64]Cf. Deere, *Surprised by the Power of the Spirit*, 45–56; Ruthven, *Charismata*, 114–15. Ruthven's discussion specifically evaluates B. B. Warfield's cessationist view; Deere's discussion is broader in scope.

[65]Deere, *Surprised by the Power of the Spirit*, 45–56.

[66]C. Van Til, *The Defense of the Faith*, 2d ed. (Philadelphia: Presbyterian and Reformed, 1963).

[67]See R. Bultmann, "Is Presuppositionless Exegesis Possible?" in *Existence and Faith: Shorter Writings*, ed. S. Ogden (New York: Meridian, 1960), 289–96.

reader is influenced by belief, God is also able to overcome human fallibility in the reading process and impress on a person the truth of the objective revelation he has given. The desire of this writer and many others in the Pentecostal movement is that we not devolve into an experience-based sect with little regard for the inspired Word, which alone is sufficient for faith and practice. We should not seek experience but God, who gives good gifts. And we should proceed according to the Scriptures rather than departing from them into a pneumatic brand of neo-orthodoxy.

In sum, the progress of redemption establishes the hope of both inner-transforming and empowering dimensions of the Spirit's work in the last days, and then declares the fulfillment of this hope in Jesus, the anointed Davidite. What is more, the larger portion of biblical revelation speaks to the charismatic nature of the Spirit and his work. Hence, there is no biblical warrant to conclude that the Spirit has changed, now that the last days have come.

2. Cessationism in Light of New Testament Teaching on Miraculous Gifts

Having set forth the redemptive-historical case for the Spirit's continuing miraculous work, we turn now to consider further New Testament evidence concerning miraculous gifts within the age of fulfillment.[68] Our purpose in examining these passages is not to lay out detailed historical-grammatical analyses, but rather to address them in terms of their bearing on cessationism. Moreover, there is some difficulty in selecting relevant texts because of the many arguments that incorporate texts with little direct bearing on *charismata*. Thus, the Bible texts we consider in this brief survey will by no means exhaust the subject, but they are salient for the issue at hand and exemplary of the broader teaching of the New Testament on the subject.

---

[68]The Lukan perspective received adequate attention during our examination of redemptive-historical fulfillment, so we restrict ourselves here to other New Testament authors.

a. Passages That Instruct Concerning the Use of Miraculous Gifts

Much has been written on 1 Corinthians 13:8–13 and whether it teaches that the temporary miraculous gifts (e.g., tongues, prophecy, words of knowledge, v. 8) continue until the Lord's return (vv. 10–12); we will therefore not duplicate here the well-known exegetical discussions.[69] Paul in this context is comparing the eternal nature of the more excellent way of love with the temporary nature of certain gifts that fulfill the needs of the church now but that will pass away when "perfection" comes (v. 10). Paul himself defines the transition from "the imperfect" to "perfection" in verses 11–12, and the primary defining characteristic of this transition is a shift from partial knowledge to full knowledge, from impeded perception ("poor reflection," v. 12a) to clear perception ("face to face," v. 12b). This profound transformation in how the believer perceives and knows can anticipate only one event, the return of the Lord.

While Richard Gaffin's point that the text does not absolutely demand continuity is well taken, it does still appear that Paul is teaching the continuity of the miraculous gifts until the Parousia.[70] And *certainly* Paul is not laying down a doctrine of cessation. Moreover, 1 Corinthians 1:7 is conceptually linked to 13:8–12 and supports the "continuity" reading, for there also the gifts are associated with an intervening period in the life of the church, during which believers "eagerly wait for our Lord Jesus Christ to be revealed."

But it is the broader context in 1 Corinthians 12–14 that finally resolves this question. Paul's discussion of the gifts in

---

[69] For example, the sense of "perfection" in verse 10. See Carson, *Showing the Spirit*, 66–72; G. Fee, *The First Epistle to the Corinthians*, 641–52; W. Grudem, *The Gift of Prophecy in 1 Corinthians*, 210–19; idem, *Prophecy in the New Testament*, 224–52; J. Ruthven, *Charismata*, 131–51; M. M. B. Turner, "Spiritual Gifts Then and Now," *VoxEv* 15 (1985): 764. R. Gaffin (*Perspectives on Pentecost: Studies in New Testament Teaching on the Gifts of the Holy Spirit* [Phillipsburg, N.J.: Presbyterian and Reformed, 1979], 109–12), a cessationist, asserts concerning 1 Corinthians 13:10–12, "The coming of 'the perfect' (v. 10) and the 'then' of the believer's full knowledge (v. 12) no doubt refer to the time of Christ's return. The view that they describe the point at which the New Testament canon is completed cannot be made credible exegetically" (109). Nor does it prescribe continuity until the Parousia, according to Gaffin.

[70] Gaffin, *Perspectives on Pentecost*, 109–10.

these chapters identifies their purpose as for the common good of the congregation (12:7; 14:1–19). There is no hint that the miraculous gifts *themselves* at Corinth were abnormal. Indeed, they appear from Acts and Paul's own testimony ("I thank God that I speak in tongues more than all of you," 14:18) to be an accepted and normal feature of new covenant life. The problem at Corinth was abuse of gifts, not their use per se.

Nor is there any connection in this context linking the gifts, including the utterance gifts (e.g., prophecy, tongues, and interpretation), exclusively to inscripturation (canon formation) or the apostolate. In fact, neither of these issues is mentioned and, given Paul's pastoral purpose in the context (to instruct concerning the proper function of the gifts), they probably did not even cross his mind. In my opinion, these cessationistic issues are born out of the contemporary church; it simply would not have occurred to people in the early church to expect or consider anything other than an empowered existence. Cessationism would have been foreign to their understanding of the age of fulfillment. The New Testament church was not looking for reasons to exclude the gifts; those early believers were seeking the gifts (12:31; 14:1, 12).

It therefore militates against Paul's purpose for theologians today to import cessationistic rationale (e.g., inscripturation and the apostolate) that is so foreign to the conceptual content of the passage. Given this context, 1 Corinthians 13:8–12 is much more naturally understood to teach that the gifts continue until the Lord's return.[71] While we await his return, the gifts are to operate on the eternal foundation of love; otherwise, they are meaningless.

The import of Romans 12:3–8 is similar to that of 1 Corinthians 12–14. Again Paul is instructing the Roman Christians concerning the proper function of the gifts in the church. The basis for their operation is again found in the proper attitude of believers (Rom. 12:3–5), which includes love (vv. 9–13). Paul approaches the subject of gifts as if it is as normal a part of Christian life as having sanctified attitudes (vv. 9–21), being good citizens (13:1–7), living righteously (13:8–14), and so on. Although the list of gifts is different from that found in 1 Corinthians

---

[71]See Grudem, *Prophecy in the New Testament*, 228–43.

12:7–11, prophecy is still included (Rom. 12:6) and is mentioned first. There is nothing in the passage or its context to indicate that some dramatic change in the operation of the Spirit was anticipated that would result in the termination of the Spirit's empowering work.

A Pauline remark that is often not mentioned in this debate, but which is telling, is found in Galatians 3:5. Almost in passing as an illustration of his point regarding faith versus works, Paul says to the Galatians, "Does God give you his Spirit and work miracles among you because you observe the law, or because you believe what you heard?" He *assumes* the normalcy of miracles here. It is an *illustration*—something concrete to which everyone can relate easily—of his larger theological point.

This ease, this comfortable acceptance of miraculous manifestations, is not unique to Paul, or even to Luke. James 5:14–16 also offers instructions concerning healing with the same tone. Prayer for physical healing and God's healing power is normal and to be expected in the life of the church. Furthermore, James encourages his readers to have faith in praying for the sick by holding up the canonical example of Elijah (vv. 17–18). He writes, "Elijah was a man just like us," and then proceeds to describe the effectiveness of his prayers. The clear implication is that the readers' prayers can be effective in the same dramatic fashion as Elijah's.

Consider also Hebrews 2:4, of which Philip Hughes insightfully writes, "It is apparent, then, that, like the believers in Corinth, 'the Hebrews' to whom this letter is addressed had been enriched with spiritual gifts."[72] Used as part of a warning concerning the grave necessity to pay attention to what God has revealed (2:1–3), these "signs, wonders and various miracles, and gifts of the Holy Spirit" are irrefutable instances of God's work within the community of his people. The author of Hebrews is reminding them of phenomena to which they were all privy.

---

[72]P. E. Hughes, *A Commentary on the Epistle to the Hebrews* (Grand Rapids: Eerdmans, 1977), 81. Among those "presumably" in operation among the recipients of Hebrews, according to Hughes, were prophecy, tongues, and healing. Moreover, experiences of the Spirit's power in miraculous gifts "may confidently be identified" as the reference of Hebrews 6:5b.

b. Passages That Record Miraculous Events

In addition to these didactic portions of the New Testament, the Gospels and Acts record numerous miracles. As in the case of the didactic passages, miracle accounts in the New Testament are absent of even the slightest indication of cessationist doctrine. The narratives that describe miracles have two primary functions: to authenticate Jesus and to authenticate the gospel message about him.[73] Miracles accompanied the apostles (2 Cor. 12:12), but as we have already seen, were not exclusively tied to them.[74] Moreover, satanic, counterfeit miracles can be used by false apostles to deceive people into believing false teaching (e.g., Mark 13:22; 2 Cor. 11:13–15; 2 Thess. 2:9–12; Rev. 13:3–4). Miraculous events in and of themselves, therefore, are not the final "proof" of authentic ministry. Indeed, proclamation of the truth about Christ is what authenticates ministry (e.g., 1 John 2:18–27; 4:13).[75] Thus, when the one true gospel of Jesus Christ is preached, signs follow to confirm the message and deliver those who are under the power of the devil (e.g., Acts 10:38; 19:11–12).

---

[73]This is not to deny the sufficiency of the preaching of the gospel. The gospel is effective without attestation by virtue of its divine origin (e.g., Rom. 1:16–17; 2 Tim. 3:16). We must disagree here with Ruthven, who states, "Characteristically, the 'word' or preaching is not 'accredited' by miracles, but rather, the preaching articulates the miracles and draws out their implications for the onlookers" (*Charismata*, 118). He favorably cites J. Jervill ("The Signs of an Apostle: Paul's Miracles," in his *The Unknown Paul: Essays on Luke–Acts and Early Christian History* [Minneapolis: Augsburg, 1984]) ,who wrote (95), "Without miracle the gospel is not gospel but merely word, or rather, words." Although Ruthven's position that miracles are part and parcel of the kingdom is correct, his view of both the function of miracles and preaching is inadequate at this point. There is much evidence to the contrary concerning the characteristic attesting function of miracles (e.g., Matt. 9:6–7; 11:1–6; 12:28; 14:25–33; Mark 2:10–11; 16:20; Luke 5:24–25; 7:18–23; 11:20; John 3:2; 5:36; 9:32–33; 10:37–38; 14:11; Acts 2:22; 14:3; Heb. 2:4). Furthermore, preaching is based on the gospel revealed in Jesus, and while miracles may lead to an opportunity for preaching in Acts, the preaching itself is not dependent on the miracle; much preaching occurs with no such precursor. Jervill's remark is therefore entirely unacceptable. The gospel is God's Word with or without the presence of miracle (see Deere, *Surprised by the Power of the Spirit*, 103ff.).

[74]Another example is found in Mark 9:38–40, where we see an anonymous person performing exorcisms.

[75]Cf. 1 John 2:18–27; 4:1–6. So also Deere, *Surprised by the Power of the Spirit*, 106–7.

The evidence that speaks more generally of miracles indicates they are part and parcel of Jesus' kingdom (e.g., Luke 7:18–23; John 9:1–12), as we have already argued. And there is nothing that militates against the view that miracles are characteristic of the entire period known as the "last days." This can lead only to one conclusion, that the notion of cessationism was not to be found anywhere in the theological universe of the early church.[76]

3. On Specific Gifts and Ministries

This essay has emphasized thus far the legitimacy of the empowering work of the Spirit, both as a work different from regeneration and as one that continues during the last days. Because of the space restrictions of the book, this section as well as subsequent ones will receive much briefer attention.

There are three main lists of gifts in the New Testament: Romans 12:6–8; 1 Corinthians 12:7–11; Ephesians 4:11–13. Many approach these gifts according to their functional differences (service, revelation, etc.), but there is a larger issue that often is not addressed by this approach. All gifts, whether "miraculous" or "mundane" (and I do not accept such a distinction), are of divine origin. In each of these lists God is clearly giving and distributing the gifts according to his will. Thus even "nonmiraculous" gifts (e.g., leadership, showing mercy, cf. Rom. 12:8) are of "miraculous" origin; that is, nothing in the life of the church is ordinary (cf. 12:6; 1 Cor. 12:4–11; Eph. 4:11). No member of the body of Christ is merely "born that way"; every ability that any member of the body of Christ possesses is specifically ordained and enabled by God. Consequently, fine distinctions between those gifts in the lists that are for today (mundane) and those that have ceased (miraculous) must rely on data other than what is found within these passages and their respective contexts. The source of all gifts is God (1 Cor. 12:4–6), who graciously imparts them according to his own will.

---

[76]See, e.g., Grudem, *Prophecy in 1 Corinthians*, passim; *Prophecy in the New Testament*, passim; Deere, *Surprised by the Power of the Spirit*, 99–115, 229–66; Ruthven, *Charismata*, passim. Although the manner of arguing for continuity may not be the same as that presented in this essay, charismatics would not disagree with the conclusions.

Discussions concerning specific gifts inevitably narrow down to the manifestation of tongues, interpretation of tongues, and prophecy, so a brief note specifically concerning these gifts is also in order here. First, these utterances are not equivalent to Scripture but rather are judged by Scripture. Paul calls on the Corinthians to judge the prophecies given during their worship services (1 Cor. 14:29; cf. 1 Thess. 5:19–22), something he would never command concerning Scripture (e.g., 2 Tim. 3:16). Thus, even during New Testament times, contemporary prophecy (in distinction to canonical prophecy) was not always vested with canonical authority.

Second, the continuing voice of the Spirit in the church does not undermine the foundational role of the apostles or the authority of biblical revelation. Those appointed to be apostles of Christ, to govern the early church, and to produce the infallible body of doctrine that came to be the New Testament canon, functioned in a unique, unrepeatable, foundational role in the building of the church (Eph. 2:19–22).[77] Moreover, their teaching, embodied in the New Testament, continues to be the only authoritative, infallible rule for faith and practice.

It is a non sequitur, however, to argue that continuing miraculous manifestations *necessarily* supplant this authority by vesting it in contemporary manifestations and/or individuals. Mainstream Pentecostals have never elevated miraculous gifts (including utterance gifts) to the level of canon (inerrant revelation with full divine authority), but rather have subjected spiritual manifestations to the authority of Scripture. In other words, the gifts are not canon-forming, they are canon-expressing. Miraculous gifts give concrete form to the canon in real-life situations just as much as the fruit of the Spirit.

Third, with regard specifically to tongues, it is often argued that this gift was restricted to human languages for the purpose of preaching.[78] However, this restriction does not fit the evidence.

---

[77]Cf. Deere, *Surprised by the Power of the Spirit*, 229–52; Grudem, *Prophecy in the New Testament*, 269–76. It is beyond the scope of our discussion to take up the continuity of the apostolic office in its broader sense.

[78]See John F. MacArthur, Jr., *Charismatic Chaos* (Grand Rapids: Zondervan, 1992), 220–45. This is the view of MacArthur and those he cites favorably. Sadly, MacArthur seems to deal only with caricatures and does not interact with more thoughtful expositions of the Pentecostal position.

In Acts 10:44–46 and 19:1–6 preaching is not mentioned, nor is there any mention of an audience. And at Corinth an interpreter was required for public utterances in tongues during the worship service (1 Cor. 14:1–28). If the gift always took the form of the human language of the hearers, why were interpreters necessary in order to make the utterance comprehensible?[79] Moreover, glossolalia functions in private contexts for personal edification apart from corporate worship (e.g., 14:13–19). Hence, the view that utterances in unidentifiable languages are just so much carnal gibberish (or even satanic) is not warranted in the light of the evidence. In some instances human languages were uttered by persons with no prior knowledge of that language (Acts 2); in others, people spoke in tongues of unknown origin ("of men and of angels," 1 Cor. 13:1), requiring interpretation in order to be comprehensible to the church at worship.

D. ON MIRACULOUS GIFTS IN CHURCH LIFE

It is one thing to identify the church as the temple of God in which God dwells by his Spirit. It is another to ask how, specifically, God's presence is manifested in the church. Pentecostals respond that his presence is manifested in both inner-transforming and empowering modes, and it is the latter that concerns us here. How should the Spirit's empowering work affect the life of the church? The Bible gives ample evidence, both through example and explicit instruction, of how the gifts should function in the life of the church today.[80]

For example, there is every reason to expect that gospel proclamation will be accompanied by miracles today. When it

---

[79]MacArthur (ibid., 227–32) engages in convoluted exegesis at this point. He dismisses all of Paul's positive remarks concerning tongues (e.g., 1 Cor. 14:18, 26–28) as "irony" actually meant to shame the Corinthians into ceasing their practice of tongues in all settings. Furthermore, speaking of both the original setting at Corinth and the church today, MacArthur asserts that tongues "cannot edify the church in a proper way" (232). This is simply bogus. The issue of contemporary cessation aside, with interpretation the edifying value of tongues was equivalent to prophecy at Corinth (14:15); even a cursory reading of 1 Corinthians reveals this.

[80]For a solid discussion of the application of miraculous gifts in the corporate life of the church, see David Lim, *Spiritual Gifts: A Fresh Look* (Springfield, Mo.: Gospel Publishing House, 1991), 183–275.

suits God's purposes, is he not free to work according to his own will? In the record of Acts (e.g., 2:19, 22, 43; 4:30; 5:12; 6:8; 8:6, 13; 13:6–12; 14:3; 15:12; 19:11–12), preaching accompanied by signs is a normal part of new covenant existence. And this is true yet today. It is the exception, not the rule, to meet a missionary from any evangelical group who has not been actively engaged (usually not by choice but by necessity) in "power encounter" evangelism. Signs and wonders do follow preaching today, although perhaps this is more common in areas being evangelized for the first time or where a new revival has sprung up after a lengthy dearth of evangelism. Also, exorcisms are more common in areas where Satan has dominated the spiritual landscape rather than biblical faith.[81]

Once the continuity of gifts is accepted, a plethora of pastoral issues emerge, not least of which is the incorporation of the gifts into public worship. It is important not to forbid all manifestations on the basis of a few abuses. Particularly useful in this regard is Paul's lengthy and well-known series of instructions on the gifts in worship found in 1 Corinthians 12–14. Worship need not be chaotic in order to be charismatic or dynamic. On the other hand, why did some in the crowd on the day of Pentecost accuse the disciples of being drunk (Acts 2:13)? The worship described by Paul in 1 Corinthians 12–14 was not characterized by passive spectating. There was active involvement of the members of the body for the common good, and not all of it was prearranged and printed in a program (1 Cor. 14:26–33a).[82]

Another important aspect of the Spirit's ministry in church life is his direct communication with believers through prayer (esp. important in Luke-Acts, as outlined above; cf. Acts 13:1–3). While the Spirit's communication to the spirit of the believer is vital, it must be submitted to the authority of God's Word. No impression of God's voice should be placed on a par with the Bible. Nevertheless, many Christians miss a vital element of the Spirit-filled life because they are closed to this kind of Spirit-to-spirit communication from God, which comes only through

---

[81]See Blomberg, "Healing," 306. He is of the opinion that as "Western societies continue to become more paganized, one may expect a continued revival of healings and exorcisms."

[82]Cf. Fee (*God's Empowering Presence*, 883–95) for more of a detailed discussion of this subject that proceeds along classical Pentecostal lines.

prayer. This source of personal guidance should not be avoided; it should be approached with biblical maturity, remembering that the Spirit gives life and guides into all truth.

E. ON DANGERS RELATED TO MIRACULOUS GIFTS

Let me begin with an analogy from the stock market. Blue-chip stocks have little risk, but also smaller dividends over time. Aggressive-growth funds carry much higher risk but the potential dividends are much greater as well.

The primary risk for those who hold the cessationist position consists in what they will miss of Spirit-filled life here on earth. They are in no danger of losing their salvation if they do not allow for the operation of miraculous gifts in the church, only the fullness of the gospel for the Christian life. However, for those who vilify charismatics as heretics, or worse, demonically inspired cultists simply because the manifestations of the Spirit are evident among them, the risks are greater. Do Pentecostals cast out demons by the power of Beelzebub?

For those who hold the Pentecostal view there are several significant dangers that I can only list here:

(1) Signs and wonders can sometimes become elevated over truth. False teachers, masquerading as apostles of Christ, often claim to perform signs and wonders to which they point in defense of their ministries. It is true that signs and wonders confirm the gospel when it is indeed preached. But those of the Pentecostal and charismatic movements must focus first on the truth of what is preached in order to discern if it is biblical. Also, remember Jesus' admonition to the seventy when they reported that even demons were subject to them, "Do not rejoice that the spirits submit to you, but rejoice that your names are written in heaven" (Luke 10:17–20).

(2) Prophetic gifts can be used to manipulate and cajole rather than to encourage. All believers have the Spirit, who is perfectly capable of speaking directly to the believer's heart without any human intermediary, especially in the case of personal guidance.

(3) Pentecostals must know that they cannot accept any group claiming to be Christian, regardless of their doctrinal commitments, simply because they are open to or support a similar

view of miraculous gifts. Some doctrinal aberrations simply should not be approved, tacitly or explicitly, even under the auspices of "charismatic renewal" or "dialogue" (e.g., the Roman doctrine of Mary as co-redemptrix and co-mediatrix).

(4) Classical Pentecostal groups should not depart from their historical evangelical moorings and fall into liberalism, becoming an existentialist sect. Here Pentecostals have much to learn from their fellow evangelicals about the courage to stand up for cardinal biblical teachings and not to allow liberal commitments to infiltrate and destroy the church.

(5) Finally, Pentecostals should not become pragmatists in which the miraculous ends justify any means, including high-tech manipulation.

F. CONCLUSION

It is the desire of most Pentecostals, with the rare sectarian exception, to engage their fellow evangelicals in open and frank dialogue, characterized by the genuine affection of Christ. I trust this essay has contributed to the dialogue in the tradition of Christian charity. As the church moves forward into the next millennium, surrounded by an increasingly wicked world, it is essential that true believers receive the Lord's own mantle—his anointing with the Spirit and power. While doctrine is necessary to know *about* God's plan of redemption and *about* having a relationship with Christ, in and of itself doctrine is not the object of our faith and is powerless to transform or empower us. For that the Spirit's work is required.

A CESSATIONIST RESPONSE TO C. SAMUEL STORMS AND DOUGLAS A. OSS

Richard B. Gaffin, Jr.

Because of the substantial overlap between the positions of Storms and Oss (especially in their disagreement with mine!) and in order to avoid unnecessary repetition, I have decided on a combined response, addressing one or the other of them individually along the way. I will focus on what, as I see it, is essential; some matters, although certainly worth discussing, will have to be left to the side.

1. At the heart of the differences between us is the conviction of Storms and Oss that the presence of miraculous gifts (such as prophecy, tongues, and healing) throughout the course of redemptive history sets the standard or at least gives us every expectation for the presence of such gifts in the life of the church today. Because Moses and the Old Testament prophets, Jesus and the apostles, and others exercised these gifts throughout the history of salvation, so their basic reasoning goes, believers may and should expect the same today.

Furthermore, in their view, the silence of Scripture about the cessation of particular gifts adds to the overwhelming burden of proof on those who hold that they have ceased. For them this biblical silence is so eloquent for their continuation that the effort to prove the contrary (in Oss's words, p. 265, n.46, and p. 271) "strains credulity," "abjectly fails," and is even called "obtuse"!

What can I possibly say in the face of such sweeping dismissals? Perhaps the following comments, picking up on several points already made in my position chapter, will not be entirely useless.

2. The view of Storms and Oss, I believe, fails to do justice to the structure of redemptive history, especially its organic wholeness and the pattern of its consummation in Christ. Perhaps a helpful point of contact between us can be Oss's general description of salvation history as the "historical unfolding of the central events in God's plan of salvation, e.g., creation, fall, history of Israel, incarnation, the cross, resurrection, ascension and exaltation, Pentecost, second coming, and new creation" (pp. 270–71, n.61). I agree with this as a summary (with the caveats that *redemptive* history does not begin until the Fall and that the new creation, while still future, has already arrived in Christ's first coming, e.g., 2 Cor. 5:17).

What is telling in this summary is the noticeable *gap* (correctly noted, I want to stress) between Pentecost and Parousia. Notice, then, that ongoing church history is *not* on the same line, for instance, with Israel's history. Church history is not in series with the other events listed; it is not a continuation of the history of which they are constituent components. Pointedly, church history is not redemptive history.

The present time of the church is "between the times," a hiatus in Christ's *one* redemptive-historical work, bracketed by his resurrection and return. In the period between Pentecost and the Parousia, so far as its forward movement is concerned, the history of salvation, in the sense of a once-for-all accomplishment, is on hold. First Thessalonians 1:9–10 neatly captures the essence of this interim: The church consists of those "turned to God from idols to serve the living and true God"—with all that service involves (we are hardly talking about a vacuum of inactivity)—just as, Paul continues, they "wait for his Son from heaven, whom he raised from the dead." Redemptive-historically speaking, the church is, categorically, the "waiting" church; that, as much as anything, is its basic identity.

Thus, if church history (with the exception of its apostolic era) is not redemptive history, we may not simply extrapolate from the latter to the former. We may not conclude that, unless there is explicit indication to the contrary, everything true during the *process* of salvation history continues beyond its *completion*. Or better, we should not think that all that is true of the process continues into the interim period (postapostolic church history), bounded by the two events that constitute that consummation (Christ's first coming, culminating in Pentecost and the founding of the church, and his second coming). Because church history and redemptive history are not on a continuum (except for their overlap during the time of the apostles), the presence of miraculous gifts throughout the Old Testament, even without express indications there of their cessation at some point in the future, carries no presumption for their continuation today. Much less is their presence, then, a compelling argument for continuation now. Nor are we entitled to say, as Storms does (p. 205), with a view to the presence of these gifts during the apostolic era, that "it is difficult to imagine how the New Testament authors could have said any more clearly than *this* what new covenant Christianity was supposed to look like." In view of the dissimilarity between salvation history and church history, silence in Scripture about the cessation of particular gifts does not, of itself, have weight as an argument.

Am I denying, then, any and all continuity between redemptive history and church history? Not at all. In fact, properly identifying those continuities (as well as discontinuities) is as much as anything the basic issue before this symposium. Critical for sorting out this issue is the distinction between the history of salvation (*historia salutis*) and the order of salvation (*ordo salutis*), between the once-for-all accomplishment of redemption (beginning with the promise of Gen. 3:15 and culminating in its fulfillment in the finished work of Christ) and its ongoing application (the believer's actual experience of the benefits of that finished redemption, regardless of time and place [see my essay, pp. 32–32, 36, 53–54]).

What is important here is not so much the terms used but how they are used. We may properly speak of the history of redemption continuing today, but only if we understand that continuation in the sense of the ongoing appropriation of redemption in the life of the church, not in terms of its once-for-all accomplishment (just as, by the way, we may speak of the history of revelation continuing today in the sense that revelation, as completed and as it has been inscripturated for the church, is continually being believed and applied through the illumining power of the Spirit; e.g., Eph. 1:17; Phil. 3:15). But, and this again is the crucial point, God's grace presently at work in manifold ways in the church is not simply on a line or in series with his grace revealed in the finished work of Christ. Developments giving rise to the Reformation (e.g., the Roman Catholic doctrine of the Mass) have made perennially clear the danger in making the one an extension of the other. Where that happens, invariably the sufficiency and historical finality of Christ's death and resurrection become eclipsed or even denied. Ultimately the gospel itself stands or falls with the distinction between redemption accomplished and applied. And only where that distinction functions properly do Christian identity and experience, both individual and corporate, come to stand in a right light.

What we must also observe (and this adds a complicating factor to the issue before us) is the essential continuity in the *ordo salutis* between the old and new covenants; the application of redemption to individuals is basically the same throughout biblical history and church history. This appears from the way in which the New Testament views faith and justification by faith: The model believer for Paul is Abraham or David, who exemplify in their experience the faith (produced by the regenerating and renewing power of the Spirit, cf. Gal. 3:29 with 4:28–29) that justifies (Rom. 4; Gal. 3). New Testament believers stand in a long line of faith (with its common focus, whether looking forward or backward, on Christ; e.g., John 8:56; Heb. 11:26; 1 Peter 1:10–11)—a line that extends at least as far back as Abel (Heb. 11:4–12:2).

This is not to deny that there are differences in saving experience between Old and New Testament believers, differences that turn on the privilege we have of living after Christ's death and resurrection have taken place and of being united by the Spirit specifically to Jesus as he is now exalted. But, as far as I can see, Scripture is not particularly concerned to spell out such differences. They resist neat, clear categorization and can only be loosely captured by comparatives like "better," "richer," "enlarged," "greater," or "fuller."[1] But continuity is deeper,

---

[1]The last three terms are used by the Westminster Confession of Faith (20:1) in describing Christian liberty.

reflected, for instance, in Gordon Fee's choosing, effectively and most appropriately, to close the main body of his recent massive study on the Holy Spirit in Paul's letters by applying to New Testament believers the prayers of David (Ps. 63:1) and Moses (Ex. 33:15–16).[2]

To sum up: On the one hand, in terms of the history of salvation (in the sense of its once-for-all accomplishment), biblical history and church history are discontinuous; on the other hand, in terms of the application of salvation, church history is the extension of biblical history. Furthermore—and this is an important consideration, though often overlooked—it is apparent that throughout biblical history, whether in corporate or individual experience, the history of redemption and its application coalesce. Consequently, without isolating them from each other, what belongs to accomplishment and what belongs to application must not be confused or the distinction between them blurred.

As an example, take David's experience in its totality. His experience of the Holy Spirit as expressed in Psalm 51:11 is certainly of a piece with his theocratic privilege of being anointed and empowered with the Spirit (1 Sam. 16:12–13). But the two are not the same. The former experience (compromised by his sin with Bathsheba and against Uriah) is at the level of *ordo salutis* and is essentially continuous with the experience of all believers; the latter, his theocratic endowment, is not, but is bound up with his distinctive role in redemptive history. David the believer and David the king are the same person. But David *as* believer and David *as* king are not the same; the two, and what pertains to each, should not be confused.

I have taken the time for this brief sketch because it serves to put the issue that divides us pointedly and in a way that needs to be addressed: Do the miraculous gifts, especially revelatory word gifts, belong to the history of salvation or the order of salvation? It is not clear to me from what either Storms or Oss has written that they make the *historia salutis-ordo salutis* distinction, much less that they consider it pertinent. But clearly their answer, in effect, is that these gifts belong to the latter, or,

---

[2]Gordon Fee, *God's Empowering Presence: The Holy Spirit in the Letters of Paul* (Peabody, Mass.: Hendrickson, 1994), 903.

they may want to say, to both, but certainly to the ongoing application of salvation/Christian experience. In my position chapter I have given a different answer, namely, that revelatory gifts belong to the former, not the latter—that is, to the once-for-all and epochal history of salvation, not to what is ongoing in salvation. Several further comments in line with this will reinforce that conclusion.

3. Oss devotes a considerable part of his chapter to a biblical-theological survey of the Spirit's work (pp. 245–60), and his position as a whole largely rests on the results. This survey supports both his particular (and interesting) construal of Pentecostal second-blessing theology as well as the continuation of miraculous gifts today. So far as the latter (continuation of gifts) is concerned, there is substantial overlap with the arguments of Storms (pp. 185–206). The primary thrust of the survey is to show that throughout redemptive history, there is a twofold working of the Spirit—his "inner-transforming" work (regeneration, conversion) and his "empowering" work (anointing, enduement with a view to exercising miraculous gifts); these two works are different, and the difference must be kept clear; the latter culminates in becoming universal under the new covenant.

What has to be questioned in this construction is not that the two works (regeneration and empowerment) are different; they plainly are and are not to be confused. But, in my judgment, confusion of a different sort is present in the construction itself; because of that, despite a number of helpful biblical-theological insights, that construction is essentially useless for what it intends to establish. Regeneration is an aspect of the application of redemption; empowerment is a redemptive-historical reality. None of us in this symposium will dispute the former. That the latter was the case under the old covenant is also clear (the various kinds of theocratic empowerment anticipated, by typifying, the once-for-all work of Christ).

Oss's construction, in other words, involves a confusion of categories. *Historia salutis* apples are mixed with *ordo salutis* oranges. The two are combined to form what becomes, in effect, a hybrid *ordo* or applicatory model for the new covenant, that is, the normative pattern for individual Christian experience, the enduring empowerment paradigm for all believers. But all of this is at the expense of at least blurring, if not missing entirely, the distinction between the finished accomplishment of salvation and its ongoing application, and what belongs to each.[3]

4. Yet the question may still be pressed: Does not the Old Testament promise and the New Testament itself document something like the eschatological mutation of theocratic anointings and salvation-historical empowerments with miraculous gifts throughout the old covenant into the (potential) experience of all new covenant believers? Again, it has to be pointed out: An affirmative answer to this question misses the redemptive-historical function of these old covenant enduements. That is, missed is the fact that these empowerings all have their focus and fulfillment not in new covenant believers and their experience but in the once-for-all work of Christ and the once-for-all apostolic-prophetic witness to that work.

But what about Numbers 11:29 ("I wish that all the LORD's people were prophets and that the LORD would put his Spirit on them!")? It seems to me that this statement is misunderstood whenever we miss what might be called its "redemptive-historical hyperbole." To read it as a promise or hope of a future when all believers will be (potential) prophets in the sense of exercising the gift in view in Romans 12, 1 Corinthians 12–14, and Ephesians 4 proves too much. For Paul is emphatic that in this sense "all are not prophets, are they?" (1 Cor. 12:29, NASB), and that the ultimate and positive reason for this restriction is by divine design (the church as one body with many and diverse parts, 12:11–27).

Moreover, the exclamation of Numbers 11:29 seems akin to Paul's declaration in 1 Corinthians 14:5 ("I wish that you all spoke in tongues but even more that you would prophesy," NASB). That and related statements in the immediate context (e.g., v. 18) hardly imply that speaking in tongues, along with prophecy, is (potentially) a gift for all believers. For, as with prophecy, he has already made clear that "all do not speak in

---

[3]Oss believes that "Pentecostal pneumatology is based on the redemptive-historical approach to biblical theology" (p. 245). To the contrary, I am arguing, that approach is most compatible with Reformed cessationist conclusions. At any rate, the latter are hardly to be explained as resulting from "the theological conditioning of an approach that operates exclusively in terms of the traditional systematic-theological categories of salvation" (p. 272, unless, perhaps, we are prepared to dismiss the accomplishment-application distinction as alien to biblical theology).

tongues, do they?" (12:30, NASB)—again for the same positive reason (the one body with different parts).

Am I then denying "the prophethood of all believers," as Oss calls it (pp. 266–67)? Not at all, but that has to be properly defined. Peter's apostolic gloss on Joel's universal apocalyptic vision, "and they will prophesy" (Acts 2:18), cannot find its fulfillment in the restrictively distributed gift of 1 Corinthians 12–14. Rather, parallel to the priesthood of all believers, it is best understood in terms of the anointing of 1 John 2:20, 27. This anointing with the Spirit, John says, is true of *all* believers, and such that "you do not need anyone to teach you" (cf. Heb. 5:12). These words, in turn, echo the fulfillment of Jeremiah's prophecy, "No longer will a man teach his neighbor, or a man his brother, saying, 'Know the LORD,' because they will all know me, from the least of them to the greatest" (Jer. 31:34).

This universal anointing is not a charismatic experience (at least not as usually understood these days!). Nor, it should be noted, does this anointing/teaching exclude a place in the church for canonical, apostolic-prophetic teaching distinct from it at the time the New Testament was being written, or, now that it has been completed, the need for the teaching rule of those set apart as undershepherds/elders (cf. 1 Peter 5:1–4).

5. Closely related to these comments, it is not at all clear to me how Storms and Oss view the apostles, their role, and their continuation in the church today. Storms seems to exclude being an apostle from the miraculous gifts, which he apparently limits to those listed in 1 Corinthians 12:8–10—an exclusion that is problematic at best (see my essay, p. 45, n.48). Note how he cites Ephesians 4:11–13 (which includes apostles) to show that all the gifts continue to the Parousia.

Oss recognizes the foundational (and therefore noncontinuing) role of the apostles, but in a footnote adds, "It is beyond the scope of our discussion to take up the continuity of the apostolic office in its broader sense" (p. 279). I am not sure what this addition intends. If it carries the suggestion that the gift mentioned in 1 Corinthians 12:28 and Ephesians 4:11 continues in some broader sense today, then what that sense is may not remain outside the scope of our discussion but begs for an explanation. In fact, it needs to recognized that there is *no* material (that is, gift or office) connection in the New Testament between the apostles appointed by Christ and the broader applications of the Greek word for apostle, meaning "messenger," "representative" (e.g., 2 Cor. 8:23; Phil. 2:25). In this wider sense, I, for example, as a minister of the gospel, am an "apostle," and we should not hesitate to say that all believers for that matter, in terms of their general office, are "apostles."

Clarity on this issue is a necessity. If there are apostles today like Paul and the Twelve—in that case, some who are vested with their inspired and infallible authority—then where are they? How are we to recognize them?[4] And if there are no apostles today, then the consequences of *that* cessation need to be faced.

Specifically, as far as arguing for the continuation of miraculous gifts, particularly revelatory word gifts, is concerned, it will not do simply to point out that the New Testament shows that others than apostles exercised them and nowhere teaches that they have ceased. That is a much too arithmetic or mechanical approach. If there is validity to my earlier comments, then what has to be shown is how these gifts, whose function throughout the entire Old Testament is redemptive-historical and in the New Testament are associated organically with the redemptive-historical role of the apostles, have subsequently surrendered that function and taken on a different, experiential and applicatory significance. But as far as I can see, the New Testament does not show that shift, either explicitly or by implication.

6. That brings me to the issue of the canon. I do not question that both Storms and Oss are committed to a closed canon and its final authority. But it is not at all clear to me on what basis they hold that commitment and how, if pressed, they would defend it. If they take the view that "the notion of cessationism was not to be found anywhere in the theological universe of the early church [i.e., the New Testament]," as Oss writes (p. 278), then neither are the notions of the cessation of the apostolate and the closing of the canon. As I noted in my response to Saucy, as far as I can see, the three notions are taught

---

[4]This, if nothing else, confronts us with what as much as anything is a massive "church order" problem, which a fragmented Christianity, especially North American evangelicalism (in large part so ecclesiologically indifferent), is just not equipped to handle.

Argument

with more or less the same degree of clarity in the New Testament, and, more importantly, stand or fall together. I need to be shown how it is possible to maintain together, in a theologically coherent fashion, both the closure of the canon and the continuation of revelatory word gifts.

In this respect, I recognize, both Storms and Oss believe prophecy is subordinate to Scripture and must be evaluated by it. I have to question, however, that they are able to make good on that conviction. Meaningful evaluation, it has to be pointed out again, is inherently impossible in view of the specificity, either as prediction or directive, that prophecy properly has on occasion—at least if it is the New Testament gift.

Here, however, my concern is related but slightly different. Oss calls prophecy (and tongues) "Spirit-prompted speech" (p. 262). How such speech differs from the inspired speech, say, of canonical prophets and apostles on the one hand, or the Spirit-controlled speech that ought to mark every believer on the other, is not made clear. Presumably, in its origination from the Spirit, it is close, if not identical, to the former, since on his view prophecy is a special gift that brings new revelations to the church (even if imperfectly uttered). Storms holds that prophecy, based on infallible revelation, is "occasionally fallible" (p. 207). But he goes on to make clear that prophecy is otherwise without error, or at least that may sometimes be the case. That would appear to mean that in its origin prophecy is inspired, God-breathed.

Storms and Oss wish to maintain prophetic speech today that is both Spirit-prompted or inspired and at the same time (whether or not infallible) subject to Scripture. But nineteenth-century debates on the doctrine of Scripture ought to have taught us the futility (and resultant serious damage in the life of the church) of trying to distinguish levels of inspiration, with different degrees of authority. Inspired speech is God's speech, his word, with his own, inalienably infallible authority.

If these comments are at all pertinent, what sense can there be in trying to maintain both a closed canon and the occurrence of inspired speech today? "Canon," after all, is not merely a literary designation or cataloging term. It carries connotations of authority. The "canon" is wherever I find God's inspired word for today. If inspired speech continues today, then, as our canon,

Scripture is not complete; no matter how highly we may otherwise view it, the Bible is but a part of that canon. That Storms is committed, in effect, to such a "Scripture plus" principle of authority seems clear from his footnote 46, where in explaining what he means by a "revelatory warrant," "revelatory insight" via prophecy, among other means, is on a par with "explicit biblical assertion." This aspect of their view is most troubling.

This is perhaps an appropriate place to take note briefly of Storms's citing of Spurgeon's experience. This incident, if it happened as reported, is an instance of Spirit-prompted insight that occurs incalculably and sporadically. But it is hardly evidence, as Storms suggests, for the lingering presence in the church, despite denial and spiritual lethargy, of the gift of prophecy or the word of knowledge. We should note that Spurgeon did not seek this insight, nor did that capacity mark his ministry (he can recall no more than a dozen such instances, remarkable as that may be). And these experiences had nothing to do with seeking anachronistically to replicate the worship scenario of 1 Corinthians 14.[5]

7. Storms and Oss take the view that in addition to its public exercise, where it must be accompanied with interpretation, speaking in tongues, as a private, devotional exercise and without interpretation, is for all believers. In addition to what has already been noted above about the restrictive distribution of the gift of tongues (by God's design that gift is *not* for every believer), this view is questionable at best because it maintains in effect that there is really not one but two gifts of tongues—a public gift given to some, a private gift (potentially) for all.

Where does Scripture teach such a two-gift construction? Certainly not in 1 Corinthians 14. There Paul does recognize that the person speaking in tongues edifies himself (v. 4, cf. v. 17), but that is likely as a "fringe benefit," as it were, for the one who has been given the gift for its public exercise—much as, for instance,

---

[5]As a (seriously meant) aside, if Spurgeon's insight is a genuine prophecy, are not Pentecostals and charismatics who are nonsabbatarians obligated to abandon that view? Does not Spurgeon's "prophecy" settle for the church a matter that, according to many evangelicals and others, Scripture does not teach or even teaches the opposite, namely, that the Lord's Day is the Christian Sabbath? Or did Spurgeon get that part wrong? Or am I missing something?

ministers in preaching or believers in witnessing are themselves edified by that activity (and are also edified in private as they prepare what to say). Further, as far as private exercise is concerned, it seems a bit of a stretch to read "speak to himself and God" (v. 28) to mean something like "go home and do it privately," especially when the immediate context has proper conduct in the church assembly in view.

Where does New Testament teaching even come close to the notion that the gift of tongues is given so that, for example, my prayer life may be more fervent and spontaneous, my fellowship with God and other believers warmer and more vital, and my witness to Christ freer and more vibrant? The widespread prevalence today of the private, devotional use of "tongues," I suspect, stems from a flawed conviction, perhaps intensified in the West by the arid rationalism of the post-Enlightenment, postmodern times in which we live—the conviction that in religious experience the nonrational and intuitive is more immediate and primal than the rational and word-bound. At least here, in this "tongues" experience if nowhere else, I can know for sure the touch of the Spirit in my life.

8. Finally, a word about power. Both Storms and Oss, it is fair to say, define the power of the Spirit primarily in terms of miraculous gifts. Oss's overall construction is controlled by the distinction between the "regenerating" and "empowering" works of the Spirit. This labeling as such suggests that the former work is less powerful or less properly a work of the Spirit's power. And Storms even goes so far as to suggest that those who hold that miraculous gifts have ceased, "believe the Holy Spirit simply inaugurates the new age and then disappears" (p. 206).

I wonder, though, if they do not have things turned around, even for the New Testament times, in which no one (at least in this symposium) questions these gifts were present (see my essay, pp. 56–59, for my views on the relationship of the Spirit and eschatology). When, for instance, Paul says, "the kingdom of God is not a matter of talk but of power" (1 Cor. 4:20), he surely has in view, at least primarily, what he has described earlier in the immediate larger context (1:18–4:21) as the "demonstration of the Spirit's power" that accompanied his gospel preaching (2:4; cf. 1 Thess. 1:5). Almost certainly, this power was not a matter of "signs and wonders," for it was exercised precisely when Paul's own observable conduct was "in weakness and fear, and with much trembling" (v. 3).[6]

In view rather is the Spirit's activity within the hearer, coincident with the preaching of the gospel—an activity that powerfully convicts and convinces. The result of this work is that the gospel is believed and faith is rooted "not on men's wisdom, but God's power" (1 Cor. 2:5). In view is the activity of the Spirit expressed more broadly a few verses later (vv. 14–15) by means of the sweeping, categorical antithesis between "the man without the Spirit" (who does not accept and cannot understand the things of God's Spirit because they can only be discerned by the Spirit) and "the spiritual man" (the person renewed and indwelt by the Spirit, who does discern these things). Here, not in miraculous gifts but in inner renewal and enlightening, is the Spirit's power in its eschatological, kingdom essence.

Take Philippians 3:10 as another example. As part of his aspiration to "gain Christ and be found in him" (vv. 8–9)—a model for all believers—Paul expresses the desire "to know Christ and the power of his resurrection and the fellowship of sharing in his sufferings, becoming like him in his death." In this declaration, we should note, the two uses of "and" are not coordinating but explanatory. Paul is not saying that the knowledge of Christ, the power of his resurrection, and the fellowship of his suffering are separate sectors of our experience, as if memorable and exhilarating times of resurrection power are offset by down days of suffering. Rather, the sequence progressively unfolds what is involved in the single and more than cognitive experience of knowing Christ (cf. v. 8, "the surpassing greatness of knowing Christ Jesus my Lord")—an experience that, in its essence, is captured as "becoming like [Christ] in his death." In a word, Paul is saying, the imprint left in our lives by Christ's resurrection power is the cross.

In other words, the same apostle, who is able to boast about "visions and revelations from the Lord" (2 Cor. 12:1), would rather boast about and delight in his weaknesses and in the

---

[6]Fee, as a Pentecostal, recognizes this point (*1 Corinthians*, 95), although he tries to qualify it by suggesting that "demonstration" implies the exercise of spiritual gifts, like tongues, that subsequently gave evidence of conversion. The work of the Spirit in view, however, is not a result of conversion but *effects* it.

hardships and persecutions he endured for Christ (vv. 9–10). For there, preeminently, he comes to understand, the power of the exalted Christ is displayed. In that suffering, "[Christ's] power is made perfect in weakness," and the proven truth is that "when I am weak, then I am strong."

To get to the heart of the matter, as I see it: Were I convinced that my faith in Christ and his promises depends on my having been left to my own resources presumably still resident in me as an unredeemed sinner (I am not saying that is the view of either Storms or Oss), then I suppose it would make sense to look, in the experience of others but especially in my own, for signs and wonders. I would long for such visible and audible miraculous phenomena as something unambiguously of God (never mind that such a quest necessarily remains ambiguous). I would crave them, at least in part, for assurance and in order to validate to myself and otherwise shore up my faith, which is so shakily grounded in myself.

But faith is not an assertion of my ever tentative subjectivity in need of "objective" props and confirmation. Ultimately it is rooted not in myself but in an eschatological act of God; it is the result of nothing less than a work of resurrection in me that has already taken place, just when I was "dead in transgressions and sins" (Eph. 2:1–10). When I understand what faith really is, then—an eschatological gift, created in me by God's Spirit, with its unerring focus on Christ and his word—there can be no greater miracle than that I (in fellowship with others) am able to say, "I believe!" (despite ever so many doubts and testings, falls and failings). Until Christ comes to raise me up bodily (together with all believers), I expect and I desire no greater work of the Spirit, no power experience of any higher magnitude, than this.

My response has had to dwell on important differences between Storms and Oss and myself. My hope, nonetheless, is that in its way it serves the concern I know they both share with me "to keep the unity of the Spirit through the bond of peace" (Eph. 4:3).

AN OPEN BUT CAUTIOUS RESPONSE TO DOUGLAS A. OSS

Robert L. Saucy

Oss has given us an excellent study on the Pentecostal theology of the work of the Spirit and miraculous gifts. The inclusion of the background and development of this position and especially the strong biblical discussion were helpful in clarifying this view. I appreciated the good biblical theology showing the development of the work of the Spirit in the Old and New Testaments. The positive affirmation that all believers have the Spirit and that the Pentecostal "receiving" of the Spirit referred only to his empowering work is also helpful. The main thesis that believers should desire the empowering of the Spirit is not only valid but central to the mission of the church and thus a valuable message for all believers. Several aspects of the Pentecostal understanding of this experience, however, are problematic for me.

1. Oss correctly asks that the debate be over substance and not the terminology of "baptism" and "filling." Confusion is always reduced when terms are clarified, especially when these terms are so crucial to the discussion. But I would have liked to see more explanation as to the difference in meaning of these two terms. On the one hand, "baptism" is essentially identified with "filling" as the empowering of the Spirit except that it is the first such experience. If we are to assume, as seems to be implied, that one who has received the baptism can subsequently grow away from the Lord and need a fresh "filling," one wonders what difference there is in such a person's relation to the Spirit and the one who has never been "baptized." If the

experience of Acts 2:4 and 4:31 are fundamentally the same (i.e., both "fillings"), why insist that the first is also "baptism"? Is the person who has been baptized but is now living away from the Lord any more empowered by the Spirit than the one who was never baptized? Oss denies what has often previously been understood of Pentecostal theology, that the baptism involves some kind of a *receiving* of the Spirit in a new way. But if it is not a new receiving or coming of the Spirit, exactly what distinguishes the one not baptized from the one who was baptized but is now walking in disobedience to the Spirit? These kinds of questions as well as others related to the biblical use of the terms "baptism" and "filling" of the Spirit demonstrate that the issue of substance is vitally related to the meaning of terms.

2. Oss rightly points to the difference between and "theological separability" of the inner-transforming and empowering works of the Spirit as the crucial issue (p. 242). I agree that these are different concepts, and yet I would caution that we do not separate them too much. The work of the Spirit in inner-transformation is essentially his ministry in producing a new life characterized by divine love (e.g., Gal. 5:22–23). His empowering for ministry is for the purpose of expressing that love in service to others. As the apostle says, the church grows (including inner-transformation) through the empowered ministry of each member, and all of this is the same love, which is the fruit of the Spirit (Eph. 4:16).

The Pentecostal understanding of the different works of the Spirit, according to Oss, rests on the distinction between the theologies of the Spirit in Luke's writings and in Paul's letters. There is no question that the different purposes of Luke and Paul require different emphases. Luke's concern with the spread of the gospel to all peoples focuses on the Spirit's empowering and direction for that task. But to limit the meaning of the coming of the Spirit in Acts to his empowering for service is to unduly restrict Luke's theology of the Spirit. While the Spirit does empower the ministry of the gospel, his coming as a result of faith in Christ is nothing less than the messianic gift of the Spirit that belongs to the fulfillment of new covenant salvation.

Luke's concept of the "baptism with the Spirit" is thus larger than receiving power for ministry as a second work of the Spirit; it is receiving the promised Spirit. To "receive" the gift of the Spirit (Acts 10:45, 47; 11:17; cf. 2:38) and be "baptized with/in the Spirit" (11:16) are essentially interchangeable terminology. The Old Testament terminology of the "pouring out" of the Spirit is also used for the same act (2:33; 10:45). To be sure, Peter uses Joel's prophecy with its charismatic effects of prophetic speech to explain the phenomena of the day of Pentecost. But the "pouring out" of the Spirit cannot be limited to his empowering for ministry or the production of miraculous manifestations. The other Old Testament uses of this terminology all carry the full concept of spiritual renewal (cf. Isa. 32:15; 44:3; Ezek. 39:29; Zech. 12:10).

Thus the coming of the Spirit at Pentecost involves more than empowerment. Luke's concept of "baptism with/in the Spirit" is clearly dependent on the meaning of Spirit-baptism in the Gospels (cf. Acts 1:4–5; also Matt. 3:11 and para.). When John the Baptist predicted the future baptism with the Spirit, he was not simply talking about empowerment for service. He was proclaiming the superiority of the salvation that would come through the Messiah when compared to that which was related to his preparatory ministry of water baptism of repentance.

This is seen further by the fact that nothing is said about ministry in relation to the Spirit's coming on the Samaritans (Acts 8:14–17), Cornelius (ch. 10), and the Ephesians (19:1–7). Instead, his coming is the gift of the Spirit related to the new covenant salvation that comes through faith in Jesus. The apostles went to Samaria not to bring the Spirit to empower the Samaritans for ministry, but to give them the gift of the Spirit that accompanied faith in Christ. Peter was sent to Cornelius to tell him how to be "saved" (11:14; 15:7–11, cf. the resultant cleansing of the heart, v. 8). The coming of the Spirit on the disciples at Ephesus likewise focused on the reception of the Spirit, not their empowerment for service. Paul's question was, "Did you receive the Holy Spirit... ?" not "Did you receive the Spirit's empowering for service?" (19:2). Even the context of Peter's proclamation concerning the reception of the Spirit at Pentecost shows that this action is related above all to salvation and the inner-transformation life, not simply to empowerment. The coming of the Spirit on those who responded to Peter's message had little to do with their ministry, but greatly transformed their personal lives (cf. 2:38–47).

Luke's theology of the reception of the Spirit is thus similar to Paul's. To receive the Spirit is to receive him as the promised gift associated with salvation in Christ. There is no specific second empowering relationship. To receive the Spirit is to receive him as the powerful God, who is desirous of empowering for all of life, including ministry. To make the coming of the Spirit in the Spirit-baptism of Acts essentially the same as the Old Testament anointing for ministry, as Pentecostalism does, is to seriously limit the full significance of what took place at Pentecost and other points in Acts.

That the baptism with the Spirit is really the gift of the Spirit that includes both the inner-transforming and empowering works of the Spirit is buttressed by the scriptural truth that *every* Christian is empowered for service. Contrary to Oss, I would argue that Paul's use of Spirit-baptism (1 Cor. 12:13) is not different from Luke's and distinct from "the anointing with Spirit and power" (p. 258). There is no doubt an emphasis on the unity of the body in the context of Paul's statement, as Oss states. But it should not be overlooked that the reference to Spirit-baptism is also set in the midst of Paul's discussion of charismatic endowment for ministry. It is, in fact, the diverse charismatic gifts that bring unity, according to Paul.

The apostle's teaching that *all* believers have been baptized with the Spirit thus demonstrates that this action belongs to salvation itself. In receiving the Spirit, believers become members of Christ's body, empowered by charismatic gifts for ministry (cf. 1 Cor. 12:4–31). The issue for believers is therefore not to seek a second distinct empowering work for ministry. It is rather to live in an obedient relationship to the Spirit so that his power can manifest itself through his "filling" or control, which both inwardly transforms and ministers to others (see the personal and ministry effect of "filling" in Eph. 5:18ff.).

3. My understanding of Spirit-baptism makes it impossible for me to see tongues as its initial evidence for all believers. As I indicated in my essay, numerous people received the gift of the Spirit in Acts with no evidence of tongues (e.g., Acts 2:38ff.). Since the occurrence of tongues takes place with the first Spirit-baptism of different groups of people (i.e., Jews, Acts 2; possibly Samaritans, ch. 8; Gentiles, ch. 10; those moving from old to new covenant salvation experience, ch. 19), it is far more convincing

to me to see tongues as the physical evidence of the coming of the Spirit marking the inauguration of the new covenant salvation for each of the new groups rather than the Spirit's empowering as a second work.[1] The Pentecostal position from Acts would carry more weight if Luke showed just one instance of a Jew coming to salvation and speaking tongues after Pentecost (even Paul's salvation and filling are recorded with no evidence of tongues) or a Gentile other than Cornelius.

The support for Initial Physical Evidence (IPE) from narrative theology ("narratology") is for me unconvincing. The record of what took place in the church by itself without explanation (and there is no explanation for IPE) cannot be prescriptive, informing the church (as Oss suggests) how it ought to be permanently structured. If Acts can be used to say tongues are permanent, then why not the permanency of apostles and the reception of canonical revelation?

As for "narrative analogy," there is no question but that Luke intends a relationship between the tongues and Spirit-baptism in the instances where tongues appear. The question is, what is the relationship? Aside from the fact that there is strong biblical evidence that Spirit-baptism cannot be limited only to the empowering work of the Spirit (thereby calling into question the relationship of tongues to the empowering work of the Spirit as posited by Pentecostal theology), it is not at all evident why three instances (or four, if we assume tongues in Acts 8) should be universalized without any explanation to that effect. It is much more convincing to see a commonality in these specific occurrences, that is, signs of the Spirit's first coming *on different groups*. If this is, in fact, the substance of the "echo effect," then the analogy of tongues with the baptism of the Spirit is neither universal for all believers nor continuing today.

4. Space necessitates only a limited response to the evidence set forth by Oss for the continuity of miraculous gifts. The arguments from the redemptive-historical perspective appear to boil down to saying that since we have entered the age of eschatological salvation, which according to Scripture is characterized by the Spirit, all of his ministries that occurred in this age should

---

[1]See my essay on the interpretation of Acts as the movement of the gospel witness from Jerusalem to all peoples (p. 133, n.61).

be understood as permanent in the church. I agree wholeheartedly with the two premises (i.e., that we have entered the eschatological age, and that it is characterized by the Spirit), but I do
not believe that the conclusion follows. Oss himself acknowledges that the apostles had a "unique, unrepeatable, foundational role" (p. 279). Furthermore, since he does not see any
prophets today who give "inerrant revelation with full divine
authority," he must also accept some change in relation to the
prophets of the New Testament, who at least in some instances
prophesied with full authority (e.g., Eph. 2:20; 3:5). These undeniable changes are sufficient to lay to rest the argument that all of
the Spirit's activities in the eschatological age are continuous.

Oss's Pentecostal position that emphasizes miracles as a
part of the present age goes far beyond the teaching of Scripture.
As I indicated in my essay, miracles such as bodily healing,
which are only temporary, do not belong to the essence of the
kingdom blessing. Moreover, the references to God's "power"
in apostolic teaching do not emphasize outward miracles, but
rather spiritual power that works inwardly. As Dunn points out,
the power of the new age in the church toward the world is fundamentally power expressed in the weakness and suffering of
this age.[2]

Scripture likewise does not support an emphasis on miracles as part of the new covenant ministry of the Spirit, as suggested by Oss. The explicit Old Testament prophecies of the new
covenant clearly focus on inner-transforming work of the Spirit.
The hearts of God's people will be changed so that they will love
God and walk in his ways (cf. Jer. 31:33; 32:38–40; Ezek. 36:26–
27). In the New Testament Jesus specifically speaks of the new
covenant in relation to forgiveness of sins (Matt. 26:28), and Paul
connects it again to the inner spiritual work of the Spirit of being
"transformed into [the Lord's] likeness with ever-increasing
glory" (2 Cor. 3:18; see also Heb. 8:8–12; 10:16–17).

Finally, it is difficult to see that the "lion's share of biblical
evidence" points to the "continuity of [the Spirit's] empowering
work [presumably miraculous manifestation] during the new
covenant epoch" (p. 272). As I demonstrated in my essay, when

---

[2]James D. G. Dunn, *Jesus and the Spirit* (Philadelphia: Westminster, 1975), 329;
see also my essay, p. 99.

we take away the miracles performed as "signs" in relation to the unique and unrepeatable roles of Jesus and the apostles, we are left with limited reference to miraculous activity in the church. This is not only in regard to teaching, but even more so in regard to actual miracles performed in the churches. It is hard to conclude from scriptural examples that "God's healing power" is "simply normal and to be expected in the life of the church" (p. 276).

Oss's point concerning the greater prominence of miraculous activity in areas where evangelism is taking place for the first time is well taken. I also agree that so-called "power encounters" with demonic spirits are part of God's work today. But consideration of the Spirit's ministry in such encounters leads to the conclusion that it is directly related to the release of someone from the bondage of Satan and sin that is at the heart of the Spirit's new covenant ministry of inner-transformation.

All this is not to deny that God works miracles today. He does. It is, however, to deny that the picture of miraculous activity seen in Scripture, especially with Jesus and the apostolic era, is to be understood as normal for all of church history. The Pentecostal perspective is to be commended for lifting up before all of the church the central truth that the Christian life and ministry depends on the supernatural work of God through the Spirit. Some of the teachings used in support of this truth, however, are difficult to sustain biblically.

A THIRD WAVE RESPONSE TO DOUGLAS A. OSS

C. Samuel Storms

Even a cursory reading of Oss's essay will reveal how closely his understanding of the work of the Holy Spirit approaches mine. Whereas there are a few differences (e.g., I do not believe tongues is the initial physical evidence of Spirit-baptism), they are largely semantic rather than substantive. One in particular deserves brief comment.

Oss makes a good case for the distinct, yet complementary, perspectives on the work of the Spirit in the writings of Luke and Paul. The former focuses on the empowering work of the Spirit that parallels the Old Testament "anointing" of prophet, priest, and king, whereas the latter highlights what Oss calls the "inner transforming" aspect of the Spirit's ministry. When Oss brings this to his interpretation of 1 Corinthians 12:13, he concludes that even if one were to concede that Paul is describing soteriological initiation, "it does not change the argument for an empowering work of the Spirit that is distinct from salvation (based on biblical theology and Lukan pneumatology)" (p. 259). I fully agree. As I argued in my essay, the Pauline doctrine of Spirit-baptism as a metaphor for conversion in no way diminishes the reality of multiple subsequent "anointings" of the Holy Spirit, designed to empower believers for charismatic ministry. Although this suggests that, for Oss, Paul and Luke employ the same terminology of Spirit-baptism to describe two different events (something I find unlikely, though not impossible), the spiritual realities that these events embody are distinct and valid. I concur with Oss that "any arguments against the Pentecostal doctrine of Spirit-baptism militate only against the label; they do not really address the substance of the issue" (p. 260).

Perhaps an illustration will help bring this down to a more manageable level. Let us suppose that you reach into the cabinet for medication to relieve a persistent headache and take hold of what you believe is aspirin. Unfortunately, the label on the bottle has long since worn off. Nevertheless, the medicine works; fifteen minutes after swallowing two tablets, your headache is completely gone. Your spouse then informs you that the medicine you took was, in fact, Tylenol. Does this news cause your headache to return? It should not. The medicinal value of the Tylenol is not diminished simply because you mislabeled it. Calling it aspirin in no way altered the physical properties of what was, in fact, Tylenol.

My point, and that of Oss as well, is that the reality of "extra-conversion" experiences of the Holy Spirit is not undermined should it be discovered that we have "mislabeled" the event. The spiritual "medicine," so to speak, still works. Whereas I prefer to reserve the terminology of Spirit-baptism for what all experience at conversion, the fact that the Pentecostal applies it to a subsequent and more restricted empowering does not in and of itself invalidate the latter phenomenon. The important issue is whether the New Testament endorses *both* the initial salvific work of regeneration and incorporation into the body of Christ on the one hand, *and* the theologically distinct (though not always subsequent) work of anointing for witness, service, and charismatic gifting on the other. Oss and I would agree that it does.

I would like to echo Oss's affirmation that "the anointed Davidite, Jesus," is portrayed in the New Testament as "pass[ing] on his own anointing to those who come under his reign" (p. 270). This, I believe, is a crucial element in properly understanding the dimensions of the Spirit's ministry in the church today that has far too long been overlooked.

Careful study of the four Gospels (and relevant texts in Acts and the letters) reveals the consistent affirmation that the power by which Jesus lived (Luke 4:1; John 1:32; 3:34–35), taught (Acts 1:1–2), preached (Luke 4:18), cast out demons (Matt. 12:22–32, esp. 28; Acts 10:37–38), resisted temptation (Luke 4:1–2), worshiped the Father (10:21), healed the sick (4:18; 5:17; 6:19; 8:48;

cf. 24:49), offered himself a sacrifice for sins (Heb. 9:13–14), and was raised from the dead (Acts 17:31; 1 Tim. 3:16) was nothing less than the energizing presence of the Holy Spirit.

In his Gospel, Luke "precisely identifies Jesus' power as the power of the Holy Spirit, and thus attributes those things Jesus did, which caused people to spread his fame far and wide (4:14b), to the *dynamis*, 'the power,' of the Spirit."[1] Jesus himself explicitly attributes his power over the demonic to the indwelling and abiding Holy Spirit. He understood that

> his ability to heal, to make people whole, to restore sight to the blind and speech to the dumb, and to overthrow the destructive forces of evil lay not in himself, lay not in the strength of his own person, but in God and in the power of God mediated to him through the Spirit. In his action God acted. In his speech God spoke. His authority was the authority of God.[2]

In other words, Jesus was himself *consciously aware* of the ultimate source of his power. He knew himself to be dependent on the power of the Spirit. The Spirit did not work secretly through him.

The significance of this for us, his disciples, becomes evident when we observe that

> the very first thing Jesus did immediately after he was resurrected from among the dead and reunited with his followers was to pass on to them, as a gift from his Father (cf. Acts 2:23), that same power by which he lived, triumphed, and broke the bands of his own human limitations. On the very day of his resurrection, he came to them locked in by their fears, "breathed"' (*enephyēsen*) on them and said, "Receive the Holy Spirit" (John 20:22).[3]

In other words, the mission of Jesus is not over. It merely passes into a new phase. Jesus continues the mission given him by his Father by sending forth his disciples in the same power with and by which the Father sent him forth—the power of the Holy Spirit.

---

[1]Gerald Hawthorne, *The Presence and the Power* (Dallas: Word, 1991), 148.
[2]Ibid., 169–70.
[3]Ibid., 235.

It should not surprise us, then, that Luke uses the exact phrase to describe the believer's experience of the Spirit as he used to describe the experience of Jesus. Both he and we (Stephen in particular) are to be "full of the Holy Spirit" (Luke 4:1; Acts 6:5). Paul deliberately juxtaposes two words in 2 Corinthians 1:21 to highlight our position and power. He declares that "he who establishes us with you in 'Christ' (*christon*) and 'christed' (*chrisas*) us is God," or, "he who establishes us with you in *the anointed one* and *anointed* us is God" (translation mine). Thus, just as Jesus said of himself, "The Spirit of the Lord is on me, because he has anointed me" (Luke 4:18), so likewise Christians are spoken of as anointed ones because we too have received the Holy Spirit and are thus set apart and empowered to serve God and authorized to act on his behalf (cf. 1 John 2:18–22, 27–28). In summary,

> The significance of the Holy Spirit in the life of Jesus extends to his followers in all of the little and the big things of their existences. The Spirit that helped Jesus overcome temptations, that strengthened him in weakness, that aided him in the hard job of taking on himself the hurts of the hurting, that infused him with a power to accomplish the impossible, that enabled him to stay with and complete the task God had given him to do, that brought him through death and into resurrection, is the Spirit that the resurrected Jesus has freely and lavishly ... given to those who would be his disciples today![4]

---

[4]Ibid., 242.

Chapter Five

CONCLUDING STATEMENTS

Intro-

Remark I

II.

III.

IV.

CONCLUDING STATEMENT (PENTECOSTAL/ CHARISMATIC VIEW)

Douglas A. Oss

These final observations are offered after having spent two profitable and edifying days of discussion with the other authors and the editor of the present work. Many thanks to Wayne Grudem, Richard Gaffin, Robert Saucy, and Sam Storms for their invaluable insights. We have been asked to offer our opinions on areas of agreement and remaining differences between the positions, as well as to submit some final advice to the church concerning miraculous gifts.

Areas of agreement and remaining differences. There are several areas when we were able to agree, though significant differences remain.

1. *Frameworks*. Gaffin's theological model for understanding miraculous gifts (and Saucy's, to some extent) is based on the "open-canon" premise. Gaffin holds that since the early church (e.g., the church at Corinth) did not yet have a New Testament, they needed the utterance gifts to function as a New Testament canon until such time as the canon was complete and available. He sees this picture in texts such as Ephesians 2:20–22. At the heart of my own framework (and Storms's as well), on the other hand, is the biblical-theological understanding of the "last days." We hold that the experiences described in the New Testament fulfill the "last days" expectation of Scripture and are characteristic of the age until the Lord's return.

Both of these "models," or "frameworks," are being used to exclude evidence from the other position. For example, Gaffin can identify any evidence I bring against cessationism as belonging

311

to the open-canon period and thus deny its continuing function. Likewise, I can deny Gaffin's arguments by appealing to the continuing nature of the "last days" and the characteristic, miraculous activity of the Spirit that *defines* this epoch. It will be up to the reader to determine which paradigm more naturally arises from the Bible and the redemptive-historical unfolding we observe in its structure. The two paradigms clash profoundly.

2. *The history of salvation and order of salvation.* Gaffin denies that a feature of the history of salvation (e.g., Old Testament anticipation of the Spirit's outpouring in power and its fulfillment at Pentecost) can become part of the order of salvation (applied to individual and church life in an ongoing sense). Thus he denies that the Spirit's *miraculous* work at Pentecost and throughout Acts is intended to become a characteristic part of the Christian life, because this would confuse the two "categories." The reader should note, however, that Gaffin does not object to all forms of continuing empowerment (e.g., bold preaching) but only to the view that miraculous gifts are characteristic of the last days. Especially important for Gaffin is to demonstrate the cessation of utterance gifts as a characteristic manifestation during this age. These manifestations, he argues, are restricted to the open-canon period except for extremely rare occasions, in which case they are inerrant.

In my opinion, Gaffin's view constitutes a hardening of the categories (history of salvation and order of salvation) that is neither demanded nor implied by Scripture. Other features of the history of salvation have continuing results in the life of the Christian and the church (e.g., the anticipation of new creation [Jer. 31:31–34; Ezek. 36:24–28] and its fulfillment in the believer). To argue that because something belongs to the history of salvation it can never have continuing results in the life of the church (e.g., experiences of the Spirit's empowering work) is to draw the lines too rigidly. Such narrowly defined categories facilitate the dismissal of evidence when it does not fit the open-canon paradigm. In sum, Gaffin holds that the Pentecostal view confuses the two categories; in my opinion, it is his unnecessarily rigid understanding of the categories that is flawed. Again, this demonstrates a fundamental paradigm collision, and the reader will need to judge each view by whether it arises naturally from within the teaching of Scripture or is imposed from without.

3. *Terminology differences.* The other three authors all agree that the phrase "baptism in the Spirit" should not be used for the empowering work of the Spirit. In my view, Luke's writings use the phrase this way. Peter could have quoted from Jeremiah 31:31–34 or Ezekiel 36:24–28 for his Pentecost sermon. But he quoted from Joel 2:28–32, which is clearly an empowerment text in the Old Testament prophetic tradition and is used to identify the experience of empowerment as the fulfillment of Jesus' statement concerning baptism in the Spirit in Acts 1:6–8. Thus, while the Pentecostal use of the label may not be traditional, neither is it patently unbiblical, as some would suggest. And in my opinion, the Pentecostal use of the label fits Luke's understanding more adequately. The other three authors suggested using "filled with the Spirit" for the empowering work, and of course this phrase is already a synonym for Spirit-baptism in Pentecostal circles. To reiterate a point in my essay, the discussion should focus on substance first and avoid debates about labels if those debates preclude substantive discussion. In other words, the substantive issue that needs to be examined is whether there is a distinct empowering work of the Spirit that is different from regeneration, labels notwithstanding.

4. *Empowerment and conversion.* Pentecostals do not suggest that the Spirit's empowering work is unrelated to conversion, only that it is theologically different from conversion and from regeneration/sanctification. In the discussion among the authors, we had no disagreement concerning the contemporary empowering work of the Spirit. All agree that the Spirit still empowers the believer. The disagreements concern the expressions or manifestations of the Spirit's power today and the place in the order of salvation for such an experience.

(a) Gaffin, and to a lesser degree Saucy, disagree that miraculous "utterance gifts" (especially prophecy, tongues, and interpretation of tongues) are characteristic of the Spirit's empowerment today. We have no disagreement concerning the continuity of healings, exorcisms, bold preaching, and so on. God does still act sovereignly in these areas, although our various expectations that he *will* act in this way seem to be disparate (Gaffin and Saucy on the cautious side; Storms and I on the enthusiastic side). The reason underlying their cessationist view of utterance gifts is that they define these gifts as "canon," sayings given to guide the church during the foundational, open-canon period. Again, the application of this theological model allows only cessationist conclusions.

Storms and I agree that utterance gifts are characteristic of the Spirit's work during the entire period of the last days. We both disagree with any definition that restricts utterance gifts to the function of canon during the open-canon period. While we do not deny that some prophecies and glossolalic utterances may have become part of the New Testament canon, the New Testament does not restrict utterance gifts to the canonical function. Indeed, one purpose of these gifts is identified plainly in the New Testament as edification (see esp. 1 Cor. 12–14). Paul writes that utterances in tongues edify both the individual (14:4) and, when interpreted, the whole church (14:5). Prophecy also has as its purpose the edification of the church. There is no indication anywhere that this edifying function of the utterance gifts was intended to cease when the New Testament canon was complete. Utterance gifts do not equal canon.

In support of the point that miraculous utterances do not equal canon, it was pointed out in our discussion that when praying in a tongue the believer's own spirit is praying, prompted by the Holy Spirit (1 Cor. 14:14, "my spirit prays, but my mind is unfruitful"). This is a common understanding of tongues in Pentecostal and charismatic circles. The question was then raised, "How can the prayer or thanksgiving of a believer's own spirit (14:14–17) be considered canonical revelation from God to the church?" This question was not resolved to everyone's satisfaction and remains open. Furthermore, Storms and I agreed over against Gaffin that tongues can be transrational communication with God (14:14), that is, the human spirit is able to communicate directly with God in a mode that transcends the intellect.

(b) The other major issue mentioned above is the place one gives to empowerment in the order of salvation. Since none of us deny its existence, where does it fit? All of us agree that empowerment is subsequent to salvation. One is not empowered until one is saved, and this dependence exists even where there is no discernible, temporal subsequence between conversion and empowerment. The other three authors argue that empowerment is something that develops gradually in the life of the believer, much like sanctification. In fact, Gaffin is more comfortable putting it under the umbrella of sanctification—which to me raises the question of the church in Corinth, which was empowered (1 Cor. 1:4–7) but hardly sanctified (cf. the remainder of the letter).

Storms and Saucy agree that empowerment is not sanctification and that it develops over time in the Christian life. Pentecostals do not disagree with this interpretation, but we emphasize the need for an identifiable and dramatic experience of the Spirit's power to signal the beginning of the process. This inaugural empowerment we call baptism in, or filling with, the Holy Spirit; continuing dramatic experiences of the Spirit's power are also called "fillings." Storms and Saucy rightly emphasize the growth that occurs in this area of the Christian life, because one dramatic experience does not put one into a permanent state of spiritual power. But the primary difference here becomes the level of intensity during the first experience. Storms and Saucy see two distinct features in the order of salvation arising from regeneration: sanctification and empowerment. Pentecostals place at the beginning of the empowerment dimension of the order of salvation a distinct, initial experience of baptism with the Spirit and power.

We all agree that regeneration is not absent from Acts. In 2:38; 11:9, 14, 15–18; 15:9, for example, there is clear indication that the outpouring of the Spirit was associated with the cleansing of the heart and new life in Christ. Nevertheless, when Luke goes on to describe the nature of the Spirit's work, his emphasis is on empowerment; cleansing and sanctification are important but do not receive the same level of treatment. Moreover, the descriptions in Acts of the Spirit's empowering work present the experiences as dramatic and immediate.

A word to the church. Pentecostals have a long history of striving for balance in the spiritual life between the fruit of the Spirit and the miraculous empowerment of the Spirit. In the course of this history there have been abuses, but there has also been God's rich blessing. For many years we have sought to embrace legitimate moves of the Spirit while eschewing bogus or abusive imitations. The following pastoral reflections come from one who was born and raised a Pentecostal, and who has seen it all.

1. I would hope that the broader evangelical community will not shy away from the empowering dimension of life in the Spirit because of abuses that may occur. If the Bible teaches that this work of the Spirit is for today, then we must work toward biblical expressions of that power and not allow this dimension to be co-opted from us by those who participate in and/or tolerate abuses that are contrary to God's Word. Our convictions in this regard should be Bible-driven, not imposed from outside Scripture by appealing to hypothetical historical and cultural reconstructions that militate against the plain meaning of the texts.

2. The Pentecostal community should reaffirm its evangelical roots and commitments. There is an alarming trend today among some Pentecostals to seek out the approval of theological liberal and even unbelieving organizations, which in some cases has led to the compromise of cardinal doctrines. In these cases, the doctrine of the Word is especially under attack because of this craving for the approval of secular and liberal groups. This in turn has led some to reject mainstream formulations of inerrancy. This shift, mostly confined to scholars for the moment, has the potential for leading people to abandon historic Pentecostalism and to turn instead to liberalism and mysticism.

The Pentecostal movement has always been a Bible-based movement, looking only to Scripture as the authority for our theology and experience. Furthermore, we have always been committed to the cardinal doctrines of evangelicalism. Now is not the time to abandon the biblical basis for our faith. Loosed from its moorings in Scripture, the Pentecostal movement will become a rudderless ship, driven by the winds of modernism and mysticism. Perhaps the lessons of the debates over biblical inerrancy among Presbyterians in the 1920 and 1930s, the stand of inerrantists in the Lutheran Church–Missouri Synod during the early and middle 1970s, and the recent courage of the inerrantists in the Southern Baptist Convention in the 1980s and 1990s will provide the Pentecostal movement with practical guidance for the future.

3. Early Pentecostals evidenced a simple, biblical faith and longing of the heart for the reality of God's purifying and empowering presence. Worship emphasized Spirit and Truth. With similar sincerity and spiritual fervor contemporary Pentecostals continue to enter God's presence and enjoy his abundant blessings.

There are two closely related subjects that deserve to be mentioned in this regard. First, spirituality must never become exclusively focused on individual or corporate experiences of God's blessing. God does not want an inwardly focused church. These experiences of the Spirit's empowering presence have a purpose, which is to empower and renew God's people to go into the marketplace and boldly witness to the gospel of Christ. Second, while the Scriptures mandate certain aspects of worship, there are phenomena in the church today that are nowhere addressed in Scripture. When God pours out his Spirit in power, believers respond in a variety of ways. We need to be tolerant of one another rather than judgmental, and we certainly should not limit God in ways that he has not limited himself. We all know that the Bible lays down boundaries that we must not cross in the name of spiritual unity; there can be no compromise, either explicitly by confession or implicitly through association, on doctrines necessary for salvation. But in the one true church, there should be a fundamental unity of the Spirit that transcends all differences.

CONCLUDING STATEMENT
(THIRD WAVE VIEW)

C. Samuel Storms

Despite the often serious disagreements that have come to light in the course of this symposium, there is much at a fundamental level concerning the person and work of the Holy Spirit on which we agree. This was especially evident during our two days of roundtable discussion in November of 1995 in Philadelphia, a time characterized by lively, yet friendly and respectful, interaction. At the close of this chapter I will address some of the common ground we share, but first I want to clarify a dozen key issues that appear in the responses to my essay by Gaffin and Saucy.

1. Central to Gaffin's cessationism is the claim that the period we know as "church history" is distinct from and discontinuous with "redemptive history." It is somewhat surprising, in view of his commitment to amillennialism, that the terminology he uses to draw this distinction sounds similar to that employed by classical dispensationalists. He describes the church age as a "hiatus," existing "between the times"; the church age is "bracketed" by Christ's two comings (p. 285). Gaffin uses this construct as a way of denying continuity between the believers' experience of the miraculous in the book of Acts (not to mention the rest of the New Testament) and the experience of God's people in subsequent church history.

I am again left wondering, "What biblical texts, either individually or collectively, assert or suggest this concept?" No one denies that redemption has been once-for-all "accomplished" and is repeatedly "applied" in the lives of those who believe. But

318

the Bible does not teach that this distinction is grounds for denying to postapostolic Christians (e.g., you and me) the availability
of those miraculous gifts so clearly described (and, I believe, *prescribed*) by Paul, Luke, and other New Testament authors. We are
one body of Christ with those who labored for the kingdom in
the book of Acts. Whereas no one in this symposium wants to
argue for apostolic succession, I want to insist on what may be
called *ecclesiastical* succession. We are the organic continuation
of the body of Christ birthed at Pentecost. The same Holy Spirit
that came to indwell and empower them (the *church*) abides to
indwell and empower us (the same *church*) now. If this is *not* the
case, the cessationist bears the burden of proving it. And explicit
(or, for that matter, implicit) biblical evidence for such has yet to
appear in this volume.

2. Gaffin interprets Spurgeon's experience as merely a
"Spirit-prompted insight that occurs incalculably and sporadically" (p. 294). However, the admission that such *postcanonical*
information came from the Holy Spirit is telling. The fact that it
may have occurred "incalculably and sporadically" is no argument for its not being a revelatory activity. My reading of 1 Corinthians 14 suggests that most prophetic ministry was
incalculable, if by that we mean unpredictable, because it was
subject to the sovereignty of God (see v. 30). The fact that such
an experience did not "mark" Spurgeon's ministry proves only
that Spurgeon probably did not have the "gift" of prophecy; it
does not prove he did not prophesy. So how *does* one explain the
dozen or so instances when it occurred? The fact that Spurgeon
did not "seek" this experience is irrelevant to whether or not it
happened and *what* it was *when* it happened.

Gaffin's appeal to Spurgeon's reference to the Sabbath hardly
undermines the relevance of the event. Gaffin asks, "Did Spurgeon get that part wrong? Or am I missing something?" (p. 294,
n.5). Yes, you are missing something. You are missing the fact that
New Testament prophecy is often a mixture that must be evaluated in the light of Scripture. Whether or not Spurgeon "got it
wrong" about Sunday being the Christian Sabbath is perhaps a
good subject to be addressed in another "Four Views" book.

3. Gaffin argues that Paul's advice to the tongues-speaker
in 1 Corinthians 14:28 to "speak to himself and God" cannot
refer to private exercise of the gift because the context pertains

to the church assembly. But if this were the case, it would seem to put Gaffin in the position of endorsing the legitimacy of *personal, uninterpreted, nonevangelistic, nonsign* speaking in tongues *in the corporate meeting of the church*, a view that I am quite certain he would not want to embrace. It is better to understand the apostle Paul as commending the use of personal, uninterpreted prayer in tongues outside the church assembly, in the privacy of one's devotional life.[1]

4. What does Paul mean by the "demonstration of the Spirit's power" that accompanied his gospel preaching (1 Cor. 2:4; 1 Thess. 1:5)? To say, as Gaffin does, that it cannot be a matter of the miraculous because "it was exercised just when Paul's own observable conduct was 'in weakness and fear, and with much trembling' (v. 3)" (pp. 295–96) is to misconstrue the nature and purpose of the miraculous. I need only point to the fact that Paul's weakness and distress induced by his "thorn in the flesh" came immediately on the heels of his most exalted revelatory experience (2 Cor. 12:1–6)! And the presence of "signs, wonders and miracles" (12:12) in his ministry were, in Paul's mind, perfectly compatible with his incomparable suffering catalogued in graphic detail only a chapter earlier (11:23–33).[2]

5. In response to my essay, Saucy asserts that the ultimate purpose of New Testament miracles is to serve as signs (p. 227). From this he concludes that other, secondary, purposes of the miraculous are not sufficient to warrant our expectation of their presence subsequent to the apostolic age. Several things here call for comment.

In the first place, whether or not the *ultimate* purpose of miracles in the ministry of Jesus and the apostles was to serve as signs has little bearing on whether miraculous *gifts* have a purpose for the church in subsequent generations. Paul's explicit

---

[1]As Fee notes, "Speaking 'by himself' (= privately) stands in contrast to 'in the assembly' in v. 28, meaning he or she should pray 'to God' in this way in private" (*God's Empowering Presence: The Holy Spirit in the Letters of Paul* [Peabody, Mass.: Hendrickson, 1994], 251).

[2]Evidence that "demonstration of the Spirit's power" in 1 Corinthians 2:4–5 refers to signs, wonders, miracles, and spiritual gifts is provided by Gary Greig in "The Purpose of Signs and Wonders in the New Testament," *The Kingdom and the Power*, ed. by Gary S. Greig and Kevin N. Springer (Ventura, Calif.: Regal, 1993), 169, n. 55.

instruction on the purpose of the *charismata* as edifying the church (1 Cor. 14:4–5, 12–13, 26), serving the common good (12:7), bringing exhortation and consolation to the body of Christ (14:3), and convicting the lost (14:24–25) is sufficient enough to warrant our confidence in God's will for the life of the church, whatever *other* purpose miracles per se might serve.

I am not sure how Saucy or anyone would go about proving the ultimate versus the secondary purpose of the miraculous. I find as many statements in the New Testament that portray the motivation for the miraculous as compassion, love, or the mere desire to demonstrate mercy to those who cry out for help (Matt. 9:27–31; 14:13–14; 15:22–28, 32–39; 17:14–21; 20:29–34; Mark 1:41–42; 5:19; 6:34–44; 8:2ff.; 9:22; Luke 7:11–17; 17:13–14). The verb translated "to have or show compassion" (*splanchnizomai*) is used eleven times in the New Testament to refer to God's compassion toward sinners, nine of which refer to Jesus' motivation in healing the sick!

6. Saucy questions my use of Acts 4:29–31 by insisting that such a prayer is valid only when "apostles" are present. He then appeals to Acts 4:33, a text, however, that speaks only of apostolic witness to the resurrection of Jesus. Acts 5:12 does refer to the apostles as those who performed signs and wonders, a fact which no one denies. But we cannot so easily dismiss the prayer of Acts 4 when we see *nonapostolic believers*, such as Stephen (6:8), Philip (8:6–7, 13), Ananias (9:17–18), disciples of John the Baptist (19:6), women at Caesarea (21:8–9), believers in Galatia (Gal. 3:5), believers in Rome (Rom. 12:6), believers in Corinth (1 Cor. 12–14), and believers in Thessalonica (1 Thess. 5:19–20), all exercising miraculous gifts.

7. Notwithstanding Saucy's valid point that our needs today may well differ in certain respects from the needs of first-century believers, this does *not* apply to edification, exhortation, and consolation. This has not changed and will not change until Jesus returns. No biblical reason can be given for thinking that their needs in this regard may be met through the ministry of the *charismata* but ours cannot. We are no less the body of Christ than they. We are no less needy in this regard than they.

8. In regard to prophecy, Saucy argues that "the Spirit's work of inspiration ... goes all the way to the actual prophecy, that is, the words spoken or written" (p. 230). But the examples

Handwritten notes at top:
- Storms says prophecy can include human error
- Saucy says all prophecy is infallible
- (p. 230)

he cites in evidence of this assertion pertain either to the Old Testament experience of prophecy or prophetic revelation that was designed by God to be inscripturated. There is no evidence that this concept of the infallible guarantee of a prophet's words applies to the exercise of the gift as it is found in the New Testament church.

9. In the case of Agabus's prophecy in Acts 21:10–11, Saucy contends that there was no error insofar as Paul himself recounts what took place (28:17) in words essentially the same as those employed by Agabus. He insists that "it will not do to argue, as Storms does, that Paul was actually describing the time when he was secretly escorted out of Jerusalem by the Romans to Caesarea (23:12–35), for Paul was already 'handed over to the Romans' before he left Jerusalem" (p. 231). But Paul's point in 28:17 is simply that he was transferred from Roman custody in Jerusalem into Roman custody in Caesarea. The fact that Paul was already, in some sense, in "the hands of the Romans" in Jerusalem does not preclude his using the same terminology in referring to his transfer to Caesarea and the jurisdiction of Felix.

The attempt to preserve the complete infallibility of Agabus's prophecy (Acts 21:10–11) simply will not hold up to the details of the text. On Saucy's reading, the Jews put Paul in chains, but twice Acts says the Romans bound him. Saucy contends that the Jews turned over the apostle to the Gentiles, but Acts says that they stubbornly refused to do so, leaving the Romans no choice but to take him from them by force.

This problem is not resolved by arguing, as Saucy does, that the word "handed over" need only mean a general or ultimate responsibility for one being transferred into another's hands. In all other 119 instances where the verb "to hand over" (*paradidomi*) appears in the New Testament, the person(s) who is said to perform the action either does it willingly, intentionally, deliberately, or counsels and commands others to do it. But in the case of Paul's capture in Jerusalem, the Jews did *not* order him to be bound, the Romans did (Acts 21:33; 22:29). The Jewish relinquishment of Paul into Roman hands was precisely the opposite of a willing, intentional, deliberate act. Far from being the cause of Paul's imprisonment by the Romans, they violently resisted it.

10. Saucy questions whether James 5 has in view the "gift" of healing, presumably because the word *charisma* ("gift") does

not occur in the passage; it only describes people praying for healing. But the term *charisma* appears nowhere in the entire book. Must we deny, for example, that James 3:1 has in view the "gift" of teaching simply because the word *charisma* is not found in *that* passage? It, too, only describes people teaching. Furthermore, why does Saucy assert that "*surely* James intends us to understand that *all* of the elders were to pray 'the prayer of faith' and that the concerted prayer would be effective" (p. 232, emphasis mine)? James says nothing about how many need to pray with that faith to which God responds with healing. Certainly we *hope* that all would. But I find it hard to believe that God is counting heads, happy to grant healing only if *all* have the requisite faith, while denying healing if only one or two do.

11. Contrary to Saucy's charge, neither I nor Jack Deere appeal without qualification to the healing ministry of Jesus. We both affirm there was something unique and unprecedented in what the Son of God accomplished, and it is misleading to suggest otherwise. But Saucy evidently believes that the disparity between healing miracles in the first century and healing miracles in subsequent church history cannot be explained if we appeal to God's compassion as a primary motivation for the healing ministry of Jesus. He asks, "Is God more compassionate at certain points of history than at others?" (p. 233).

The answer of course is "no." God is as compassionate today as he was then and no more or less compassionate now than he will be in the age to come. But whether or not he manifests that compassion equally at all times is subject both to his secret and sovereign purpose as well as the depth of zeal and faith with which his people pray. Ultimately, of course, our inability to fully understand why God does or does not heal can never justify diminishing commitment in praying for the sick. *Confusion is never an excuse for disobedience, nor is the lack of experience.*

Similarly, God is always gracious. But he does not always save the souls to whom we witness or for whom we pray. But still we must pray. If more souls should be saved in one generation of the church than another, we must not think that God has diminished in his love for the lost or that we now have an excuse not to pray with the same fervency and frequency as did those in times of great spiritual harvest.

Matthew tells us that when Jesus saw the great multitude he had *compassion* for them and *healed* their sick (Matt. 14:14).

My question is simple: As the exalted Son of God looks down from the right hand of the Majesty on High, does he feel differently toward the sick and infirm? Is he now apathetic toward their pain? No one denies that miraculous healing now is less frequent than it was then. But what shall be our response to this? Personally, I am not content to deal with this problem by minimizing, if not denying, compassion as a preeminent factor in why God heals the sick. I would rather ground my confidence in the immutability of God's character, lay prayerful hands on the sick with the unfailing assurance that whereas the church may have changed, God has not, and live with the mystery of unanswered prayer until Jesus returns.

12. Contrary to what Saucy writes (p. 233), I nowhere suggest nor do I believe that the "primary" function of tongues is self-edification. I argue extensively from 1 Corinthians 14 that tongues function as a form of petitionary prayer, a means of expressing gratitude to God, a means for praising and blessing the mighty works of the Father, and perhaps also a means for conducting spiritual warfare. Yes, tongues also edify the speaker. It will not do simply to assert (wrongly, I believe) that this is inconsistent with the primary function of all gifts. I clearly affirm that the ultimate purpose of the *charismata* is the "common good" of the Christian community (1 Cor. 12:7). But Saucy must yet reckon with Paul's inescapable assertions in 14:4–5 relative to the self-edifying influence of tongues, as well as his own private exercise of the gift, for which he gives profuse thanks to God, in 14:14–19.

Let me conclude with a few brief comments. Notwithstanding our obvious disagreements, we are of one mind on several key points. First of all, it seems clear to me that all the participants in this symposium rejoice that our God still heals in response to the prayers of his people. Furthermore, we stand united against the antisupernaturalistic philosophy so prevalent in our day. None of us questions the historical reality of those miracles described in Scripture nor does anyone doubt that God can and occasionally does perform mighty acts of power according to his sovereign purposes.

Second, we all agree that the power of God is equally as evident in the cultivation of practical holiness and the fruit of the Spirit as in the manifestation of gifts or miracles. I need only point to Romans 15:13, 19 as one example of this. Whereas the apostle Paul appeals to the "power" (*dynamis*) of the Spirit as the source for his "signs and wonders" (v. 19), he no less attributes the Christian's "joy," "peace," and "hope" (v. 13) to the same "power." It is the power of the Spirit by which blind eyes are opened, both physically (John 9) and spiritually (2 Cor. 4:1–6). It is the power of the Spirit by which demons are cast out (Matt. 12:28) and persecution is endured (Gal. 5:22–23). The church cannot afford to lose sight of either of these truths.

Third, I heartily and happily concur with Gaffin's belief that there is no power experience of any higher magnitude than that of the new birth. Of all the miracles that have occurred or may yet occur, none can compare with, nor should any evoke greater gratitude than, the miracle of eternal life. I trust that all our readers concur.

Still, differences remain. We have heard the claim in this symposium that the contemporary validity of revelatory gifts threatens the finality of the canon. I believe this is an emotionally-charged argument that lacks either biblical or theological support. Cessationists in general contend that their reluctance to admit the validity of revelatory gifts is in part because of their desire to maintain the centrality and authority of the written Word in the life of the believer. This is an admirable desire that I myself fully embrace. But I cannot help but wonder, "Which view more greatly honors the authority of Scripture: the one that aims to reproduce the pattern of church life and experience expressed in the New Testament, or the one that relegates substantial portions of the New Testament record to contemporary irrelevance?"

I believe we honor and uphold the centrality and authority of Scripture when we recognize its principles, patterns, and practices as binding on us today. We do not honor the authority of Scripture by employing a theological grid that serves only to filter out the miraculous and charismatic elements of life and ministry. We honor and uphold biblical authority by submitting our conscience and our church life to the text, irrespective of how far short our experience may fall from the New Testament standard.

All of us wish that contemporary church life was a more complete reflection of the New Testament ideal. But we cannot, we *must* not, respond to the discomfort and confusion this often creates with anything less than *more* prayer for the sick, *greater* zeal for spiritual gifts, and *deeper* desire for the hand of God to perform those signs and wonders that bless his people and magnify his name. Nothing will contribute more to the entrenchment of powerlessness in the church than a theology that empties prayer of meaningful expectancy.

CONCLUDING STATEMENT (OPEN BUT CAUTIOUS VIEW)

Robert L. Saucy

The works of God as the infinite invisible Spirit have always evoked wonder and a certain incomprehension on the part of God's people. Combined with fallibility on the part of all interpreters, the ultimate incomprehensibility of God's works inevitably leads to diversity in their attempted explanations. As is evident to the reader of this work, the understanding of miraculous spiritual gifts in the contemporary church is no exception. Despite some remaining differences among us, however, I want to say that participation in this symposium has been a genuine blessing for me. Unity in the church has many dimensions and coming together around the Scriptures in search of truth for the sake of God's work cannot help but increase a sense of oneness, even when final agreement is not reached.

I would like to begin these concluding words with a few comments by way of explanation and rejoinder to some of the responses to my original essay. The responses indicated that both continuationists viewed my position as reductionistically limiting the purpose of all miracles to authenticating "signs" (see Storms, p. 161, and Oss, p. 165). Such was not what I intended to propose, as I trust that the entire essay helped to make clear. The contexts of my statements that were disputed by the responders related to contexts dealing specifically with times in biblical history when extraordinary miraculous activity accompanied God's inspired prophetic ministers (esp. Jesus and the apostles). My intention even here was not to limit the performance of the miracles to a single purpose, but rather to say that in these instances their *primary* purpose was to authenticate the bearers of divine revelation and their message.

A word of clarification is also needed concerning my description of Pentecostal Spirit baptism as bringing a "definitive new relationship" to the Spirit, which Oss views as a misunderstanding of this tradition. My statement was based on Pentecostal explanations of Spirit baptism, such as the following by Ralph Riggs and Donald Gee:

> As the Spirit of Christ, He had come at conversion, imparting the Christ-life, revealing Christ, and making Him real. At the Baptism in the Spirit, *He Himself in His own person* comes upon and fills the waiting believers.... His coming to the believer at the Baptism is the coming of the Third Person of the Trinity, in addition to the coming of Christ.[1]

> The New Testament appears to indicate as an unmistakable historical fact that after the first entry of the Spirit in regeneration there can be and should be also *a special personal reception by believers of the Holy Spirit in his original and unique person.* This experience is called the "baptism in the Holy Spirit."[2]

To my mind these statements convey the idea that at conversion the believer does receive the Spirit, but apparently more related to *his work* in bringing Christ and his life. In Spirit baptism, however, the Spirit comes in *his own person* in a way that was somehow different from his coming in regeneration. Perhaps the wording of my description of this second work was not the most propitious. However, it is difficult for me to see how these Pentecostal explanations do not, in fact, teach something of a new relationship of the believer to the person of the Spirit.

More in the nature of a rejoinder and perhaps challenge to both continuationist positions, I would like to respond to two significant issues mentioned in responses of Storms and Oss to my position. Despite the attempt by Storms to deny apostleship

---

[1]Ralph M. Riggs, *The Spirit Himself* (Springfield, Mo.: Gospel Publishing House, 1949), 79–80 (emphasis added).

[2]Donald Gee, *Die Früchte des Geistes*, 6; cited by Frederick Dale Bruner, *A Theology of the Holy Spirit* (Grand Rapids: Eerdmans, 1970), 75 (emphasis added).

as a gift, I still believe that its inclusion in the discussion of gifts in Ephesians 4 (which Storms did not deal with) makes it more likely that it should be included among the gifts. To make it simply an office raises the question as to why the other offices, i.e., elder, bishop, and deacon, are not included in these passages.

Be that as it may, most continuationists appear to acknowledge that the apostles in their miracle-working were different from others in the church both in the New Testament and subsequently (see Storms, p. 159). This applies also to Jesus, and yet both continuationists seem to suggest that the church is empowered to do the same miracles as Jesus (Oss, pp. 269–70; Storms, pp. 306–8). Surely if the miracle-working of the apostles was different, then that of Jesus was also.

My point is that if one acknowledges a difference with regard to miracles between Jesus and the apostles over against others in the church, then this difference begs for some explanation. At times continuationists recognize the *special position and task* of Jesus and the apostles and their consequent difference in miracle-working power, even as Storms does in his quote from Deere (p. 159). But little attention is then given to the relation of the miracles to the special ministries of these individuals: For example, why were there so many and powerful miracles? What purpose did they serve? The point I am attempting to make is reflected in the failure of most continuationists to deal with what I have termed the "unevenness" of miracles in Scripture and the difference between miraculous activity in the Gospels and Acts and later church history.

No one denies that God has worked miracles throughout history, including that of the church. But to point out, as continuationists do, that miracles occurred among God's people at many different times in no way refutes what seems incontrovertible from Scriptural evidence, namely, that there were significant times in the history of redemption when God's plan called for special ministries accompanied by extraordinary miraculous power and activity. (Perhaps "concentrations" of miracles is preferable to "clusters" as a description of this historical reality.)

Now either such unevenness of miracles both in Scripture and history must be denied altogether or an explanation must be sought for this phenomenon. The continuationist continues to demand scriptural teaching to substantiate a change in the miracle-working between the New Testament era and the later church. As I suggested in my essay, the eschatological position of the possible coming of Christ precluded the biblical writers from giving an explicit description of a postapostolic church. But I would suggest that consideration of the rationale for the special miraculous activity of Jesus and the apostles does provide biblical evidence for a change in miraculous activity in the later church.

I would challenge the continuationists for more clarity in their position as to whether Jesus and the apostles are the pattern for the church or not. And if they are not, that is, if Jesus and the apostles truly did have a special position with a special task, then they should provide a clear explanation for the extraordinary miracles that does not apply to those not in the same position and ministry. This does not necessarily mean cessationism, but it would help clarify the issue of miracles in the church and preclude simply using Jesus and the apostles as models for the contemporary church without further explanation.

Despite continuing disagreements, considerable areas of agreement bind us together even on the topic of miraculous gifts. All concur with the thrust of the classical Pentecostal concern that the Spirit works *both* in the believer's personal spiritual transformation and in empowerment for ministry of spiritual gifts. Scripture reveals the "filling" of the Spirit for ministry (esp. in Acts) as well as for personal walk and growth. A considerable chasm remains in relation to the sharpness of the division between these two works of the Spirit as found in the classical Pentecostal tradition, and also the distinction between the reception of the Spirit in his work of renewal and his reception for empowerment. Yet despite disagreement over the meaning of Spirit baptism and the ministry of the Spirit in empowerment, all acknowledge that the Spirit's primary work is the production of Christlikeness in God's people.

With regard to miracles, all happily concurred that our God is a miracle-working God. According to his sovereign will and for the furtherance of his purpose and glory, he continues to work miracles today. Much disagreement remains, however, over the biblical teaching concerning the *purpose* of miracles and consequently their *extent* in this postapostolic period of the church.

The significant use of the "redemptive-historical" perspective in support of both cessationism and continuationism has been most interesting to me. Obviously both understandings and applications of this important biblical theme cannot be completely valid. I suggest that further study is needed on the historical development *within* eschatological salvation. It is not enough simply to state the truth that the age of eschatological salvation characterized by the Spirit's ministry has dawned and then go on to insist that all of the Spirit's work is present uniformly throughout the age. Nor is it sufficient to acknowledge that the prophesied kingdom of Christ is presently manifest during this age. Since eschatological salvation includes final perfect glorification, it is clear that this salvation and the kingdom are not totally present today. The understanding of what aspects of that perfect kingdom and the ministry of the Spirit are normal for this age, what awaits the future coming of Christ, and exactly how we taste of the "powers of the coming age" today (Heb. 6:5) are all vital questions that merit further study in relation to the issue of miracles today.

Disagreement over the manifestation of miraculous gifts today also rests on the lack of concurrence on the nature of many of these gifts. For example, does the valid working of the gift of healing result in a complete instantaneous healing or only a partial restoration that could involve process? Even more importantly, are most miraculous healings, and for that matter most miracles reported from the church around the world today, the result of the operation of spiritual gifts or the result of believers' prayers without any relationship to a gifted individual? Perhaps it would be better at times to accept the gracious work of God without attempting to pour it into a debatable theological category.

One such area where this could be helpful is God's present leading of his people. After much discussion the participants in the symposium seemed to agree that somehow God does guide or reveal his mind to us today in matters that transcend the explicit teaching of Scripture—for example, in specific directions in personal or even church decisions. Strong divergence, however, remains over the *nature* and *place* of contemporary "prophecy" in this guidance. While I remain personally convinced that all biblical prophecy is inspired infallible utterance, I am not at all sure what difference there is between *some* "fallible prophecy" accepted by many continuationists and the "guid-ance" or "leading" of God that the church has always taught, except that "prophecy" may appear to be more miraculous. In this area, I believe that care should be taken that our disagree-ments are really substantive and not merely semantic.

Finally, what should the church do in light of the present diversity of biblical interpretation and practice that unfortu-nately for some bespeaks of confusion and strife? As I have already indicated, the church must continue to study *communally* the remaining issues. Participation in the symposium reminded me again that communication with understanding is not always easy. Following scriptural advice, careful listening should always precede response.

I also urge us all to make it clear that the focus of our churches is on the central truths of the evangelical faith that make us one in Christ and his salvation. Ultimately the goal of the Spirit's activity is that we all be "conformed to the likeness of his Son" (Rom. 8:29). Historically God's work of revival has always centered on the vital truths of salvation, that is, turning from sin and obeying Christ in holiness of life. Thoughtful care must be taken to ensure that no concomitant phenomena eclipse the real import of God's work either in reality or in reputation. We should all be concerned when fascination with miraculous knowledge and manifestations of miraculous power take prece-dence in the church over concern for the salvation of the lost and discipleship in the spiritual and ethical fruit of the Spirit.

Furthermore, I would encourage critical biblical evaluation of all "miraculous" manifestations. This advice is naturally expected from one with an "open, but cautious" position. Not finding explicit teaching in Scripture for either cessationism or continuationism, I am compelled to consider carefully the phe-nomena of God's work in the light of what is known from Scrip-ture about miraculous gifts in order to help me determine the question of their manifestation today. This, by the way, is why consideration of the miracles of church history is not "irrelevant" to me, as it was to one responder. But even belief in the contin-uation of miraculous gifts does not preclude the responsibility of the church to carefully evaluate all miraculous activity in the light of the biblical patterns of the nature and practice of these gifts. I suggest that even with our differences, greater unity could be attained in the church today if there was more willingness to seriously consider all of the scriptural teaching on this subject and act upon it.

In conclusion, I would like to add two strong impressions that I left with as a result of the fellowship with the others as we discussed together the topic of this book. Our interaction renewed my realization that our disagreements are among "brothers and sisters in Christ." I recognize that genuinely false miracle-workers are alive and well in the world, preying on God's people and those outside of the church. Detecting them is not always easy, and we must do everything in our power to protect our churches from them. The fellowship that we enjoyed, however, was clearly among believers. We did not agree on all points, but our dialogue helped us to see that we shared a common heart. This recognition conditioned not only the content of our dialogue, but especially the attitude in which it was pursued. Getting to know the heart of those with whom we differ and seeing God's presence at work in them as well as oneself is a boon toward fruitful dialogue.

Not only did I recognize the work of God in those with whom I disagreed, but I also came to a new appreciation for the reality of differences within the body of Christ. With all believers, I long for the day when all of God's people are united. The presence of sin, however, will no doubt delay that reality until the time of glorification. In the meantime, we should all recognize that divergent views are frequently the result of emphasizing certain aspects of God's total truth. This emphasis may proceed beyond scriptural bounds to exaggerated error at times, but it is helpful to recognize that the emphasis was often initiated in search of a reality that the church needed to hear. In the case of miraculous spiritual gifts, continuationists continually remind us of the supernatural power and experiential aspects of our Christian faith. Cessationists, on the other hand, stress that true Christianity rests on, and is always to be evaluated by, the once-for-all delivered revelation of the completed canonical Scripture. The church does not yet perceive the correct relationship of these elements, but surely both emphases are to be included in it.

CONCLUDING STATEMENT (CESSATIONIST VIEW)

Richard B. Gaffin, Jr.

1. Evident throughout a two-day discussion the authors and editor of this volume were able to have together, after exchanging main chapters and responses, was the firm commitment of all of us to the unique and final authority of Scripture as God's own Word. We all share a desire not to be involved with anything or have any experience that might detract from or compromise that authority. This common commitment encourages me personally. More importantly, it holds great promise for the church today concerning the issues addressed in this volume.

Consider this disconcerting situation: Especially in recent decades the work of the one Spirit, given to unify the church (e.g., 1 Cor. 12; Eph. 4:3), has become the occasion (notice I did not say, the source!) of disunity and even divisions in the church. What is the way out of this impasse of claim and counterclaim about experiences of the Spirit's working?

Certainly the answer does not lie, at least ultimately, in those experiences themselves. Slogans like "theology divides; tongues unite," or "500 million Pentecostals can't be wrong" (as I have heard it put) have a neat ring but are not really helpful, especially in a world religions scene where something like "tongues" experiences are not a uniquely Christian phenomena. Surely, if I may state what for many is obvious but which has a way of getting overlooked, for believers in Jesus Christ, all experience, including those attributed to his Spirit, must be assessed by his inscripturated Word to see whether they are genuine. Nothing about the experience itself, not even the results that may follow (however praiseworthy and beneficial in themselves, like an increase in love for others, a zeal for the gospel, fervency in prayer), may claim the final word. Only sound doctrine, that is, teaching faithful to Scripture, has that right. Where there is a readiness on all sides to maintain that standard without compromise, we have every reason to be hopeful and to expect that the Spirit will honor that commitment and grant greater unity to the church, not only in understanding his work but also in experiencing it.

In a recent book on Pentecostal spirituality (in view are developments within the charismatic movement as well as Pentecostal denominations),[1] Harvey Cox concludes that, with the waning of "scientific modernity and conventional religion," we are witnessing a new "struggle for the soul of humankind." In this battle the emerging contenders, as he sees it, are "fundamentalism" and "experientialism."[2] Among the former, for instance, are "those Christians who believe in the verbal inerrancy of the Bible";[3] the latter embraces a wide array of intuitive, less analytical spiritualities for which experience is primary.

Reminiscent of struggles in American Protestant Christianity earlier in this century, the issue for Cox is a rerun of "Shall the fundamentalists win?" Especially noteworthy is his observation that in this updated version, "the larger struggle between fundamentalists and experientialists is being played out even within the parameters of pentecostalism."[4] A major theme of the book is that nothing has been more decisive in fostering experientialism than the emergence in this century of Pentecostal spirituality. But, he believes, within Pentecostalism itself it is an "open question" at present whether experientialism or fundamentalism will prevail.[5]

I am at the opposite end of the religious-theological spectrum from Cox and reject most of what he says about Christian "fundamentalism" as a caricature. But I strongly suspect that in its basic contours his analysis of current trends in spirituality

---

[1] H. Cox, *Fire From Heaven: The Rise of Pentecostal Spirituality and the Reshaping of Religion in the Twenty-First Century* (Reading, Mass: Addison-Wesley, 1995).

[2] Ibid., 300, 309.

[3] Ibid., 302.

[4] Ibid., 310.

[5] Ibid., 319.

and of the struggle that is going on is accurate. What will prevail as our final authority, within Pentecostalism and beyond—Scripture or experience? Cox, of course, hopes for the latter (with Scripture as just one, relative contributing resource). Let us pray that this will not be the case.

This mention of prayer is not simply a pious aside. In fact, there is need today, as perhaps never before, that believers pray for the Holy Spirit to make them sensitive to Scripture and to the discerning of our times. The simple, supposedly "open" prayer, "Lord, give me more of your Spirit," will not do. Nor will the prayer for prophecy or tongues or other revelatory word gifts, especially if such prayer is voiced on the unreflecting or carelessly examined assumptions that these New Testament gifts are for today and that others are evidently receiving them. In our day premature prayer for the Spirit is not an imaginary danger.

There is sound, biblical wisdom in the words of a venerable catechism, "Prayer is an offering up of our desires unto God, for things agreeable to his will. . . ."[6] The qualification introduced by the second phrase is absolutely essential. Prayer is not a blank check at my disposal but is to be filled out only according to God's will revealed in Scripture. Otherwise, our desires, no matter how well intended, too easily become self-fulfilling wishes that evade or even overturn his will. The desire to speak in tongues and to receive other revelatory word gifts would become appropriate only after it could first be convincingly established, by sound, Spirit-led reflection on Scripture, that God intends these gifts for today. Only then would the prayer *for* the Spirit be pleasing *to* the Spirit.

At the same time, I recognize, those, like myself, who are convinced from Scripture that these gifts do not continue, as well as those who are not convinced from Scripture that they do, need to be careful that these convictions are true to Scripture. Our ongoing prayer for the Spirit in this respect (as all others) ought to be that we be kept from resisting the Spirit as he speaks in Scripture.

May God more and more grant his church in our time experience that flows from a common, Scripture-based praying for the Spirit.

---

[6]Westminster Shorter Catechism, answer 98.

2. While the commitment to biblical authority shared by the participants in this volume is promising, I am still left with the inescapable impression that the view represented by Oss and Storms is, in important respects, in tension with that commitment.

According to a sound formulation of orthodox Protestant theology, there are four major attributes of Scripture: authority, clarity (perspicuity), necessity, and sufficiency.[7] These "perfections" (as they have sometimes been called) are inseparable and mutually conditioning; they stand or fall together. One of my continuing difficulties with the viewpoint of Oss and Storms is that while it affirms the authority of Scripture, it denies its sufficiency. Or, to be fairer, their view has an inadequate and too restricted understanding of its sufficiency. Obviously, the Bible does not give specific answers about all sorts of individual life concerns and daily decisions that have to be made (whom to marry, what ministry opportunity to take, whether our church should expand its building, what the real problem in a particular counseling situation is, and the like). But from this obvious fact it seems no less obvious to them that such specific revelations are needed and so are given by God today. Moreover, they believe, the Bible itself provides the precedent for these continuing revelations.

But does this conclusion follow? Is it really the case, in other words, that the sufficiency of Scripture as it has been affirmed, in the main, since the Reformation needs to be reconsidered and more carefully qualified? Presupposing the revelation of himself that God gives in creation (general revelation), does Scripture in fact teach not, as the Reformers were convinced, "Scripture alone" but a "Scripture plus" principle of revelation? Oss and Storms in effect answer these questions affirmatively and reach the questionable conclusion that, because the Bible is being supplemented by ongoing revelations today, it is in that respect an insufficient revelation.

In his response to Saucy, Oss even seeks to turn the tables by proposing that the Westminster Confession of Faith itself, one of the classic creeds in the Reformation tradition, supports his view of continuing revelation. In particular, he cites references

---

[7]For a helpful overview, see C. Van Til, *An Introduction to Systematic Theology* (Phillipsburg, N.J.: Presbyterian and Reformed, 1974), 134–36.

in chapter 1 to "new revelations of the Spirit" (sec. 6) and "private spirits" (sec. 10) to suggest that that document is at least open to the view that revelations, subordinate to Scripture, continue today.

Despite what may have even been the personal views of some who helped to produce the Confession (although this raises a historical question of its own, the answer to which is not as clear as Oss thinks), the Confession will not bear the interpretation Oss wishes to give it. Everything said in chapter 1 ("Of the Holy Scripture") stands under the affirmation in section 1:

> Therefore it pleased the Lord, at sundry times, and in divers manners, to reveal himself, and to declare that his will unto the church; and afterwards ... to commit the same wholly unto writing ... those former ways of God's revealing his will unto his people being now ceased.

Here the Confession is clear that not only has inscripturated and canonical revelation ceased, but that the rest of the media used throughout the history of revelation (note the allusion to the opening words of Heb. 1:1 in the KJV) have likewise ceased. Not just one way (inscripturation) but "those former ways" (note the plural) of revealing God's will, whatever they are, have ceased.

Furthermore, section 6 asserts that Scripture teaches, either expressly or by sound inference, that "the whole counsel of God concerning all things necessary for his own glory, man's salvation, faith and *life*" (italics added). In other words, Scripture reveals all we need to have not only concerning the gospel and sound doctrinal and ethical principles, but also for the practical and pressing life issues about which we have to make decisions. There is no area of concern in our lives, the Confession is saying, for which Scripture is not an adequate revelation.

Moreover, the Confession continues, "nothing is at any time to be added" to biblical revelation. Consequently, the appended phrase in question, "whether by new revelations of the Spirit [cf. 'private spirits,' sec. 10], or traditions of men," hardly intends to qualify this sweeping negative declaration by allowing for further revelations today. Rather, it is best understood as specifying the respective fronts over against which the Confession is concerned to distance itself: Rome's tradition principle on the one hand, and the continuing revelations claimed throughout the radical wing of the Reformation on the other.[8] In discovering God's will for today, in seeking and expecting guidance for my life, the Confession is emphatic: There is no place for either authoritative human tradition or new revelation.

In fact, the view of Oss and Storms is in continuity with the radical Reformation front that the Westminster Confession opposes. Better than their view, the Confession grasps the wholeness and completeness of the process of revelation tethered to the finished history of redemption. Only where that tie is appreciated will it also be recognized that the period following Pentecost and the apostolic founding of the church is devoid of new revelations (apart, perhaps, from unexpected and unsought exceptions that prove the rule). Only then, too, will it be appreciated that for this present interim, until Christ returns, such specific revelations are no longer necessary because canonical Scripture thoroughly suffices as "a lamp to my feet and a light to my path" (Ps. 119:105; note the individualizing, though not individualistic, singular, "my").

May God more and more grant his church in our time an appreciation for the redemptive-historical rationale that controls his revelatory activity, and so with that appreciation, an unwavering confidence in the sole, exclusive sufficiency of Scripture as the guide for both faith and life.

3. Finally, nothing about the Spirit's working is more essential than the eschatological aspect. The Spirit presently given to the church, in images used by Paul, is the "deposit" and "firstfruits" toward the eschatological future. That has been more and more widely recognized in this century, especially by biblical scholars. But there is much less agreement about where in the Spirit's total activity in creation and salvation the eschatological dimension is to be found.

Pentecostals and charismatics stress revelatory word gifts and healings as manifesting the presence of the eschatological kingdom and the Spirit's power. But as I have tried to show earlier (pp. 56–59), such phenomena, where they occur, are but provisional pointers, less-than-eschatological epiphenomena. Paul seems clear enough about that in 1 Corinthians 13:8–12: Word

---

[8]See B. B. Warfield, *The Westminster Assembly and Its Work* (New York: Oxford Univ. Press, 1931), 224.

gifts like prophecy and tongues (including the kind of knowledge they bring) "cease" and "pass away." That cannot possibly
be said of what is eschatological; by their very nature, eschatological realities *endure*. That enduring work of the Spirit is the
resurrection-renewal already experienced by believers. And that
renewal manifests itself in "fruit" like faith, hope, and love, joy,
and peace (to mention just some). That fruit, however imperfectly displayed for the present, is eschatological at its core. In
such fruit, not in word gifts and healings, we experience the
eschatological "touch of the Spirit" in our lives today.

May God more and more grant the church today a proper
assessment of the eschatological nature of the Spirit's activity.
Perhaps then the debate between continuationists and cessationists will take on less escalated and more biblical proportions.
Perhaps then, too, the Spirit, intent as he is on the unity of the
church, will bring us closer to a genuine resolution of the differences that presently divide us.

CONCLUSION

Wayne A. Grudem

This is the end of the book, but it is obviously not the end of the discussion. Important differences remain unresolved. Yet the authors also share some significant areas of agreement, and it is appropriate to state these clearly and to be thankful for them.

AREAS OF AGREEMENT

1. *Commitment to Scripture.* The authors agreed in their commitment to Scripture as the inerrant word of God and our absolute authority in all the matters we discussed. In practical terms, this means that the authors of these essays want to reaffirm to those who share their positions that Christians must continually be subject to the teachings of Scripture in every area of life and ministry.

2. *Fellowship in Christ.* The authors frequently expressed thankfulness for the fact that they could discuss these matters *as brothers in Christ together*. One of the significant results of our two-day conference was that we all (and I include myself as editor) left our conference with a greater appreciation for the genuine love for Christ and concern for the purity of the church that we saw in those with whom we disagreed. I think Dr. Saucy spoke for all of us in his concluding statement when he said that "the church must continue to study *communally* the remaining issues." It is fair to say that at the end of the conference we all hoped that the Lord would give a similar experience to those who use this

book as a basis for discussing these matters—that they too would grow in appreciation for the depth of commitment to Christ and desire to seek the good of the church that is found in the hearts of people who differ over these specific matters.

3. *The importance of experiencing a personal relationship with God.* All the authors shared a commitment to the importance of a genuine, vital, personal, and relational experience of God in our Christian lives day by day, an experience that includes prayer, worship, and hearing the voice of God speak both to our hearts and our minds through the words of Scripture in all our specific life situations. Regarding miracles, all the authors agreed that the greatest and most wonderful miracle that we have ever experienced is our new birth in Christ, and that Christians would do well to remember this with thanksgiving in the context of these other discussions. Regarding the power of the Holy Spirit, we also agreed that personal growth in holiness and faith is one clear evidence of the Holy Spirit's power at work, and that this truth should never be neglected.

4. *A measure of agreement on specific details about miracles and the work of the Holy Spirit.* Although the authors disagreed on many details and on matters of emphasis and expectation, they nonetheless agreed on some specific details in these matters:

(a) *Healing and miracles*: God does heal and work miracles today.

(b) *Guidance:* The Holy Spirit does guide us (but more study is needed on how the Holy Spirit uses our impressions and feelings in this matter).

(c) *Empowering:* The Holy Spirit does empower Christians for various kinds of ministry, and this empowering is an activity that can be distinguished from the inner-transforming work of the Holy Spirit by which he enables us to grow in sanctification and in obedience to God. This empowering work of the Holy Spirit is not a new doctrine; previous generations sometimes called it "unction" or "anointing." The Holy Spirit can give us such empowering for ministry in varying degrees, not only in preaching, but also in prayer, evangelism, counseling, and other activities we do in the church for the advancement of God's kingdom.

(d) *Revelation:* God in his sovereignty can bring to our minds specific things, not only (i) by occasionally bringing to mind specific words of Scripture that meet the need of the moment, but also (ii) by giving us sudden insight into the application of Scripture to a specific situation, (iii) by influencing our feelings and emotions, and (iv) by giving us specific information about real life situations that we did not acquire through ordinary means (though Dr. Gaffin holds this last category is so highly exceptional that it is neither to be expected nor sought; he prefers a term other than "revelation" to describe these four elements). On this specific point there was the least agreement among the four authors.

AREAS OF DISAGREEMENT

One of the marks of constructive theological dialogue is the ability of people who differ to agree at the end on what their differences are and how to express those differences. In that sense, we achieved a beneficial result from these essays and discussions by clarifying the specific areas in which genuine differences still remain:

1. *Expectation.* Because of differences in understanding the way in which the Holy Spirit ordinarily works during the church age, the authors differed significantly in their *expectations* of how often we should expect the Holy Spirit to work in a miraculous way to heal, to guide, to work miracles, to give unusual empowering for ministry, and to bring things to mind (or reveal things to us).

2. *Encouragement.* Because of differences in understanding what we should expect the Holy Spirit to do today, the authors also differed in how much they think we should *encourage* Christians to seek and pray for miraculous works of the Holy Spirit today.

3. *What should we call these things?* Although the authors did agree that God can sometimes bring things suddenly to our minds, Dr. Storms and Dr. Oss prefer to call this the gift of prophecy, but Dr. Gaffin does not; to him the gift of prophecy is restricted to the giving of Scripture-quality words—a gift that ended when the New Testament canon was completed. According to Dr. Saucy,

God can bring things to mind today, but this should usually be called personal guidance, not prophecy. However, Saucy is also open to the (unlikely) possibility that God can give an "inspired" and inerrant prophecy even today; but even if it were to happen, it would not be part of the canon, which is closed.

Although all the authors agreed that God can still work miracles (including healing), Storms and Oss maintain that people today can have that gift, Gaffin limits it to the apostolic age, and Saucy, while open to that gift today, would examine claims to miracles with great care and caution (he felt that, historically speaking, miracles seem to be especially prominent in church-planting situations).

Regarding the gift of speaking in tongues plus interpretation, according to Gaffin and Saucy these two gifts, when put together, constitute Scripture-quality revelation from the Holy Spirit. Gaffin believes that these gifts only functioned during the "open canon" situation when the New Testament was incomplete. When asked what is happening in the lives of Christians who claim to speak in tongues today, Gaffin is not sure but believes this activity is probably just an ordinary human ability to speak in nonsense syllables. He is also open to being shown from Scripture that this activity is helpful to certain people in their prayer lives, though he would still not call it the gift of speaking in tongues. To Saucy, while Scripture does not rule out tongues today, many modern expressions do not conform to the scriptural practice or purpose of tongues.

Storms and Oss, on the other hand, hold that speaking in tongues is not a revelation from God but is a form of human prayer and praise—it is the Christian's own *human spirit* praying to God through syllables that the speaker does not understand. Storms and Oss believe that this gift continues today. Oss adds that tongues, as prompted by the Holy Spirit, can also be used by God to convey a message to the church, though not a Scripture-quality word. Both Storms and Oss also hold that the gift of interpretation is simply the ability to understand what the tongue-speaker is saying in those words of prayer or praise.

Regarding any empowering work of the Holy Spirit after conversion, Oss calls this "baptism in the Holy Spirit" the first time it happens; the other authors use different terms such as empowering or filling or anointing by the Holy Spirit (see below).

4. *The main purpose of miracles*. Though all authors agreed that there may be several purposes for miracles, both Gaffin and Saucy see the initial authentication of the gospel message in the first century as the primary purpose of miracles, while Storms and Oss believe that other purposes, such as bearing witness to the gospel message in all ages, ministering to the needs of God's people, and bringing glory to God even in the present day, should receive equal emphasis.

5. *Is there a single empowering work of the Holy Spirit after conversion?* While Oss sees a pattern in the book of Acts whereby Christians experienced a single empowering work of the Holy Spirit (or baptism in the Holy Spirit) distinct from conversion, and sees speaking in tongues as the sign that signifies this, the other authors do not see such a pattern or encourage Christians to seek such a single experience distinct from their conversion and distinct from experiences of empowering that may occur multiple times throughout the Christian life.

6. *To what degree should we see church life in the New Testament as a pattern to seek to imitate today?* This was perhaps the single, most fundamental disagreement among the authors. Storms and Oss, throughout our conversations, continued to emphasize that in all other areas of the Christian life (such as evangelism, moral conduct, doctrine, church government and ministry, etc.), we seem to take the patterns of the New Testament as patterns we should imitate in our lives today. They challenged Gaffin and Saucy to explain why it was only in the area of miraculous works of the Holy Spirit that they were unwilling to take the New Testament as God's pattern for us today.

Gaffin and Saucy, on the other hand, kept returning to the fact that everyone agreed that there was a uniqueness to the apostles; that is, there are no more apostles today (in the sense of the "apostles of Jesus Christ" who founded the early church and wrote or authorized the writings of the words of Scripture). And seeing that the presence of the apostles, together with the "open canon" situation, makes the New Testament age somewhat different from today, Gaffin and Saucy noted that Storms and Oss did admit to some important ways in which the New Testament is *not* a pattern for us. If so, and if they also agree that there was an unusual concentration of miraculous power in the lives of the apostles even during the time of the New Testament, then why do they hesitate to admit to a significant difference today specifically in this area of miraculous activity, an area that was so closely connected to the apostles themselves?

Should we expect today the same frequency and power of miracles that we see in the lives of the apostles in the New Testament? Storms and Oss think we should expect only a little less; Saucy thinks we should expect quite a bit less; and Gaffin thinks we should expect even less than that. These discussions ended in an impasse.

7. *Results in church life*. Because of these previous six differences, when we discussed specific styles of ministry and church life, we realized that the churches in which these various views are believed and taught look significantly different. Churches holding to the views advocated by Storms and Oss include much more teaching and encouragement of people to pray for, seek, and exercise miraculous gifts (healing, prophecy, tongues and interpretation, miracles, distinguishing between spirits, and perhaps some others). But churches holding to views expressed by Gaffin, and to some extent by Saucy, do not encourage people to seek or pray for these gifts and do not ordinarily provide "space" for them to occur either in large assemblies or in smaller home fellowship groups in the life of the church. In this way, the kind of leadership that each author would give if he were the pastor of a church is different in focus and emphasis. Clearly, these matters do make some difference in the life of the church.

TWO FINAL QUESTIONS

At the conclusion of this book I wish to ask and comment on two final questions as the editor.

What is the deepest concern of Christians in this area? In working on this book over several months, I began to ask myself, "What is the foundational concern of most Christians in this area?"[1] If we think about the vast majority of ordinary Christians in the churches represented by these four views—Bible-believing

---

[1]This question, and the answer to it, were first suggested to me by Zondervan editor Jack Kuhatschek as we discussed plans for this book. But I did not realize the foundational importance of this question until I began writing this conclusion for the book.

churches where the Word of God is regularly taught and believed—what is really important to them? What is their deepest concern in all of this discussion about the Holy Spirit and his gifts?

I don't think that the differences we usually talk about among our churches are their deepest concern. I do not think most Christians care deeply whether the pastor wears a coat and tie or a sweater or a robe, or whether the church has an Anglican liturgy or a Baptist order of service or charismatic spontaneity with tongues and prophecies. I don't think they care deeply whether the church leads music with an organ or with a guitar, or teaches that you should be baptized in the Holy Spirit or filled with the Holy Spirit. These matters are of some importance, but they are not matters of deepest concern.

I think what people really want is *to be in the presence of God.* They want to have a deeper personal experience of God as they participate in church life week by week. They want times of prayer that are not just forty-five minutes of prayer requests and five minutes of prayer, and not just quickly praying through a long list of requests, but times when they can pray long enough—in an unhurried way—so that they not only talk to God but also hear his still, small voice bearing witness to their hearts. And they want times of worship where, when they are singing, they are allowed to focus their attention on God for an extended time—where no one is interrupting them to tell them to greet their neighbor, or to sing loudly on the next verse, or to listen to the announcements, or to listen to the choir, or to fill out the registration card in the pew. These things, of course, have a place, but they all shift our focus from God alone to the people around us, and they interrupt our times of deepest reverence in the worship of God alone.

Christians instinctively long to be in an assembly of God's people where they can focus their attention on God long enough that their eyes and minds and hearts are aware of nothing but his presence, where their voices are singing his praise (or perhaps silent in his presence), and where they are free to feel the intensity of their love for him and to sense in their spirits that God is there, delighting in the praises of his children. That is what Christians today really long for. They long to come to church and be allowed to worship and pray until they sense in their spirits that they are in the manifest presence of God.

When churches have allowed people to have such extended times of prayer and worship, this longing of Christians has been fulfilled, and these churches have grown remarkably. No denomination or viewpoint on spiritual gifts should have a monopoly on such times of worship and prayer. Cessationist churches and "open but cautious" churches, as well as Pentecostal, charismatic, and Third Wave churches, can provide such times of prayer and worship, each in its own style and within guidelines that protect their doctrinal convictions regarding spiritual gifts.

Of course, I am not saying that we need to diminish the importance we give to sound Bible teaching, in which we hear God's voice speaking to us. In many of our churches this is done well; in other churches it is not, and people go away spiritually hungry week after week because they have not been fed on the Word of God. Yet I am saying that I think many churches need, in addition to such teaching, much more emphasis on extended, uninterrupted times of prayer and worship. I think people are longing to come to church and to know in their experience that they have spent extended time in the manifest presence of God.

Could we minister together? My second comment has to do with relationships among pastors who differ over these issues, taking myself and the four authors as a test case. In reflecting on all that has now been written and said, I have wondered what would happen if, by some unusual work of God's providence, the five of us somehow found ourselves together in a church where we were the only five elders and where we would agree to share the pulpit ministry equally among ourselves. Would it work? Would we stay together, or would we inevitably form five different churches?

I don't know what the other authors might say, but my answer is this: I think we would have to work hard to find some "neutral" vocabulary that we as elders could use to refer to certain experiences and phenomena in the life of the church. I think we would have to work hard at allowing a variety of kinds of home fellowship groups with different emphases and different styles (and perhaps different things happening!). I think that we would have to spend regular hours in prayer and earnest discussion together to be sure that the overall focus of the church was on Christ and the advancement of his kingdom. I think that we would have to work hard at letting the congregation know that, though we differed on certain doctrinal matters, we greatly appreciated each other's gifts and ministries.

But after acknowledging those challenges, and yet knowing these other four men as I do, I really think that it would work. I think that we could live and minister and pray together. I think we could offer pastoral care to one another and to each other's families. I think that we would frequently know times of incredible depth of intercession together for the work of the church. In fact, if this were to happen, I think that it might even be the most exciting and enjoyable time of ministry that any of us had ever known. And I think that the Lord himself would take delight in it and would enjoy fellowshiping with us and blessing us, and would tell us,

> How good and pleasant it is
>   when brothers live together in unity!
> It is like the precious oil poured on the head,
>   running down on the beard,
> running down on Aaron's beard,
>   down upon the collar of his robes.
> It is as if the dew of Hermon
>   were falling on Mount Zion.
> For there the LORD bestows his blessing,
>   even life forevermore.

PSALM 133

AUTHOR INDEX

SUBJECT INDEX

Abel, 287
Abraham, 150, 287
Acts
  not pattern for all ages, 37–38, 102,
    227–29
  pattern for all ages, 74–77, 88–91, 193,
    319
adoption, awareness of, 183
Agabus, 49–50, 68, 208, 231, 322
agreement, areas of, 341–43
AIDS, 215, 233
Ananias, 193
angels, 189
Anglican liturgy, 347
anointing by the Holy Spirit, 255, 257,
  269–70, 289, 291, 305, 308, 342, 344
anointing with oil, 213
anointing with power, 181
antisupernaturalism, 26, 324
apostles, 39–40, 66, 101, 302
  as foundation, 66, 78, 291
  do not continue, 152, 303
  not a pattern for today, 329, 330
  unusual miracles, 102, 109, 159–60
apostles and prophets
  as foundation, 42–44, 48–49, 91, 112,
    124
apostleship
  a gift, 101–102, 152, 291, 328–29
  an office, 157–58
  not a gift, 156–58
  qualifications, 157
apostolic age
  a pattern for today, 171, 325, 345–46
  not a pattern for today, 100, 118, 138,
    152, 226, 234, 285–86, 345–46
apostolic succession, 44
application of Scripture, 343
Assemblies of God, 11, 14, 15, 241
Assemblies of God Seminary, 15, 244
Association of Vineyard Churches, 12
assurance, 183

Augustine, 115–16, 161–62
authority of Bible
  see: Scripture: authority
authors' conference, 16–17, 311, 318, 327,
  332, 333, 334, 341

baptism in the Holy Spirit, 30–41, 225,
  347
  cessationist view, 30–41
  Christians should not seek, 99, 345
  Christians should seek, 165, 235, 345
  connected with tongues, 261–62
  definition, Pentecostal, 243
  different from filling with Holy Spirit,
    298–99
  different in Luke and Paul, 259
  different views, 344–45
  dramatic experience, 315
  has happened to all believers, 98, 301
  ideally received at conversion, 255
  in 1 Corinthians 12:13, 258–60
  more than empowering in Luke, 299–
    300
  open but cautious view, 97–99
  Pentecostal/charismatic view, 164–65,
    240–64, 328
  real issue is not terminology, 260, 305–
    6, 313
  same meaning for Luke and Paul, 305
  sometimes received at conversion,
    242, 255
  terminology important, 298–99
  terminology useful today, 235, 240
  the wrong label? 259, 305–6, 313
  Third Wave view, 175–85
baptism of Jesus, 253
Baptist churches, 347
Bereans, 147
Bible teaching, 348
Bible: authority
  see: Scripture: authority

354

SCRIPTURE INDEX

(including extrabiblical literature)